Selected Writings
of
James Madison Pendleton

Volume I

Historical and Autobiographical

JAMES MADISON PENDLETON
(1811-1891)

Selected Writings
of
James Madison Pendleton

In Three Volumes

Volume I

Historical and Autobiographical

- *James Madison Pendleton and His Contribution to Baptist Ecclesiology*
- *Reminiscences of a Long Life*
- *The Funeral of Dr. J. M. Pendleton*

Compiled and Edited by Thomas White

he Baptist Standard Bearer, Inc.
Number One Iron Oaks Drive • Paris, Arkansas 72855

Thou hast given a *standard* to them that fear thee;
that it may be displayed because of the truth.
— *Psalm 60:4*

Printed in 2006

by

THE BAPTIST STANDARD BEARER, INC.
No. 1 Iron Oaks Drive
Paris, Arkansas 72855
(479) 963-3831

THE WALDENSIAN EMBLEM
lux lucet in tenebris
"The Light Shineth in the Darkness"

ISBN# 1579780466

SELECTED WRITINGS OF JAMES MADISON PENDLETON
IN THREE VOLUMES

VOLUME ONE — HISTORICAL AND AUTOBIOGRAPHICAL

- James Madison Pendleton and His Contribution to Baptist Ecclesiology
  by THOMAS WHITE

- Reminiscences of a Long Life
  by JAMES MADISON PENDLETON

- Article on the Death of J. M. Pendleton
  by M. M. RILEY

VOLUME TWO — ECCLESIASTICAL

- Selected Writings on Various Aspects of the New Testament Church
  by JAMES MADISON PENDLETON

VOLUME THREE — THEOLOGICAL

- Selected Writings on Various Topics of Theology
  by JAMES MADISON PENDLETON

TABLE OF CONTENTS
VOLUME I
Historical and Autobiographical

	PAGE
Acknowledgements	ix
Introduction	xi
James Madison Pendleton and His Contribution to Baptist Ecclesiology . . . . *by* Thomas White	1
Reminiscences of a Long Life . . . . *by* James Madison Pendleton	279
The Funeral of Dr. J. M. Pendleton . . . . . *by* M. M. Riley	443

Acknowledgements

I must extend a thank you to those who made this process possible. First, I would like to thank Bill Lee and his associates at the Baptist Standard Bearer who agreed to publish this project. His work to preserve our Baptist heritage will positively impact generations to come. I must also thank the Southern Baptist Historical Library and Archives in Nashville, Tennessee which houses many of these rare resources on microfilm. Also I want to thank Jennifer Faulk for her dedicated service and selfless help in retyping many of these articles. Many teachers and friends have encouraged and guided my study of James Madison Pendleton, including Dr. John Hammett, Dr. Keith Harper, Dr. Paige Patterson, and Dr. James Hilton. Without them, I would not be the person I am today and this project would never have reached completion. Last, I would like to thank my family who put up with hours of endless work on projects just like this one. Besides my Lord Jesus Christ, Joy is the love of my life, and our daughter Rachel is, of course, the apple of her daddy's eye. God has truly blessed me far beyond anything I could have ever imagined. To Him be praise forever and forever. Amen.

INTRODUCTION

This book is volume one in a three volume series. The first volume contains the only PhD dissertation to focus on James Madison Pendleton. The dissertation is titled, "James Madison Pendleton and His Contributions to Baptist Ecclesiology" and was originally written for Southeastern Baptist Theological Seminary in the spring of 2005. Minor changes and revisions have been made to the original publication but the work is substantially the same. This volume also includes Pendleton's autobiography titled *Reminiscences of a Long Life*, and a newspaper article "The Funeral of Dr. J. M. Pendleton." This volume provides much information about the life and influence of Pendleton. The second volume in the work contains many of his writings on ecclesiology. The doctrine of the church and more specifically the doctrine of baptism dominate much of the second volume. The third volume contains miscellaneous theological articles from Pendleton and demonstrates the pastoral concern of a man who truly personified the pastor/theologian.

Of particular interest in volume one is the dissertation's discussion of the extent of Landmarkism. The term Landmarkism has been linked to many views which have little to do with it. This dissertation, among other things, attempts to pinpoint a precise definition of the central aspect of Landmarkism. In this definition, one will not find the mention of a denial of the universal church, nor an insistence upon closed communion, nor the belief of Baptist church succession. This definition restricts Landmarkism to the denial of Pedobaptist ministers as Gospel ministers and the denial of Pedobaptist churches as true churches. This is the essential meaning of Landmarkism. All else is mere peripheral additions.

The key error of Landmarkism when properly defined can be easily determined. Landmarkism places the proper mode and proper subject of baptism in the "being" of a church and not in the "well-being" of a church. This placement affects all that follows ecclesiologically. With proper mode and subject of baptism in the "being" or definition of the existence of a church, all Pedobaptist organizations are no longer churches. With Pedobaptist no longer possessing churches but societies, they cannot commission or ordain gospel ministers. Since a person cannot call themselves to the ministry because that call must be affirmed by the local church, Pedobaptist societies do not have gospel ministers. This is the outworking of Landmarkism which, ironically, began from Calvin's definition of the true church—the word preached and the sacraments rightly administered. Calvin intended the ordinances to be "rightly" administered meaning without infusing grace which corrupts justification by faith alone while the Landmark movement extended that definition to include the ordinances administered according to Scripture in mode and subject.

A clear understanding of this movement can allow one to solve the Landmark riddle. The ordinances must be kept in the definition of the "being" of a church in order to distinguish the church from parachurch organizations and Bible study groups. The correction to Landmarkism comes by placing "rightly administering the ordinances" in the "well-being" of a church which allows one to consistently affirm what Scripture teaches without un-churching all Pedobaptist gatherings. This author believes that the proper mode and subject belong to the "well-being" of a church. With this definition, Baptists maintain that Pedobaptist gatherings are true churches and possess gospel ministers while maintaining that Baptist churches are closer to the New Testament and thus, purer churches than Pedobaptist churches. Understanding the error of Landmarkism does not undermine the usefulness of Pendleton or the Landmark

INTRODUCTION

emphasis on the local church. Pendleton's dedication to every detail of Scripture and his focus on proper ecclesiology can provide many insights to the reader in an age where the specifics of how church should occur have been substantially lost.

One final note worthy of notice is the bibliography of this dissertation which is the most complete listing of Pendleton's works. Months of effort scrolling through cloudy microfilm displaying issues of the *Tennessee Baptist* and other Baptist newspapers from the middle of the 1800s have resulted in listing more than seven hundred articles which Pendleton wrote. Perhaps this list will demonstrate the importance of Pendleton during his lifetime and help some future researcher to better understand our Baptist heritage.

At the request of his son, Pendleton wrote his autobiography titled, *Reminiscences of a Long Life*, which was published in 1891. Pendleton began writing this book on his seventy-ninth birthday, November 20, 1890, and finished it within two months.[1] This work is the most comprehensive account of Pendleton's life. One cannot read this work without admiring the man who wrote it. It seems as if every page demonstrates his concern for people, his devotion to the Lord, and his love for his wife.

The final chapter was finished by Pendleton's son after Pendleton's death, which occurred on March 5, 1891, at 12:40 p.m.[2] It was fitting that Pendleton's final sermon and breath came where he spent much of his ministry—Bowling Green, Kentucky. He preached his last sermon there on the 25th day of January in 1891.

In addition to providing wisdom for young ministers, this work demonstrates Pendleton's disagreement with the practice of slavery and the civil war. Pendleton considered

---

[1]James Madison Pendleton, *Reminiscences of a Long Life* (Louisville, KY: Baptist Book Concern, 1891), 185.
[2]Unsigned article, "Editorial Notes of the Death of J. M. Pendleton," *Western Recorder* (March 12, 1891).

himself an emancipationist but not an abolitionist, desiring the gradual removal of slavery and not its immediate reversal. Pendleton not only disliked slavery but also rejected the right of the South to secede from the Union. These views forced him to flee North under threats to his life. He eventually wrote his systematic theology titled *Christian Doctrines: A Compendium of Theology* for the benefit of uneducated black ministers in the South.

The final article included in this volume discusses the death and funeral of J. M. Pendleton. The reader will notice that T. T. Eaton and W. H. Whitsitt who fought so vehemently against each other during the controversy over Baptist origins were both present and involved in the funeral proceedings of J. M. Pendleton. Two bitter enemies both had a sincere admiration for Pendleton. After years of studying his work and writings, this author continues to have a deep rooted appreciation for the man known as James Madison Pendleton. Although, I am not a Landmarker, it is my sincere desire that through Pendleton's writings, the reader will develop a desire for proper ecclesiology, a better appreciation of Baptist history, and a deeper understanding of Scripture.

JAMES MADISON PENDLETON AND HIS CONTRIBUTION TO BAPTIST ECCLESIOLOGY

BY

Thomas White

TABLE OF CONTENTS
VOLUME I
*James Madison Pendleton and
His Contribution to Baptist Ecclesiology*

PAGE

ABSTRACT 5

INTRODUCTION

    § Purpose of the Dissertation 9

    § Overview of the Dissertation 11

    § Definition of Terms 13

CHAPTER 1. THE LIFE AND WORKS OF JAMES MADISON PENDLETON

    § Childhood 1811–1831 25

    § Beginning the Ministry 1831–1849 28

    § The Expanding Ministry 1849–1857 30

    § Relocation to Murfreesboro, TN 1857–1861 44

    § Relocation to the North 1862–1865 59

    § Upland, Pennsylvania 1865–1883 60

CHAPTER 2. BAPTISM: THE CENTRAL ASPECT OF PENDLETON'S ECCLESIOLOGY

    § Introduction 67

    § The Importance of Baptism in Pendleton's Ecclesiology 68

    § Pendleton's Formulation of Proper Baptism . . . 73

    § Pendleton Among His Contemporaries 103

    § Pendleton's Unique Contribution 113

    § Current Discussion of Baptism 115

    § Pendleton's Lasting Influence 117

CHAPTER 3. CONGREGATIONAL CHURCH POLITY AND LOCAL CHURCH AUTONOMY

§ Introduction 120
§ Pendleton's View of Congregational Church Polity . 121
§ Pendleton's View of Local Church Autonomy . . . 130
§ Pendleton's Rejection of Other Forms of Church Government 133
§ The Graves-Howell Controversy 142
§ Pendleton Among His Contemporaries 145
§ Pendleton's Unique Contribution 152
§ Current Discussions on Church Polity 153
§ Pendleton's Lasting Influence 156

CHAPTER 4. THE LORD'S SUPPER: WITH WHOM SHOULD WE COMMUNE?

§ Introduction 158
§ Pendleton's Theology of the Lord's Supper 159
§ Disagreement with Graves Over Denominational Communion 169
§ Pendleton Among His Contemporaries. 178
§ Pendleton's Unique Contribution 183
§ Current Discussions on the Lord's Supper 185
§ Pendleton's Lasting Influence 187

CHAPTER 5. CONCLUSION: EVALUATION OF JAMES MADISON PENDLETON

§ Purpose of the Dissertation 189
§ Evaluation of Pendleton's Unique Contributions to Baptist Ecclesiology 189
§ Evaluation of Pendleton's Lasting Influence on Baptist Ecclesiology 193

BIBLIOGRAPHY

§ Pendleton's Works 199
§ Other Sources 247

ABSTRACT

The purpose of the dissertation is to research the life and works of James Madison Pendleton looking specifically at his contributions to Baptist ecclesiology. Pendleton, a member of the "Landmark Triumvirate," had never been the focus of a dissertation which allowed this investigation to provide additional insight into the Landmark movement of the 1850s and the establishment of Baptist identity during the same time frame.

The method of the dissertation is as follows. In the introduction, the reader is briefly exposed to James Madison Pendleton and the need for the dissertation. This section identifies the outline of the dissertation as following Pendleton's reasons for being a Baptist. Pendleton gave three initial reasons and later added a fourth. The first two relate to baptism, the third to church government, and the fourth to the Lord's Supper. The introduction also discusses two areas of needed clarification. The definition of the term Landmarkism and the definitions of terms relating to communion have varied in scholarly works. Thus, for the purpose of clarity, this dissertation discusses and defines them in the introduction.

Chapter one attempts to interweave the life and works of James Madison Pendleton by chronologically tracing his life and discussing relevant works during the time in which they were written. Pendleton lived from 1811 to 1891 and wrote sixteen books and over seven hundred articles all of which could not be discussed individually. An additional provision to help future researchers can be found in the bibliography which lists all of Pendleton's articles.

Chapter two identifies baptism as the central aspect of Pendleton's ecclesiology. Pendleton's ecclesiology is affected by his doctrine of baptism because he includes proper administration of ordinances as a requirement for the *being* of a church. The implication follows that churches not practicing proper baptism are not churches but religious societies. From this crux, Pendleton developed what he considered the central tenet of Landmarkism which was the non-recognition of Pedobaptist ministers as Gospel ministers. He reasoned that Pedobaptist churches practiced improper baptism which meant they were not New Testament churches. A Gospel minister needs to be ordained by a church and needs to be properly baptized. Since Pedobaptist ministers meet neither of these requirements, they are not Gospel ministers. This discussion identifies proper baptism as the line of demarcation between a true church and a religious society.

Chapter three addresses the issue of church government demonstrating that Pendleton supported congregational church government and local church autonomy. Pendleton based his support of congregational church government on Baptist principles of regenerate church membership and scriptural mandates for the congregation to elect church officers, accept or reject members, and discipline members. This chapter also discusses the Graves-Howell controversy and evaluates Pendleton's actions related to that controversy which influenced the Southern Baptist view of local church autonomy.

Chapter four identifies Baptist beliefs concerning the Lord's Supper as Pendleton's final reason for being a Baptist. Pendleton believed that this area of ecclesiology distinguished Baptists because they do not believe in transubstantiation or consubstantiation and because they require proper baptism for participation in the Lord's Supper. This issue also related to Landmarkism as Pendleton argued for consistency. Many Baptists who exchanged pulpits with Pedobaptists refused to admit them to the Lord's table. This practice drew criticism from Pedobaptists. Pendleton argued that Baptists should be consistent by continuing to refuse Pedobaptists admittance to the Lord's table on the basis that they are unbaptized and to no longer exchange pulpits with them. Additionally, the debate over close communion or denominational communion placed Graves and Pendleton on opposing sides. This chapter demonstrates that although close communion is often associated with Landmarkism, Pendleton did not believe it to be one of the tenets of Landmarkism and that Pendleton supported the practice of denominational communion.

Chapter five attempts to summarize the conclusions of the dissertation. Each individual chapter identifies areas of unique contribution or lasting influence from Pendleton. This final chapter draws those conclusions together presenting a succinct discussion of Pendleton's contributions and influence.

INTRODUCTION
PURPOSE OF THE DISSERTATION

James Madison Pendleton (1811–1891) served as a Baptist pastor for forty-six years, taught theology at Union University for four years, served as editor of *The Southern Baptist Review* for five years, and served as co-editor of the *Tennessee Baptist* for three years. He wrote more than 700 articles for various Baptist papers.[1] He also published fifteen books, two of which, *Christian Doctrines: A Compendium of Theology*, and *Church Manual: Designed for the Use of Baptist Churches*, are still in circulation. Rufus Spain noted that these two works best represent Baptist theology in the latter half of the nineteenth century.[2] Pendleton was a towering figure in nineteenth century Baptist life.

Perhaps his most famous role came as a member of the "Landmark triumvirate."[3] This group, which also included J.

---

[1]This author has personally collected 738 articles, yet there are references to other issues of the *Tennessee Baptist* which no longer exist that contain additional articles. The best estimate is that Pendleton wrote between 750–800 articles during his life. The articles still in existence are available on microfilm contained at the Southern Baptist Historical Library in Nashville, Tennessee.

[2]Rufus B. Spain and Samuel S. Hill, *At Ease in Zion: Social History of Southern Baptists 1865–1900* (Tuscaloosa: University of Alabama, 2003), 2.

[3]For more information on Landmarkism, see LeRoy B. Hogue, "A Study of the Antecedents of Landmarkism" (Th.D. diss., Southern Baptist Theological Seminary, 1966); James E. Tull, "A Study of Southern Baptist Landmarkism in the Light of Historical Baptist Ecclesiology" (Ph.D. diss., Columbia University, 1960); James E. Tull, "The Landmark Movement: An Historical and Theological Appraisal," *Baptist History and Heritage* 10 (January 1975): 3–18; Philip Bryan, "An Analysis of the Ecclesiology of Associational Baptists, 1900–1950" (Ph.D. diss., Baylor University, 1973);

R. Graves and A. C. Dayton, contributed to the rise and continuation of the movement called Landmarkism that caused great controversy in Baptist history.[4] Landmarkism contributed to the Graves-Howell controversy, the Whitsitt controversy, and a split of the convention in 1905 resulting in the American Baptist Association.[5] Despite the impact of Landmarkism, Pendleton's contribution to it has not been

---

Hugh Wamble, "Landmarkism: Doctrinaire Ecclesiology Among Baptists," *Church History* 33 (December 1964): 429–47; Louis Keith Harper, "Old Landmarkism: A Historical Appraisal," *Baptist History and Heritage* 25 (April 1990): 31–40; W. C. Taylor, "James Madison Pendleton: World Landmark of Baptist Devotion to Truth and Loyalty to New Testament Churches" (Louisville: The W. C. Taylor Letters, 1990–1991); and Edward C. Briggs, "Landmark Views of the Church in the Writings of J. M. Pendleton, A. C. Dayton, and J. R. Graves," *The Quarterly Review* 35 (April 1975): 47–57.

[4]For more information on J. R. Graves, consult the following: Harold S. Smith, "A Critical Analysis of the Theology of J. R. Graves" (Th.D. diss., Southern Baptist Theological Seminary, 1966); Harold S. Smith, "The Life and Work of J. R. Graves (1811–1891)," *Baptist History and Heritage* 10 (January 1975): 19–27; Marty G. Bell, "James Robinson Graves and the Rhetoric of Demagogy: Primitivism and Democracy in Old Landmarkism (Baptist)" (Ph.D. diss., Vanderbilt University, 1990); Michael Henry Bone, "A Study of the Writings of J. R. Graves (1820–1893) as an Example of the Nature and Function of Absolutes in Religious Symbol System" (Ph.D. diss., Boston University, 2001); Myron James Houghton, "The Place of Baptism in the Theology of James Robinson Graves" (Th.D. diss., Dallas Theological Seminary, 1971); Barry William Jones, "James R. Graves, Baptist Newspaper Editor: Catalyst for Religious Controversy, 1846–1893" (Ph.D. diss., Ohio University, 1994); T. A. Patterson, "The Theology of J. R. Graves, and Its Influences on Southern Baptist Life" (Th.D. diss., Southwestern Baptist Theological Seminary, 1944); and O. L. Hailey, *J. R. Graves: Life, Times and Teachings* (Nashville: O. L. Hailey, 1929). For more information on A. C. Dayton, see James E. Taulman, "Amos Dayton Cooper: A Critical Biography" (Th.M. thesis, Southern Baptist Theological Seminary, 1965); and James E. Taulman, "The Life and Writings of Amos Cooper Dayton (1813–1865)," *Baptist History and Heritage* 10 (January 1975): 36–43.

[5]Timothy George, "Southern Baptist Ghosts," *First Things* 93 (May 1999): 23, noted Landmarkism as a main movement in Baptist history and stated that "Landmarkism is still alive and well in the Baptist hinterland...."

thoroughly researched. Specifically, Pendleton's disagreement with Graves over what beliefs are part of Landmarkism needs further attention. Thus, a thorough study of Pendleton's position will reveal new insights into the core of Landmarkism and its influence on Baptist ecclesiology.

The insufficient research is reflected in the fact that Pendleton has never been the sole study of a dissertation. Two Th.M. theses focused on Pendleton, yet neither of these comprehensively studied his articles.[6] Furthermore, only a handful of articles have been written on Pendleton, and most articles discussing Landmarkism utilize the definitions provided by J. R. Graves in his work *Old Landmarkism: What Is It?*[7] Although Graves is rightly recognized as the key leader of the movement, this author believes Pendleton represents a less extreme view of Landmarkism. This dissertation will present Pendleton's view of Landmarkism along with his contributions to Baptist ecclesiology.

OVERVIEW OF THE DISSERTATION

Before presenting the content of the dissertation it will be necessary to define important terms. Thus, immediately following this overview, Landmarkism and the terms relating to communion will be defined. Following these definitions, chapter one will provide an introduction to the life and works of Pendleton. This author will attempt to provide a short biography of Pendleton discussing relevant facts pertaining to the writing of his articles and books. By interweaving the biography with a summary of his works, this author desires to provide additional insight into the context of Pendleton's works.

---

[6]James Emmett Hill Jr., "James Madison Pendleton's Theology of Baptism" (Th.M. thesis, Southern Baptist Theological Seminary, 1958); and William Clyde Huddleston, "James Madison Pendleton: A Critical Biography" (Th.M. thesis, Southern Baptist Theological Seminary, 1962).

[7]J. R. Graves, *Old Landmarkism: What Is It?* (Texarkana: Bogard Press, 1880).

The second chapter will probe Pendleton's formulation of the doctrine of baptism, which formed the central aspect of his ecclesiology and took up more space in his writings than any other topic.[8] This chapter will first summarize Pendleton's theology of baptism. The chapter will also identify Pendleton's unique contribution by comparing Pendleton's work with that of his contemporaries. By interacting with modern works, this chapter will identify any lasting influence on the theology of baptism. This chapter will demonstrate that Pendleton's unique contribution was pinpointing the issue of baptism as the central issue in pulpit affiliation, non-recognition of Pedobaptist churches, and non-recognition of Pedobaptist ministers.

The third chapter will focus on Pendleton's support for church independence and congregational church government. This chapter will begin by summarizing Pendleton's reasons for holding to congregational church polity. Additionally, this chapter will discuss the implications of Pendleton's emphasis on church independence and congregational polity. Following the summary of his theology, works from Pendleton's contemporaries will be examined to discover if Pendleton made any unique contribution to the issue of church polity. The final section will attempt to identify any lasting contribution made by Pendleton to congregational church polity by interacting with modern works on the issue.

---

[8]The following works contain his teachings on baptism: James Madison Pendleton, *Christian Doctrines: A Compendium of Theology* (Philadelphia: American Baptist Publication Society, 1906); *Church Manual: Designed for the Use of Baptist Churches* (Philadelphia: American Baptist Publication Society, 1867); *Distinctive Principles of Baptists* (Philadelphia: American Baptist Publication Society, 1882); *An Old Landmark Re-set* (Nashville: Graves & Marks, 1854); *Three Reasons Why I Am a Baptist* (Cincinnati: Moore, Anderson & Company, 1853); *Three Reasons Why I Am a Baptist with a Fourth Reason Added on Communion* (St. Louis: National Baptist Publishing, 1856). In addition to these books, Pendleton wrote a number of articles dealing with baptism. See the bibliography for a complete list of articles.

The fourth chapter will examine Pendleton's doctrine of the Lord's Supper. This chapter will begin by giving an analysis of Pendleton's position on the doctrine, and then it will discuss Pendleton's contemporaries, identifying any unique contributions made by Pendleton. This section will specifically address the conflict between J. R. Graves and Pendleton over communion and Landmarkism. It will demonstrate that Pendleton saw nothing wrong with including members of other Baptist churches in communion. Pendleton stated in a letter to J. J. D. Renfroe that the Landmark doctrine concerns the non-recognition of Pedobaptist ministers and does not involve denominational communion among Baptist church members.[9] Graves, on the other hand, wanted to make close communion part of the Landmark doctrine. The last section in this chapter will attempt to relate Pendleton to modern theologians, noting any lasting contributions. This chapter will demonstrate that Pendleton was unique by being the only member of the "Landmark triumvirate" who allowed denominational communion. However, in the area of formulation of the theology of the Lord's Supper, Pendleton popularized previously stated positions.

The final chapter will attempt to draw conclusions and evaluate Pendleton's unique contributions. After evaluating Pendleton's unique contributions, the author will summarize Pendleton's lasting influence in relation to Baptist ecclesiology.

DEFINITION OF TERMS

Landmarkism

Two major disagreements exist over Landmarkism. The first disagreement concerns whether Graves and company created a new strand of thought or simply resurrected an old belief.

---

[9]James Madison Pendleton, "Introduction," in *Vindication of the Communion of Baptist Churches,* by J. J. D. Renfroe (Selma: John L. West, 1882), 5.

Pendleton's famous tract was titled, "An Old Landmark Reset." From the title one would gather that the Landmark members thought their beliefs were not new. In Cathcart's *Baptist Encyclopedia*, Landmarkism falls under the topic of "Old-Landmarkism." Furthermore, the article states, "the doctrine of landmarkism is not a novelty, as some suppose . . . because William Kiffin, of London, one of the noblest of English Baptists, advocated it in 1640. . . ."[10] In addition to Cathcart, LeRoy B. Hogue concluded that Landmarkism began long before Graves's support of it.[11] Finally, Bryan stated, "The Landmark movement, often called 'Old Landmarkism,' attempted to preserve historic distinctive Baptist principles."[12] These men believed that Landmarkism reestablished historical Baptist principles.

However, others believed that Landmarkism represented new and original thought. James E. Tull in his dissertation sought to demonstrate that rather than resurrecting an ancient Landmark, Graves gave birth to a new one.[13] Concurring with Tull were Hugh Wamble and Harold Smith.[14] Wamble attempted to summarize the beliefs of Landmarkism, but he specifically stated, "I would like to make it clear that, despite Landmarkers' claim that their ecclesiology is the authentic Baptist view, Landmarkism differs at central points from ecclesiology held by Baptists

---

[10]William Cathcart, "Old-Landmarkism," in *The Baptist Encyclopedia*, ed. William Cathcart (Philadelphia: Louis H. Everts, 1881), 867–8.

[11]LeRoy B. Hogue, "A Study of the Antecedents of Landmarkism" (Th.D. diss., Southern Baptist Theological Seminary, 1966).

[12]Bryan, "An Analysis of the Ecclesiology of Associational Baptists, 1900–1950," 11.

[13]James E. Tull, "A Study of Southern Baptist Landmarkism in the Light of Historical Baptist Ecclesiology" (Ph.D. diss., Columbia University, 1960).

[14]Hugh Wamble, "Landmarkism: Doctrinaire Ecclesiology Among Baptists," *Church History* 33 (December 1964): 429–47; and Harold S. Smith, "A Critical Analysis of the Theology of J. R. Graves" (Th.D. diss., Southern Baptist Theological Seminary, 1966).

prior to 1850."¹⁵ Thus, others believed that Landmarkism represented an aberration from traditional Baptist thought.

Truth exists in both of the previous claims. Depending upon the precise definition of Landmarkism, one can affirm or reject its claim to historical precedence. Certain beliefs identified with Landmarkism, such as (1) proper baptism being essential to the essence of church, (2) the belief that immersion alone is proper baptism, and (3) the belief in close communion, can be traced to long before Graves. However, a succinct discussion and definition of Landmarkism as put together by Graves and Pendleton had not existed before the 1850s. Thus, if Landmarkism is defined as the rejection of Pedobaptist groups as churches and the rejection of Pedobaptist ministers as Gospel ministers, then perhaps this system is new. In summary, the primary tenets of Landmarkism existed long before Graves and Pendleton; however, the specific system of defending these beliefs and their implications of rejecting Pedobaptist churches and ministers was new, if only in developing new implications.

The second disagreement over Landmarkism concerns a definition of the movement. The previous discussion has indicated the importance of a working definition. This author makes no claim to be the last word on the discussion but merely to introduce the reader to the issue and establish the definition which will be used for this study. Landmarkism has been defined by the *Encyclopedia of Southern Baptists* in the following way:

> The distinctive tenets of this movement fall into the category of ecclesiology, fitting into a very logical system centered around the primacy of the local church. Since a valid church is an assembly of baptized (immersed) believers, then pedobaptist organizations cannot be recognized as true churches, but only as religious

---

¹⁵Wamble, "Landmarkism: Doctrinaire Ecclesiology Among Baptist," 430.

societies. Such groups cannot give authority to preach, and therefore their ministers should not be recognized as regular gospel ministers. Upon this follows a rejection of their ordinances. Even an occasional immersion must be designated alien and nugatory, since it lacks proper authority.[16]

At this point Patterson correctly defined Landmarkism; however, later in this same publication he also added close communion and church succession as Landmark distinctives.[17] This idea of church succession was written on by G. H. Orchard who taught that there had been a line of churches holding Baptist beliefs going all the way back to biblical times.[18] Although some people who supported Landmarkism held these beliefs, others who denied Landmarkism held to the succession of Baptist churches.[19] Graves would have agreed with Patterson's definition and did so in his work *Old Landmarkism: What Is It?* However,

---

[16]W. Morgan Patterson, "Landmarkism" in *Encyclopedia of Southern Baptists*, ed. Norman Cox (Nashville: Broadman Press, 1958), 757.

[17]Patterson, "Landmarkism," 757. However, Patterson later recognized that Pendleton did not hold to these views. He wrote, "Yet it must be remembered that Pendleton differed from other Landmarkers in significant ways. His understanding of Landmarkism seemed to be limited to his concept of pulpit affiliation. Also, unlike many Landmarkers, he accepted the concept of the universal church, never adhered to Baptist successionism, and was able to work within the organizational framework of the conventions and societies of Baptists in a way many Landmarkers were never able to do." See W. Morgan Patterson, "The Influences of Landmarkism Among Baptists," *Baptist History and Heritage* 10 (January 1975): 56.

[18]George Herbert Orchard, *A Concise History of the Foreign Baptists* (Nashville: Graves & Marks, 1855). This view was later espoused by J. M. Carroll, *The Trail of Blood* (Lexington: American Baptist Publishing Company, 1931).

[19]Graves, *Old Landmarkism*, 86. Those who held to this view but did not adhere to Landmarkism, include R. B. C. Howell, who said "that the Apostolic Church was Baptist and that through several channels it may be readily traced in a state of comparative purity down to our time." See R. B. C. Howell, *The Terms of Communion at the Lord's Table* (Philadelphia: American Baptist Publication Society, 1846), 262.

Tull notes four areas where Pendleton disagreed with Graves: "(1) Pendleton never relinquished the idea of the universal church; (2) refused to equate the Kingdom of God with the aggregate of Baptist churches; (3) refused to subscribe to the theory of church succession; and (4) thought the theory of nonintercommunion was trivial and unimportant."[20] Pendleton believed the central point of Landmarkism concerned the non-recognition of Pedobaptist ministers as Gospel ministers.

Three primary sources must be consulted in developing any definition for Landmarkism—the Cotton Grove Resolutions, *Old Landmarkism* by Graves, and *An Old Landmark Re-set* by Pendleton. The "Cotton Grove Resolutions" included the following:

1. Can Baptists, consistently with their principles or the Scriptures, recognize those societies not organized according to the pattern of the Jerusalem Church, but possessing different governments, different officers, a different class of members, different ordinances, doctrines and practices, as churches of Christ?

2. Ought they to be called gospel churches, or churches in a religious sense?

3. Can we consistently recognize the ministers of such irregular and unscriptural bodies as gospel ministers?

4. Is it not virtually recognizing them as official ministers to invite them into our pulpits, or by any other act that would or could be construed into such a recognition?

---

[20]James E. Tull, *High-Church Baptists in the South* (Macon: Mercer Press, 2000), 44. On the issue of church succession, there is no clear refutation of the church succession theory in Pendleton's writings. Tull did not document his statement; however, after studying Pendleton's work, this author concludes that Tull accurately noted an absence of church succession in Pendleton's writings.

5. Can we consistently address as brethren those professing Christianity, who not only have not the doctrine of Christ and walk not according to his commandments, but are arrayed in direct and bitter opposition to them?[21]

On July 28, 1851, the Big Hatchie Association met in an annual session at Bolivar, Tennessee and answered questions one, two, three, and five in the negative. Question four was answered affirmatively. This established the first formal statement of the tenets of Landmarkism.

Graves in *Old Landmarkism: What Is It?* added further beliefs to Landmarkism. One addition to which Pendleton objected was titled, "inconsistencies and evils of intercommunion among Baptists." Graves also indicated a belief in the succession of the kingdom and a denial of the universal church.[22] Many later scholars have attributed some form of succession of the kingdom or succession of Baptist churches to the definition of Landmarkism.[23] This author

---

[21]Graves, *Old Landmarkism*, 14.

[22]Ibid., 84. Graves said, "Nor have I, or any Landmarker known to me, ever advocated the succession of any particular church or churches; but my position is that Christ, in the very 'days of John the Baptist,' did establish a visible kingdom on earth, and that this *kingdom* has never yet been 'broken in pieces,' nor given to another class of subjects—has never for a day 'been moved,' nor ceased from the earth, and never will until Christ returns personally to reign over it." Graves said concerning the local church, "He [Christ] has no invisible kingdom or church, and such a thing has no real existence in heaven or earth. It is only an invention employed to bolster up erroneous theories of ecclesiology" (28).

[23]See Robert Torbet, who attributed this view to Graves, Pendleton, and Landmarkism in "Landmarkism" presented at the Second National Theological Conference in Green Lake, Wisconsin, June 6–11, 1959. John Steeley, "The Landmark Movement in the Southern Baptist Convention," in *What is the Church?*, ed. Duke McCall (Nashville: Broadman Press, 1958), 136, said, "A major emphasis of Graves which serves to identify the Landmarkism of his time relates to church succession, expressed in the claim of Baptists to this distinction . . . It is not, of course, a peculiarity of Landmarkers alone that they claim apostolic succession for Baptist churches. Other Baptists who are not Landmarkers believe that such a succession may be traced or at least may be inferred. It is rather the *a priori* method of establishing such a claim. . . ." Hugh Wamble

believes Pendleton would have disagreed with directly linking church succession to Landmarkism although he never denied the view. Three reasons support this belief. First, Pendleton never used church succession as his primary argument to combat Campbellism or establish Landmarkism as others did. Second, Pendleton recognized that church succession flowed through the early Anabaptist who baptized by pouring. By acknowledging the true church flowed through those who practiced baptism by pouring, he would have weakened his position on baptism by immersion.[24] Three, R.B.C. Howell and other opponents of Landmarkism held to some form of church succession while earnestly rejecting Landmarkism.

Much confusion over Pendleton's position on the universal church may have come from a work titled *Landmarkism* published in 1899.[25] This work was not published until eight

---

"Landmarkism: Doctrinaire Ecclesiology Among Baptists," 439, stated, "Landmarkers contend that Baptist churches have existed continuously since the time of Jesus Christ." Chad Hall, "When Orphans Become Heirs: J. R. Graves and the Landmark Baptists," *Baptist History and Heritage* 37 (Winter 2002): 112–27, attributed the view of successionism to the Landmark movement. Lastly, Bill Leonard, *Baptist Ways: A History* (Valley Forge: Judson Press, 2003), 183–4, claimed that closed communion and church successionism are part of the basic beliefs of Landmarkism.

[24]S. H. Ford, "History of the Baptists in the Southern States by B. F. Riley, D. D. — Misstatements — Old Landmarkism — Succession — Irregular Immersions," *Ford's Christian Repository and Home Circle* (July 1899): 420, claimed that Pendleton said, "The ana-Baptist [sic] question [did they sprinkle] really has nothing to do with the landmark question; nor has the church succession question. . . . I doubt not there have been in all ages, from the days of the apostles, persons who have believed for substance as Baptists do now; but that there has been a regular succession of churches, I am by no means certain. . . . It has not been established to my satisfaction; but I am a 'landmarker.'"

[25]Confusion over Pendleton's other positions can be clearly seen in works which assume that Pendleton, being one of the Landmark founders, accepted Grave's formulation of Landmarkism. For example, H. Leon McBeth, *The Baptist Heritage* (Nashville: Broadman Press, 1987), 449, stated, "he never embraced the total system as did Graves" but McBeth went on to say, "Pendleton's [*Church*] *Manual* advances Landmark views

years after his death, yet the cover of the book appears as though Pendleton authored the work. At the bottom of the cover notations state that other authors produced articles for the publication. These authors include J. N. Hall, J. R. Graves, Judson Taylor, and J. B. Moody. As for Pendleton's part, this book merely reproduced his *Old Landmark Re-set*. However, this little book has led to much confusion because it contains a strong denial of the universal church. This denial comes from the inclusion of the last article titled, "The New Issue: The Invisible Church Idea" by J. N. Hall. Hall wrote, "For our part we deny this whole 'invisible, universal church' idea. There is but one sort of a church in the New Testament; and that is a local and visible church."[26] Hall never clarifies the "we" but by positioning this article as the last article in the book, he gave the impression that the previous writers concurred.

For the purposes of this dissertation, a less extreme definition of Landmarkism, Pendleton's definition, will be utilized. Landmarkism consisted of the following beliefs:

---

of Baptist life on closed communion, alien immersion, and Baptist successionism." This dissertation contends that Pendleton did not advocate Baptist successionism and did not hold to the closest form of communion. However, McBeth was not alone. Jesse Fletcher, *The Southern Baptist Convention: A Sesquicentennial History* (Nashville: Broadman & Holman, 1994), 62, included Pendleton as supporting Baptist successionism. William Brackney, *The Baptists* (New York: Greenwood Press, 1988), 65, included a Pendleton quote in a section supporting Graves's view of close communion which implied Pendleton's agreement. Robert Torbet, *A History of the Baptists* (Valley Forge: Judson, 1950), 281, implied that both Graves and Pendleton held to the closest form of communion. He said, "they have not admitted members of different Baptist churches to share together in the observance of the Lord's Supper, for they have held that the ordinance is only for the members of the local church." Thus, much confusion exists concerning Pendleton's differentiation from Graves. Although it is not the sole purpose of this dissertation, Pendleton's and Graves's views will be distinguished in following discussions.

[26]J. N. Hall, "The New Issue," in *Landmarkism, Liberalism and the Invisible Church* (Fulton: National Baptist Publishing House, 1899), 75. This collection does not note an editor.

1. proper administration of the ordinances is essential to the existence of a true local church;
2. proper baptism is by immersion only of believers only;
3. without proper baptism, Pedobaptist societies cannot be considered true churches;
4. Pedobaptist societies not being true churches, their preachers are not properly ordained or commissioned and cannot be considered Gospel ministers;
5. with no valid churches or ministers, Pedobaptist immersions (alien immersions) cannot be accepted; pulpits cannot be exchanged with Pedobaptists; and communion cannot be extended to Pedobaptists;
6. emphasis is placed on the primacy of the local church.

The Landmarkism supported by Pendleton ended at this point. He recognized the universal church (but did not emphasize it), allowed for denominational communion, and did not endorse a strict view of church succession. This position will be demonstrated later in this presentation.

TERMS RELATING TO COMMUNION

Because one section of this dissertation focuses on communion and because Pendleton and Graves disagreed on this issue, precise definitions of the terms relating to communion are necessary. Communion can be discussed in three categories. The first category is that of close communion. This has also been known as closed, strict, and restricted communion.[27] Close communion for the current

---

[27]Pendleton used "close" in *Three Reasons Why I Am a Baptist with a Fourth Added on Communion*, 199. Edward Hiscox used "close" but acknowledged the terms "strict or restricted" in *The New Directory for Baptist Churches* (Philadelphia: Judson Press, 1894), 448. W. T. Conner used "close" in *Christian Doctrine* (Nashville: Broadman, 1937), 289. J. R. Graves used the terms "strict or restricted" communion in *Intercommunion: Inconsistent, Unscriptural and Productive of Evil*

discussion will mean that only members of a particular local church are allowed to participate in communion. Christians of similar beliefs belonging to other churches, or members of other denominations are not allowed to partake in communion.[28] The second category is denominational communion.[29] This practice has also been referred to as "transient communion" or "closed intercommunion."[30] However, this dissertation will use "denominational communion" to refer to that view which allows non church members to partake in communion on the condition of like faith and practice. Such a person should be one that could be accepted into that particular church's membership. The third category is open communion.[31] This type communion allows any Christian to partake in communion because it belongs to Christ and is thus open to all children of God. This practice has also been referred to as "mixed communion."[32]

(Memphis: Baptist Book House, 1881), 10, 14. J. L. Dagg used the term "strict" in *Manual of Church Order* (Charleston: Southern Baptist Publication Society, 1858; reprint, Harrisonburg: Gano Books, 1990), 225. Among current scholarship, McBeth used the term "closed" in *The Baptist Heritage*, 81, and Slaydon Yarbrough, *Southern Baptists: A Historical, Ecclesiological, and Theological Heritage of a Confessional People* (Nashville: Fields, 2000), 109, related the terms "close" and "closed" stating that they both mean "only members of the particular congregation are allowed to partake."

[28]This author recognizes that not all authors have used this term to signify the closest form of communion. For example, McBeth left open the possibility of intercommunion among Baptist churches (denominational or transient communion). He defined closed communion as "meaning that only those who had received believer's baptism by immersion might join in the supper" (81).

[29]Graves, *Intercommunion*, 11, used "denominational communion."

[30]Dagg, *Manual of Church Order*, 214, used "transient communion." Yarbrough, *Southern Baptists*, 110, used "closed intercommunion."

[31]This term has been widely used. See for example: Dagg, *Manual of Church Order*, 214; Hiscox, *The New Directory for Baptist Churches*, 447; Yarbrough, *Southern Baptists*, 110; and McBeth, *The Baptist Heritage*, 81.

[32]Thomas F. Curtis, *Communion: The Distinction Between Christian and Church Fellowship and Between Communion and Its Symbols: Embracing a Review of the Arguments of Robert Hall and Baptist W. Noel in Favor of*

An additional term that needs clarification is "intercommunion."³³ Intercommunion has been utilized in multiple ways. One may participate in intercommunion which crosses denominational lines. This would fall under the category of open communion. One may participate in intercommunion which only crosses church membership lines but remains within the same the denomination. This would fall under the category of denominational communion. This dissertation will attempt to clarify which meaning is intended when cited from other writers. The primary usage for this word will be in describing discussions between J. R. Graves and J. M. Pendleton. Their disagreement over intercommunion centered on crossing church lines and not denominational lines. Graves and Pendleton both agreed that Baptists should not commune with Pedobaptists. Thus, "open communion" was not acceptable for either; however, Graves and Pendleton disagreed over "denominational communion." Pendleton supported denominational communion while Graves supported close communion. This dissertation will use the term "denominational communion" when referring to communion which crosses the line of local church membership, except when quoting others who use the term "intercommunion" when referring to this practice.

Mixed Communion (Philadelphia: American Baptist Publication Society, 1850).

³³See Graves, *Intercommunion* for both uses of this word.

CHAPTER 1

THE LIFE AND WORKS OF JAMES MADISON PENDLETON

Childhood 1811–1831

James Madison Pendleton was born on November 20, 1811, to John and Frances Pendleton at Twyman's Store in Spotsylvania County, Virginia, during the presidency of the person after whom he was named—James Madison.[1] In the autumn of 1812, Pendleton's family moved to Christian County, Kentucky. Here Pendleton was reared by "pious Baptist" parents where he attended "the neighborhood schools, at such times as he could be spared from labor."[2] In addition to having pious parents, the entire atmosphere of Kentucky exuded a religious atmosphere. At the turn of the century, just before the birth of Pendleton, a spiritual renewal emerged in the Kentucky area. In June of 1800, many devout members of Muddy River, Red River, and Gasper River congregations met at the Red River meeting house. From this point forward, the Cumberland region of Kentucky would experience what would be called "the great

---

[1] James Madison Pendleton, *Reminiscences of a Long Life* (Louisville, KY: Baptist Book Concern, 1891), 8. Keith Eitel, "James Madison Pendleton," in *Baptist Theologians*, eds. Timothy George and David Dockery (Nashville: Broadman Press, 1990), 188, mistakenly identified November 11, 1811, as the date of James Madison Pendleton's birth. For a more complete biography, see B. F. Proctor, *The Life of Rev. James Madison Pendleton* (Louisville: Baptist Book Concern, 1904); Pendleton, *Reminiscences of a Long Life*; and William Clyde Huddleston, "James Madison Pendleton: A Critical Biography" (Th.M. thesis, Southern Baptist Theological Seminary, 1962).

[2] J. H. Spencer, *A History of Kentucky Baptists* (Cincinnati: J. H. Spencer, 1885), 523.

revival."³ The revival in Kentucky along with other areas was also known as "the second great awakening."⁴ Christian County, Kentucky, where Pendleton grew up, was in the Cumberland region.⁵ The revival occurred before Pendleton's birth, but the effects of the revival lingered. One man characterized it by saying, "It is a very comfortable thing to be in a country where religion has obtained the pre-eminent influence. That is those that have it shows [sic] it, and those that have it not wish to be considered religious for the credit it gives in the society."⁶ The religious nature of this society encouraged Pendleton to consider religious matters.

During his teenage years, Pendleton demonstrated an acute interest in spiritual matters. Just before turning fifteen, Pendleton used money earned from selling wool to buy his first purchase—a Bible. Pendleton said, "I prized it highly and found great use for it."⁷ After turning fifteen, he decided to give great attention to religion, resolving to read his Bible and pray every day. After an extended time of reading his Bible, contemplating his own sinfulness, and attempting to

---

³John B. Boles, *The Great Revival: Beginnings of the Bible Belt* (Lexington: University of Kentucky, 1972), 52. For an account of the events leading up to this revival, consult Mark Noll, *The Rise of Evangelicalism* (Downers Grove: InterVarsity, 2003), and for an account of the revival, consult, Iain Murray, *Revival & Revivalism: The Making and Marring of American Evangelicalism 1750–1858* (Bath: Bath Press, 1994).

⁴For further research on the 2d Great Awakening see: Boles, *The Great Revival*; Paul Conkin, *Cane Ridge: America's Pentecost* (Madison: University of Wisconsin Press, 1990); James Rogers, *The Cane Ridge Meeting-house* (Cincinnati: Standard, 1910); Winthrop Hudson & John Corrigan, *Religion in America: An Historical Account of the Development of American Religious Life* (New York: Macmillan, 1992); William Warren Sweet, *Religion on the American Frontier* (New York: Cooper Square Publishers, 1964); Ralph Morrow, "The Great Revival, the West, and the Crisis of the Church," in *The Frontier Re-examined*, ed. John F. McDermott (Urbana: University of Illinois Press, 1967); and Donald Matthews, "The Second Great Awakening as an Organizing Process, 1780–1830," *American Quarterly* 21 (Spring 1969): 23–43.

⁵Boles, *The Great Revival*, xviii.
⁶Ibid., 68.
⁷Pendleton, *Reminiscences of a Long Life*, 22.

save himself, Pendleton read a sermon by Samuel Davies from 1 Cor 1:22–24. After reading this sermon, he went into the woods to pray, and understood for the first time the mercy of salvation through Jesus Christ.[8] At age seventeen, on the second Sunday in April, 1829, Pendleton went before Bethel Church in Christian County, Kentucky, and told of his conversion experience which had occurred a few weeks earlier in those nearby woods.[9] He was baptized by John S. Wilson the following Tuesday, April 14, in a creek not far from the meeting house.

Pendleton's formal education was limited.[10] Because his father, in addition to being a farmer, taught school, Pendleton learned much at home but did not begin attending the neighborhood school until the age of nine or ten.[11] Although work on the farm often interrupted his studies, Pendleton learned well, and in 1831 at age nineteen, he tried his hand at teaching in the western part of Christian County.[12] This lasted for only three months, and he returned home discouraged and with only three dollars in his pocket.[13] By the end of the year, Pendleton moved to Russellville, Kentucky, to study Latin grammar under Robert T. Anderson.[14] Early in 1833, Pendleton accepted an invitation to minister in Hopkinsville, where he would remain until 1836. This afforded him the opportunity to study at the Academy under the charge of James D. Rumsey, "who had a

---

[8]Ben Bogard, *Pillars of Orthodoxy, or Defenders of the Faith* (Louisville: Baptist Book Concern, 1900), 256.
[9]Pendleton, *Reminiscences of a Long Life*, 27–8.
[10]Huddleston, "James Madison Pendleton: A Critical Biography," 16.
[11]Pendleton, *Reminiscences of a Long Life*, 15.
[12]Ibid., 34.
[13]Bob Compton, "J. M. Pendleton: A Nineteenth-Century Baptist Statesman (1811–1891)," *Baptist History and Heritage* 10 (January 1975): 30.
[14]Pendleton, *Reminiscences of a Long Life*, 37. Anderson founded a school there in 1830. It was said of him, "In this profession he was preeminent, and was of incalculable benefit to the Baptists of Bethel Association, as well as others." See Spencer, *A History of Kentucky Baptists*, 381.

fine reputation as a classical scholar."[15] Pendleton would focus his study on Latin and Greek. After moving in 1836, no further record of formal education exists. However in 1865, Denison University in Ohio conferred upon Pendleton the honorary title of Doctor of Divinity.[16]

BEGINNING THE MINISTRY 1831–1849

Pendleton did not begin as the polished pulpiteer which was to characterize his career. He began by leading prayer meetings during which he largely read Scripture. He did not consider these engagements preaching, but in February of 1830, to Pendleton's astonishment, his home church licensed him to preach.[17] He commented, "I thought it quite uncalled for and did not believe it possible for me to preach."[18] It was the fourth Sunday in September, 1831, when Pendleton preached what he considered his first sermon at a church called West Union about ten miles west of Hopkinsville. Pendleton commented on his effort, "To call what I said a 'sermon' would be flagrant injustice to that term."[19] He felt himself utterly incompetent to preach. His exhortations were very short, consisting of only a few sentences, and when he had said all he could think of to say, he "sought relief from his embarrassment in prayer."[20] Some agreed with Pendleton's assessment of his preaching. One local pastor stated, "You say some pretty good things, but your preaching is neither adapted to comfort the saint nor alarm the sinner."[21] However, Pendleton did not give up but continued to improve.

---

[15]Pendleton, *Reminiscences of a Long Life*, 40. No further information can be found about this academy.
[16]J. J. Burnett, *Sketches of Tennessee's Pioneer Baptist Preachers* (Nashville: Marshall & Bruce, 1919), 406.
[17]Huddleston, "James Madison Pendleton: A Critical Biography," 24.
[18]Pendleton, *Reminiscences of a Long Life*, 31.
[19]Ibid., 35.
[20]Ibid., 33.
[21]Bogard, *Pillars of Orthodoxy, or Defenders of the Faith*, 258.

In 1833 while studying in Hopkinsville, Pendleton simultaneously served at two churches, Bethel Church and Hopkinsville, who each gave him a hundred dollars a year. He commented, "Some may think that this was poor pay; but my deliberate opinion is that the pay was better than the preaching."[22] The arrangement with these churches was that he would preach one Saturday and two Sundays in the month to each of the Hopkinsville and Bethel churches.[23] Before long, Pendleton's church at Hopkinsville, of which he had become a member, called for his ordination. The ordination council consisted of four men and met on November 2, 1833.[24]

In the latter part of 1836, Pendleton was called to pastor the First Baptist Church of Bowling Green, Kentucky. He officially began January 1, 1837, and continued serving this church for twenty consecutive years with the exception of a few months, spent in Russellville, Kentucky, around 1850.[25] He was the first man in southern Kentucky to devote himself to full-time ministry, making four hundred dollars a year.[26] In August of 1837, Pendleton went with John Waller to the Russell Creek Associational meeting at Columbia in Adair County, Kentucky, on a trip that would change his life forever.

The trip to the Russell Creek Association would cover over seventy miles on horseback. The two gentlemen stayed the night in Glasgow, which was almost half way, with Richard Garnett, and Pendleton was introduced to his daughter,

---

[22]Pendleton, *Reminiscences of a Long Life*, 40.
[23]Spencer, *A History of Kentucky Baptists*, 524.
[24] Pendleton, *Reminiscences of a Long Life*, 42.
[25]Spencer, *History of Kentucky Baptists*, 524. In January 1850, Pendleton kept a commitment to Alfred Taylor by helping him with his church at Green River. The church at Bowling Green, having been without a pastor, invited Pendleton to resume his former place of service. Pendleton accepted and moved back to Bowling Green. See Compton, "J. M. Pendleton: A Nineteenth-Century Baptist Statesman (1811–1891)," 30.
[26]Eitel, "James Madison Pendleton," 190.

Catherine S. Garnett. Catherine, her brother, and another gentleman accompanied Pendleton to the associational meeting. After the meeting concluded, Pendleton had a thirty-mile ride back to Glasgow during which he became acquainted with Catherine. He wrote, "I was impressed with the excellences of her character and her general intelligence."[27] In October 1837, Pendleton went to Louisville for the formation of the General Association of Kentucky Baptists. On his way home, he went about twenty miles out of the way to visit Catherine. On this visit, he informed her of his love for her and proposed to marry her. This took her by surprise. Thus, Pendleton urged her not to answer immediately. Before the end of the year, Catherine returned with a favorable answer to Pendleton's proposal, and on March 13, 1838, James Madison Pendleton and Catherine S. Garnett were united in holy matrimony.[28] Beginning a family would not take long as the Pendletons gave birth to their first child on January 8, 1839. She was named Letitia after a dear friend. On May 5, 1840, John Malcom Pendleton was the second child born to the Pendletons, and on March 11, 1844, Fannie, the third child, was born.[29]

THE EXPANDING MINISTRY 1849–1857

Pendleton's ministry began to expand through the writing of both articles and books. In fact, over this eight year time span, he would write over two hundred articles and publish two books. Although his work received mixed reviews, he continued to publish. Part of his success can be attributed to timing and cultural influences which provided the setting for Pendleton's position. Some of the influences which contributed to Pendleton's success included: (1) an increased number of Christians from the "Great Revival" searching for the right church, (2) controversy over evangelism and

---

[27]Pendleton, *Reminiscences of a Long Life*, 52.
[28]Bogard, *Pillars of Orthodoxy, or Defenders of the Faith*, 260.
[29]Huddleston, "James Madison Pendleton: A Critical Biography," 29.

missions, and (3) the search for denominational identity.[30] A summary of Pendleton's writings will demonstrate the exact nature of his influence.

At first Pendleton's published writings focused on the issue of slavery but would eventually expand to other topics. This section will utilize three divisions to discuss his work: (1) the beginning of the slavery issue, (2) miscellaneous works, and (3) Pendleton's part in the Landmark movement.

The Beginning of the Slavery Issue

Pendleton's deep interest in emancipation resulted in more than twenty articles for a newspaper named *The Examiner* published in Louisville signed "A Southern Emancipationist."[31] However, Pendleton's position was not a popular one, and during the summer of 1849, he submitted his resignation from his pastorate at the First Baptist Church of Bowling Green over the issue of emancipation of slaves. The resignation was refused, and he remained pastor.

The issue of slavery affected the First Baptist Church of Bowling Green and the rest of the nation. Living in the southern part of Kentucky near the Tennessee state line and later in Nashville, Pendleton found himself surrounded by a majority who supported the cause of slavery. One writer said, "From the 1830s through the secession crisis, religion took on a major role in the proslavery crusade. When northern abolitionists contended that slavery per se was a sin,

---

[30]For a complete study, see Eugene T. Moore, "The Background of the Landmark Movement" (Th.M. thesis, Southwestern Baptist Theological Seminary, 1947); and LeRoy B. Hogue, "A Study of the Antecedents of Landmarkism" (Th.D. diss., Southern Baptist Theological Seminary, 1966). Other factors could include: the American Bible Society's translation of βαπτίζω; Kentucky resident John Taylor's emphasis on the local church through his *Thoughts on Missions*; and attempts to battle Alexander Campbell. For a good history of the Campbellite movement from their perspective, see W. E. Garrison and A. T. DeGroot, *The Disciples of Christ* (St. Louis: Christian Board of Publications, 1948).

[31]Pendleton, *Reminiscences of a Long Life*, 93.

Southern clergymen responded that the institution was a moral one. In response to this anti-slavery attack, Southern clerics forged an impregnable union between religion, morality, and slavery."[32]

Basically three positions existed on the issue. First, there were those who supported the institution of slavery. Second, there were those who felt that slaves should be slowly freed. Pendleton held this position which supported the gradual emancipation of slaves. Third, there were those called abolitionists who believed that slavery should be immediately ended.[33] This issue divided families, states, and the nation. By supporting the gradual emancipation of slaves, Pendleton received criticism from anti-slavery and pro-slavery proponents.[34]

---

[32]Mitchell Snay, *Gospel of Disunion: Religion and Separatism in the Antebellum South* (Chapel Hill: University of North Carolina, 1997), 53. Mark Noll, *America's God* (New York: Oxford University Press, 2002), 386–401, discussed "The Bible and Slavery" specifically addressing the biblical defense of slavery (388–9).

[33]For further research on the issue of slavery see: Mitchell Snay, "Gospel of Disunion: Religion and the Rise of Southern Separatism, 1830–1861" (Ph.D. diss., Brandeis Unviersity, 1984); Edward Crowther, "Southern Protestants, Slavery, and Secession: A Study in Southern Religious Ideology, 1830–1861" (Ph.D. diss., Auburn University, 1986); Conrad Engelder, "The Churches and Slavery: A Study of the Attitudes Toward Slavery of the Major Protestant Denominations" (Ph.D. diss., University of Michigan, 1964); J. Morgan Kousser & James M. McPherson, eds., *Region, Race, and Reconstruction: Essays in Honor of C. Vann Woodward* (New York: Oxford University Press, 1982); Bertram Wyatt-Brown, *Southern Honor: Ethics and Behavior in the Old South* (New York, Oxford University Press, 1982); Noll, *America's God*; Edward R. Crowther, "Holy Honor: Sacred and Secular in the Old South," *Journal of Southern History* 58 (November 1992): 619–36; Mitchell Snay, "American Thought and Southern Distinctiveness: The Southern Clergy and the Sanctification of Slavery," *Civil War History* 35 (December 1989): 311–28; and E. T. Winkler, "Introduction to Notes and Questions for the Oral Instruction of Colored People," in *Teaching Truth, Training Hearts*, ed. Thomas Nettles (Amityville: Calvary Press, 1998), 125–34.

[34]Pendleton was sometimes accused of owning slaves. He responded, "By the will of my father, I became the owner of a colored boy, but I gave him

Miscellaneous Works

Pendleton continued to write for the *Baptist Banner* under its new name, the *Western Recorder*.[35] Two particular articles concerning "An Able Ministry" began what would be a recurring theme throughout his writing career.[36] On February 5, 1853, Pendleton introduced a series of articles designed to benefit local Baptist pastors. The first article, titled "Short Sermons," appeared in this year and addressed the issue of "The Piety of the Thessalonian Church."[37] Throughout his life span, he would publish at least forty-nine other short sermons in the *Tennessee Baptist*. Furthermore, he published two books which were collections of sermons.[38] Although there is no way to measure the use of these sermons by local ministers, it is likely that they had considerable influence.[39] Many preachers of this time worked

---

permission to go to Liberia and was attempting to prepare him for the enjoyment of freedom, when he was attacked with disease and died." Furthermore, he added, "It is to me a consoling thought, that while a member of my family he became, as I believe, a sincere Christian." See James Madison Pendleton, "Corrections," *Baptist Banner* (October 3, 1849). After Pendleton's mother died, he was left in a difficult position. By the will of his father, in the distribution of the estate, he again became a slaveholder. The law would not allow Pendleton to free her so he hired her out and paid her the amount for which she was hired and added to it ten percent. As soon as law permitted, he released her. Pendleton said, "I was not a slave-holder *morally* but *legally*." See Pendleton, *Reminiscences of a Long Life*, 127–8.

[35]The *Baptist Banner* was a religious newspaper published in Louisville, Kentucky. In 1851, the name changed to the *Western Recorder*.

[36]James Madison Pendleton, "An Able Ministry," *Western Recorder* (June 11, 1851); and "An Able Ministry Continued," *Western Recorder* (June 18, 1851).

[37]James Madison Pendleton, "Short Sermons Number 1: The Piety of the Thessalonian Church," *Tennessee Baptist* (February 5, 1853).

[38]James Madison Pendleton, *Notes of Sermons* (Philadelphia: American Baptist Publication Society, 1886); and *Short Sermons on Important Subjects* (St. Louis: National Baptist Publishing, 1859).

[39]The *Tennessee Baptists* had a circulation in January of 1859 of more than thirteen thousand which made it the largest Baptist weekly in the world. J. R. Graves, "The Goal Won at Last," *Tennessee Baptist* (January 8,

during the week to provide for their families and could not devote themselves to full-time ministry. Thus, such works were attractive and useful to them.

Pendleton was also asked to defend Baptist beliefs during this time frame. He said, "I was called on to preach a dedication sermon at Liberty Church, Logan County, and I gave my reasons for being a Baptist."[40] He later expanded this sermon into a book called *Three Reasons Why I Am a Baptist*.[41] The preface, written May 4, 1853, said, "Many brethren have expressed a desire that these Reasons should be published, giving it as their opinion, that the publication would promote scriptural views of Baptism and Church Government."[42] The following three were his reasons for being Baptist:

> (1) because Baptists regard the baptism of infants as unscriptural, and insist on the baptism of believers in Christ—and of believers alone; (2) because Baptists consider the immersion in water, of a believer, essential to baptism—so essential that there is no baptism without it; and (3) because Baptists practice the congregational

---

1859). Additionally other articles indicate the popularity of Pendleton's sermons. O. H. Morrow, "Pendleton's Sermons," *Tennessee Baptist* (July 21, 1860) stated concerning *Short Sermons on Important Subjects*, "I had but one dollar on earth, I gave it cheerfully for the book... I hope that Bro. Pendleton will live to write many more such volumes; and I hope to possess another dollar, and yet another as they may be offered for sale."

[40]Pendleton, *Reminiscences of a Long Life*, 103.

[41]James Madison Pendleton, *Three Reasons Why I Am a Baptist* (Cincinnati: Moore, Anderson & Company, 1853). This was his first work designed to be published as a book, and before his death, this book would be published under two additional titles. *Three Reasons Why I Am a Baptist with a Fourth Reason Added on Communion* (St. Louis: National Baptist Publishing, 1856); and *Distinctive Principles of Baptists* (Philadelphia: American Baptist Publication Society, 1882).

[42]Pendleton, *Three Reasons Why I Am a Baptist*, iii.

form of church government, which is the New Testament model.[43]

In 1854, two series of articles began in the *Tennessee Baptist* which would later be accumulated and published as books. "Thoughts on Christian Duty" began with the first of twenty articles on May 6, 1854.[44] These twenty articles later made up the chapters of the book by the same title.[45] Next, Pendleton began writing "Questions to the Impenitent." He directed these articles to unbelievers challenging them to put their faith in Jesus Christ. This series of eighteen articles was published as a book three years later.[46]

Some of his more lengthy articles were published in the *Southern Baptist Review*.[47] Perhaps the most helpful are two articles written on "The Scriptural Meaning of the Term Church."[48] These articles provide insight into Pendleton's definition of the church and his understanding of the local versus the universal church. He disagreed with Graves and Dayton over the existence of the universal church. Pendleton wrote, "In the New Testament the term church in its application to the followers of Christ refers either to a particular congregation of saints, or to the redeemed in the aggregate. It is used in the latter sense in Ephesians 1:22;

---

[43]Ibid., 1, 82, and 148. Pendleton later added a fourth reason which was because Baptists alone scripturally observe the Lord's Supper. See Pendleton, *Three Reasons Why I Am a Baptist with a Fourth Reason Added on Communion*, 172.

[44]James Madison Pendleton, "Thoughts on Christian Duty Number 1: The Christian Profession," *Tennessee Baptist* (May 6, 1854).

[45]James Madison Pendleton, *Thoughts on Christian Duty* (Nashville: Southwestern Publishing House, 1857).

[46]James Madison Pendleton, *Questions to the Impenitent* (St. Louis: St. Louis Baptist Publishing, 1857).

[47]Pendleton served as editor for this publication which existed approximately five years.

[48]James Madison Pendleton, "The Scriptural Meaning of the Term Church," *The Southern Baptist Review* 1 (January 1855): 6–17 and "The Scriptural Meaning of the Term Church," *The Southern Baptist Review* 1 (February–March 1855). 65–83.

3:21; 5:25, 27."[49] Thus, Pendleton believed in the existence of the universal church.

Pendleton also provided a working definition for the church. He commented, "A congregation of saints, organized according to the gospel, whether that congregation is large or small, is a New Testament church."[50] This definition would undergo further development in his *Church Manual* published in 1867.[51]

Additional articles demonstrated Pendleton's thoughts on "The Atonement of Christ," which would later be expanded into a book by the same name but not published until 1885.[52] He also wrote an article titled "Justification," which would be published thirty-two years later in his *Christian Doctrines* almost word for word, demonstrating surprising continuity between his early and mature theological formulation.[53]

Pendleton's articles give clues into his views on a variety of issues not addressed in his books. For example, Pendleton supported extemporaneous preaching which probably means he practiced it while preaching.[54] He supported female education on multiple occasions and enrolled his daughter in

---

[49]Pendleton, "The Scriptural Meaning of the Term Church," 8–9.
[50]Ibid., 9.
[51]In his *Church Manual: Designed for the Use of Baptist Churches* (Philadelphia: American Baptist Publication Society, 1867), 7, Pendleton stated, "A church is a congregation of Christ's baptized disciples, acknowledging him as their Head, relying on his atoning sacrifice for justification before God, and depending on the Holy Spirit for sanctification, united in the belief of the gospel, agreeing to maintain its ordinances and obey its precepts, meeting together for worship, and cooperating for the extension of Christ's kingdom in the world."
[52]James Madison Pendleton, "The Atonement of Christ," *The Southern Baptist Review* 2 (January–February 1856): 41–61; and James Madison Pendleton, *The Atonement of Christ* (Philadelphia: American Baptist Publication Society, 1885).
[53]James Madison Pendleton, "Justification," *The Southern Baptist Review* 2 (January–February 1856): 149–63.
[54]James Madison Pendleton, "Extemporaneous Preaching," *The Southern Baptist Review* 1 (April–May 1855): 262.

college.⁵⁵ He also began a series of twenty-one articles on Acts called "Conversations on the Acts of the Apostles."⁵⁶

One last major event occurred in 1856. This was the publication of a new version of Pendleton's *Three Reasons Why I Am a Baptist*. After the book had sold approximately thirteen thousand copies, Pendleton decided to add two appendices and make a few minor changes.⁵⁷ Pendleton's fourth reason for being Baptist was "Baptists alone scripturally observe the Lord's Supper."⁵⁸ In this section, Pendleton denied the legitimacy of transubstantiation and consubstantiation. He further stressed that the Lord's Supper was "a Church ordinance, to be observed as a memorial of the death of Christ."⁵⁹ As a church ordinance, the Lord's Supper should be observed only by the members of a visible church of Christ. Because Pendleton did not believe that Pedobaptist churches were visible churches of Christ, they could not properly partake in communion and could not commune with Baptist churches. More will be said about his views of communion in the chapter of this dissertation which addresses that issue.

Pendleton's Part in the Landmark Movement

The issue of immersion was central in the Landmark movement. Most Baptists agreed that improper baptism (non-immersion) should not be accepted but confusion emerged over accepting the baptism of a believer by

---

⁵⁵James Madison Pendleton, "Plea for Thorough Female Education," *The Southern Baptist Review* 2 (July–August 1856): 369–84; and James Madison Pendleton, "Letter Entitled, 'Mary Sharpe College, Winchester, Tennessee,'" *Tennessee Baptist* (April 1, 1854).

⁵⁶James Madison Pendleton, "Conversations on the Acts of the Apostles: Number 1," *Tennessee Baptist* (August 23, 1856).

⁵⁷The first appendix was his fourth reason for being a Baptist which addressed communion, and the second appendix discussed the perpetuity of circumcision as it relates to Jewish people.

⁵⁸Pendleton, *Three Reasons I am a Baptist, with a Fourth Reason Added, on Communion*, 172.

⁵⁹Ibid., 177.

immersion performed by a Pedobaptist. The term used to describe such baptisms was "alien immersion."[60] Graves had been discussing the question of the validity of alien immersions since 1846, and on June 24, 1851, Graves met with others and developed the "Cotton Grove Resolutions."[61] Pendleton's involvement began in 1852. Pendleton said, "Everything went on in the ordinary style till February, 1852, when Rev. J. R. Graves, of Nashville, held a meeting with us."[62] Graves had established his position on the issue and requested to leave and not conduct the revival meetings if Pendleton held to a different view. Pendleton asked him to stay and preach saying, "I have never given the matter of alien immersion a thorough study, and I shall be glad to hear you preach on that subject."[63] By the end of the meeting, Graves's preaching had convinced Pendleton to the point that he announced full agreement with Graves. Additionally, Graves had so excited the Pedobaptists on the issue of baptism that several sermons were preached on the subject after his departure.[64] In fact, the attacks against Graves encouraged Pendleton to defend him more vehemently.[65]

---

[60]For a complete study of alien baptism, see Philip Edward Rodgerson, "A Historical Study of Alien Baptism Among Baptists Since 1640" (Th.D. diss., Southern Baptist Theological Seminary, 1952).

[61]J. R. Graves, *Old Landmarkism: What Is It?* (Texarkana: Bogard Press, 1880), 14.

[62]Pendleton, *Reminiscences of a Long Life*, 96.

[63]As in O. L. Hailey, *J. R. Graves: Life, Times and Teachings* (Nashville: O. L. Hailey, 1929), 73.

[64]Pendleton, *Reminiscences of a Long Life*, 103. Pendleton does not give the names of those who preached the sermons. He wrote, "Several sermons were afterward preached by Methodist and Presbyterian ministers." One of those ministers was W. Randolph, pastor of the Methodist church in Bowling Green whom Pendleton would later debate. See unsigned article, "To the Public," *Tennessee Baptist* (May 15, 1852).

[65]James Madison Pendleton, "Letter to Brother Graves," *Tennessee Baptist* (June 5, 1852). Pendleton commented, "And here is to say once for all, that when a minister visits this place at my solicitation, as you did, and conducts a meeting on principles which meet my hearty approbation, as you did, if after his departure, he is calumniated and persecuted, as you

Pendleton also wrote several articles commenting on the meeting after its conclusion. In an article titled "Revival Intelligence," he stated that "for one week Brother G. preached exclusively to professors of religion."[66] This resulted in a spirit of forgiveness and humbleness. The meeting resulted in about seventy souls converted to God. Those who were converted included Pendleton's thirteen year old daughter. Pendleton said, "I know of no man who conducts a protracted meeting so much to my satisfaction as Brother Graves."[67] This meeting began a long friendship and foreshadowed the denominational fighting which lay ahead.

The first stage of this long controversy began when some including W. Randolph, pastor of the Methodist church in Bowling Green, made several harsh comments concerning Graves. Randolph believed Graves had misused the official doctrinal statement of the Methodist church known as the *Disciplines* during the revival. Pendleton challenged Randolph to a public debate. After the debate, various authors wrote letters to the *Christian Advocate* to which Pendleton responded through the *Western Recorder* and *Tennessee Baptist* newspapers.[68] This discussion would lessen within a few months but reemerge again in the future.

Two years lapsed between Pendleton's initial rejection of alien immersion and his systematic defense of Landmarkism. This printed defense emerged as four articles in the *Tennessee Baptist* titled "Ought Baptists to Recognize Pedobaptist Preachers as Gospel Ministers?"[69] This question

---

have been, I will defend him, though I hear a thousand thunders rolling through the Pedobaptist heavens."

[66]James Madison Pendleton, "Revival Intelligence," *Western Recorder* (March 17, 1852).

[67]Ibid.

[68]James Madison Pendleton, "Letter to Brother Graves," *Tennessee Baptist* (March 27, 1852); "To the Public," *Western Recorder* (May 26, 1852); and "Letter to Brother Graves," *Tennessee Baptist* (June 5, 1852).

[69]James Madison Pendleton, "Ought Baptists to Recognize Pedobaptist Preachers as Gospel Ministers?," *Tennessee Baptist* (July 22, 1854); "Ought

Pendleton answered in the negative. The first three articles put forth the position and the fourth article responded to several objections which had been raised. These four articles were accumulated and published in one tract which Graves titled, *An Old Landmark Re-set*.[70] The title of this tract, which referred to a couple of Old Testament texts, provided the name "Landmarkism" for the movement.[71]

In order to understand the argument, one must first understand what the pamphlet claimed. Thus, a short summary of the work will be given before addressing the debate it sparked.

In *An Old Landmark Re-set*, Pendleton indicated his presuppositions from the beginning. He quoted from Edward Dorr Griffin, who was the third President of Williams College in Massachusetts and a prominent Pedobaptist. Griffin wrote, "If nothing but immersion is baptism, there is no visible church except among the Baptists."[72] This statement taken from a Pedobaptist served as the starting point. Griffin and Pendleton agreed that proper baptism was essential to the existence of a visible church. Griffin, of course, did not believe that immersion was the only form of proper baptism.

Baptists to Recognize Pedobaptist Preachers as Gospel Ministers? Number Two," *Tennessee Baptist* (August 5, 1854); "Ought Baptists to Recognize Pedobaptist Preachers as Gospel Ministers? Number Three," *Tennessee Baptist* (August 12, 1854); and "Ought Baptists to Recognize Pedobaptist Preachers as Gospel Preachers?" *Tennessee Baptist* (December 16, 1854).

[70]Pendleton, *Reminiscences of a Long Life*, 103, stated that Graves gave the document its title. Pendleton, *An Old Landmark Re-set*. This work has been re-published from Bogard, *Pillars of Orthodoxy, or Defenders of the Faith*, 266–311. References will be from the reprint edition.

[71]The two passages to which this referred are the King James Version of Prov 22:28, "Remove not the ancient landmark, which thy fathers have set;" and Prov 23:10, "Remove not the old landmark; and enter not into the fields of the fatherless." All Scripture unless otherwise noted will be from the New King James Version.

[72]Edward Dorr Griffin, "Letter on Open Communion," in *Conversations Between Two Laymen on Strict and Mixed Communion*, ed. J. G. Fuller (Boston: Lincoln & Edmands, 1832): 247.

Pendleton, believing that proper baptism must be by immersion of believers, worked out the implications of his belief.

Pendleton built a logical argument upon his presupposition that proper baptism was essential to the existence of a visible church. First, he sought to prove that proper baptism must be by immersion of believers. Second, he implied that only Baptists practice proper baptism. He then concluded that Baptists were the only valid visible churches of Christ. If Baptists were the only valid visible churches of Christ, then they should not invite Pedobaptists to preach in Baptist pulpits. He presented multiple reasons for not exchanging pulpits with Pedobaptists.

The first reason for not inviting Pedobaptists to preach in Baptist pulpits was consistency. Pendleton asked how a church may share the pulpit yet not share communion. It seemed inconsistent to allow someone to preach in a church yet not allow that person to participate in communion. However, he understood that in many small towns the pastors of the Baptist churches and the pastors of the Pedobaptist churches involved in this practice were friends. Thus, he urged Baptists to stand firm on their biblical convictions and not to allow other factors, including friendship, to affect doctrine. He proposed that Baptists not share pulpits or communion with Pedobaptists. This, he claimed, was the only way to be consistent and obey Scripture.

Not only was it inconsistent for Baptists to share the pulpit with Pedobaptists and not share communion, but Pendleton believed that Baptists should not share the pulpit with Pedobaptists because they were not gospel ministers. Pendleton wrote, "If Pedobaptist societies are not churches of Christ, whence do their ministers derive their authority to preach?"[73] In Pendleton's view, a minister of the Gospel must

---

[73]Pendleton, *An Old Landmark Re-set*, 274.

be ordained by a Gospel church. With no Gospel church to ordain their ministers, Pedobaptist societies could not have Gospel ministers. Additionally, Pendleton claimed that Pedobaptists would not recognize someone as a minister of the Gospel who had not been baptized. He was doing no different since he did not believe that Pedobaptists had been properly baptized.[74] Pedobaptists challenged Pendleton's position by noting the apostle Paul's words in Phil 1:15–18 where he rejoiced over those who preached the Gospel, even out of envy and strife. Pendleton responded that Paul did not call them Gospel ministers. The discussion revealed a central question—the question of authority. Did the authority to be a Gospel minister come from the local church, come from the call of God, or come from preaching the proper message?

Pendleton, contending that Paul's words did not mean that such men were true ministers of the Gospel, formed a distinction between a "*kerusso*" and an "*euangelizo*" preacher.[75] The former would be considered a minister of the Gospel and must be authorized by the local church. The latter could be any person who presents the Gospel message. Pendleton implies that while all can be "*euangelizo*" only those ordained by the local church can be "*kerusso*" preachers. Thus, Pedobaptist preachers are not ministers of the Gospel and should not be invited to preach in Baptist pulpits.

Those who disagreed with Pendleton responded either directly to him or through various papers. Pendleton would then respond as he did to the editor of the *Presbyterian Herald*. He said,

---

[74]Ibid., 277.

[75]Ibid., 309. Such a distinction among the Greek words was not unfounded. A distinction can also be found in Edward Hiscox, *The New Directory for Baptist Churches* (Philadelphia: Judson Press, 1894), 94. Hiscox says, "The minister is the *kerux*, the herald, who preaches the Gospel, who proclaims the glad tidings to men. The pastor is the *poimen*, who folds and feeds and leads the flock." Hiscox discusses James as a pastor while Paul and Barnabas were ministers.

Where there is no baptism, there are no visible churches. There is no baptism among Pedo-baptists. Therefore, there are no visible churches. Where there are no visible churches, there is no gospel authority to preach. There are no visible churches among Pedo-baptists. Therefore, there is no gospel authority to preach.[76]

A Methodist minister challenged Pendleton in the *Christian Advocate*. He argued that God gave validity to Methodist ministers by using them. He cited Isaac Watts as his primary example. Pendleton quickly responded, "As to singing Watts' Hymns I have only to say that, so far as I know, church action is not necessary to authorize a man to make Hymns; but church action is necessary to authorize a man to preach."[77] Pendleton continued to believe that the "Landmark" stood and that Baptists should not invite Pedobaptists into their pulpits.

After the publication of Pendleton's tract, the tone of discussion remained cordial among Baptists. This can be seen by S. H. Ford who called Pendleton, "A man whom we highly esteem for his talents, his integrity, and piety, and with whom we are sorry to have to differ."[78] However, over the next two years, the tone shifted to bitterness and animosity. For example, an unsigned article stated, "Brethren Graves and Pendleton have each taken their position and shown their hand in answer to the call we made upon them to cease fanning the fires of strife in our denomination. Bro. Graves, it seems, is to do the fighting,

---

[76]James Madison Pendleton, "Reprint of Letter of J. M. Pendleton to Dr. Hill, Editor of Presbyterian Herald," *Tennessee Baptist* (September 2, 1854).

[77]James Madison Pendleton, "Ought Baptists to Recognize Pedobaptist Preachers as Gospel Preachers?" *Tennessee Baptist* (December 16, 1854).

[78]S. H. Ford, "Elder J. M. Pendleton and High Churchism," *Western Recorder* (January 10, 1855).

and Bro. Pendleton the ridiculing. They both seem determined on war, but each in a different way."[79]

As the discussion continued it became more personal and more divisive. One example was the personal feud which arose between J. R. Graves and R. B. C. Howell over the issue of church discipline in the First Baptist Church of Nashville, Tennessee. Then the Civil War would send Pendleton North which all but ended his support of Landmarkism in periodicals. Additionally, Graves complicated the issue of Landmarkism by adding tenets to it. The inclusion of close communion, church successionism, and the denial of the universal church created contention because Pendleton did not support those additions. Thus, at the end of his life, Pendleton stated that he held to Landmarkism, but the Landmarkism to which he held was different from the beliefs that Graves and others might include in the movement. His participation in this movement was minimal after the Civil War.

RELOCATION TO MURFREESBORO, TENNESSEE 1857–1861

Having expanded his ministry through writing, drastic change came in January 1857. Pendleton was offered the Chair of Theology at Union University. He "promptly declined the appointment" and informed the trustees that he was "utterly incompetent, having never been to a theological school."[80] He went on to comment that he knew nothing of theology except what he had learned from the Bible. This he thought would end the discussion; however, the trustees replied that "they wanted a man who had learned his theology from the Bible."[81] Pendleton also insisted that could not give up preaching, so arrangements were made for him to

---

[79]Unsigned article, "The Tennessee Baptist Irreconcilable," *Western Recorder* (October 31, 1855).
[80]Pendleton, *Reminiscences of a Long Life*, 108.
[81]Ibid.

take over the pulpit of the Baptist Church in Murfreesboro. Thus, he accepted the invitation.

The announcement of Pendleton's appointment said, "The upmost unanimity prevailed among the Trustees and Faculty. He is regarded by both as preeminently the man for the position. He is a model sermonizer, and not only ripe but a sound theological scholar."[82] With the move came the heartache of leaving the church he had served for almost twenty years. Regarding the First Baptist Church of Bowling Green, Kentucky, Pendleton commented, "God bless this church! Its prosperity will always contribute to my happiness, and its trials, should trials be its lot, will touch a sympathetic chord in my heart. I leave this church without an unkind feeling toward any member."[83] Thus, Pendleton moved to Tennessee.

While teaching theology, Pendleton used texts written by Thomas Hartwell Horne, Henry Jones Ripley, John Dagg, and John Dick.[84] He commented that many times he found himself teaching things of which he knew nothing except what he had learned himself without the aid of anyone. These books and Pendleton's own systematic formulation reveal much about his theological position.[85] Pendleton's soteriology followed the strand of Baptist thought influenced

---

[82]Unsigned announcement, "Theological Chair at Union University," *Tennessee Baptist* (December 6, 1856).

[83]James Madison Pendleton, "Leaving Kentucky," *Tennessee Baptist* (January 10, 1857).

[84]Pendleton, *Reminiscences of a Long Life*, 111. Thomas Hartwell Horne, *An Introduction to the Critical Study of Knowledge of the Holy Scriptures* (Philadelphia: E. Littell, 1825); Henry Jones Ripley and Henry Ware, *Sacred Rhetoric; or Composition and Delivery of Sermons* (Boston: Gould and Lincoln, 1849); John Dagg, *Manual of Theology* (Charleston: Southern Baptist Publication Society, 1857); and John Dick, *Lectures on Theology* (Philadelphia: J. Whetham, 1836).

[85]See James Madison Pendleton, *Christian Doctrines: A Compendium of Theology* (Philadelphia: American Baptist Publication Society, 1906) for his formulation.

by Andrew Fuller denying limited atonement.[86] Pendleton's views on Scripture place him with the majority of American Protestants affirming reliance on Scripture alone.[87]

Before his ministry ended, Pendleton obtained a national reputation and a place in history among Baptist theologians.[88] His lasting significance is "closely tied to the impact of Southern Baptist Landmarkism."[89] By focusing on the local church, he helped bring distinctive ecclesiological principles of Baptists to the forefront and contributed to developing a denominational identity. His impact primarily came through his writing in the pages of the *Tennessee Baptist* and publishing books. He was not considered the Baptist statesman that John Dagg was, nor as great a theologian as Charles Hodge,[90] and did not obtain the notoriety in the pulpit that Charles Spurgeon obtained; however, Pendleton appealed to the common man and especially to Baptists. Before his death it was stated of Pendleton, "No publications are more sought for, than those which issue from his pen, by Baptists. . . . Doctor Pendleton

---

[86]For a discussion of Calvinism among Baptists, see E. Brooks Holifield, *Theology in America* (London: Yale University, 2003), 278–90; and Thomas Nettles, *By His Grace and for His Glory* (Grand Rapids: Baker, 1986).

[87]Burnett, *Sketches of Tennessee's Pioneer Baptist Preachers*, 406. Pendleton particularly focused on the original languages, reading the New Testament through in Greek twenty-seven times, but he also read it more than once in Latin and French. For a discussion of the reliance on Scripture during this time frame, see Noll, *America's God*, 370–1. For a discussion of Baptist views on Scripture, see L. Russ Bush, and Thomas Nettles, *Baptists and the Bible*, Revised and Expanded (Nashville: Broadman & Holman, 1999). This work states, "Pendleton is firm in his conviction that the Spirit's governance of inspiration extended to the very words of the text" (199).

[88]Burnett, *Sketches of Tennessee's Pioneer Baptist Preachers*, 406.

[89]Eitel, "James Madison Pendleton," 198.

[90]See E. Brooks Holifield, *The Gentlemen Theologians: American Theology in Southern Culture 1795–1860* (Durham: Duke University Press, 1978). Holifield does not mention Pendleton but does both Dagg and Hodge.

has a well deserved and well earned national reputation, which few men have attained."[91]

In the midst of moving and teaching, Pendleton wrote seventy-nine articles in 1857, and over the next five years, he wrote over 460 articles. These articles provide insight into Pendleton's activity. His writings during this period can be divided into four sections. First, miscellaneous works help to construct a complete view of Pendleton. Second, Pendleton interacted with some influential contemporaries. Third, the Graves-Howell controversy emerged, and fourth, the continued issue of slavery came to a boiling point. These categories will serve as areas of discussion.

Miscellaneous Works

These articles fall into no particular category but provide insight into Pendleton's thinking. One article stated that Christian men had no reason to join secret societies.[92] Another article addressed the recently accepted rules for conduct at Union University and another condemned the wearing of expensive jewelry and clothing.[93] These articles demonstrate Pendleton's conservative nature on practical issues.

In another article Pendleton expressed his friendship with Graves. "I know no man who has had so much opposition to encounter. I know no man at whom so many darts have been thrown. Some of those darts have occasionally struck me, because I was standing by your side, but I have never

---

[91]Joseph H. Borum, *Biographical Sketches of Tennessee Baptist Ministers* (Memphis: Rogers and Co., 1880), 513.

[92]James Madison Pendleton, "Query—Secret Societies," *Tennessee Baptist* (August 8, 1857). This article identifies a point of contention between Pendleton and R. B. C. Howell, who was a Mason.

[93]James Madison Pendleton, "Union University," *Tennessee Baptist* (August 15, 1857). The rules worthy of notation are a shift to not allowing students to partake of any intoxicating drink, nor attend public balls or dancing parties, nor carry deadly weapons. James Madison Pendleton, "Thoughts on Jewelry," *Tennessee Baptist* (August 22, 1857).

regretted that I was standing there. I stand there still. . . ."[94] This relationship would strengthen in 1858 when Pendleton and A. C. Dayton would join Graves as joint editors of the *Tennessee Baptist*. Pendleton commented on the change: "My becoming editor did not impose on me the necessity of writing more than I had done; for I had been for several years engaged to supply two columns a week for the paper. . . ."[95] With this new relationship, Pendleton changed the signature of his articles from "J. M. P." to just "P."[96]

Pendleton began several new series in the *Tennessee Baptist*. They included: "Sunday Morning Thoughts;"[97] "Thoughts on the Lord's Supper;"[98] "Thoughts on Giving;"[99] "Letters to Young Preachers;"[100] and "Conant's Revision of Matthew."[101] Another article of interest was titled "There is No Danger."[102] This article addressed fears that Landmarkism would divide

---

[94]James Madison Pendleton, "Letter to Brother Graves," *Tennessee Baptist* (October 3, 1857).

[95]Pendleton, *Reminiscences of a Long Life*, 112.

[96]James Madison Pendleton, "New Relation," *Tennessee Baptist* (May 15, 1858).

[97]James Madison Pendleton, "Sunday Morning Thoughts," *Tennessee Baptist* (May 15, 1858). He wrote twenty-four articles under this title in 1858–59, and on October 8, 1859, he changed the name to "Sabbath Morning Thoughts" and the series continued for another twenty-nine articles.

[98]James Madison Pendleton, "Thoughts on the Lord's Supper: Number 1," *Tennessee Baptist* (October 29, 1859). Pendleton wrote twenty-one articles on this subject during 1859–1861.

[99]James Madison Pendleton, "Thoughts on Giving: Number 1," *Tennessee Baptist* (November 26, 1859). Pendleton wrote fourteen articles on this subject during 1859–1860.

[100]James Madison Pendleton, "Letters to Young Preachers: Number 1," *Tennessee Baptist* (April 14, 1860). Pendleton wrote fifteen letters on this subject during 1860–61.

[101]James Madison Pendleton, "Conant's Revision of Matthew: Number 1," *Tennessee Baptist* (January 26, 1861). Pendleton wrote eleven articles on this subject during 1862.

[102]James Madison Pendleton, "There is no Danger," *Tennessee Baptist* (June 5, 1858). Pendleton would again put forth his opinion that no danger existed in another article. "Where Is the Danger?," *Tennessee Baptist* (October 1, 1859).

the Southern Baptist Convention. Pendleton did not feel there was any way this issue would divide the Convention.[103] One article demonstrating that Pendleton believed a person could not be saved without hearing the Gospel was titled, "Are the Heathen Saved Without the Gospel?"[104]

He also published multiple books during this time frame. *Thoughts on Christian Duty* was originally published in the *Tennessee Baptist* and designed to benefit Christians in the process of sanctification.[105] *Questions to the Impenitent* demonstrated two consistent themes which mark Pendleton's life.[106] First, he desired to see people accept the Gospel message of Jesus Christ, and second, his writings were practical. This book confronted its readers with the reality of the decision to accept or reject Christ. *Christianity Susceptible of Legal Proof* contained fifty-two pocket-sized pages and was printed in 1858.[107] In it, Pendleton discussed the reliability of the witness of the disciples and the Scriptures.

In January 1859, Pendleton's friend and co-worker, Joseph H. Eaton, President of Union University, died. Pendleton preached the funeral, and the *Sermon on the Death of J. H. Eaton* was later published.[108] Not only did this loss affect

---

[103]Many people blame Landmarkism for an eventual split. For further research see David O. Moore, "The Landmark Baptists and Their Attack Upon the Southern Baptist Convention Historically Analyzed" (Ph.D. diss., Southern Baptist Theological Seminary, 1950).

[104]James Madison Pendleton, "Are the Heathen Saved Without the Gospel?," *Tennessee Baptist* (November 26, 1859).

[105]Pendleton, *Thoughts on Christian Duty*, 3. Pendleton said in the preface, "The author supposed that something of the kind would be beneficial to those who had just entered on the Christian life, and he undertook the task because no one else seemed inclined to undertake it."

[106]James Madison Pendleton, *Questions to the Impenitent* (St. Louis: St. Louis Baptist Publishing, 1857).

[107] James Madison Pendleton. *Christianity Susceptible of Legal Proof* (Nashville: Southwestern Publishing House, 1858).

[108]James Madison Pendleton, *Sermon on the Death of J. H. Eaton*, (Nashville: Southwestern Publishing House, 1859). Pendleton preached the funeral sermon on Acts 7:59, "Lord Jesus, receive my Spirit."

Pendleton personally, but because he became acting chairman, it also affected him professionally. Pendleton stated, "For two years I acted as Chairman of the faculty and therefore presided on commencement occasions, and handed to the graduates their diplomas in testimony of their scholarship."[109] Thus, during 1859, Pendleton served as acting president of Union University, as pastor of the First Baptist Church of Murfreesboro, as co-editor of the *Tennessee Baptist*, as editor of *The Southern Baptist Review*, as teacher of theology at Union University, as author of *Short Sermons on Important Subjects*,[110] and as author of 130 articles.

Interaction With Contemporaries

Pendleton first interacted with Francis Wayland by writing a review of his *Notes on the Principles and Practices of Baptists*.[111] This review provided insight into the cultural factors behind Landmarkism's success and pointed to areas of agreement between Pendleton and Wayland. While Pendleton agreed with the majority of the work, he harbored personal feelings against Wayland for his actions in a controversy with the American Bible Society in 1836 in

---

[109]Pendleton, *Reminiscences of a Long Life*, 113.

[110]Pendleton, *Short Sermons on Important Subjects*. This work contained fifty sermons written from 1855 to 1859 "specifically useful to one class of readers—young preachers." In these sermons, Pendleton utilized the exegetical method to expound short passages of Scripture. He said, "If the sermons have not grown out of the texts, I have unfortunately failed to carry my intention into effect" (5). Most of these sermons concluded with a section called "remarks" which applied truths to the believer's lives.

[111]James Madison Pendleton, "A Review of *Principles and Practices of Baptists*," *The Southern Baptist Review* 3 (January 1857): 51–73. Francis Wayland, *Notes on the Principles and Practices of Baptist Churches* (New York: Sheldon & Co., 1857).

which Wayland supported the decision of the Society to translate the word "*baptizo*" as baptize instead of immerse.[112]

Pendleton agreed with Wayland on baptism, local church independence, and the call to the ministry. Wayland indicated that the church carried the authority for appointing ministers of the Gospel. This pleased Pendleton as it supported one of his points in *An Old Landmark Re-set*. In an interesting note, both Pendleton and Wayland agreed that restricting music to choirs should not be practiced and longed for a time when Baptist congregations would cease to praise God by proxy and personally sing praises to His name. Pendleton concluded his review by stating, "We, therefore, give it a hearty recommendation, though we may not endorse every sentiment it contains."[113]

Another article containing Pendleton's remarks on a contemporary was his "Review of Dagg's *Church Order*."[114] Dagg, who was perhaps the premier Southern Baptist theologian of this time, also did extensive work in the area of ecclesiology. Pendleton seemed pleased that this book had been written as it filled some gaps in Dagg's *Manual of Theology*. He said, "We are glad that the former volume has been succeeded by the present [*A Manual of Church Order*], for there was a vacuum that needed to be filled. True, it is not, in all respects, filled just as we would have it, but this circumstance shall not be made the occasion of captious

---

[112]Pendleton stated, "Our prejudice may have originated partly on other accounts. We do not deny that while we have ever admired Dr. Wayland's intellectual greatness, we have for years deplored his want of nerve and decision as a Baptist. How could we do otherwise than regret his preparing the obnoxious resolution adopted by the American Bible Society in 1836—a resolution which virtually makes the common English Version the standard of all translations on which said Society bestows its patronage?" See Pendleton, "A Review of *Principles and Practices of Baptists*," 51–2.

[113]Ibid., 72–3.

[114]James Madison Pendleton, "Review of Dagg's *Church Order*," *The Southern Baptist Review* 5 (January 1859): 36–55. John Dagg, *Manual of Church Order* (Charleston: Southern Baptist Publication Society, 1858; reprint, Harrisonburg: Gano Books, 1990), 225.

complaint."[115] Pendleton did not express anger even over a twelve page section specifically criticizing his tract "An Old Landmark Re-set."[116]

Dagg criticized Pendleton for starting with a premise furnished by a Pedobaptist rather than one furnished from Scripture itself.[117] He also disagreed with Pendleton concerning ministers, writing "that ministers of the word, as such, are officers of the universal church; and that their call to the ministry by the Holy Spirit, is complete in itself, without the addition of outward ceremony."[118]

Pendleton specifically responded to Dagg's placement of the officers as officers of the universal church by questioning why local Baptist churches ordained preachers if they are officers of the universal church. Concerning Dagg's comments, Pendleton concluded, "More than four years have passed away since the Landmark was written; but we are not yet inclined to retract a single sentence. . . ."[119]

Graves-Howell Controversy

In 1858, the controversy between Graves and Howell began over the Southern Baptist Convention Bible Board and the formation of the Southern Baptist Sunday School Union. Graves desired the formation of the Southern Baptist Sunday School Union of which Dayton would be president and Graves recording secretary. Howell expressed concern about this group competing with the Southern Baptist Publication Society of Charleston which had published several of his books, and he further expressed concern about a Southern Baptist agency under Landmark control. Howell acted by writing a harsh letter criticizing the Landmark movement to

---

[115]Pendleton, "Review of Dagg's *Church Order*," 36.
[116]Dagg, *Manual of Church Order*, 286–98.
[117]Ibid., 289. See pp. 31–2 in this dissertation for further discussion of this premise.
[118]Ibid., 292.
[119]Pendleton, "Review of Dagg's *Church Order*," 46.

the editor of the *Christian Index*. This sparked a series of attacks on Howell by Graves through the pages of the *Tennessee Baptist*.[120] Howell responded by bringing Graves before the church for church discipline in a trial that lasted from October 12–18, 1858, and concluded with Graves's exclusion from the church membership.[121] Graves appealed to the Baptist General Association of Tennessee, claiming that his group now constituted the true First Baptist Church and won his appeal by a vote of 164 to twenty-seven.[122] This controversy continued to be fought in print[123] and came to a head at the Southern Baptist Convention of 1859 where Howell was elected president but immediately declined to serve in an effort to avoid division.[124]

---

[120]For a complete study, see Kenneth Vaughn Weatherford, "The Graves-Howell Controversy" (Ph.D. diss., Baylor University, 1991). For a summary, see chapter 11 on "Landmarkism" in *Tennessee Baptists: A Comprehensive History 1779–1999*, by Albert W. Wardin (Brentwood: Tennessee Baptist Convention, 1999). For Howell's article and Graves response, see *Tennessee Baptist*, February 28, 1858.

[121]The church found Graves guilty and excluded him. However, Graves's followers declared that they were the true First Baptist Church because the disciplinary proceedings had not been handled correctly. In February 1859, Dayton and seven other men, including three deacons, were also excluded for supporting Graves. Before it was over, forty-seven would be excluded over this issue. See Wardin, *Tennessee Baptists: A Comprehensive History 1779–1999*, 187.

[122]Ibid.

[123]Unsigned article, "The Baptist Watchman," *Tennessee Baptist* (February 27, 1858); unsigned article, "The Baptist Church in Murfreesboro to the First Baptist Church in Nashville, Tennessee," *Tennessee Baptist* (October 23, 1858); James Madison Pendleton, "The South Western Baptist," *Tennessee Baptist* (March 20, 1858); "Startling Disclosures," *Tennessee Baptist* (March 27, 1858); and "The Charges Against J. R. Graves," *Tennessee Baptist* (September 18, 1858). For the other viewpoint of the controversy, see R. B. C. Howell et al., *Both Sides* (Nashville: Southwestern Publishing House, 1859).

[124]Fletcher, *The Southern Baptist Convention: A Sesquicentennial History* states on page 65 that it took two ballots before Howell received a majority. After Howell declined to serve, it took four more ballots before Richard Fuller was elected. However, the 1859 *Proceedings of the Southern Baptist Convention* state on page 13 that Howell won on the first ballot and that Fuller was elected after Howell's resignation. For a full discussion

During this controversy, Pendleton could not remain neutral and defended Graves in an article titled, "The Charges Against J. R. Graves." In this article, Pendleton stated, "They are serious charges, but the specifications under them are frivolous, childish, ridiculous."[125] Pendleton wrote numerous articles on this issue during 1858–59.[126] He suggested that for the sake of peace neither Howell nor Graves should run for president of the 1859 Southern Baptist Convention but that a third party, Jeter, be nominated.[127]

The Slavery Issue Continued

Soon after he became co-editor of the *Tennessee Baptist*, allegations claiming Pendleton disagreed with the institution of slavery emerged. Pendleton addressed those allegations in

---

of Howell's election, consult James Hilton, "Robert Boyte Crawford Howell's Contribution to Baptist Ecclesiology: Nineteenth Century Baptist Ecclesiology in Controversy" (PhD diss., Southeastern Baptist Theological Seminary, 2005), 214–18.

[125]Pendleton, "The Charges Against J. R. Graves."

[126]James Madison Pendleton, "That Correspondence," *Tennessee Baptist* (October 9, 1858); "Proceedings of the First Baptist Church at Its Meeting of the Night of the 12th of Oct. 1858," *Tennessee Baptist* (October 23, 1858); "Strange Injustice," *Tennessee Baptist* (October 23, 1858); "Bro. Hendren's Letter," *Tennessee Baptist* (November 27, 1858); and "How Unreasonable," *Tennessee Baptist* (December 11, 1858); "Letter to the Church in Murfreesboro," *Tennessee Baptist* (January 22, 1859); "Inconsistency," *Tennessee Baptist* (February 12, 1859); "Read This All Ye People," *Tennessee Baptist* (February 26, 1859); "The Council," *Tennessee Baptist* (March 12, 1859); "Look Here," *Tennessee Baptist* (April 9, 1859); "Southern Baptist Convention," *Tennessee Baptist* (April 9, 1859); "A False Impression Made," *Tennessee Baptist* (April 23, 1859); "Southern Baptist Convention," *Tennessee Baptist* (May 21, 1859); "The Interview Sought, and Avoided," *Tennessee Baptist* (June 4, 1859); "The Last Charge Against J. R. Graves," *Tennessee Baptist* (June 11, 1859); "How Mr. Graves Stands at Home," *Tennessee Baptist* (July 23, 1859); and "On Howell's Election Again," *Tennessee Baptist* (July 23, 1859).

[127]James Madison Pendleton, "A Good Thing," *Tennessee Baptist* (April 30, 1859).

the pages of the *Tennessee Baptist*.[128] He said concerning his discussion with Graves over slavery, "I now state that the greatest objection I have had to him during that period—and that I now have to him—is, that he is more in favor of slavery than I think he ought to be. We are both decided in our opposition to abolition. I, imbibing at an early period the sentiments of Henry Clay, am in favor of gradual Emancipation. . . ."[129] Pendleton never wavered from his view that slavery should be gradually removed. In fact, he informed the trustees of Union that he would submit his resignation at any time if they felt him to be injuring the institution.[130] They did not want his resignation, and he did not submit it.

During 1860, the warning signs of a coming disaster steadily rose. In his autobiography, Pendleton noted, "The election of Mr. Lincoln to the Presidency in 1860 was the occasion of the secession of most of the Southern States from the Union."[131] The issues of slavery and secession dominated the next two years of Pendleton's life. On secession, Pendleton differed with both Graves and Dayton. He said, "My friend Graves visited me and spent hours in trying to persuade me to declare myself in favor of the Confederacy."[132] Pendleton responded to Graves, "The only question with me was, 'What is right?' Having settled this question in favor of the United States, I took my stand, and there were very few who stood

---

[128]James Madison Pendleton, "J. R. Graves on Slavery," *Tennessee Baptist* (May 8, 1858); "What Is an Abolitionist?," *Tennessee Baptist* (August 14, 1858).

[129]Pendleton, "J. R. Graves on Slavery."

[130]Pendleton, *Reminiscences of a Long Life*, 114. Pendleton does not give the date of this communication. It could have been anytime between 1858–61. He said, "The Trustees did not wish me to offer my resignation, and I did not. I therefore continued in my place till the institution suspended in April, 1861."

[131]Ibid., 117.

[132]Ibid., 119.

with me."[133] This issue continued to escalate through 1860 before coming to a head in 1861.[134]

Signs of Pendleton's impending departure began to appear in 1861 with the hiring of Thornton Stringfellow to write a series of articles supporting the institution of slavery for *The Southern Baptist Review*.[135] During this time, Pendleton made no contributions to the periodical. Another sign of the end came in a letter that Graves published as an open letter to Pendleton. Graves said, "We rejoice to see the change the political mind of Tennessee is undergoing—*Nashville is overwhelmingly for secession today*. All the men I left Union men, I find now think with me, *save one*—i.e. all I have yet conversed with."[136] Thus, Graves felt that every "Union" man but Pendleton had been convinced to side with the Confederacy.

The official reason given for Pendleton's departure was financial. "The receipts of this paper since 1861 have not justified the editorial labor employed and for the last quarter scarcely paid for the white paper."[137] However, one wonders if the lack of receipts really created the necessity of letting Pendleton go. This may not have been the cause for the following reasons: (1) the receipts supported the hiring of Thornton Stringfellow, (2) Graves did not release his "secular editor" or his "corresponding editor" but released Pendleton,

---

[133]Ibid., 119–20.
[134]James Madison Pendleton, "The Slavery Question," *Tennessee Baptist* (March 3, 1860); "Enemies at Work," *Tennessee Baptist* (March 24, 1860); "The 'Mississippian,'" *Tennessee Baptist* (April 21, 1860); "Please Spare Me," *Tennessee Baptist* (May 19, 1860); "Another False Impression," *Tennessee Baptist* (May 26, 1860); "Prof. J. M. Pendleton," *Tennessee Baptist* (June 2, 1860); "More About Slavery," *Tennessee Baptist* (June 9, 1860); and "Slavery Again," *Tennessee Baptist* (August 11, 1860).
[135]Huddleston, "James Madison Pendleton: A Critical Biography," 60.
[136]Senior Editor, "Letter to Pendleton," *Tennessee Baptist* (April 20, 1861). Emphasis in original.
[137]Unsigned article, "Our Associate," *Tennessee Baptist* (July 6, 1861). This author believes that Graves wrote the article.

and (3) Pendleton did not continue to write for the publication as he had done before being hired.

Perhaps the real reason for Pendleton's removal from the editorial staff of the *Tennessee Baptist* was his view on secession.[138] Pendleton stated his support for gradual emancipation in such a way that most southerners in favor of slavery could at least tolerate his position. What could not be tolerated was his denial of the right of the South to withdraw from the Union or revolt against the Union.

Pendleton stated, "But I deny that the right of revolution can exist under a Republican form of government. This view, so far as I know, is original with me."[139] He supported his beliefs by stating that it is the right of the majority to rule, and thus the majority has no need to revolt. Conversely, the minority has no right to rule or revolt as they have willingly conceded power to the majority. He concluded, "Believing the Confederacy, whether regarded as secession or revolution, had no right to exist, I had no sympathy with it, and heartily wished its overthrow by the Army and Navy of the United States."[140]

Pendleton replied to his dismissal in an article entitled, "A Few Parting Words," in which he began by commenting on his contributions to the paper. He said, "I have been connected with the paper either as Correspondent or Editor for about eight years and have written for it, perhaps, not less than eight hundred articles."[141] He apologized for leaving several of his series without proper conclusion—"Letters to Young Preachers," "Thoughts on the Lord's Supper," and "Conant's Revision of Matthew." Pendleton closed his article by saying,

---

[138]Burnett, *Sketches of Tennessee's Pioneer Baptist Preachers*, 407, attributes Pendleton's departure to the disagreement over "States' rights."
[139]Pendleton, *Reminiscences of a Long Life*, 121.
[140]Ibid.
[141]James Madison Pendleton, "A Few Parting Words," *Tennessee Baptist* (July 13, 1861).

And now, not willing to stir up the deep fountain of feeling within, and betray what might be thought an unmanly weakness, I say to the Senior, the Corresponding, and the Secular Editor, the Publishers, and all the patrons of the *Tennessee Baptist* and *Southern Baptist Review* one word, and lay down the pen editorial—that word is FAREWELL.[142]

Thus, an end came to Pendleton's articles in the *Tennessee Baptist* and *The Southern Baptist Review*.[143] About the same time it was decided that Union University, like many schools in the South, would disband for a time because of the war.[144]

Pendleton experienced uncertainty during this time. He stated, "Everything being disorganized by the war, my means of support were cut off, and I went to work on my farm. I knew of nothing else I could do; so I worked during the week and preached on Sunday to the very few that were willing to hear me."[145] In addition to wondering about provisions for his family, his life was at risk. He said, "I suppose I was in greater danger of personal violence than I thought at the time. It is said that a citizen offered to head any company that would undertake to hang me. . . ."[146] In another publication, he said, "When the war broke out almost everybody in Murfreesboro turned against the Union, and because I did not there was something said about hanging me."[147] Pendleton's autobiography discussed the nightly

---

[142]Ibid.

[143]Pendleton's removal from the *Tennessee Baptist* directly affected his employment with the *Southern Baptist Review* because both were published by Graves, Marks & Co. Thus, Graves controlled both publications.

[144]Union University re-opened in 1868 only to close again in 1873. Southwest Baptist University in Jackson, Tennessee would be renamed Union University shortly after T. T. Eaton, the son of the former Union president, donated his library of 6,000 books to the institution in 1907.

[145]Pendleton, *Reminiscences of a Long Life*, 123.

[146]Ibid. 122.

[147]James Madison Pendleton, "Mistakes Corrected," *Western Recorder* (September 30, 1865).

provision made in case the mob should arrive. There was always a window left open and something to eat packed in a bag to allow for a quick escape. Finally, Pendleton made the decision to leave the South.

RELOCATION TO THE NORTH 1862–1865

Between 1862–65, Pendleton moved twice, began a new ministry, and lost two family members to death. It all began on the last day of August, 1862, when Pendleton left Murfreesboro. He recalled his departure:

> As the Federal forces had possession of the railroad to Nashville, it was deemed safer for me to go on the train. My family went in a barouche in charge of Rev. G. W. Welch, a theological student. The horse was well known in and around Murfreesboro and not much progress was made on the way before a "halt" was called by one of a guerrilla band. He made inquiries of Mr. Welch and finally said, "You are not the man I thought you were," and permitted him to proceed. My wife heard all that passed, and has never had a doubt that the man supposed that I, as usual, was driving my horse, and intended to capture me.[148]

Next, in October of 1862, Pendleton's oldest son, John Malcom, was killed while fighting for the Confederacy.[149] In November of the same year, Pendleton began duties as pastor at the First Baptist Church in Hamilton, Ohio, where he served for three years. On November 2, 1863, Pendleton received a communication which said, "Mother is dangerously ill—come by first train."[150] After getting there as soon as possible, Pendleton was greeted by the words, "She

---

[148]Pendleton, *Reminiscences of a Long Life*, 129.
[149]Ibid., 66.
[150]Ibid., 135.

died yesterday."[151] Feeling that his Hamilton pastorate was unsuccessful, Pendleton would move again.

UPLAND, PENNSYLVANIA 1865–1883

Convinced that Hamilton was not the place for him, Pendleton desired to move west and pastor in Illinois. However, providence would not allow it. Pendleton attended the meeting of the Philadelphia Association in October 1865. He was invited to preach for the Upland Baptist Church in Upland, Pennsylvania, which currently had no pastor. The next Sunday, Pendleton preached in Camden, New Jersey, and the following Sunday returned to Upland Baptist Church. Pendleton said, "The church, at the evening service, was requested to remain after the congregation was dismissed."[152] Although Pendleton did not know it, that night the church voted, and John P. Crozer put a letter in Pendleton's hands informing him that he had been called as their pastor. Pendleton responded before returning to Ohio by accepting the call to become their pastor. These years can best be discussed in two sections—Pendleton's practical ministry at Upland and a discussion of Pendleton's books.

Ministry at Upland

Pendleton's ministry at Upland is not documented in as much detail as his time in Murfreesboro. His autobiography and books provide what little information is available. While at Upland, Pendleton turned his attention to writing books.[153] In 1873, the Upland meeting house, as Pendleton called it, needed to be enlarged after experiencing revival

---

[151]Ibid., 136.
[152]Ibid., 139.
[153]Pendleton served on the Board of Managers and more specifically the Committee of Publication for the American Baptist Publication Society for approximately eighteen years beginning in 1865.

and adding about two hundred members.[154] During his ministry at Upland, Upland Baptist planted two churches—South Chester and Village Green.

Pendleton offered his resignation to Upland Baptist Church in June of 1883. He did so in part because "judicious ministers had expressed the opinion that a man should not be pastor after reaching seventy years of age."[155] Although Pendleton had exceeded this mark by almost two years, he felt no regret in staying longer because there had been a small revival in which he baptized more than forty people in 1882. Pendleton also told the church, "I leave you as I came among you, nothing but a poor sinner, 'saved by grace,'" and as the final day of his ministry at Upland approached, he felt great sorrow from the fact that he was closing his "work in the ministry of the gospel."[156] From this point forward, Pendleton would devote his attention to writing.

Published Books

Pendleton's *Church Manual: Designed for the Use of Baptist Churches* was published in 1867 and devoted 162 pages to the theological discussion before providing a very practical set of appendices amounting to nineteen pages. Pendleton began this discussion by acknowledging the existence of the universal church, calling it the redeemed in the aggregate. He acknowledged that this was the intended meaning of

---

[154]Pendleton would not call the building a church because a church is made up of believers. The building was extended by thirty feet and a new baptistry was constructed. One hundred and twenty of the converts in the revival were over twenty years old. Pendleton, *Reminiscences of a Long Life*, 144–6.

[155]Pendleton, *Reminiscences of a Long Life*, 160.

[156]Ibid. For more information on Pendleton's ministry at Upland, consult Garnett Pendleton, *Semi-Centennial of Upland Baptist Church, 1852–1902, Oct. 8 to 12* (Philadelphia: n.p., 1902); and Upland Baptist Church Minutes, Upland, Pennsylvania.

several passages in Ephesians. This acknowledgment was not a typical Landmark belief.[157]

Of particular emphasis was Pendleton's definition of a church. He said,

> A church is a congregation of Christ's baptized disciples, acknowledging him as their Head, relying on his atoning sacrifice for justification before God, and depending on the Holy Spirit for sanctification, united in the belief of the gospel, agreeing to maintain its ordinances and obey its precepts, meeting together for worship, and cooperating for the extension of Christ's kingdom in the world.[158]

After giving a definition of a church, he stated two categories of prerequisites for joining a church, "moral" and "ceremonial." Under moral requirements, Pendleton addressed repentance, faith, and regeneration. Under the ceremonial requirements, Pendleton discussed only one—baptism.

The remainder of the book discussed the officers of a church, the doctrine of a church, the ordinances of a church, the government of a church, the discipline of a church, and the duties of a church. The final appendices of this book provided a very practical guide to managing the normal business of a church. He began with business meetings, giving an abridged version of *Robert's Rules of Order*. The next section included examples of minutes and letters. The third section gave a sample marriage ceremony, while the fourth addressed the province of associations and councils stressing the church as the highest authority.[159]

---

[157]James Madison Pendleton, *Baptist Church Manual* (Nashville: Broadman & Holman, 1966), 5.

[158]Pendleton, *Baptist Church Manual*, 7.

[159]The last section provides various statements of faith but could not have been completed by Pendleton as it mentions the Baptist Faith and Message of 1925 and 1963.

In 1878, Pendleton published *Christian Doctrines: A Compendium of Theology* to fill a void in theological education. He "wished to write a book suitable to the comprehension of colored ministers in the South and at the same time acceptable to other classes of readers."[160] It would be impossible to measure accurately the success of this book; however, it is significant that copies of the work are still circulating. Additionally Pendleton commented, "It is specially gratifying to me that the circulation of the volume has reached about eleven thousand copies, and that it is used as a text-book in most of the colored Theological Institutes of the South."[161]

Time and space do not allow for a complete summary of this work, but the book offers insight into Pendleton's theological methodology. He desired to have a completely biblical theology. He commented, "But it has been my purpose to present the views of theologians so far only as those views accord with the teachings of the Scriptures. The Bible is the only authoritative standard in matters of faith and practice .... Every page has been written in the interest of scriptural truth, and for its maintenance."[162]

Pendleton published *Distinctive Principles of Baptists* twenty-nine years after publishing *Three Reasons*. Although the content of this work only slightly differed from the earlier editions, the tone in dealing with the issues was much milder.[163] The only notable distinction in the content of the work was that the fourth reason on communion omits any discussion on intercommunion between Baptist churches.

---

[160]Pendleton, *Reminiscences of a Long Life*, 152. Pendleton also says that this is "my best and most important book."

[161]Ibid., 153. His autobiography was written in 1891 and thus measures the success of *Christian Doctrines* for just over 12 years.

[162]James Madison Pendleton, *Christian Doctrines: A Compendium of Theology* (Valley Forge: Judson Press, 2000), 5–6. The book discusses most areas of systematic theology in 426 pages.

[163]Huddleston, "James Madison Pendleton: A Critical Biography," 66, agrees with this analysis of the situation.

Pendleton addressed transubstantiation and consubstantiation but left out some material from the discussion.

Two other changes emerged in the clarity and tone of the work. Pendleton appeared to have developed greater clarity concerning the issues. Chapter three in *Distinctive Principles of Baptists* was entitled "Baptists hold that, according to the scriptural order, persons must come first to Christ and then to the church and its ordinances."[164] Although this order was implied throughout the other works, Pendleton clearly stressed this as the difference between Baptists and other religious societies. Graves concurred stating "blood before water, Christ before the Church."[165] The second clear difference was the tone throughout. In this work, Pendleton claimed that Baptists are clearly different from other religious societies and should remain distinct. In the earlier works, Pendleton claimed that Baptists are the only people on the face of the earth who correctly follow the New Testament and maintain a proper church. Pendleton did not compromise, but his wording was less harsh.

Pendleton spent the winter of 1883 contributing to *Brief Notes on the New Testament* in which he wrote the commentary on Acts, Epistles, and Revelation.[166] He began this work on July 4, 1883, and finished his comments on March 4, 1884. While spending the winter of 1884–85 in Austin, Texas, with his daughter and son-in-law, Pendleton expanded upon an article written for the *Southern Baptist Review* entitled "The Atonement of Christ" to write his book of 173 pages by the same title, which was published in

---

[164]Pendleton, *Distinctive Principles of Baptists*, 159.
[165]Graves, *Old Landmarkism*, 43.
[166]James Madison Pendleton, and Geo W. Clark, *Brief Notes on the New Testament* (Philadelphia: American Baptist Publication Society, 1884). Geo. W. Clark wrote the comments on the Gospels. Pendleton worked vigorously on this project because he feared he would die and leave it unfinished. Pendleton, *Reminiscences of a Long Life*, 163.

1885.[167] Pendleton claimed that this work was the result of a half century of study on the subject.[168] In six chapters, he addressed the nature, the necessity, the value, the extent, the results, and practical aspects of the atonement. Pendleton believed in an enlarged of view of the atonement which offered salvation to all and of which the central idea was satisfaction.

Pendleton left Austin and headed for Murfreesboro, Tennessee, where he spent the summer and the next winter with friends. From Murfreesboro and later from Bowling Green, Pendleton wrote his *Notes of Sermons* which would be published in 1886. This book developed from fifty-five years in the ministry and was designed to "be useful to preachers who have not enjoyed the advantages of regular theological education."[169] Beyond printing sermons, Pendleton hoped that this book would help preachers learn proper exposition and construction of sermons. Two particular characteristics remained true throughout. First, he remained exegetical, attempting to draw the message directly from the Scripture passage which was being discussed. Second, he attempted to apply all of the messages to the listener by making "remarks" at the conclusion of each sermon.

The next years were spent with Pendleton and his wife traveling back and forth to spend time with friends and family. At the request of his son, Pendleton wrote his autobiography titled, *Reminiscences of a Long Life*, which was published in 1891. Pendleton began writing this book on his seventy-ninth birthday, November 20, 1890, and finished it within two months.[170] This work is the most comprehensive account of Pendleton's life. One cannot read this work without admiring the man who wrote it. It seems

---

[167]Pendleton, "The Atonement of Christ," 41–61. James Madison Pendleton, *The Atonement of Christ* (Philadelphia: American Baptist Publication Society, 1885).
[168]Pendleton, *The Atonement of Christ*, 7.
[169]Pendleton, *Notes of Sermons*, 4.
[170]Pendleton, *Reminiscences of a Long Life*, 185.

as if every page demonstrates his concern for people, his devotion to the Lord, and his love for his wife.

The final chapter was finished by his son after the death of James Madison Pendleton, which occurred on March 4, 1891, at 12:40 p.m.[171] It was fitting that Pendleton's final sermon and breath came where he began his ministry—Bowling Green, Kentucky. He preached his last sermon there on the 25th day of January in 1891. Those speaking at his funeral held on March 6, 1891, included such notable figures as T. T. Eaton and William H. Whittsitt.[172] Pendleton was buried in Fairview cemetery about one mile outside of Bowling Green. Mrs. Pendleton was buried in the same location on September 21, 1898.[173]

---

[171]The following article identifies March 5 as the death of Pendleton, Unsigned article, "Editorial Notes of the Death of J. M. Pendleton," *Western Recorder* (March 12, 1891). However, March 4, 1891 is affirmed by M. M. Riley, "Funeral of Dr. J. M. Pendleton," *The Baptist*, March 12, 1891; Unsigned article, "Dr. J. M. Pendleton" *The National Baptist* (March 12, 1891); and Unsigned article, "Death of Rev. J. M. Pendleton D. D." *Religious Herald* (March 12, 1891).

[172]Ibid., 198. There seems to be some confusion. Pendleton, *Reminiscence of a Long Life* notes March 6 as the date of the funeral services. March 7, 1891 is used in unsigned article, "Editorial Notes of the Death of J. M. Pendleton," *Western Recorder* (March 12, 1891) and in Huddleston, "James Madison Pendleton: A Critical Biography," 92. Interestingly, Whitsitt was involved in a controversy while President at the Southern Baptist Theological Seminary over the origin of Baptists in which Landmarkers were his chief opponents and more specifically, T. T. Eaton led the charge as editor of the Kentucky paper. See Walter Shurden, *Not A Silent People: Controversies That Have Shaped Southern Baptists* (Nashville: Broadman Press, 1972), 26.

[173]Huddleston, "James Madison Pendleton: A Critical Biography," 92.

CHAPTER 2

BAPTISM: THE CENTRAL ASPECT OF PENDLETON'S ECCLESIOLOGY

Introduction

Although Pendleton wrote about many areas, he focused most of his work in the area of ecclesiology. His writings in ecclesiology began around the time of the revival held at the First Baptist Church of Bowling Green by J. R. Graves in February, 1852. During this revival, Graves confronted Pendleton with views on baptism, to which Pendleton admittedly had not given much thought. By the end of the meeting, Pendleton announced full agreement with Graves and because of the excitement generated, preached several sermons on the matter after Graves departed.

Two seeds sprouted from this same era in the form of two publications. The first was a book which resulted from a dedication sermon delivered at Liberty Church in Logan County. During this address, Pendleton gave his reasons for being a Baptist which would later be expanded into a book.[1] The three reasons given for being a Baptist were: (1) baptism of believers, (2) baptism by immersion, and (3) congregational form of church government. This book was published in 1853.[2]

---

[1] James Madison Pendleton, *Reminiscences of a Long Life* (Louisville, KY: Baptist Book Concern, 1891), 103.

[2] James Madison Pendleton, *Three Reasons Why I Am a Baptist* (Cincinnati: Moore, Anderson & Company, 1853).

The second major publication was written in four articles published during 1854 in the *Tennessee Baptist* and entitled, "Ought Baptists to Recognize Pedobaptist Preachers as Gospel Ministers?"[3] These articles were later published in a pamphlet under the title *An Old Landmark Re-set*.[4] This work and the movement known as "Landmarkism" continued to dominate Baptist discussions for years to come.

From 1852 to 1854 Pendleton, out of necessity, developed his views on ecclesiology. These views were recorded in two articles at the beginning of 1855 titled "The Scriptural Meaning of the Term Church."[5] Within the formation of the doctrine of ecclesiology, another more specific doctrine emerged as the central aspect—the doctrine of baptism.

THE IMPORTANCE OF BAPTISM IN PENDLETON'S ECCLESIOLOGY

Demonstrating the importance of baptism in Pendleton's writings can be accomplished by scanning his corpus of work. Pendleton discussed baptism in over half of his books, and in many of his articles.[6] Additionally, only two Th.M. theses

---

[3]James Madison Pendleton, "Ought Baptists to Recognize Pedobaptist Preachers as Gospel Ministers?," *Tennessee Baptist* (July 22, 1854); "Ought Baptists to Recognize Pedobaptist Preachers as Gospel Ministers? Number Two," *Tennessee Baptist* (August 5, 1854); "Ought Baptists to Recognize Pedobaptist Preachers as Gospel Ministers? Number Three," *Tennessee Baptist* (August 12, 1854); and "Ought Baptists to Recognize Pedobaptist Preachers as Gospel Preachers?" *Tennessee Baptist* (December 16, 1854).

[4]James Madison Pendleton, *An Old Landmark Re-set: or Ought Baptists Invite Pedobaptists to Preach in Their Pulpits?* (Nashville: Graves & Marks, 1854).

[5]James Madison Pendleton, "The Scriptural Meaning of the Term Church," *The Southern Baptist Review* 1 (January 1855): 6–17; and "The Scriptural Meaning of the Term Church," *The Southern Baptist Review* 1 (February–March 1855): 65–83.

[6]James Madison Pendleton, *Christian Doctrines: A Compendium of Theology* (Philadelphia: American Baptist Publication Society, 1906); *Church Manual: Designed for the Use of Baptist Churches* (Philadelphia: American Baptist Publication Society, 1867); *Distinctive Principles of Baptists* (Philadelphia: American Baptist Publication Society, 1882); *An*

have been written about Pendleton, and one is titled *James Madison Pendleton's Theology of Baptism*.[7] One final emphasis can be found in *Three Reasons Why I Am a Baptist with A Fourth Reason Added*. This book dedicated 148 of 214 pages to the discussion of baptism. Furthermore, baptism provided two of the three original reasons for Pendleton being a Baptist. However, the question must be asked, Why did baptism receive so much attention? The answer comes from Pendleton's formulation of ecclesiology and more specifically from his definition of a church.

A close look at Pendleton's definition of a church demonstrates why baptism became a central issue. His definition of the church was clearly stated in his *Church Manual*. He stated:

> A church is a congregation of Christ's baptized disciples, acknowledging him as their Head, relying on his atoning sacrifice for justification before God, and depending on the Holy Spirit for sanctification, united in the belief of the gospel, agreeing to maintain its ordinances and obey its precepts, meeting together for worship, and cooperating for the extension of Christ's kingdom in the world.[8]

Should one desire a shorter definition, Pendleton provided that as well: "A church is a congregation of Christ's baptized disciples, united in the belief of what he has said, and covenanting to do what he has commanded."[9] Both

---

Old Landmark Re-set (Nashville: Graves & Marks, 1854); *Three Reasons Why I Am a Baptist* (Cincinnati: Moore, Anderson & Company, 1853); *Three Reasons Why I Am a Baptist with a Fourth Reason Added on Communion* (St. Louis: National Baptist Publishing, 1856); and over twenty articles discussing baptism which can be found in the bibliography.

[7]James Emmett Hill Jr., "James Madison Pendleton's Theology of Baptism" (Th.M. thesis, Southern Baptist Theological Seminary, 1958).

[8]James Madison Pendleton, *Baptist Church Manual* (Nashville: Broadman & Holman, 1966), 7.

[9]Ibid.

definitions include "Christ's baptized disciples." To Pendleton, this meant that anyone not receiving proper baptism was not a member of the visible church and any church not practicing proper baptism was not a church—instead they were a society.

Pendleton's early thought matched his later thought on this issue. He said in early 1855 that proper baptism was a necessary qualification for church membership. He went further by stating, "There can, according to the gospel, be no visible church without baptism. Baptism draws the line of demarkation [sic] between the church and the world. It is the believer's first public act of obedience to Jesus Christ."[10] When asked if the hand of fellowship should be extended before or after baptism, Pendleton responded, "There really cannot be church fellowship without baptism. There cannot be a church without baptism, nor membership in a church. Strictly and properly speaking the hand of church fellowship should be given after baptism."[11] When the pastor presented a person upon a profession of faith, the pastor and congregation realized that acceptance was conditional upon baptism. He offered the following wording, "You who are in

---

[10] Pendleton, "The Scriptural Meaning of the Term Church," 13. This position put Pendleton in a historic line going back to early Anabaptists, who taught believers' baptism. Martin Luther disagreed with this position saying, "This they interpret to mean that no man should be baptized before he believes. I must say that they are guilty of a great presumption. For if they follow this principle they cannot venture to baptize before they are certain that the one to be baptized believes. How and when can they ever know that for certain? Have they now become gods so that they can discern the hearts of men and know whether or not they believe?" See Martin Luther, "Concerning Rebaptism" in *Martin Luther's Basic Theological Writings*, ed. Timothy Lull (Minneapolis: Fortress Press, 1989), 351.

[11] James Madison Pendleton, "The Hand of Fellowship," *Tennessee Baptist* (October 20, 1860). This became a typical Baptist position. Edward Hiscox, *The New Directory for Baptist Churches* (Philadelphia: Judson Press, 1894), 69, agreed by saying that "baptism constitutes the ritual or ceremonial qualification for that sacred fellowship. Except by baptism no person can be received as a member of the Church, without violating the prescribed conditions, and vitiating the divine method."

favor of receiving this individual as a candidate for baptism, and when baptized as a member of the church, make it known. . . ."[12]

In a follow up article on "The Scriptural Meaning of the Term Church," Pendleton elaborated on baptism. He supported the view that baptism was a church ordinance as opposed to a gospel ordinance or a ministerial ordinance. He said, "It is almost universally conceded that baptism is administered to initiate the baptized into the church."[13] Because baptism initiated the baptized into the church, and the church alone was responsible for the acceptance, discipline, and removal of its members, baptism must be a church ordinance. He stated, "If, therefore, baptism is not a church ordinance—if churches have no control over its administration—their right to decide on applications for membership is materially infringed—not to say taken away."[14]

The majority of Pedobaptists and Baptists believed that baptism served as the door to the church, and thus, it was a church ordinance. Thomas Summers, a prominent Methodist, said, "Baptism is an ordinance instituted by Christ, consisting in the application of water by a Christian minister, to suitable persons, for their initiation into the

---

[12]Pendleton, "The Hand of Fellowship."

[13]Pendleton, "The Scriptural Meaning of the Term Church," 67. The view in a less dogmatic form can be seen in Edwin C. Dargan, *Ecclesiology: A Study of the Churches* (Louisville: Chas. T. Dearing, 1897), 200, who wrote, "Still we cannot say that there is any definite command which lays the performance of these two ordinances upon the churches; yet, it appears to be the natural, if not necessary, deduction from the whole trend and tenor of the New Testament teaching." However, not all agreed on this issue. Dagg said, "The opinion has been held, almost as a theological axiom, that baptism is the door into the church. It is not the door into the spiritual universal church; for men enter this by regeneration, and are, therefore, members of it before they are fit subjects for baptism. It is not the door into a local church; for, though it is a prerequisite to membership, men may be baptized, and remain unconnected with any local church." See John Dagg, *Manual of Church Order* (Charleston: Southern Baptist Publication Society, 1858; reprint, Harrisonburg: Gano Books, 1990), 135.

[14]Pendleton, "The Scriptural Meaning of the Term Church," 68.

visible church, and consecration to the Father, Son, and Holy Ghost."[15] Summers continued, "[T]he church in every age has perpetuated this institution."[16] Edward Dorr Griffin, who was the third President of Williams College in Massachusetts and a prominent Pedobaptist, stated, "I agree with the advocates for close communion. . . . that baptism is the initiatory ordinance which introduces us into the visible church; of course, where there is no baptism there are no visible churches."[17] Both Griffin and Summers concurred that baptism initiated members into the visible church. Pendleton stated, "On this point, however, there is no controversy between Baptists and Pedobaptists, for both believe in the priority of baptism to church-membership."[18]

The disagreement arose over what constituted proper baptism. Griffin wrote, "If nothing but immersion is baptism, there is no visible church except among the Baptists."[19] Yet, he attempted to prove that infant baptism was scriptural. Neither Summers nor Griffin believed that "nothing but immersion is baptism." They would accept Pedobaptists' and

---

[15]Thomas O. Summers, *Baptism: A Treatise on the Nature, Perpetuity, Subjects, Administrator, Mode, and Use of the Initiating Ordinance of the Christian Church* (Nashville: E. Stevenson & J. E. Evans, 1856), 13. Summers served as co-editor of the "Southern Christian Advocate," and editor of the Nashville "Christian Advocate." He became professor of systematic theology at Vanderbilt University in 1874 and served as dean of the theology faculty.

[16]Ibid., 18.

[17]Edward Dorr Griffin, "Letter on Open Communion," in *Conversations Between Two Laymen on Strict and Mixed Communion*, ed. J. G. Fuller (Boston: Lincoln & Edmands, 1832): 244. This view continues to be presented. See for example the Baptist Faith and Message or Stanley Grenz, *The Baptist Congregation* (Vancouver: Regent, 1985), 33, where the entire discussion of baptism is under a chapter titled, "Baptism—the Initiatory Ordinance." Hiscox, *The New Directory for Baptist Churches*, 77, also agreed and went farther. He said, "Nor is it expedient, or promotive of good order for ministers to baptize persons who wish to unite with churches of other denominations. Such persons should receive the ordinance from the pastors of the churches with which they are to unite."

[18]Pendleton, *Distinctive Principles of Baptists*, 171–2.

[19]Griffin, "Letter on Open Communion," 247.

Baptists' baptisms as valid. In contrast, Pendleton believed that believer's baptism by immersion was the only proper baptism. Since Pendleton believed that valid baptism must be by immersion of believers, he concluded that Pedobaptists had no visible churches. The essential issue was what is proper baptism. For the Pedobaptists, sprinkling, pouring, or immersing of a person in childhood or adulthood constituted valid baptism. For Pendleton, proper baptism was by immersion only of believers only.

In summary, Pendleton believed that the being of a visible church required proper baptism. He did not believe that Pedobaptists administered proper baptism, and thus, they were not visible churches but societies. As far back as Calvin, the marks of a church included "rightly administering the ordinances."[20] Thus, the proper administration of baptism formed the line of demarcation between true churches and religious societies.

Pendleton's Formulation of Proper Baptism

Pendleton spent many pages distinguishing proper baptism from improper baptism. A working definition is essential for clarity and can be found in his more concise treatment of baptism in *Christian Doctrines*. He said, "Baptism is the immersion in water, by a proper administrator, of a believer in Christ, into the name of the Father and of the Son, and of

---

[20]John Calvin, *Institutes of the Christian Religion*, in *Library of Christian Classics*, trans. by F. L. Battles, ed. John T. McNeill (Louisville: Westminster John Knox Press, 1960), 1023, said, "Wherever we see the Word of God purely preached and heard, and the sacraments administered according to Christ's institution, there, it is not to be doubted, a church of God exists." This view was adopted by Baptists, as can be seen in the London Confession of 1644 and in the Orthodox Creed of 1679. The Orthodox Creed stated, "the marks by which she [the church] is known to be the true spouse of Christ, are these, viz. Where the word of God is rightly preached, and the sacraments truly administered, according to Christ's institution. . . ." These confessions can be found in William Lumpkin, *Baptist Confessions of Faith* (Valley Forge: Judson Press, 1969).

the Holy Spirit."[21] From this definition, four elements emerge which will serve as the categories for this discussion. They are: (1) proper subject, (2) proper mode, (3) proper administrator, and (4) proper form.

Proper Subject

In *Three Reasons Why I Am a Baptist*, Pendleton gave as his first reason that Baptists insist on the baptism of believers only and reject infant baptism.[22] Pendleton continued his emphasis of this point throughout his life, listing it first when writing *Distinctive Principles of Baptists* almost thirty years later. Pedobaptists saw their position as equally important and insisted upon the baptism of infants. Charles Hodge stated,

> Those, therefore, who, having been themselves baptized, and still professing their faith in true religion, having competent knowledge, and being free from scandal, should not only be permitted but urged and enjoined to present their children for baptism, that they may belong to the Church, and be brought up under its watch and care. To be unbaptized is a grievous injury and reproach; one which no parent can innocently entail upon his children.[23]

---

[21]Pendleton, *Christian Doctrines*, 342. Believer's baptism was also the primary distinction between the Anabaptists and the Magisterial Reformers. William Estep, *The Anabaptist Story* (Grand Rapids: Eerdmans, 1996), 201, stated, "If the most obvious demarcation between the reformers and the Roman Catholics was biblical authority, that between the Reformers and the Anabaptists was believers' baptism. Believers' baptism was for the Anabaptists the logical implementation of the Reformation principle of *sola Scriptura*. Almost as soon as the Anabaptist movement could be distinguished within the context of the Reformation itself, believers' baptism became the major issue."

[22]Pendleton, *Three Reasons Why I Am a Baptist with a Fourth Reason Added on Communion*, 5.

[23]Charles Hodge, *Systematic Theology*, vol. 3 (Peabody: Hendrickson, 2001), 579.

The content of Pendleton's discussion of the subject of baptism varied in his works. In *Church Manual* and *Christian Doctrines*, he argued the positive case that believers alone are the proper subjects of baptism. However, in his *Distinctive Principles of Baptists* and *Three Reasons Why I Am a Baptist*, Pendleton focused on refuting the practice of infant baptism. Pendleton also went to great lengths in his articles to refute infant baptism. For the purposes of this dissertation, the positive case will be presented first and then the refutation of the practice of infant baptism.

Pendleton began his defense of believers baptism with a discussion of the commission Christ gave to his disciples. Pendleton quoted Matt 28:18–20, stating that it proves teaching or making disciples should precede baptism. He next discussed Mark 16:15–16 which establishes the priority of faith to baptism and Luke 24:46–47 which connects the repentance and remission of sin with the commission of Christ. His conclusion from this description of Christ's commission was that "No man can, in obedience to this commission, baptize an unbeliever or an unconscious infant."[24] Providing examples of commands given in the Bible where nothing more or less than what was commanded should be done, Pendleton argued that only those who have "been made disciples," "believed," and "repented" can be baptized.[25] He concluded that "the commission of Christ, in enjoining the baptism of disciples, believers, forbids in effect the baptism of all others."[26]

---

[24]Pendleton, *Baptist Church Manual*, 80.

[25]He specifically notes Noah and the commands concerning the Ark, Abraham and the commands surrounding the burnt offering, and commands surrounding the institution of the Passover as times when nothing more than what was commanded should be done.

[26]Pendleton, *Christian Doctrines*, 353. Pendleton, *Distinctive Principles of Baptists*, 17, stated, "The Commission given by the Savior to his apostles just before his ascension to heaven furnishes no plea for infant baptism." Dagg likewise began his discussion of baptism with the "Great

Pendleton continued to establish the precedent of belief before baptism through the support of several passages in Acts. He noted that at Pentecost repentance came before baptism, that Philip preached Christ to the people and then believers were baptized, and that with Peter and with Paul belief was required before baptism. After discussing Acts, Pendleton stressed that "believers alone are scriptural subjects of baptism."[27]

Pendleton also addressed the remainder of the New Testament attempting to demonstrate that the entire New Testament upholds the position that belief precedes baptism.[28] He noted, "The baptized are referred to as 'dead to sin,' rising from the baptismal waters to 'walk in newness of life.'"[29] This characteristic, Pendleton believed, could not be applied to speechless infants or non-believers. Pendleton concluded this discussion by noting Eph 4:5 which states,

---

Commission" of Jesus and continued to reference it throughout his defense of believer's baptism by immersion. See Dagg, *Manual of Church Order*, 13.

[27]Pendleton, *Baptist Church Manual*, 87. Pendleton's view represents the thought of Baptist confessions from the London Confession of 1644 to the Baptist Faith and Message of 2000.

[28]A similar argument can be seen in Balthasar Hubmaier, "On the Christian Baptism of Believers," in *Balthasar Hubmaier: Theologian of Anabaptism,* trans. and ed. H. Wayne Pipkin and John H. Yoder (Scottsdale: Herald Press, 1989), 95–149. Hubmaier stated that the order used by John the Baptist was "(1) word, (2) hearing, (3) change of life or recognition of sin, (4) baptism, (5) works" (106). Hubmaier also commented that the order used by the Apostles was "first, preaching; second, faith; and third, outward baptism" (115). Believers baptism was a key theme of the entire Anabaptist movement. See Estep, *The Anabaptist Story*, 201–36.

[29]Pendleton, *Christian Doctrines*, 356. Most defenses of believers' baptism include the symbolism of death to sin as Christ died and rising to walk in newness of life as Christ was resurrected. Hiscox, *The New Directory for Baptist Churches*, 425, stated that baptism symbolized, "the death, burial, and resurrection of Christ, who died for our sins, and rose again for our justification." He continued by stating that every candidate declares, "his own death to sin, and a rising to newness of life in Christ." Dagg, *Manual of Church Order*, 38, supported the same position quoting Rom 6:3–4.

"one Lord, one faith, one baptism." He wrote, "The one Lord is the object of the one faith, the one faith embraces the one Lord, and the one baptism is a profession of the one faith in the one Lord."[30] Thus, Pendleton believed that the New Testament supported only believers as the proper subjects for baptism because faith must precede baptism.[31]

While presenting the positive case for believers as the subject for baptism, Pendleton addressed one major challenge from Pedobaptists who stated that if infants are not to be baptized because they cannot believe, they will not be saved.[32] He responded by saying, "If the salvation of infants depends on their faith, they cannot be saved. They are incapable of faith. They are doubtless saved through the mediation of Christ, but it is not by faith."[33] Pendleton continued that the apostles baptized only accountable agents and that infants

---

[30] Pendleton, *Christian Doctrines*, 357.

[31] This can be seen in many other writers. Some of the classic presentations are these by Balthasar Hubmaier, "On the Christian Baptism of Believers;" J. M. Frost, *The Moral Dignity of Baptism* (Nashville: Sunday School Board, Southern Baptist Convention, 1905); Emil Brunner, *The Divine-Human Encounter*, trans. Amandus W. Loos (Philadelphia: Westminster, 1943); Karl Barth, *The Teaching of the Church Regarding Baptism* (London: SCM, 1948); H. Wheeler Robinson, *Baptist Principles* (London: Carey Kingsgate, 1960); and George Beasley-Murray, *Baptism in the New Testament* (Grand Rapids: Eerdmans, 1973).

[32] This resulted from a belief in "original guilt" or "infant guilt" by which infants had to be baptized in order to remove their original guilt in order for them to go to heaven should they die in infancy. Richard P. McBrien, *Catholicism* (San Francisco: Harper Collins, 1989), 188, said, "Cyprian of Carthage was the first to argue that infants are baptized because of the 'contagion of death' inherited from Adam." This belief can also be traced to Augustine. Neville Clark, "Theology of Baptism," in *Christian Baptism*, ed. Alec Gilmore (Chicago: Judson Press, 1959), 320, states, "Upon the basis provided by Tertullian and Cyprian in their doctrine of original sin, Ambrose and Augustine superimposed a theology of original guilt. From such guilt infant baptism guaranteed deliverance." For further research see Dale Moody, *Baptism: Foundation for Christian Unity* (Philadelphia: Westminster, 1967). The original remarks of Augustine can be seen in Augustine, "On Original Sin," in *Nicene and Post-Nicene Fathers*, ed. Philip Schaff, vol. 5 (Peabody: Hendrickson, 1999), 237–57.

[33] Pendleton, *Baptist Church Manual*, 83.

cannot be considered accountable agents. "What conscience has an infant? There can be no operation of conscience prior to accountability. Baptism, then, in its administration to unconscious babes, cannot be what an inspired apostle declares it to be."[34] Thus, until a child reached an age of accountability, they were covered by the grace of God, did not need to be baptized, and could not be legitimately baptized.

In addition to presenting the positive case for believer's baptism, Pendleton also refuted the case for infant baptism. He began his rebuttal by stating, "The account given of John's baptism and of the personal ministry of Christ affords no justification of infant baptism."[35] Pendleton argued that John the Baptist preached repentance, and that being a descendant of Abraham was not enough to qualify one for baptism. Similarly, the disciples of Christ "baptized no infants during his ministry."[36] One text receiving special attention was John 4:1 which states that "Jesus made and baptized more disciples than John." Making and baptizing disciples were two different activities with making disciples coming before baptism. Pendleton posed the question, "Could

---

[34]Pendleton, *Christian Doctrines*, 356. The argument that children cannot be made disciples because they cannot yet believe was challenged by Luther who wrote, "When they say, 'Children cannot believe,' how can they be sure of that? Where is the Scripture by which they would prove it and on which they would build? They imagine this, I suppose, because children do not speak or have understanding. But such a fancy is deceptive, yea, altogether false, and we cannot build on what we imagine." See Luther, "Concerning Rebaptism," 353–4. However, Luther's point has not convinced many.

[35]Pendleton, *Distinctive Principles of Baptists*, 13. The first chapter is titled, "Baptists regard the baptism of unconscious infants as unscriptural, and insist on the baptism of believers in Christ; and of believers alone." In this chapter, Pendleton does not address Scripture's account of John in the womb. Luther noted Scripture's account of John the Baptists leaping in the womb to prove that children can believe and have faith. He said, "Inasmuch as John had faith, though he could not speak or understand, your argument fails, that children are not able to believe." See Luther, "Concerning Rebaptism," 354. Despite Luther's point, most believe that John represents a special situation.

[36]Pendleton, *Distinctive Principles of Baptists*, 14–5.

unconscious infants be made disciples?"³⁷ He concluded that since an infant could not be made a disciple, an infant should not be baptized.

Pendleton also addressed the difficult issue of household baptisms by writing, "The argument from household baptisms in favor of infant baptism is invalid."³⁸ This discussion began with Cornelius who was described in Acts 10:2 as, "a devout man and one who feared God with all his household." This household was eventually baptized after hearing the Gospel. Pendleton raised the question, "Can infants fear God?"³⁹ The next household baptism discusses Lydia in Acts 16. Verse 15 says, "And when she and her household were baptized, she begged us, saying, 'If you have judged me to be faithful to the Lord, come to my house and stay.' So she persuaded us." Pendleton said concerning this verse, "No one denies that Lydia was a believer; she was therefore a proper subject of baptism. But it is inferred by Pedobaptists that, as her household was baptized, infants must have been baptized;" however, he went on to argue

---

³⁷Pendleton, *Three Reasons Why I Am a Baptist with a Fourth Reason Added on Communion*, 8. Even Zwingli, who supported infant baptism, did not think infants could believe. He rejected this idea which Luther supported by stating, "Baptism cannot confirm faith in infants because infants are not able to believe." Zwingli, as cited in Timothy George, *Theology of the Reformers* (Nashville: Broadman & Holman, 1988), 142–3.

³⁸Pendleton, *Three Reasons Why I Am a Baptist with a Fourth Reason Added on Communion*, 25. This argument is made by Calvin who stated "Nor is their silly objection plausible that there is no evidence of a single infant's ever being baptized by the hands of the apostle! For even if this is not expressly related by the Evangelists, still, because infants are not excluded when mention is made of a family's being baptized, who in his senses can reason from this that they were not baptized?" See Calvin, *Institutes of the Christian Religion*, 1331. Additionally, Charles Hodge wrote, "When, therefore, the Apostles baptized the head of a family, it was a matter of course, that they should baptize his infant children." Hodge specifically noted the household baptisms in Acts. See Hodge, *Systematic Theology*, vol. 3, 556. For another of Pendleton's contemporaries, see Summers, *Baptism*, 32–4.

³⁹Pendleton, *Three Reasons Why I Am a Baptist with a Fourth Reason Added on Communion*, 22.

"that Lydia had neither husband nor children."[40] Part of his justification lies in the statement that "she was engaged in secular business—was 'a seller of purple, of the city of Thyatira,' which was about three hundred miles from Philippi. If she had a husband and infant children, is it not reasonable to suppose that her husband would have taken on himself the business in which she was engaged, allowing her to remain at home with the infant children?"[41] Furthermore, the custom of the day suggested calling a house by the man's name. If Lydia had no husband, it explained why they referred to the house of Lydia. Pendleton concluded by saying that the burden of proof now lies on the Pedobaptists to demonstrate that she had infant children.

The next example of a household baptism came from the baptism of the jailer in Acts 16:31–34:

> So they said, "Believe on the Lord Jesus Christ, and you will be saved, you and your household." Then they spoke the word of the Lord to him and to all who were in his house. And he took them the same hour of the night and washed their stripes. And immediately he and all his family were baptized. Now when he had brought them into his house, he set food before them; and he rejoiced, having believed in God with all his household.

From this verse, Pendleton emphasized that believing was required before baptism and that the jailer rejoiced "having believed in God with all his household." Again the ability to

---

[40]Pendleton, *Distinctive Principles of Baptists*, 26–7.
[41]Pendleton, *Three Reasons Why I Am a Baptist with a Fourth Reason Added on Communion*, 23. Hodge, *Systematic Theology*, vol. 3, 556, stated, "Lydia 'was baptized and her household'" in his defense of infant baptism. He concluded his discussion of household baptisms by saying, "It is to be remembered that the history of the Apostolic period is very brief, and also that Christ sent the Apostles, not to baptize, but to preach the Gospel, and, therefore, it is not surprising that so few instances of household baptism are recorded in the New Testament." From this statement, Hodge moved to church history attempting to support infant baptism.

believe in something did not lie with infants; thus, infants could not be baptized.

The final household baptism is discussed in 1 Cor 1:16. Paul wrote, "Yes, I also baptized the household of Stephanas." Fortunately, Paul commented further on the household of Stephanas in 1 Cor 16:15, "I urge you, brethren—you know the household of Stephanas, that it is the firstfruits of Achaia, and that they have devoted themselves to the ministry of the saints."

Pendleton stated, "Infants could not addict [devote] themselves to the ministry of the saints."[42] In concluding this section on the household baptisms, Pendleton added, "In view of such considerations as have now been presented, the reasonings of Pedobaptists from household baptisms are utterly inconclusive. They cannot satisfy a logical mind."[43] Pendleton denied that the household baptisms supported infant baptism in any way.

In addition to the household baptisms, Pendleton discussed other relevant New Testament passages.[44] He discussed 1 Cor 7:14: "For the unbelieving husband is sanctified by the wife, and the unbelieving wife is sanctified by the husband;

---

[42]Pendleton, *Three Reasons Why I Am a Baptist with a Fourth Reason Added on Communion,* 24. Hiscox, *The New Directory for Baptist Churches,* 477, agreed with Pendleton. Hiscox wrote concerning the "addicting themselves to the ministry" saying that "This could not have been spoken of baptized infants, but well describes the Christian activities of adult believers. No infants can be found in the household of Stephanas."

[43]Pendleton, *Distinctive Principles of Baptists,* 28. Hiscox, *The New Directory for Baptist Churches,* 473–7, discussed the household baptisms in Acts. Hiscox stated, "This argument, like the others in its support, is founded on the faintest and most illogical inference. It is inferred that these households certainly had infant children in them, and that such children certainly were baptized; both of which are wholly gratuitous" (473).

[44]Pendleton, *Distinctive Principles of Baptists,* 30. This section is not in *Three Reasons Why I Am a Baptist with a Fourth Added on Communion,* and thus represents new material developed with the maturation of Pendleton's theology.

otherwise your children would be unclean, but now they are holy." After discussing the various translations of this verse, Pendleton quoted Albert Barnes, a "well-known Pedobaptist" who claimed, "There is not one word about baptism here; not one allusion to it; nor does the argument in the remotest degree bear upon it. The question was not whether children should be baptized, but it was whether there should be a separation between man and wife where the one was a Christian and the other not."[45] He also discussed 1 Cor 15:29, Gal 3:27, Col 2:12, and 1 Pet 3:21 as all demonstrating that infants could not be the proper subjects of baptism. In concluding this section, he quoted from several Pedobaptist authors such as William Wall, Moses Stuart, and Leonard Woods attempting to prove the "utter absence of New Testament authority for infant baptism."[46] Pendleton concluded by leading into his next discussion, "Strange as it is for Pedobaptists to go to the Old Testament for justification of one of their practices under the New Testament economy, yet, as they do so, it is necessary to follow them."[47]

---

[45]Albert Barnes, *Notes on the New Testament, Explanatory and Practical: 1 Corinthians* (Grand Rapids: Baker Book House, 1949), 117–8. As in Pendleton, *Three Reasons Why I Am a Baptist with a Fourth Reason Added on Communion*, 29.

[46]Pendleton, *Distinctive Principles of Baptists*, 37–9. William Wall was of the Church of England and wrote *History of Infant Baptism*. Moses Stuart was Professor of Sacred Literature at Andover Theological Seminary and wrote *Is the Mode of Christian Baptism Prescribed in the New Testament?* Leonard Woods was one of the first professors at Andover Theological Seminary. He taught Christian Theology from 1808 until 1846 and wrote *Lectures on Infant Baptism*.

[47]Pendleton, *Distinctive Principles of Baptists*, 39. It is common for the defense of infant baptism to utilize the Old Testament for support. For example, Zwingli believed that baptism is the circumcision of the Christians. George stated, "This comparison was, of course, well worn by patristic and medieval usage; Luther referred to it as well. No one, however, had developed it as thoroughly as Zwingli." See George, *Theology of the Reformers*, 141.

Pendleton also refuted the Old Testament arguments given in favor of infant baptism. He said, "The argument from the supposed identity of the Jewish commonwealth and the gospel church is of no force."[48] Pendleton began by quoting Pedobaptist authors to explain their position that the Jewish and Christian churches are "the same in substance" or have "substantial oneness."[49] For example, John Calvin linked the Old Testament church to the New Testament church by arguing the following: (1) Abraham was father of all who believe, (2) the covenant with the Jews was not made void, (3) the promise to Abraham is to be fulfilled literally, and (4) there is no difference between baptism and circumcision.[50] Additionally, this argument forms the central argument of Charles Hodge who stated, "In order to justify the baptism of infants, we must attain and authenticate such an idea of the Church as that it shall include the children of believing parents."[51] His third proposition was that the "commonwealth of Israel was the church" and his fourth was "the Church under the New Dispensation is identical with that under the Old."[52] Hodge attempted to establish oneness so that he could prove infants were part of the Jewish church and should thus be part of the Christian church. Pendleton refuted this position with his definition of the term church. He said, "It means 'a congregation,' 'an assembly' . . . They were separated from the world—a spiritual people. Baptists

---

[48]Pendleton, *Distinctive Principles of Baptists*, 39. The argument presented rested mainly on the fact that the Greek word *ecclesia* was not a newly invented word, but it was the term by which the LXX had rendered the Hebrew word *qahal*. They inferred that these words denote the same thing, the congregation of the Lord. Dagg, *Manual of Church Order*, 156–64, also responded to this argument by demonstrating the difference between the two and by stating that "If the first covenant had been faultless, then should no place have been sought for the second" (164).

[49]Pendleton, *Three Reasons Why I Am a Baptist with a Fourth Reason Added on Communion*, 31–4, and in *Distinctive Principles of Baptists*, 40. See also Summers, *Baptism*, 23–6.

[50]Calvin, *Institutes of the Christian Religion*, 1335–8.

[51]Hodge, *Systematic Theology*, vol. 3, 547.

[52]Ibid., 548–52.

say that in this sense of the term 'church' there was no church before the Christian dispensation."[53]

In order to defend his position better, Pendleton spent nineteen pages covering four subheadings all seeking to prove that the "Jewish theocracy" and the "kingdom of God" (New Testament church) are not identical. His view is best summarized by a listing of his four subheadings.

> (1) When the Jewish theocracy had been in existence for centuries, the prophets predicted the establishment of a new kingdom; (2) another fact fatal to the identity contended for is that those who were regular members of the old Jewish Church could not become members of the Christian Church without repentance, faith, regeneration, and baptism; (3) it deserves special notice that the covenant of the Jewish Church and the covenant of the Christian Church are different; and (4) the supposed identity of the Jewish Church and Christian Church involves absurdities and impossibilities.[54]

Recognizing the importance for Pedobaptists of relating infant baptism to circumcision and thus, the Jewish church to the Christian church, Pendleton attempted to establish that no parallel exists.

The next section states, "The argument from circumcision fails."[55] Again Pendleton utilized four sub-points to explain

---

[53]Pendleton, *Distinctive Principles of Baptists*, 42–3.

[54]Pendleton, *Distinctive Principles of Baptists*, 44–63; *Three Reasons Why I Am a Baptist with a Fourth Reason Added on Communion*, 35–54.

[55]Pendleton, *Distinctive Principles of Baptists*, 63. Dagg, *Manual of Church Order*, 173–8, and 191–5, also refuted the argument from circumcision. Dagg stated one additional reason that Pendleton did not include: "Since, the covenant of circumcision instituted no ecclesia, and cannot admit gentile infants among the covenant seed, the doctrine of infant church-membership cannot be affected by the question." Hiscox said of the argument from circumcision, "What connection there is between these two institutions would require a philosopher to discover. And yet this has been the argument chiefly relied on by theologians, scholars, and divines in this country especially, for generations past, to prove the divine

his position. He said that (1) the circumcised needed to be baptized before they could become members of the church of Christ, (2) that circumcision was confined to one sex,[56] (3) that the eighth day was appointed for the circumcision of infants while there is not an appointed day for the baptism of infants, and (4) that the Jerusalem council virtually denied the substitution of baptism for circumcision.[57] Thus, Pendleton denied the validity of the argument from circumcision.

After discussing the scriptural issues, Pendleton examined "the historical argument" and began by writing, "What does church history say of infant baptism? Much, I admit; but

---

authority for infant baptism." See Hiscox, *The New Directory for Baptist Churches*, 486–7. Hiscox offered a rebuttal similar to Pendleton's.

[56]Calvin responded to this argument with the following, "A similar sleight-of-hand is their cavil that, if baptism must be conformed to circumcision, women ought not to be baptized. For if it is quite certain that the sanctification of the Israelite offspring was attested by the sign of circumcision, there is no doubt that it was intended that from it men and women equally be sanctified. Only the bodies of the males were imprinted with it, which could be imprinted by nature, yet in such a way that the women might be through them, so to speak, companions and partners of circumcision. Therefore, setting aside these absurdities of theirs, let us cling to the resemblance between baptism and circumcision, which we see most completely in accord with respect to the inner mystery, the promises, the use, and the efficacy." See *Institutes of the Christian Religion*, 1339. Just as Pendleton's point did not convince Pedobaptists, Pedobaptists formulations such as Calvin's have not convinced Baptists. For example, Paul Jewett criticized the covenant argument by stating, "The nub of our criticism of 'the argument from the covenant" for infant baptism has been that it stresses the covenant idea as the unifying concept of redemptive history to the point of suppressing the *movement* of redemptive history, a movement from the age of anticipation and promise to the age of realization and fulfillment." See Paul Jewett, *Infant Baptism and the Covenant of Grace* (Grand Rapids: Eerdmans, 1978), 235–6.

[57]Pendleton, *Distinctive Principles of Baptists*, 64–72. On point number four, Pendleton elaborated by saying that the council could have easily stated that baptism replaced circumcision or completely abolished circumcision, but instead they allowed it to continue for reasons of nationality only, not reasons of salvation.

there is no proof that it was practiced before the latter part of the second century."⁵⁸ Pendleton responded to two claims for early support of infant baptism. The first response addressed Irenaeus who wrote, "For he [Christ] came to save all persons by himself: all, I mean, who by him are regenerated [or baptized] unto God; infants, and little ones, and children and youth and elder persons."⁵⁹ Pendleton disputed the translation of the Latin word *renascor* as baptize claiming that it means "born again" or "regenerated."⁶⁰ The next person discussed was Tertullian. The Pedobaptists asserted that Tertullian opposed infant baptism, which proved the existence of it. Pendleton disputed this claiming that Tertullian used the word *parvulos* which should be translated as "little children."⁶¹ Pendleton concluded, "If infant baptism rests for its support on the practice of the first two centuries, it rests on a foundation of sand."⁶²

---

⁵⁸Pendleton, *Distinctive Principles of Baptists*, 72. It was important for Pendleton to lay out the historical origin of infant baptism because men such as Martin Luther had claimed an earlier origin. Luther said, "Since our baptizing has been thus from the beginning of Christianity and the custom has been to baptize children, and since no one can prove with good reasons that they do not have faith, we should not make changes and build on such weak arguments." See Luther, "Concerning Rebaptism," 353.

⁵⁹Irenaeus, "Against Heresies," *Ante-Nicene Fathers*, vol. 1 (Peabody: Hendrickson, 1999), 391.

⁶⁰Pendleton, *Distinctive Principles of Baptists*, 72. For support of his position, Pendleton quoted Winer, *Christian Review*, vol. 3, 213, and Philip Doddridge, *Miscellaneous Works* (London: William Ball, 1839), 493.

⁶¹Pendleton, *Distinctive Principles of Baptists*, 74. This quote from Tertullian states, "And so, according to the circumstances and disposition, and even age, of each individual, the delay of baptism is preferable; principally, however, in the case of little children. For why is it necessary —if (baptism itself) is not so necessary —that the sponsors likewise should be thrust into danger?" See Tertullian, "On Baptism," in *Ante-Nicene Fathers*, vol. 3 (Peabody: Hendrickson, 1999), 678.

⁶²Pendleton, *Three Reasons Why I Am a Baptist with a Fourth Reason Added on Communion*, 65. Dagg, *Manual of Church Order*, 199, stated, "Other learned men have examined the same writings, and have arrived at the conclusion, that infant baptism was wholly unknown until about the close of the second century;—that it originated in Africa, and in the third century became prevalent there, but did not supplant the primitive

The next noteworthy discussion centered on the Council of Carthage in A.D. 253. At the council, a bishop named Fidus presented a question concerning whether a child should be baptized before it was eight days old.⁶³ Pendleton said, "The very fact that such a question was sent to the Council shows that infant baptism was a new thing."⁶⁴

Pendleton demonstrated that at various times people protested against infant baptism. Part of the evidence came from the Council of Mela, in Numidia around A.D. 416. The council stated, "Also, it is the pleasure of the bishops to order that whoever denieth that infants newly born of their mothers, are to be baptized, or saith that baptism is administered for the remission of their own sins, but not on account of original sin, derived from Adam, and to be expiated by the laver of regeneration, *be accursed.*"⁶⁵ The fact

---

baptism in the Oriental churches, until the fifth century." Hiscox, *The New Directory for Baptist Churches*, 479, agreed with Pendleton by saying, "Infant baptism was unknown until the first part of the third century after Christ."

⁶³Pendleton, *Three Reasons Why I Am a Baptist with a Fourth Reason Added on Communion*, 68. Fidus was one of the sixty-six bishops present at the Council of Carthage. See Alexander Campbell, *Christian Baptism with Its Antecedents and Consequents* (Bethany: Published by the author, 1851; reprint, Nashville: Gospel Advocate, 1951), 293–4. Cyprian records the council's conclusion, "And therefore, dearest brother, this was our opinion in council, that by us no one ought to he hindered from baptism and from the grace of God, who is merciful and kind and loving to all. Which, since it is to be observed and maintained in respect of all, we think is to be even more observed in respect of infants and newly-born persons, who on this very account deserve more from our help and from the divine mercy, that immediately, on the very beginning of their birth, lamenting and weeping, they do nothing else but entreat." See Cyprian, "The Epistles of Cyprian," in *Ante-Nicene Fathers*, eds. Alexander Roberts and James Donaldson, vol. 5 (Peabody: Hendrickson, 1999), 353–4.

⁶⁴Pendleton, *Distinctive Principles of Baptists*, 77.

⁶⁵Pendleton, *Three Reasons Why I Am a Baptist with a Fourth Reason Added on Communion*, 71. David Benedict, *A General History of the Baptist Denomination in America and Other Parts of the World* (New York: Lewis Colby, 1848), 10, discussed this council of fifteen people which Augustine led. Benedict stated the declaration of the council as follows:

that this statement needed to be issued demonstrated that some opposed infant baptism.

Pendleton mentioned several practical objections to infant baptism. Among those, he stated that its advocates cannot agree why it should be practiced, and that those baptized as infants do not always grow up to demonstrate a regenerate life. Furthermore, if universally practiced, infant baptism would do away with believer's baptism. To conclude, Pendleton said, "Baptists regard infant baptism as utterly destitute of scriptural support; and, in view of its many evils, they are most decided in their opposition to it."[66]

In various articles, Pendleton addressed more specific matters. To Presbyterians such as Peter Edwards who claimed to agree with Baptists on the baptism of adults, Pendleton responded, "The reason why Pedobaptists baptize believers is not found in the positive fact that they are believers, but in the negative fact that they were not baptized in infancy."[67] Pendleton further recognized the problem of blurring the line between the church and world through infant baptism. He wrote, "We might, if so disposed, show that infant baptism is not only corrupting in its influence, but that its obvious tendency is to abolish the distinction everywhere recognized in the word of God

---

"We will that whoever denies that children by baptism are freed from perdition and eternally saved, that they be accursed."

[66]Pendleton, *Distinctive Principles of Baptists*, 89.

[67]James Madison Pendleton, "Peter Edwards on Baptism," *The Southern Baptist Review* 4 (June 1858): 422–3. Peter Edwards was for several years a Baptist and Pastor of the Baptist Church at Portsea. He later became a Presbyterian and his work was encouraged and printed by the Presbyterian Board of Publication. Peter Edwards, *Candid Reasons for Renouncing the Principles of Antipedobaptism* (Aberdeen: George King, 1841), 9–10, stated, "Pedobaptists agree with them in this, that believers are proper subjects of baptism; but deny that such only are proper subjects. They think, that, together with such believing adults who have not yet been baptized, their infants have a right to baptism as well as their parents." He continued to claim agreement with Baptists on adult baptism.

between the church and the world."[68] Pendleton firmly rejected infant baptism and supported baptism as a church ordinance for believers only and by immersion only.

Proper Mode

In Pendleton's later work, the first heading in his discussion of baptism was titled the "Act of Baptism." He preferred not to use the word "mode" because it implied multiple valid methods while he believed that true baptism required immersion of believers. He emphasized the necessity of having all aspects correct by calling it the "act of baptism." Pendleton stated, "Immersion is so exclusively the baptismal act, that without it there is no baptism; a believer in Christ is so exclusively the subject of baptism, that without such a subject there is no baptism."[69]

The first and most important support of immersion as the proper baptismal method to Pendleton was the meaning of the word in the New Testament. One could not assume this argument because prominent Pedobaptists such as Charles Hodge argued otherwise. Hodge said, "In the Classics; in the Septuagint and the Apocryphal writings of the Old Testament; in the New Testament; and in the writings of the Greek fathers, the word βάπτω, βαπτίζω, and their cognates, are used with such latitude of meaning, as to prove the assertion that the command to baptize is a command to immerse, to be utterly unauthorized and unreasonable."[70] Understanding that Pedobaptists contested the translation of βαπτίζω, Pendleton presented his case for translating it as "immerse."

---

[68]Pendleton, "Dr. Alexander's Doubts of the Propriety of Infant Baptism," 34.
[69]Pendleton, *Baptist Church Manual*, 64. All Baptist confessions of faith since 1644 support immersion as the proper form of baptism.
[70]Hodge, *Systematic Theology*, vol. 3, 526–7. Mark Noll, "Charles Hodge" in *Evangelical Dictionary of Theology*, ed. Walter Elwell, 2d ed. (Grand Rapids: Baker, 2001), 561, calls Hodge, "The most influential American Presbyterian theologian of the nineteenth century."

Pendleton stated that the Greek lexicons give "immerse, dip or plunge as the primary and ordinary meaning of βαπτίζω."[71] This word in the English translation had been "anglicized" but not translated. This resulted from King James's rules of translation. The King's third rule stated, "the old ecclesiastical words (were) to be kept, as the word church not to be translated congregation."[72] The fourth rule had even greater implications on the possible translation of the term baptize. It stated, "When any word hath divers significations, *that* to be kept which hath been most commonly used by the most eminent Fathers, being agreeable to the propriety of the place and the analogy of faith."[73] Even if the evidence clearly demonstrated that *baptize* should be translated as *immerse*, this rule would not have allowed the translators to do so. Augustine's and Aquinas's use of the term forced a vague translation.

Pendleton further elaborated on why *baptism* was not translated as *immerse* by stating, "King James virtually forbade the translation of *baptize* and *baptism*."[74] Pendleton clarified by saying, "There is no historical evidence that the king was opposed to *immersion*; but he was bitterly opposed to the 'Genevan Version' of the Bible in which *baptism* was rendering [sic] *washing*."[75] Whatever the reason, the lack of a translation made an appeal to the lexicons and historical understanding of the word essential in order for Pendleton to prove its correct meaning.

---

[71]Pendleton, *Three Reasons Why I Am a Baptist with a Fourth Reason Added on Communion*, 83.

[72]As stated in Pendleton, *Christian Doctrines*, 343. For a complete list of King James's rules see W. Fiddian Moulton, *The History of the English Bible* (London: Charles H. Kelly, 1911), 196. This rule is also discussed by F. F. Bruce, *The English Bible: A History of Translations* (New York: Oxford University, 1961), 98.

[73]As stated in Pendleton, *Three Reasons Why I Am a Baptist with a Fourth Reason Added on Communion*, 85. Moulton includes the same information in *The History of the English Bible*, 196.

[74]Pendleton, *Baptist Church Manual*, 66.

[75]Ibid., 69.

Pendleton stated, "not only Lexicographers, but distinguished Pedobaptist scholars and theologians, admit that *baptizo* means to *immerse*."[76] Pendleton quoted from John Calvin first. In the *Institutes of the Christian Religion*, Calvin stated, "But whether the person being baptized should be wholly immersed, and whether thrice or once, whether he should only be sprinkled with poured water—these details are of no importance, but ought to be optional to churches according to the diversity of countries. Yet the word 'baptize' means to immerse, and it is clear that the rite of immersion was observed in the ancient church."[77] From this quotation Pendleton stressed the concession of Calvin that *baptize* means to *immerse*. Thus, if one wanted to follow the New Testament example, immersion was the only option.

Pendleton strengthened his case by quoting the opinions of other non-Baptists. Moses Stuart, a Congregationalist who taught at Andover Seminary, stated, "*Bapto* and *baptizo* mean to *dip, plunge,* or *immerse*, into anything liquid. All lexicographers and critics of any note are agreed in this."[78] Thomas Chalmers, a respected Presbyterian, provided additional support. Chalmers wrote, "The original meaning of the word *baptism*, is *immersion*, and though we regard it as a point of indifferency, whether the ordinance so named be performed in this way or by sprinkling—yet we doubt not, that the prevalent style of the administration in the apostle's days, was by an actual submerging of the whole body under water."[79] Pendleton quoted these and many other non-Baptists who agreed with his position on the meaning of βαπτίζω.

---

[76] Pendleton, *Three Reasons Why I Am a Baptist with a Fourth Reason Added on Communion*, 91.

[77] Calvin, *Institutes of the Christian Religion*, 1320.

[78] Moses Stuart, *Is the Mode of Christian Baptism Prescribed in the New Testament?* (Nashville: Graves, Mark & Rutland, 1856), 41.

[79] As in Pendleton, *Christian Doctrines*, 346. See also Thomas Chalmers, *Lectures on the Epistles of Paul the Apostle to the Romans* (New York: Carter, 1845), 152.

Pendleton typically avoided using the endorsements of Baptist preachers and scholars for immersion; however, he did specifically note Spurgeon's beliefs on the matters. In the *Tennessee Baptist,* Pendleton demonstrated that Spurgeon believed baptize means to immerse.[80] Spurgeon stated, "If it means sprinkle, let our brethren translate it sprinkle. But they dare not do that; they know they have nothing in all classical language that would ever justify them in doing that, and they have not the impudence to attempt it."[81]

Pendleton also sought to prove that "the classical usage of *baptizo* establishes the position that immersion is the baptismal act."[82] In doing so, Pendleton recognized the work of Alexander Carson and T.J. Conant, proving that the classical usage was that of immersion.[83] He also relied on Moses Stuart who quoted Pindar, Hippocrates, Aristotle, Plato, Josephus, Plutarch, and others to support immersion as the proper meaning of βαπτίζω.[84] In concluding this section, Pendleton said, "No man of established reputation as a Greek scholar will deny that *baptizo*, at the beginning of the Christian era, meant 'to *immerse*,' and that usage had confirmed that meaning."[85] After stressing this point, Pendleton drew the conclusion that because immersion was the sense in which the writers of the New Testament understood the word, they would not have used the word to

---

[80]James Madison Pendleton, "Spurgeon on Baptism," *Tennessee Baptist* (October 10, 1857).
[81]Charles H. Spurgeon, *The New Park Street Pulpit* (Pasadena: Pilgrim Publication, 1975), 267–8.
[82]Pendleton, *Baptist Church Manual*, 72.
[83]Alexander Carson, *Baptism in Its Mode and Subjects* (Philadelphia: American Baptist Publication Society, 1848). Thomas Jefferson Conant, *The Meaning and Use of Baptizein, Philologically and Historically Investigated for the American Bible Union* (New York: American Bible Union, 1860).
[84]Stuart, *Is the Mode of Christian Baptism Prescribed in the New Testament?*, 52–64.
[85]Pendleton, *Distinctive Principles of Baptists*, 109–10.

depict sprinkling or pouring. Thus, the proper act of baptism required immersion.

Not only the meaning of the word βαπτίζω, but the actual design of the ordinance further supported the argument for immersion. Pendleton wrote, "The design of baptism furnishes an argument in favor of the proposition I am establishing."[86] Pendleton linked the design of baptism to the death, burial, and resurrection of Jesus in a symbolic fashion. If baptism symbolically represents Jesus' death, then sprinkling or pouring failed to accomplish the task as well as immersion. In order to prove that baptism symbolized Jesus' death and resurrection, Pendleton quoted and discussed Rom 6:3–5, "Or do you not know that as many of us as were baptized into Christ Jesus were baptized into His death? Therefore we were buried with Him through baptism unto death, that just as Christ was raised from the dead by the glory of the Father, even so we also should walk in newness of life. For if we have been united together in the likeness of His death, certainly we also shall be in the likeness of His resurrection. . . ." He also cited Col 2:12 and 1 Peter 3:21 to link baptism symbolically to the death, burial, and resurrection of Christ. He summarized that baptism taught the three great facts of the New Testament—Christ died, was buried, and rose again.

Another argument used for immersion being the proper translation came from "the places selected for the administration of baptism and the circumstances attending

---

[86]Pendleton, *Three Reasons Why I Am a Baptist with a Fourth Reason Added on Communion*, 104. This was an important argument because men like Charles Hodge differed. Hodge, specifically addressing the "argument from the design of the ordinance," stated in his *Systematic Theology*, vol. 3, 539, "From all this it appears that the truth symbolized in baptism may be signified by immersion, affusion, or sprinkling; but that the ordinance is most significant and most conformed to Scripture, when administered by affusion or sprinkling."

its administration, as referred to in the New Testament."[87] The first discussion centered on the baptisms John performed. John baptized in the Jordan River. The Jordan River was approximately eighty to one hundred feet wide and up to twelve feet deep in the center. This provided plenty of water to perform the act of baptism by immersion. Furthermore, John baptized in Enon, near Salim, possibly because a stream existed there which also contained suitable water for immersion.[88] Pendleton also discussed the baptism of the Ethiopian eunuch in Acts 8:38-39: "And both Philip and the eunuch went down into the water, and he baptized him. Now when they came up out of the water. . . ." From the description "down into the water" and "up out of the water" the passage indicates that both men were in the water. This was not necessary for sprinkling or pouring but was necessary for immersion. Thus, Pendleton stated, "Philip and the eunuch were men of good sense, and therefore did not go into the water for purposes of 'pouring or sprinkling.'"[89]

Pendleton discussed in detail the Greek preposition εἰς which can have different meanings in different situations. One of his contemporaries, Thomas Summers, translated this

---

[87]Pendleton, *Three Reasons Why I Am a Baptist with a Fourth Reason Added on Communion*, 110.

[88]Pendleton, *Distinctive Principles of Baptists*, 123–4. In the same work, Pendleton addressed the objections of his contemporary N. L. Rice, who claimed the need for substantial water came from the people who were to be baptized. Pendleton stated that this is merely hypothesis and not stated in the New Testament (123–8). See "Dr. N. L. Rice and Immersion," *Tennessee Baptist* (August 18, 1855). Rice (1807–1877) was pastor of various churches, President of Westminster College for a time, and professor of didactic and polemic theology in the theological seminary in Danville, Kentucky. He debated Alexander Campbell over the issue of baptism and this is recorded in a book titled, *Baptism: the Design, Mode and Subjects* (St. Louis: Keith and Woods, 1855).

[89]Pendleton, *Distinctive Principles of Baptists*, 129. Hodge in his *Systematic Theology*, vol. 3, 535, argued that "There is no known stream in that region of sufficient depth to allow of the immersion of a man." Pendleton did not comment specifically on this, but if the stream contained enough water to go "down into," it would seem to be deep enough for immersion.

word as "to" instead of "into" in order to explain properly such passages as Acts 8:38–39.⁹⁰ Summers said, "When *eis* means *into*, it is used before the noun as well as before the verb."⁹¹ Since εἰς is used but once in Acts 8:38, Philip and the eunuch did not go *into* the water but *to* the water according to Summers. But Pendleton showed that if this Greek construction required the translation of *to* instead of *into*, many verses in the New Testament would not make sense. For example in Matt 8:31–33, the demons did not go "into" the swine but merely "to" the swine. Also in Matt 9:17, the wine was put "to" the bottles instead of "into" the bottles. Pendleton quoted Calvin in his discussion of the Ethiopian eunuch. On Acts 8:38 Calvin asserts, "Here we see the rite used among men of old time in baptism; for they put all the body into the water."⁹² Thus, Pendleton gave good reasons for concluding that *"eis"* meant *"into"* specifically in the case of Ethiopian eunuch going *"into"* the water.

Additionally, Pendleton claimed to have history on his side, stating, "History bears testimony to the practice of immersion, except in cases of sickness and urgent necessity, for more than thirteen hundred years."⁹³ Again Pendleton

---

⁹⁰Summers, *Baptism*, 100. Hodge, *Systematic Theology*, vol. 3, 531, takes a different approach attempting to defend that when εἰς was translated "into" immerse was not the meaning because "According to ancient accounts, the common way of baptizing was for the person to step into water, when water was poured on his head, and then he came up out of the water, not in the least incommoded by dripping garments."

⁹¹Summers, *Baptism*, 100.

⁹²John Calvin, "Commentary Upon the Acts of the Apostles," *Calvin's Commentaries*, vol. 18 (Grand Rapids: Baker Books, 1999), 364.

⁹³Pendleton, *Three Reasons Why I Am a Baptist with a Fourth Reason Added on Communion*, 127. Pendleton did not make further comment on the clause, "except in cases of sickness and urgent necessity." Some Pedobaptists argued that history did not support immersion conclusively. Hodge in his *Systematic Theology*, vol. 3, 537, stated, "But it is denied that immersion is essential to baptism; that it was at any time or in any part of the Church the exclusive method; and more especially is it denied that immersion is now and everywhere obligatory or necessary to the integrity of Christian baptism."

referred to Pedobaptists to prove his point. He quoted from Richard Baxter, "It is commonly confessed by us to the Anabaptists, as our commentators declare, that in the apostles' times the baptized were dipped over head in the water. . . ."[94] Next, he quoted John Wesley who said, "Mary Welsh, aged eleven days, was baptized, according to the custom of the first church and the rule of the Church of England, by immersion."[95] He also quoted John Calvin who commented on John 3:22–23, "From these words we may infer that John and Christ administered baptism by plunging the whole body beneath the water."[96] With all of the support for *immersion*, Pendleton asked how the practice of sprinkling began.

To explain how sprinkling began, Pendleton quoted a lengthy passage from Wall's *History of Infant Baptism*.

> Now, *Calvin* had not only given his Dictate, in his Institutions, that *the difference is of no moment, whether thrice or once; or whether he be only wetted with the water poured on him*: But he had also drawn up for the use of his church at *Geneva* (and afterward published to the world) *a form of administering the sacraments,* where, when he comes to the order of baptizing, he words it thus: *Then the minister of baptism pours water on the infant; saying, I baptize thee,* etc. There had been, as I said, some Synods in the Dioceses of France that had spoken of affusion without mentioning immersion at all; that being the common practice; but for an Office or Liturgy of any

---

[94] Pendleton, *Distinctive Principles of Baptists*, 136. This author has been unable to find the original source. The quotation is included in Campbell, *Christian Baptism with Its Antecedents and Consequents*, 146, with no citation of the original source. Richard Baxter (1615–1691) allied himself with the Puritan movement and is best known for two writings, *The Saints' Everlasting Rest*, and *The Reformed Pastor*.

[95] John Wesley, *The Journal of John Wesley*, ed. Nehemiah Curnock, vol. 1 (London: Epworth Press, 1938), 166. As in Pendleton, *Distinctive Principles of Baptists*, 136.

[96] John Calvin, "Commentary on the Gospel According to John," *Calvin's Commentaries*, vol. 17 (Grand Rapids: Baker Books, 1999), 130.

church; this is, I believe the first in the world that prescribes affusion absolutely.[97]

Pendleton claimed that the *Edinburgh Encyclopedia* said that the lawfulness for sprinkling resulted from a verbal conversation of Pope Stephen II in 753; however, it was not a law until 1311 that immersion or sprinkling were both acceptable.[98]

Pendleton next attempted to answer ten Pedobaptist objections to baptism by immersion. These objections can be broken down into three categories which are: (1) lexical objections, (2) contextual objections, and (3) pragmatic objections. Under lexical objections, it is argued that "John baptized, not in, but at, Jordan," that John baptized "with water" and not in water, and the phrase "diverse washings" in Heb 9:10 indicates more than one baptism.[99] Pendleton countered the first two objections with lexical arguments demonstrating that the Greek preposition "en" must be translated "in" otherwise the Greeks would have no such preposition. Concerning Heb 9:10, Pendleton stated, "It surely will be conceded that these regulations involved

---

[97]William Wall, *The History of Infant Baptism*, vol. 1 (Oxford: Oxford University Press, 1862), 580–1, as in Pendleton, *Three Reasons Why I Am a Baptist with a Fourth Reason Added on Communion*, 132–3.

[98]Pendleton, *Distinctive Principles of Baptists*, 142–3. The original source could not be located, but Campbell, *Christian Baptism,* 147, verifies Pendleton's account by giving a direct quotation. Campbell quotes, "The first law for sprinkling was obtained in the following manner: Pope Stephen II, being driven from Rome by Adolphus, king of the Lombards, in 753, fled to Pepin, who, a short time before, had usurped the crown of France. Whilst he remained there, the monks of Cressy, in Britany, consulted him whether, in case of necessity, baptism poured on the head of the infant would be lawful. Stephen replied that it would. But though the truth of this fact be allowed—which, however, some Catholics deny—yet pouring, or sprinkling, was admitted only in case of necessity. It was not till the year 1311 that the legislature, in a council held at Ravenna, declared immersion or sprinkling to be indifferent."

[99]Pendleton, *Three Reasons Why I Am a Baptist with a Fourth Reason Added on Communion,* 137, 138, and 144.

'divers immersions.' There were 'divers' occasions for immersing, and 'divers' objects were immersed."[100]

The contextual objections argued that the fact that the Holy Spirit is said to be poured out militates against immersion.[101] Charles Hodge stated, "The Spirit is frequently said to be poured out on men; but men are never said to be dipped or immersed into the Holy Spirit."[102] Pendleton responded to this argument by saying, "If so, it militates equally against sprinkling. If pouring is baptism, why is not the Spirit sometimes said to be baptized?"[103] Pedobaptists also objected that Saul was baptized standing up (Acts 9:18), to which Pendleton responded that standing up was the first action in a series of actions. Additionally, Pendleton questioned why Saul should have stood up to be sprinkled. Pendleton addressed two other minor objections, that Acts 10:7 implied water was to be brought to the baptism, and that the baptism of the Israelites unto Moses in the cloud and in the sea is irreconcilable with immersion, by elaborating on how Baptists interpret the passages to support immersion.[104]

The pragmatic objections to immersion included that the jailer in Acts 16:30–34 could not have been immersed in prison, that immersion is indecent and dangerous, and that three thousand persons could not have been immersed on the day of Pentecost. To the first, Pendleton explained that he believed the jailer left the jail and his house to be baptized, and Pendleton dismissed the second objection. The most important of this category is the objection that three thousand could not have been baptized in one day. Hodge stated concerning Pentecost, "Against the idea of full immersion in these cases there lies a difficulty, apparently

---

[100]Pendleton, *Distinctive Principles of Baptists*, 155.
[101]Ibid., 150.
[102]Hodge, *Systematic Theology*, vol. 3, 532.
[103]Pendleton, *Three Reasons Why I Am a Baptist with a Fourth Reason Added on Communion*, 140.
[104]Pendleton, *Distinctive Principles of Baptists*, 150–4.

insuperable, in the scarcity of water."[105] More generally, Hodge objected, "'Then went out to him [John] Jerusalem, and all Judea, and all the region round about Jordan, and were baptized of him in Jordan, confessing their sins' (Matt. 3:5–6); it seems physically impossible that he should have immersed all this multitude. When all the circumstances are taken into view, the presumption in favour of immersion, even in this class of passages, disappears."[106] Pendleton used N. L. Rice's argument for "much water" to refute that there was insufficient water for the task and used the story of a monk who caused 10,000 to be baptized in one day to prove that baptizing such a great number was possible.[107] After addressing all of the objections, Pendleton concluded his discussion by saying, "Whatever else may be said of these objections, it cannot be said that they have *weight*."[108] To summarize, Pendleton believed "the immersion in water of a believer in Christ is essential to baptism—so essential that without it there is no baptism."[109]

Proper Administrator

This issue of having a proper administrator arose as some Baptist churches accepted baptism by immersion from Pedobaptist churches. Generally two reasons were given for not accepting Pedobaptist immersions. First, the two groups often understood the symbolism of baptism in different ways, and second, the administrators of Pedobaptist immersions were not considered valid administrators.

---

[105]Hodge, *Systematic Theology*, vol. 3, 534.
[106]Ibid., 532.
[107]N. L. Rice, *Baptism: the Design, Mode and Subjects* (St. Louis: Keith and Woods, 1855). See also Benedict, *A General History of the Baptist Denomination in America and Other Parts of the World*, 302, or Jonathon Davis, *History of the Welsh Baptists* (Pittsburgh: D. M. Hogan, 1835), 14.
[108]Pendleton, *Distinctive Principles of Baptists*, 158.
[109]Pendleton, *Three Reasons Why I Am a Baptist with a Fourth Reason Added on Communion*, 147–8. Identical phrase also in Pendleton, *Distinctive Principles of Baptists*, 158.

Pendleton argued against Pedobaptist immersions.[110] He believed that only a proper administrator should perform the act of baptism.[111] By proper administrator, he meant that the person must be set aside or ordained by a true, visible, local church for administering the ordinance of baptism in accordance with the commands of Christ. The church setting the administrator aside or ordaining him should support the proper act of baptism and the administrator must have been baptized properly. Thus, the church performing the ordination must be a true, local congregation of believers and that church must be ordaining a proper person to have a proper administrator.[112] The ultimate authority rests with the church who empowers a proper administrator to perform a baptism according to the commands of Christ. If a properly ordained person baptized someone and the administrator later became a reprobate, it would not matter because the ordinance was administered under the authority of the church and not the person.

This belief meant that baptisms by immersion performed by Pedobaptist ministers were not valid. Pendleton did not hold this position alone. J. R. Graves and Basil Manly Sr. also

---

[110]Pendleton's rejection of Pedobaptist immersions resulted in part from the fact that this was baptism outside the "church." Rejection of baptism outside the church goes as far back as Cyprian who called a council at Carthage on September 1, 256. At this council, "87 bishops unanimously declared that baptism outside the Church was entirely null and void." Stanley Lawrence Greenslade, "Cyprian" in *Early Latin Theology*, vol. 5, Library of Christian Classics (Philadelphia: Westminster Press, 1956), 148.

[111]This theological discussion bears similarities to the Donatist controversy with Augustine. The Donatists believed that proper baptism required a proper administrator. See W. H. C. Frend, *The Donatist Church* (Oxford: Clarendon Press, 1952); and G. G. Willis, *Saint Augustine and the Donatist Controversy* (London: S P C K, 1950).

[112]Proper ordination is a key link in Landmark beliefs. For more information see William Thomas Lane, "Ordination: Its Significance and Meaning for the Southern Baptist Convention Studied in the Context of the Landmark Controversy" (Ph.D. diss., Southern Baptist Theological Seminary, 1959).

held this position.¹¹³ Although Manly openly rejected Landmarkism, he published a letter on May 28, 1857, stating his opposition to Pedobaptist immersions. He said, "They never immerse when the candidate can be persuaded to any other method."¹¹⁴ Additionally the lesser known Joseph Walker, editor of the *Christian Index* in Macon, Georgia, published a tract on the invalidity of Pedobaptist immersions and the impropriety of their recognition by Baptist churches.¹¹⁵ Pendleton recommended that everyone spend one dollar and purchase seven copies of this pamphlet.¹¹⁶

The requirement of proper ordination and thus proper baptism for a proper administrator had deeper implications. This question of authority related to the other duties of a minister of the gospel. A person had to be properly ordained in order to administer the sacraments or serve as the preacher in a church. To those who said there was no scriptural connection between baptism and preaching, Pendleton published twenty questions.¹¹⁷ He strongly

---

¹¹³James Madison Pendleton, "Brother Manly on Immersions of Pedobaptists," *Tennessee Baptist* (June 27, 1857). Basil Manly Sr. (1798–1868) was pastor of the prominent First Baptist Church in Charleston, SC, presided over the University of Alabama at Tuscaloosa from 1838–1855, and fought for the establishment of the Southern Baptist Theological Seminary.

¹¹⁴Basil Manly Sr. "Immersion administered by Pedobaptist," *South Western Baptist* (May 28, 1857).

¹¹⁵Joseph Walker, *An Essay on the Impropriety of Admitting Persons into Baptist Churches on Paedobaptist Immersions, with a Review of a Letter of Rev. Richard Fuller on the Same Subject* (Macon: Telegraph Steam Press, 1858).

¹¹⁶James Madison Pendleton, "Pedobaptist Immersions," *Tennessee Baptist* (May 1, 1858).

¹¹⁷James Madison Pendleton, "An Old Landmark Re-set," *Tennessee Baptist* (January 17, 1855). The questions were: (1) Why was Jesus baptized before he preached?; (2) Did the priority of baptism in this case mean nothing?; (3) Were not the twelve apostles baptized before they were sent forth to preach?; (4) Were not the seventy disciples?; (5) Why was Saul of Tarsus baptized before he became a preacher?; (6) According to the gospel are not preachers sent forth by churches?; (7) If so, have not the churches jurisdiction of preachers?; (8) If so, are not preachers members of

believed that in order to be a proper administrator of the ordinance, or a minister of the Gospel, one must have been properly baptized and ordained by a proper church.

Pendleton also addressed the issue of a baptism administered by an evangelist and even an unbaptized evangelist. Some argued that an evangelist must at times baptize in the field without the concurrence of the church. Such a case existed in Acts 8 with the Ethiopian eunuch. Pendleton stated, "Evangelists go forth on their mission by authority of the churches. The churches prompted by a courtesy induced by the necessity of the case, allow their evangelists, for the time being, to decide for them on applications for baptism."[118] Thus, the evangelist baptizes by and under the authority of the church which sends him. However, an unbaptized evangelist possesses no such authority. The churches must set apart and send the evangelist.[119] Pendleton noted certain Methodists who agreed

---

the churches?; (9) If so have they not been baptized? Or can unbaptized persons be church members?; (10) Had there been Pedobaptist preachers in the apostolic age, would Paul have recognized them as gospel ministers?; (11) Why do not Baptist churches ordain unbaptized men to the work of the ministry?; (12) Would this be wrong if there is no necessary scriptural connection between baptism and preaching?; (13) If an unbaptized man has the right to preach, has he not a right to administer the ordinances of the gospel?; (14) Does the expression, 'let him that heareth say come,' refer to preaching?; (15) If it does, must it not embrace all that hear?; (16) If so, when the wicked hear are they to become preachers too?; (17) If they are, why did Paul command the things which he had taught to be committed by Timothy 'to faithful men?'; (18) Does not the recognition of an unbaptized person as a gospel minister virtually reduce baptism to a nullity?; (19) Is it not saying that such a person's disobedience to Christ is a small matter?; and (20) If such a person sincerely thinks that sprinkling or pouring is baptism, does sincerity alone account for a neglect of one of Christ's commands?

[118]Pendleton, "The Scriptural Meaning of the Term Church," 68.

[119]James Madison Pendleton, "The Validity of Baptism Administered by an Unbaptized Evangelist," *Tennessee Baptist* (June 21, 1856).

that proper church ordination was essential to administer the ordinance of baptism or the Lord's Supper.[120]

Proper Form

Pendleton's definition of baptism asserted that believers should be baptized in the name of the Father, of the Son, and of the Holy Spirit.[121] He understood that this was the baptismal formula given by Jesus in Matt 28:19. Pendleton did not explicitly state that using only part of the formula would nullify the validity of baptism. Instead, he positively stated the benefits of utilizing the correct formula. He said, "There is a visible, symbolic expression of the new relation to the three Persons of the Godhead—a relation really entered into in repentance, faith, and regeneration."[122] Thus, Pendleton supported the understanding of entering into a relationship with the triune God by the use of the proper formula.

PENDLETON AMONG HIS CONTEMPORARIES

The discussion of Pendleton's Contemporaries will be broken down into three sections. The first section will identify and discuss Baptist contemporaries of Pendleton. The second section will discuss non-Baptist contemporaries of Pendleton, and the third section will evaluate Pendleton's place among his contemporaries. The selections chosen are representative of the literature during this time frame and provide a foundation for evaluation of Pendleton's theology of baptism.

Pendleton's Interaction with Other Baptist Contemporaries

---

[120]James Madison Pendleton, "Old Landmark Methodists," *Tennessee Baptist* (December 13, 1856).

[121]The Second London Confession of 1677, the Philadelphia Confession of 1742, the Orthodox Creed of 1679, and the New Hampshire Confession of 1833 support Pendleton's position.

[122]Pendleton, *Distinctive Principles of Baptists*, 171.

Several Baptist writers existed who deserve detailed discussion. John Dagg, Edward Hiscox, J. Newton Brown, R. B. C. Howell, and A. C. Dayton all contributed to the area of ecclesiology, and with Pendleton, dominated Baptist discussions in this area of theology. Furthermore, Pendleton demonstrated knowledge of their works and commented on them. Thus, with these particular writers not only the views of baptism, but also the implications of baptism upon the larger area of ecclesiology will be discussed.

Pendleton interacted with one of his most famous colleagues, John Dagg, through an article in the *Southern Baptist Review* which reviewed Dagg's work.[122] Dagg wrote a *Manual of Church Order* which demonstrated his agreement with Pendleton on the doctrine of baptism. Dagg emphasized the importance of baptism by discussing it in his first chapter and concluding that chapter by writing, "It will be shown hereafter, that in a Church, organized like the primitive churches, none but baptized persons can be admitted to membership. On this account, the present chapter on baptism has been introduced, as a necessary preliminary to the subsequent discussions on church order."[123]

Dagg and Pendleton agreed that baptism is the immersion of believers; however, Dagg believed one could be a minister without proper baptism. Dagg addressed Landmarkism under "Miscellaneous Topics."[124] In this section, Dagg differed with Pendleton by allowing Pedobaptist ministers to preach in the pulpit of Baptist churches. He also recognized Pedobaptist ministers as ministers of the Gospel. The primary difference between the two rested in the placement of a minister's service. Dagg said, "We have maintained, in chapter VIII., that ministers of the word, as such, are officers

---

[122]Pendleton, "Review of Dagg's *Church Order*," 36–55.
[123]Dagg, *Manual of Church Order*, 73. John Dagg (1794–1884) wrote a *Manual of Theology* and *Manual of Church Order* which were widely read. He served as pastor of Fifth Baptist Church of Philadelphia, president of the Alabama Female Atheneum, and president of Mercer University.
[124]Dagg, *Manual of Church Order*, 286–98.

of the universal church."[125] Pendleton placed their ministry under the authority of the local church. Thus, Dagg bypassed the need for ordination and the setting apart by a true church by placing these responsibilities under the Holy Spirit instead of the local church. Dagg said, "Many Pedobaptist ministers give convincing proof that the Holy Spirit has called and qualified them to preach the gospel, and that it is therefore not only their right, but their duty, to fulfill the ministry which God has committed to them."[126] This statement from Dagg implied that Pedobaptist ministers have the right to baptize. Since Pedobaptists have the right to baptize, Dagg addressed what baptisms should be accepted by Baptist churches. Although Dagg expressed that infant sprinkling would not qualify, he left this and the acceptance of alien immersion up to the discretion of the local church.[127]

Another contemporary who was equally important on the issue of ecclesiology was Edward Hiscox. Hiscox's work was perhaps the only ecclesiology which rivaled Pendleton's in its longevity and popularity.[128] Hiscox agreed with Pendleton wholeheartedly on the meaning of baptism and utilized the same method of quoting Pedobaptists to prove that the "immersion or dipping of a candidate in water, on a

---

[125]Ibid., 292.

[126]Ibid., 294.

[127]Dagg expressed disapproval of infant sprinkling, and addressed the issue of rebaptism. He divided this into two sections with the first being that of an improper subject and the second of improper administrator. He stated that rebaptism may not be necessary in either case and that the local church must decide. On the subject of infant baptism, Dagg said, the candidate must decide whether or not he or she has done their duty and the local church must decide whether or not to accept the baptism. He continued, "If the candidate's satisfaction with his baptism would suffice, persons baptized in infancy might obtain admission into our churches without other baptism" (284). See Dagg, *Manual of Church Order*, 282–5.

[128]Edward T. Hiscox, *Baptist Church Polity, Doctrines, Confessions of Faith* (Nashville: Historical Commissions, 1856). This particular book would undergo two additional publications. *The Hiscox Standard Baptist Manual* (Valley Forge: Judson Press, 1865); and *The New Directory for Baptist Churches*.

profession of faith in Christ, administered in the name of the Father, Son, and Spirit" was the valid form of baptism.[129] Hiscox avoided a direct rebuttal of the conclusions of Landmarkism. He did, however, disagree with Pendleton when he said:

> To insist on the invalidity of all except denominational ordination is to enter the list for a defense of sacramentarianism, and to stand challenged before the Christian world for the proof of an unbroken succession of sacred orders. This would be as impossible to prove, as it would be useless if proven. We cannot accept the baptism of other denominations because it is *not baptism*, but *sprinkling*. It is defective both in substance and in form. It is quite otherwise with ordination, since both the form and the substance in the various communions are virtually the same. And if they be not, there is no authoritative Scriptural standard by which to be guided, as in the case of baptism.[130]

Thus, Hiscox recognized Pedobaptist ministers as Gospel ministers. However, Hiscox did not automatically accept alien immersion performed by those Pedobaptist ministers. The acceptance or rejection of alien immersion came from the understanding of the person receiving alien immersion and applying for membership in the local Baptist church.[131]

---

[129]Hiscox, The New Directory for Baptist Churches, 389.

[130]Ibid., 384.

[131]Ibid., 76–7. Hiscox identifies three way a person may be accepted into membership in a local Baptist congregation: (1) baptism, (2) letter, and (3) experience. Although he does not directly address alien immersion, he stated the following, "Persons cannot be received to membership on the credit of letters from other denominations. Such letters are accepted as testimonials of previous Church standing and Christian character; but the applicants are to be received by *baptism*—if not already baptized—or otherwise on their Christian *experience*, related in person before the Church." This allows the church to judge each applicant individually as to the validity of their salvation and baptism. See Hiscox, *The New Directory for Baptist Churches*, 73–9.

John Newton Brown, another Baptist contemporary of Pendleton, agreed that infant baptism was an error. Pendleton quoted from Brown, "Infant baptism is an error from beginning to end; corrupt in theory, and corrupting in practice; born in superstition, cradled in fear, nursed in ignorance, supported by fraud, and spread by force; doomed to die in the light of historical investigation. . . ."[132] Pendleton went on to say, "The Lord bless Bro. Brown . . . I rejoice that he has expressed himself so fully, so clearly, and so powerfully. I never felt more like going all the way to Philadelphia to shake a brother's hand."[133] However, Brown did not clearly address the issue of pulpit affiliation or acceptance of Pedobaptist ministers.

R.B.C. Howell, pastor of the First Baptist Church of Nashville, Tennessee, and a prominent Baptist, published a book called *Evils of Infant Baptism* to which Pendleton referred.[134] Howell in this work and in his book on communion offered the following definition of baptism: "To be buried with Christ in baptism is to be immersed; and after mature, protracted, and anxious examination, we have arrived at the settled, and unalterable conclusion, that immersion in water, by an authorized administrator, of a properly qualified candidate, in the name of the Father, and of the Son, and of the Holy Ghost, and this alone, is Christian

---

[132] J. Newton Brown, "Preliminary Historical Essay," in *Memorials of Baptist Martyrs*, by Joseph Belcher (Philadelphia: American Baptist Publication Society, 1854), 13, as in James Madison Pendleton, "Who Will Accept the Challenge?," *Tennessee Baptist* (July 22, 1854). John Newton Brown (1803–1868) served as pastor of several churches, professor of theology and ecclesiastical history at New Hampton Theological Institution; however, he is best known for his contributions to the New Hampshire Confession of Faith, which he popularized by including it in his widely used *Church Manual*.

[133] Pendleton, "Who Will Accept the Challenge?"

[134] James Madison Pendleton, "Review of Dr. Summers on Baptism," *The Southern Baptist Review* 1 (October–December 1855): 575–607. He noted Howell's work in this article. R. B. C. Howell, *The Evils of Infant Baptism* (Charleston: Southern Baptist Publication, 1852).

baptism."[135] Howell made no direct comment on the acceptance of alien immersion in these works.

Perhaps the work which most completely agreed with Pendleton was written by A. C. Dayton.[136] Graves published several articles written by Dayton in a little book and wrote an introduction to it. In that introduction, Graves argued along the same lines as Pendleton and came to similar conclusions. In this work, Graves and Dayton demonstrate complete support of Pendleton on the issue of baptism, the rejection of alien immersions, and the implications for recognition of churches and ministers.[137] Other than his fellow Landmarkers, some of Pendleton's beliefs, usually concerning alien immersion or Pedobaptist ordination, were rejected by his Baptist contemporaries.

Pendleton's Interaction with Non-Baptist Contemporaries

The first contemporary in this category is Alexander Campbell. Campbell was a Baptist for seventeen years (1813–1830) but later took hundreds of Baptist churches with him while forming a new denomination known as the Disciples of Christ or the Church of Christ.[138] Pendleton

---

[135]R. B. C. Howell, *The Terms of Communion at the Lord's Table* (Philadelphia: American Baptist Publication Society, 1846), 152–3.

[136] Amos Cooper Dayton, *Pedobaptist and Cambellite Immersions* (Nashville: Graves, & Marks, 1858). Dayton (1813–1865) was one-third of the "Landmark Triumvirate" with Pendleton and Graves. His best known work is *Theodosia Earnest, or, The Heroine of Faith* (Chicago: Church and Goodman, 1866).

[137]Edwin C. Dargan, *Ecclesiology: A Study of the Churches* (Louisville: Chas. T. Dearing, 1897), 216, noted that Dayton's book is the only book devoted to the subject of Pedobaptist immersions. Dargan stated, "Drs. Graves, Pendleton and Dayton, with others defend the strict view, while Drs. Wayland, Waller, Fuller, Jeter and Burrows have upheld the other." The strict view denied the legitimacy of Pedobaptist immersions.

[138]H. Leon McBeth, *The Baptist Heritage* (Nashville: Broadman Press, 1987), 375. For more information on this topic see Austin Bennett Amonette, "Alexander Campbell Among the Baptists: An Examination of the Beginning, Ambiguity, and Deterioration of Their Relationship, 1812–

personally felt the influence of Alexander Campbell as "half the Baptist churches of Kentucky switched to the new Disciples movement."[139] McBeth noted four areas of disagreement between Campbell and the Baptists: (1) Campbell taught that faith is only historical belief, (2) Campbell taught that baptism by immersion completed the process of salvation, (3) Campbell denied the authority of the Old Testament upon Christians, and (4) Campbell rejected all use of confessions of faith.[140] Only the second is relevant to the current discussion.

Pendleton wrote against Campbell claiming that "Mr. C. has written voluminously, and it has been his misfortune to contradict himself more frequently than any theologian of the present generation."[141] Pendleton also specifically criticized Campbell's belief that immersion precedes the remission of sins.[142] Campbell believed that "three things are essential to the Christian profession—that a person must believe, and repent, and be baptized. . . ."[143] Pendleton argued that baptism was not essential to salvation.

In addition to writing against Alexander Campbell, Pendleton spent a great deal of time specifically addressing Pedobaptists who disagreed with his position. It is especially important to note Pendleton's interaction with these Pedobaptist for two reasons. First, his interaction with them

---

1830" (Ph.D. diss., New Orleans Baptist Theological Seminary, 2002) and for a good history from a Disciples perspective, see W. E. Garrison and A. T. DeGroot, *The Disciples of Christ* (St. Louis: Christian Board of Publications, 1948).

[139]McBeth, The Baptist Heritage, 377.

[140]Ibid., 377–80.

[141]James Madison Pendleton, "Campbellism Examined," *The Southern Baptist Review* (February 1855): 87.

[142]Ibid., 102. Pendleton specifically disagrees with Jeremiah Jeter, *Campbellism Examined* (New York: Sheldon & Blakeman, 1857), 197, who said "Mr. Campbell has been frequently, but, I think unfairly charged with teaching *baptismal regeneration*."

[143]Campbell, *Christian Baptism*, 84.

further elaborates on their arguments and his rebuttal forms a more complete look at Pendleton's theology of baptism. Second, his interaction demonstrates that although some Baptists may have thought the case for believers' baptism by immersion had been adequately proven, some Pedobaptists continued to disagree.

Perhaps the most outspoken was Thomas Summers. Pendleton reviewed Summers's work *Baptism, a Treatise on the Nature, Perpetuity, Subjects, Administration, Mode and Use of the Initiating Ordinance of the Christian Church, with an Appendix, Containing Strictures on Dr. Howell's "Evils of Infant Baptism."*[144] In this review, Pendleton focused on the mode and subject of baptism attempting to refute almost every claim made by Summers. As one would expect, Pendleton concluded by stating, "Dr. S. upon an examination of this subject will find that he does not understand it at all."[145]

Another major opponent of Pendleton was Presbyterian Peter Edwards. Pendleton reviewed his work in *The Southern Baptist Review*. He stated, "The inevitable tendency of Pedobaptism is to supersede the baptism of believers, and drive it from the world. Let all parents become Pedobaptists, and what is the result?"[146]

Another opponent with whom Pendleton corresponded was William Wallace Hill. Pendleton quoted Hill as saying, "Baptism is symbolic of the cleansing of the soul from sin; and that this cleansing is the distinctive work of the Spirit of God! . . . The child has the same need of cleansing which the

---

[144]Thomas O. Summers, Baptism, a Treatise on the Nature, Perpetuity, Subjects, Administration, Mode and Use of the initiating Ordinance of the Christian Church, with an Appendix, Containing Strictures on Dr. Howell's "Evils of Infant Baptism." (Richmond: John Early, 1852).

[145]Pendleton, "Review of Dr. Summers on Baptism," 607.

[146]Pendleton, "Peter Edwards on Baptism," 420. The quote here cited was utilized elsewhere by Pendleton. See for instance "Infant Baptism," *Tennessee Baptist* (February 12, 1859).

adult has."¹⁴⁷ In response to this, Pendleton questioned how baptism could be symbolic of a change and bring about a real change at the same time—the real change making it a necessity for children.¹⁴⁸

One important figure existed with whom Pendleton seemingly failed to interact on the issue of baptism. Charles Hodge lived from 1797–1878 and taught at Princeton almost his entire life. His three volume *Systematic Theology* was published during 1871–3 and presented the Presbyterian case for infant baptism by sprinkling.¹⁴⁹ Perhaps Pendleton failed to interact with Hodge because by the time Hodge's *Systematic Theology* had been printed, Pendleton had already written against similar arguments from earlier writers. Hodge's views have been noted throughout this chapter, but two quotes summarize his position. He said concerning the mode of baptism, "The ordinance is most significant and most conformed to Scripture, when administered by affusion or sprinkling."¹⁵⁰ Concerning the subject of baptism, Hodge stated, "To be unbaptized is a grievous injury and reproach; one which no parent can innocently entail upon his children."¹⁵¹ Thus, Hodge supported infant baptism by pouring or sprinkling.

Evaluation of Pendleton's Interaction

It seems that the arguments of Pendleton and those who agreed with him had some success. Pendleton noted that at one instance, fourteen Methodists were properly baptized.¹⁵² On another occasion, he wrote about a Methodist minister

---

¹⁴⁷James Madison Pendleton, "Dr. Hill on Baptism," *Tennessee Baptist* (February 2, 1856).
¹⁴⁸Ibid. William Wallace Hill was editor of the *Presbyterian Herald* in Louisville, Kentucky.
¹⁴⁹Charles Hodge, *Systematic Theology* (Peabody: Hendrickson, 2001). Pendleton did interact with him on church government.
¹⁵⁰Hodge, *Systematic Theology*, vol. 3, 539.
¹⁵¹Ibid., 579.
¹⁵²James Madison Pendleton, "Methodists Getting Right," *Tennessee Baptist* (February 9, 1856).

who joined Pendleton's church and changed his views requesting proper baptism.[153] Finally, an article appeared in which Pendleton responded to an author who blamed Baptists for the decline in infant baptism. Pendleton attributed the decline to a better understanding of the Scriptures.[154] Joseph Frey and others like him wrote books on why they had changed their view on this issue to become Baptists.[155]

Despite some success, Pendleton and those who believed as he did never completely defeated the support for infant baptism. Pendleton's own work continually demonstrated interaction with many who agreed and others who disagreed. The debate over the mode and subject of baptism has yet to be settled and probably never will be.

Pendleton's interaction with his Baptist contemporaries also met with mixed success. While substantial agreement on baptism existed, disagreement over the implications of Landmarkism remained. Landmarkism flourished in some areas and gained followers; however, theologians such as Dagg and Hiscox were not convinced by Pendleton's arguments. It appears that Pendleton had more success in convincing the populace than the mature theologian to follow the beliefs of Landmarkism. Regardless of his success, Pendleton's interaction does show him to be a responsible theologian, who was aware of opposing views and engaged in theological disputations.

PENDLETON'S UNIQUE CONTRIBUTION

Pendleton's formulation of the doctrine of baptism was not unique. He along with many others held that proper baptism

---

[153]James Madison Pendleton, "The Baptism of a Methodist Minister," *Tennessee Baptist* (November 11, 1856).
[154]James Madison Pendleton, "Why Infant Baptism Is Neglected," *Tennessee Baptist* (April 13, 1861).
[155]Joseph Samuel Frey, *Essays on Christian Baptism* (New York: Printed by the author, 1843).

must be by immersion of believers only, that baptism composed the door to the visible church, and that proper baptism must occur before participation in the Lord's Supper. Pendleton neither uniquely formulated this doctrine nor added anything unique to this doctrine. He restated the case for baptism by immersion of believers only. The reason he wrote on the issue was to continue countering Pedobaptist writings. As Pedobaptists stated their position, Pendleton and others like him refuted their views. Although he added little new material, his consistent rebuttal of Pedobaptist views was needed and did contribute to developing a distinct Baptist identity.

Pendleton did, however, uniquely contribute to ecclesiological issues through his insistence upon proper baptism. First, Pendleton forced a reconsideration of the essence or being of the church. If the existence or "being" of a visible church required the word preached and the sacraments rightly administered, as had been the popular view since the days of John Calvin, then Pendleton's position that Pedobaptists societies were not proper churches stands.[156] Pendleton's formulation forced those who did not wish to unchurch all Pedobaptists to place the ordinances rightly administered in the "well being" of a church instead of the "being" of a church or to leave out or redefine the word "rightly."[157] Thus, he

---

[156]The differentiation between the "being" of a church and the "well being" of a church is an important one. Pendleton required proper baptism for the "being" of a church which allowed him to label Pedobaptist churches as societies. If the word preached and the sacraments rightly administered belongs to the "well being" of a church and not its "being," then Pedobaptist churches would still be churches—just imperfect churches. Furthermore, Pendleton knew of the distinction between "well being" and "being." He stated, "The truth is a church may exist without officers. It has been well said that 'officers are essential to the *well being*, not the *being* of a church.'" See Pendleton, "The Scriptural Meaning of the Term Church," 17.

[157]A. H. Strong, *Systematic Theology*, vol. 3 (Philadelphia: Judson Press, 1909), 890, defined the individual church as "that smaller company of regenerate persons, who, in any given community, unite themselves voluntarily together, in accordance with Christ's laws, for the purpose of

contributed by spurring future generations to consider carefully their ecclesiology and specifically their definition of the "being" of a church.

Second, Pendleton uniquely contributed to the doctrine of baptism by demonstrating its implication for Pedobaptist ministers. According to the definition of a church accepted by Pendleton and others, Pedobaptist ministers could not be properly ordained because they had not been properly baptized and were not members of true churches. Without proper baptism and without proper ordination, Pedobaptist ministers could not be considered Gospel ministers, and thus, Pendleton rejected alien immersion. This author has found no other person that formulated this argument as Pendleton did. The principle of not recognizing Pedobaptist ministers as Gospel ministers arose through the famous "Cotton Grove Resolutions;" however, Pendleton pinpointed baptism as the central issue and uniquely presented a systematic defense of this position.

Third, Pendleton uniquely contributed by systematizing the formulation opposing pulpit exchange. This contribution will be discussed in greater length under the section on the Lord's Supper as it relates to consistency in that area; however, it must be mentioned here because it is from the implication that Pedobaptist ministers are not Gospel ministers and that Pedobaptist churches are not Gospel churches that the prohibition against pulpit exchange emerged. Again the central issue to determine legitimate from illegitimate grew out of proper baptism.

---

securing the complete establishment of his kingdom in themselves and in the world." In his discussion, he specifically said, "We do not define the church as a body of 'baptized believers,' because baptism is but one of 'Christ's laws (890).'" While Strong never stated that Landmarkism or Pendleton caused him to leave "baptized believers" out of his definition, one can be sure that Strong was aware of the controversy and recognize that this may be his attempt to avoid it.

Thus, while Pendleton's formulation of the doctrine of baptism contributed nothing unique, his conclusions did. By applying the principle of Pedobaptist baptism as being improper, he drew conclusions about Pedobaptist churches, Pedobaptist ministers, and pulpit exchange with Pedobaptists. If another writer so clearly stated these differences and took the implications of the doctrine of baptism to this extreme before Pendleton, this author has yet to read that writer. Perhaps J. R. Graves, who is so often given the credit for Landmarkism, originated the idea, but Pendleton put these ideas systematically on paper.

CURRENT DISCUSSIONS OF BAPTISM

Many works on this issue are currently in print and several publications within the past five years address the issue of baptism.[158] Some Baptists support the view that baptism is no longer an important doctrine.[159] Furthermore, at least one author has attempted to reformulate the Baptist discussion

---

[158] Walter B. Shurden, ed., *Proclaiming the Baptist Vision: Baptism and the Lord's Supper* (Macon: Smyth & Helwys, 1999); R. Wayne Stacy, ed., *A Baptist's Theology* (Macon: Smyth & Helwys, 1999); Lennart Johnson, *Baptist Reconsideration of Baptism and Ecclesiology* (New York: P. Lang, 2000); Rebecca R. Tellinghuisen, "Children and Believer's Baptism: Questions of Proper Age, Readiness and the Role of Faith Development Theory" (M.A. thesis, North American Baptist Seminary, 2000); Stanley E. Porter and Anthony R. Cross, *Dimensions of Baptism* (New York: Sheffield Academic Press, 2000); Larry Dyer, *Baptism: The Believer's First Obedience* (Grand Rapids: Kregel, 2000); Tom Wells, *Does Baptism Mean Immersion? A Friendly Inquiry Into the Ongoing Debate* (Laurel, Miss: Audubon Press, 2000); Brian Russell, *Baptism: Sign and Seal of the Covenant of Grace* (London: Grace Publications, 2001); and Fred Malone, *The Baptism of Disciples Alone: A Covenantal Argument for Credobaptism Versus Paedobaptism* (Cape Coral: Founders Press, 2003).

[159] For example Bill J. Leonard, "At the River," in *Proclaiming the Baptist Vision: Baptism and the Lord's Supper*, ed. Walter B. Shurden (Macon: Smyth & Helwys, 1999), 15, posed the question, "Does baptism mean anything at all?" Another article in this same book written by Todd Wilson is titled, "Why Baptists Should Not Rebaptize Christians from Other Denominations." Wilson does not believe even those sprinkled as children should be rebaptized.

of baptism.¹⁶⁰ However, many authors still support the traditional Baptist position on baptism.¹⁶¹ In addition to those works which focus specifically on baptism, the subject is discussed in some recent systematic theology texts written by Baptists. These texts reveal that this doctrine does not currently receive the same emphasis that Pendleton gave it.¹⁶² Thus, whether right or wrong, the majority of Baptists no longer discuss the issue with the same zeal as Pendleton.

Those who disagree with the Baptist position continue to write works supporting their view as well.¹⁶³ Their argument

---

¹⁶⁰R. Wayne Stacy, "Baptism," in *A Baptist's Theology*, ed. Wayne Stacy (Macon: Smyth & Helwys, 1999). His reformulation preferred "sign" to "symbol," preferred to discuss the life long process of conversion, and preferred to discuss the adoption into the community. He said, "Baptists need some 'rite of Christian commencement'—baptism at birth, baby dedication, or something similar—to signify the beginning of this process, some 'ritual of adoption' into the people of God . . . ."(170).

¹⁶¹Erroll Hulse, "Where I Buried Old Erroll Hulse: A Journey in Believer's Baptism," in *Why I Am a Baptist*, eds. Thomas Nettles and Russell Moore, (Nashville: Broadman & Holman, 2001); R. Stanton Norman, *More Than Just a Name* (Nashville: Broadman & Holman, 2001); Malone, *The Baptism of Disciples Alone*; and Russell, *Baptism: Sign and Seal of the Covenant of Grace*.

¹⁶²Millard Erickson, *Christian Theology* (Grand Rapids: Baker, 1998), 1114, said, "While it may not be the only valid form of baptism, it is the form that most fully preserves and accomplishes the meaning of baptism." Wayne Grudem, *Systematic Theology* (Grand Rapids: Zondervan, 1994), 967, wrote, "The position advocated in this book is that baptism is not a 'major' doctrine that should be the basis of division among genuine Christians, but it is nonetheless a matter of importance for ordinary church life, and it is appropriate that we give it full consideration." James Leo Garrett, *Systematic Theology: Biblical, Historical, & Evangelical* vol. 2 (Grand Rapids: Eerdmans, 1995) provided the arguments for both sides and allows the reader to make his or her own decision.

¹⁶³Just within the past five years the following were published: Wangerin Walter Jr., *Water, Come Down!* (Minneapolis: Augsburg Fortress Publisher, 1999); Paul Turner, *Your Child's Baptism* (Chicago: Liturgy Training Publications, 1999); James E. Davison, *Living Water: A Guide to Baptism for Presbyterians* (Louisville: Geneva Press, 2000); Dianne Ahern, *Today I Was Baptized* (Ann Arbor: Aunt Dee's Attic, 2000); Colin Ogilvie Buchanan, *Infant Baptism in Common Worship* (Cambridge: Grove Books, 2001); Mary Lee Wile, *Christ's Own Forever: Episcopal Baptism of Infants*

continues to center around the "covenant of grace" which is the relationship any child with at least one believing parent has with God.[164] In addition, several Pedobaptist books provide practical support for parents or God-parents with children about to go through the experience of infant baptism.[165] For the purposes of this dissertation, it is enough to note that no new argument for infant baptism to which Pendleton did not respond in his day has been discovered.

PENDLETON'S LASTING INFLUENCE

It is difficult to determine the lasting influence of a theologian and even more difficult to pinpoint any lasting contribution in a specific area of doctrine. As the conclusion of this dissertation will demonstrate, Pendleton's influence continues in certain areas more than others, especially through his *Church Manual* and the continuing influence of Landmarkism.[166] For example, in 1900 his *Church Manual*

---

and Young Children; Parent/Godparent Journal (np: Living the Good News, 2003); Greg Strawbridge, ed., *The Case for Covenantal Infant Baptism* (Phillipsburg, NJ: P&R Publications, 2003); and Tom Sheridan, *The Gift of Baptism: A Handbook for Parents* (Chicago: ACTA Publications, 2003).

[164]Pierre Charles Marcel and Philip Edgcumbe Hughes, *The Biblical Doctrine of Infant Baptism* (London: J. Clarke, 1953; reprint, Eugene: Wipf & Stock, 2002), 200, stated, "With the rejection of the covenant of grace every possible foundation of infant baptism disappears. The advocates of infant baptism ought to be fully persuaded of this and, consequently, to render themselves completely conversant with the doctrine of the covenant." See also Douglas Wilson, *To A Thousand Generations: Infant Baptism Covenant Mercy for the People of God* (Moscow: Canon Press, 1996) which attempts to tie infant baptism to circumcision.

[165]Wile, Christ's Own Forever: Episcopal Baptism of Infants and Young Children; Parent/Godparent Journal; and Sheridan, The Gift of Baptism: A Handbook for Parents.

[166]Landmarkism "altered the texture of Baptist life in the South" according to Holifield, *Theology in America*, 277. However, Holifield included neither Graves nor Pendleton in *The Gentlemen Theologians: American Theology in Southern Culture 1795–1860*. Thus, in Holifield's view the influence came more through the movement than through the men who started it. Hudson, *Religion in America*, 168, specifically noting

was revised by Franz Marshall McConnell and titled *Pendleton's Church Manual: Designed for the Use of Baptist Churches.*[167] Again in 1941, J. E. Cobb revised Pendleton's work and titled his work, *Baptist Church Manual.*[168] Cobb stated in the preface, "The author of this manual recognizes that the manual most generally used among our particular group of Baptists is that of Dr. J. M. Pendleton."[169] In 1955 a new publication of Pendleton's *Church Manual* was released by Judson Press, and in 1966 another new publication was released by Broadman Press.[170] Thus, his influence has continued in the area of ecclesiology.

However, lasting influence, especially in the doctrine of baptism, does not appear to be present. Influence can still be traced through his work in ecclesiology, but there is no continuing influence to mention in the doctrine of baptism. This author has checked several systematic theology texts without locating any influence from Pendleton in the area of baptism[171] and no mention at all of Pendleton in other

---

Graves and Pendleton, stated that "Although the major Baptist bodies repeatedly repudiated the Landmarkists, their 'High Church' views gained wide currency in the South by the end of the century." Donald Matthews, *Religion in the Old South* (Chicago: University of Chicago, 1977), 133–5, does not even note Pendleton in his discussion of the influence of Landmarkism on religion in the South. Matthews said of Graves, "Although he offended many Baptists with his sometimes unfair, always abrasive tactics, he attracted many supporters in the antebellum South" (134). Norman Maring and Winthrop Hudson, *A Baptist Manual of Polity and Practice* (Chicago: Judson Press, 1963) does not note Pendleton.

[167]Franz Marshall McConnell, *Pendleton's Church Manual: Designed for the Use of Baptist Churches* (Dallas: B. J. Robert Book Company, 1900).

[168]J. E. Cobb, *Baptist Church Manual* (Little Rock: Baptist Publishing House, 1941).

[169]Cobb, Baptist Church Manual, i.

[170]James Madison Pendleton, *Church Manual* (Philadelphia: Judson Press, 1955); and James Madison Pendleton, *Baptist Church Manual* (Nashville: Broadman Press 1966).

[171]Garrett, *Systematic Theology: Biblical, Historical, & Evangelical*, vol. 2, mentions Pendleton five times but not once under the doctrine of

works.[172] As the influence of Landmarkism has diminished, so have Pendleton's contributions in the area of baptism. He was a faithful transmitter of traditional Baptist views on baptism, but the areas in which he made unique contributions or formulations have not been incorporated into the mainstream of Baptist thought.

---

baptism. Dale Moody, *The Word of Truth* (Grand Rapids: Eerdmans, 1981) mentions Pendleton only once in his connection with Landmarkism.

[172]Strong, *Systematic Theology*; Edgar Young Mullins, *The Christian Religion in Its Doctrinal Expression* (Nashville: Broadman Press, 1917); Conner, *Christian Doctrine*; Grudem, *Systematic Theology*; and Erickson, *Christian Theology*. All have no mention of Pendleton.

CHAPTER 3

CONGREGATIONAL CHURCH POLITY AND LOCAL CHURCH AUTONOMY

Introduction

The issues of congregational church government and independence of the local church played a major role not only in the ecclesiology of Pendleton but also in his friendship with J. R. Graves. Pendleton stated this issue as his third reason for being a Baptist. He wrote, "I am a Baptist because Baptists adopt the form of church government recognized in the New Testament—that is to say, the congregational form of government."[1] In addition to it being his third reason for being a Baptist, Pendleton discussed the issue in at least four books and thirteen articles.[2] Throughout his life, Pendleton demonstrated a consistent belief in and a consistent formulation of congregational church government and local church

---

[1] James Madison Pendleton, *Three Reasons Why I Am a Baptist with a Fourth Reason Added on Communion* (St. Louis: National Baptist Publishing, 1856), 148.

[2] James Madison Pendleton, *Distinctive Principles of Baptists* (Philadelphia: American Baptist Publication Society, 1882); *An Old Landmark Re-set* (Nashville: Graves & Marks, 1854); *Three Reasons Why I Am a Baptist* (Cincinnati: Moo

re, Anderson & Company, 1853); *Three Reasons Why I Am a Baptist with a Fourth Reason Added on Communion*; *Church Manual: Designed for the Use of Baptist Churches* (Philadelphia: American Baptist Publication Society, 1867); and *Christian Doctrines: A Compendium of Theology* (Philadelphia: American Baptist Publication Society, 1906). Consult bibliography for a list of articles.

autonomy.³ However, some controversy arose when Pendleton defended Graves against the discipline of the First Baptist Church of Nashville.⁴ This issue will receive further discussion later. First, it is important to understand Pendleton's formulation of congregational church government and local church autonomy.

PENDLETON'S VIEW OF CONGREGATIONAL CHURCH POLITY

Meaning of the Term ἐκκλησία

Pendleton stressed the importance of properly understanding the term ἐκκλησία, the Greek word almost always translated "church" in the New Testament. After defining the Greek term ἐκκλησία as "a congregation or assembly," he stated that the term did not always indicate the purpose for which a certain group assembled.⁵ For example in Acts 19:32, 41, the term ἐκκλησία identified an "assembly" of people which met in Ephesus. Additionally, in verse 39 of the same chapter, it referred to a lawful "assembly."⁶ After giving these examples of alternate uses of ἐκκλησία, Pendleton noted that the term

---

³This can be demonstrated by comparing *Three Reasons Why I Am a Baptist* to the latest edition of the work, *Distinctive Principles of Baptists*. These two works contain identical content. Thus at the end of his life, Pendleton did not desire to change his previous formulation.

⁴For additional information concerning Graves's discipline, see Kenneth Vaughn Weatherford, "The Graves-Howell Controversy" (Ph.D. diss., Baylor University, 1991).

⁵James Madison Pendleton, "The Scriptural Meaning of the Term Church," *The Southern Baptist Review* 1 (January 1855): 8. For a detailed discussion consult K. L. Schmidt, "ἐκκλησία" in *Theological Dictionary of the New Testament*, ed. Gerhard Kittel and trans. Geoffrey W. Bromiley, vol. 3 (Grand Rapids: Eerdmans, 1965), 501–36; or H. E. Dana and L. M. Sipes, *A Manual of Ecclesiology* (Kansas City: Central Seminary Press, 1944).

⁶Pendleton, *Christian Doctrines*, 329. John Dagg, *Manual of Church Order* (Charleston: Southern Baptist Publication Society, 1858; reprint, Harrisonburg: Gano Books, 1990), 75, agreed with Pendleton. Dagg referred to the same verse, Acts 19:39, stating that it "was used to denote the assembly of citizens in the democratic towns of Greece."

is compounded of two words, καλέω meaning "to call" and the preposition ἐκ meaning "out" for a combined inference of "to call out." The word originally expressed the idea of an assembly of Greek citizens who were summoned and *called out* by a herald.[7] However, the connotation of *called out* probably did not carry over to the use of the word by the apostles. Pendleton stated, "It is questionable whether the apostles in their use of the term *ekklesia* meant anything more than congregation or assembly. However true it is that a congregation of saints is called out from the world, it is not certain that the sacred writers intended by the word *ekklesia* to express the idea of a congregation *called out*."[8]

In the New Testament, ἐκκλησία "is usually, if not always, employed to designate a particular congregation of saints, or the redeemed in the aggregate."[9] Furthermore, the most prominent use of ἐκκλησία in the New Testament comes in its application to a local assembly of believers such as "the churches of Galatia," "the churches of Macedonia," "the churches of Asia," and "the churches of Judea." Pendleton placed no size restriction on the New Testament church, citing the house church of Aquila and Priscilla, and

---

[7]Schmidt, "ἐκκλησία," 513.

[8]Pendleton, "The Scriptural Meaning of the Term Church," 8. Schmidt, "ἐκκλησία," 530, supports this position.

[9]Pendleton, *Christian Doctrines*, 329. Pendleton included similar wording in his *Church Manual*, 5. The clause "redeemed in the aggregate" would be significant not only for Pendleton's time but in Kansas City in 1963, when the Baptist Faith and Message was being voted upon. The proposed Baptist Faith and Message contained new wording on the church, "which includes all of the redeemed of all ages." This reference to the universal church was objected to by many with Landmark sentiments. However, "Hobbs, with Albert McClellan's coaching, called the group's attention to a J. M. Pendleton quotation acknowledging New Testament use of *church* to mean the redeemed in aggregate. Since Pendleton had been a leader of the Landmark movement, that settled matters." Jesse Fletcher, *The Southern Baptist Convention: A Sesquicentennial History* (Nashville: Broadman & Holman, 1994), 209.

Nymphas,[10] and Jesus' words in Matt 18:20, "For where two or three are gathered together in My name, I am there in the midst of them." Although other restrictions established the boundaries to determine a proper church, Pendleton stated that "it may be said that when two or three are gathered together there may be a church of Christ."[11] As for a complete definition of the church, Pendleton gave the following:

> A church is a congregation of Christ's baptized disciples, acknowledging him as their Head, relying on his atoning sacrifice for justification before God, and depending on the Holy Spirit for sanctification, united in the belief of the gospel, agreeing to maintain its ordinances and obey its precepts, meeting together for worship, and cooperating for the extension of Christ's kingdom in the world.[12]

---

[10]1 Cor 16:19 states, "The churches of Asia greet you. Aquila and Priscilla greet you heartily in the Lord, with the church that is in their house." Col 4:15 states, "Greet the brethren who are in Laodicea, and Nymphas and the church that is in his house."

[11]Pendleton, "The Scriptural Meaning of the Term Church," 9.

[12]James Madison Pendleton, *Baptist Church Manual* (Nashville: Broadman & Holman, 1966), 7. Pendleton's definition demonstrates agreement with the majority of Baptists and especially with notable Baptist theologians. For example, Dagg, *Manual of Church Order*, 74, stated, "A Christian Church is an assembly of believers in Christ, organized into a body, according to the Holy Scriptures, for the worship and service of God." Edward Hiscox, *The New Directory for Baptist Churches* (Philadelphia: Judson Press, 1894), 20, gave the following as the definition of a church, "A Christian church is a company of regenerate persons, baptized on a profession of faith in Christ; united in covenant for worship, instruction, the observance of Christian ordinances, and for such service as the gospel requires; recognizing and accepting Christ as their supreme Lord and Lawgiver, and taking His Word as their only and sufficient rule of faith and practice in all matters of conscience and religion." A. H. Strong, *Systematic Theology*, vol. 3 (Philadelphia: Judson Press, 1909), 890, defined the individual church as "that smaller company of regenerate persons, who, in any given community, unite themselves voluntarily together, in accordance with Christ's laws, for the purpose of

With this definition, Pendleton clearly established the purpose of the New Testament assembly. In his opinion, the New Testament church existed for the purposes of fulfilling Christ's commands and consisted only of believers in Christ.

Regenerate Church Membership

---

securing the complete establishment of his kingdom in themselves and in the world."

Part of the argument for regenerate church membership resulted from Pendleton's argument for the baptism of believers only.[13] He felt that baptism formed the door to the church, and if the door to the church was restricted to believers, then regenerate church membership logically followed. Pendleton's definition of the church included proper baptism of Christ's disciples. He wrote, "If this definition of the term 'church' is correct, it is manifest that membership is preceded by important qualifications."[14] He pointed out two categories of qualifications—*moral* and *ceremonial*.[15] The moral qualification is regeneration which consists of repentance and faith. Pendleton stated that these were "private matters between God and the soul."[16] The ceremonial qualification was baptism which represented a public confession of a private decision. The private qualification established that the church would only consist of regenerate members who publicly confessed their regeneration before being admitted as members. Pendleton stated, "That baptized believers are the only persons eligible to church-membership is clear from the whole tenor of the Acts of the Apostles and of the Apostolic Epistles. Everywhere it is seen that baptism preceded church-relations; nor is there an intimation that it was possible for

---

[13]Regenerate church membership, although present in splinter groups throughout history, was strongly supported by the Anabaptist movement and was characteristic of Baptists from their inception. A discussion of regenerate church membership is included in Henry Vedder, *A Short History of the Baptists* (Philadelphia: American Baptist Publication Society, 1907), 57–70, which discussed Montanism, Novatians, Donatists, and Arianism in the chapter entitled, "The Struggle for a Pure Church."

[14]Pendleton, *Christian Doctrines*, 330–1. Other Baptists have agreed with Pendleton on this point.

[15]This can be seen in his *Baptist Church Manual*, 7–8; *Christian Doctrines*, 331; and "Scriptural Meaning of the Term Church," 9. Hiscox, *The New Directory for Baptist Churches*, 63, gave four conditions: regenerate heart; confession of faith; reception of baptism; and a Christian life. Dagg, *Manual of Church Order*, 79, 95, listed the moral characteristic of salvation and the ceremonial characteristic of baptism.

[16]Pendleton, *Baptist Church Manual*, 12.

an unbaptized person to be a church member."[17] If baptism is required for local church membership, and if baptism is only of believers, then the local church can consist only of the regenerate.[18]

Pendleton's argument for a regenerate church membership developed over time. Only in *Distinctive Principles of Baptists* published in 1882 did Pendleton devote a complete chapter to its discussion. He stated, "Baptists are distinguished from all other religious denominations by their belief that no one is eligible to a church relation who has not first been brought into a personal, spiritual relation to Christ by faith in his name."[19]

Authority of the Congregation

Based upon the definition of a church as a gathered body of believers which governs itself, Pendleton clarified the areas of authority which fell to the congregation. The fact that the congregation's authority was limited to its own assembly will be discussed after identifying three basic categories of congregational authority within the local assembly.[20] Pendleton believed that the congregation was responsible for: (1) election of its officers, (2) acceptance of members, and (3)

---

[17]Pendleton, *Distinctive Principles of Baptists*, 171.

[18]Henry Lee Anderson, "The Ecclesiology of Ante-Bellum Baptist Churches in the South" (Th.D. diss., New Orleans Baptist Theological Seminary, 1960), 28, stated concerning regenerate church membership, "No tenet was followed more universally and was more obviously adhered to than the emphasis upon the necessity of a personal experience of faith with Christ as a prerequisite to church membership. This concept was so fundamentally basic to Baptists thought and was so universally incorporated into all the sources that it would scarcely seem necessary to examine the sources further. . . ."

[19]Pendleton, *Distinctive Principles of Baptists*, 159.

[20]Pendleton was not alone in holding to congregational church rule or local church autonomy. Norman, *More Than Just a Name*, 119, said, "Writings on Baptist distinctives all contend for Congregationalism as the most appropriate form of church government. . . . Further, Baptists believe that each church is independent of every other church."

church discipline, including the dismissal of members.[21] These three individual sections will now be discussed.

Election of Officers

Pendleton believed that the election of the first deacons in Acts 6 was unmistakably given over to the congregation. He said, "The democratic principle was fully recognized. This is too obvious to be denied."[22] Additionally, he noted from Acts 15:22–23 that first it pleased the whole church to send chosen men of their own company, and secondly, that the letters written were by the apostles, elder, and *brethren*. This means that "the laity of the church at Jerusalem acted as well as the apostles and elders."[23] Even John Calvin affirmed the authority of the congregation to elect its elders.[24]

Pendleton believed that there were only two officers in the New Testament. "Pastors and Deacons are the only permanent church officers."[25] Discussing the election of these officers, he wrote, "Being independent sovereignties, under Christ, the churches have the right to choose their own officers. The right is exclusively their own."[26] Thus, the New

---

[21]This belief can also be seen in Dagg, Hiscox, Strong and others as well as in the Baptist confessions of faith.

[22]James Madison Pendleton, "The Scriptural Meaning of the Term Church," *The Southern Baptist Review* 1 (February–March 1855): 74.

[23]Pendleton, *Three Reasons Why I Am a Baptist, with a Fourth Reason Added, on Communion*, 163.

[24]John Calvin, *Institutes of the Christian Religion*, in *Library of Christian Classics*, trans. by F. L. Battles, ed. John T. McNeill (Louisville: Westminster John Knox Press, 1960), 1066. He stated that Acts 14:23 demonstrated congregational affirmation "by a show of hands in every church." This is his interpretation of χειροτονέω. In addition, he noted that Cyprian implied congregational affirmation by insisting that the choosing of the bishop be done in the presence of the people.

[25]Pendleton, "The Scriptural Meaning of the Term Church," 78.

[26]Ibid.

Testament established a congregational duty to elect its pastors and deacons.[27]

Acceptance of Members

Pendleton asserted that a church has the right to admit members into its fellowship. Rom 14:1 stated, "Receive one who is weak in the faith, *but* not to disputes over doubtful things." In discussing this verse, Pendleton commented, "To whom is this command addressed? . . . To all that be in Rome, beloved of God, called to be saints."[28] His point stressed that members of the church bore the responsibility for admitting or rejecting members.

Another example of the authority of the church to accept members comes from the New Testament example of church discipline given in 2 Corinthians. After the discipline had worked successfully, Paul urged the church at Corinth to allow a member back into its fellowship. Pendleton stated that 2 Cor 2:6 gave two key insights. First, the penalty was sufficient, and second, the punishment was inflicted by the "many." This implied the rule of the majority of the church.[29] Furthermore, in 2 Cor 2:6–8 Paul urged the church to reaffirm their love to the offender. "The power and the right to restore was with the church, and Paul solicits an exercise of the power and of the right."[30] Pendleton, citing previous discussions, stated that the church demonstrated the power

---

[27]Although the London Confession of 1644 in article thirty-six mentions the offices of pastors, teachers, elders, and deacons, the majority of confessions believed in only two offices and that bishop, elder, and pastor all referred to the same office. The Second London Confession and New Hampshire Confession both indicate that bishops or pastors refer to the same position.

[28]Pendleton, *Christian Doctrines*, 338. Also in "The Scriptural Meaning of the Term Church," 72. This was the traditional Baptist position which can be seen in the London Confession of 1644, the Second London Confession of 1677, the Philadelphia Confession of 1742, and the Orthodox Creed of 1679.

[29]Pendleton, *Christian Doctrines*, 340.

[30]Pendleton, *Distinctive Principles of Baptists*, 194.

to exclude members and to admit excluded members which also implied the power to admit any applying members.[31]

Discipline and Dismissal of Members

Matt 18:15–17 established the rules to be followed and the right of a congregation to discipline members. It stated:

> Moreover if your brother sins against you, go and tell him his fault between you and him alone. If he hears you, you have gained your brother. But if he will not hear, take with you one or two more, that "by the mouth of two or three witnesses every word may be established." And if he refuses to hear them, tell it to the church. But if he refuses even to hear the church, let him be to you like a heathen and a tax collector.

In addition to Matthew 18, the right of a church to dismiss members was given in 2 Thess 3:6, "But we command you, brethren, in the name of our Lord Jesus Christ, that you withdraw from every brother who walks disorderly and not according to the tradition which he received from us." Pendleton believed that these passages established the church as the final authority for the discipline and dismissal of members. As to who should handle discipline, he wrote, "'Tell it to the church.' What church? The aggregate body of the redeemed? This is equally impossible and absurd. I ask again, What church? Evidently the local congregation to which the parties belong."[32] Furthermore, the action of the local body was final: "But can there be no appeal from the

---

[31]The view that the congregation had the right to accept members goes as far back as 1527 with Hubmaier. See Balthasar Hubmaier, "Baptismal Order," in *Anabaptism in Outline*, ed. Walter Klaassen (Scottdale: Herald Press, 1981), 121–2. He wrote of a applicant, "the bishop then presents him to his church."

[32]Pendleton, *Distinctive Principles of Baptists*, 206.

action of a single local church to an 'Association' or a 'Presbytery' or a 'Conference'? No; there is no appeal."[33]

Providing additional evidence of the right of a congregation to exercise discipline, Pendleton noted 1 Cor 5:1–5 and commented, "Paul 'judged' that the incestuous man ought to be excluded, *he* did not exclude him."[34] Furthermore, no one person could exclude another individually, but the church had to be "gathered together." Paul later stated in 1 Cor 5:15 "put away from yourselves the evil person." Unlike Calvin, who saw justification in this passage for discipline by presbytery,[35] Pendleton stressed that this command went not to the elders but "to the church of God which is at Corinth."[36] It was the church which possessed the right and final authority in church discipline. Pendleton concluded, "Now, if the New Testament churches had the power and the right to do these three things, they must have had the power and the right to transact any other business coming before them."[37]

---

[33]Ibid., 207. This would become an issue of discussion in the Graves-Howell controversy which will be addressed later in this chapter. Graves appealed to the association but not concerning the matter of discipline. He appealed the matter based on the claim that his church was the true First Baptist Church of Nashville. Pendleton supported his appeal.

[34]Pendleton, *Three Reasons Why I Am a Baptist, with a Fourth Reason Added, on Communion*, 157.

[35]John Calvin, *Calvin's Commentary: 1 Corinthians*, vol. 20 (Grand Rapids: Baker, 1999), 182–3. Calvin wrote, "As, however, a multitude never accomplishes anything with moderation or seriousness, if not governed by counsel, there was appointed in the ancient Church a Presbytery, that is, an assembly of elders, who by the consent of all, had the power of first judging in the case. From them the matter was brought before the people, but it was as a thing already judged of."

[36]Pendleton, "The Scriptural Meaning of the Term Church," 73. Pendleton also stated regarding these verses, "It deserves notice too, that the members of the Corinthian church could not, in their *individual capacity*, exclude the incestuous man." See Pendleton, *Baptist Church Manual*, 105.

[37]Pendleton, "The Scriptural Meaning of the Term Church," 74. Pendleton's position here followed the established position in the 1644 London Confession, and the Second London Confession or the Philadelphia Confession. Although autonomy and congregational polity were not

Pendleton's View of Local Church Autonomy

In Baptist history, there have been different views on the autonomy of the local church and its connection to the association. LeRoy Moore identifies three strands of belief concerning the connectedness of the church. They are: (1) connectional, (2) localist, and (3) individualist. The connectional strand can be seen in the churches of the Philadelphia Baptist Association who rejected congregational isolationism.[38] Walter Shurden notes that some associations even took a place of superiority over the local church.[39] Pendleton and the Landmark position would fall under the "localist" strand and reject associational superiority.

Pendleton's formulation of local church autonomy developed from the equality of churches. He stated, "If one church is equal to another then it is obviously absurd to say that the action of one church binds any other church, not to say all churches."[40] The church was independent or autonomous on many levels. Perhaps the most confusing case arose when one church disciplined a member who left to join another church. Should the church to which the member applied have the right to accept him? Pendleton stated, "One church has a perfect right to receive members who have been excluded from another, and ought to do it provided they have been

---

expressly mentioned in the New Hampshire Confession, J. Newton Brown, *The Baptist Church Manual: Containing the Declaration of Faith, Covenant, Rules of Order and Brief Forms of Church Letters* (Philadelphia: American Baptist Publication Society, 1853) clearly indicated in material following the confession that he held to these principles. They were once again added in the 1925 Baptist Faith and Message. See also D. A. Carson, "Church, Authority in the," in *Evangelical Dictionary of Theology*, ed. Walter Elwell, 2d ed. (Grand Rapids: Baker, 2001), 249–51.

[38]LeRoy Moore, "Crazy Quilt: Southern Baptist Patterns of the Church," *Foundations* 20 (1977): 12–3.

[39]Walter B. Shurden, *Associationalism Among Baptists in America: 1707–1814* (New York: Arno Press, 1980), 151–9.

[40]James Madison Pendleton, "Church Independence," *Tennessee Baptist* (October 6, 1860).

unjustly excluded."⁴¹ However, Pendleton did not endorse the acceptance of an unfit member or a justly disciplined and unrepentant member because it infringed upon the law of Christ.

Church independence did not mean total independence. Pendleton wrote, "It is an independent sovereignty—not independent of Christ—but independent of every other church. And therefore, no other church can interfere with its government."⁴² Pendleton believed that the autonomy of the local church did not separate the church from Christ. The law came from Christ who was the lawgiver and no church had the right to make laws contrary to those given by Christ. Thus, no church had the right to refuse membership to a person who scripturally qualified for membership. He wrote, "There is no law making power vested in the membership of any gospel church."⁴³ There was, however, an independence from every other church.

> When a church acts in accordance with the law of Christ, what it binds on earth is bound in heaven, and what it looses on earth is loosed in heaven. That is to say, it is approved, ratified, sanctioned in heaven. When a church acts otherwise, Heaven disapproves, censures, and condemns. It would be well for all to remember that churches, while independent of one another, are neither independent of Christ nor his law.⁴⁴

Pendleton stressed the limitation of local church sovereignty. He commented, "In these days, much is said about the

---

⁴¹Pendleton, "The Scriptural Meaning of the Term Church," 76.

⁴²James Madison Pendleton, "Church Democracy," *Tennessee Baptist* (July 19, 1856). This was not the case with all associations at all times. The Philadelphia Association at one time allowed for appeal to them of local church decisions and the Sandy Creek Association made certain decisions on behalf of the local churches. See Shurden, *Associationalism Among Baptists in America 1707–1814*, 151–2.

⁴³Pendleton, "Church Democracy."

⁴⁴James Madison Pendleton, "Sovereignty of Churches," *Tennessee Baptist* (November 12, 1859).

sovereignty of churches. Jesus Christ is the Sovereign Head of all his churches. If sovereignty resides in the Head of the Churches, how can it reside in Churches?" [45] He believed that independence was limited and concluded, "Whatever things are wrong among Baptists, their form of church government is certainly right. Here they stand, as on a rock, and can afford to let the waves of controversial wrath rise, and dash, and break in harmless impotence at their feet."[46]

In addition to the biblical arguments, Pendleton presented several logical advantages of independence. He discussed the following advantages at some length: it is best suited to every form of civil government; it is in accord with the tendencies of the age;[47] it gives suitable prominence to the membership of a church; it provides an advantage in the appointment of church officers; it furnishes the most effectual preservative from doctrinal error; it secures, also, more satisfactory corrective discipline; and it cherishes a sense of individual responsibility.[48] Pendleton felt that this view of independence set the Baptist denomination apart. He said,

---

[45]Pendleton, "Sovereignty of Churches." This opinion would be carried on in Baptist thought. Edwin C. Dargan, *Ecclesiology: A Study of the Churches* (Louisville: Chas. T. Dearing, 1897), 42, wrote, "Of course the churches, all of them, were under the supreme headship of Christ...."

[46]Pendleton, "Church Democracy."

[47]If the church followed society, this could be considered a negative; however, Pendleton believed that congregation polity in local churches influenced society. He stated in *Distinctive Principles of Baptists*, 213–4, "How much the practical workings of church independence have had to do in developing the doctrine of popular rights it is impossible to say, but there is every reason to believe that they have promoted the development." Mark Noll, *America's God* (New York: Oxford University Press, 2002), 244–7, briefly discussed the debate between Baptists and Methodists noting the appeal by Baptists to American freedom. For more information, see Nathan Hatch, *The Democratization of American Christianity* (New Haven: Yale University, 1989).

[48]The discussion of these advantages is contained in *Distinctive Principles of Baptists*, 211–23.

"Among whom, except Baptists, is the doctrine of church independency fully exemplified?"[49]

Some of Pendleton's most powerful and persuasive arguments did not come in the positive presentation of his beliefs but in his defense against what he considered improper views. Thus, this presentation will now discuss his refutation of other views.

PENDLETON'S REJECTION OF OTHER FORMS OF CHURCH GOVERNMENT

Improper Understanding of ἐκκλησία

Pendleton believed that some other forms of church government had improperly understood the New Testament word ἐκκλησία. Pendleton gave three results of an improper understanding of this word. First, Pendleton noted that an improper understanding of the scriptural term "church" has led to "the adulterous union between church and state."[50] He claimed that throughout history many justified the union for various reasons.[51] However, "If a church was considered, as it is, a congregation of baptized believers, independent of

---

[49]Ibid., 225.

[50]Pendleton, "The Scriptural Meaning of the Term Church," 80.

[51]Augustine, at first, had reservations about invoking the aid of the state against schimastics in Northern Africa; however, after seeing the success of the emperor, he changed his mind and accepted the union of church and state. See Hermann Doerries, *Constantine and Religious Liberty*, trans. Roland Bainton (New Haven: Yale University, 1960), 57. Zwingli saw union in the church and the state. Timothy George, *Theology of the Reformers* (Nashville: Broadman & Holman, 1988), 134, stated, "In Zurich, perhaps more than in any of the other Reformed cities, church and civic community were one indivisible body, governed by the spiritual and secular officers who both accepted the principle of Scriptural authority as the basis of their joint governance." Luther and Calvin, as magisterial reformers, also allowed the state a measure of authority over church affairs.

every other congregation, its union with the state would not be regarded as a practicable thing."[52]

Second, Pendleton noted that an improper understanding of the scriptural term church has led to the belief of "a church as an organization commensurate with the territory of a nation."[53] With this, Pendleton did not have in mind the union of church and state, rather the idea of a denominational church, such as the Presbyterian church of the United States. He explained, "The idea seems to be that many local communities make up a great church which extends throughout the nation."[54] He believed that the Scriptures knew nothing of this type formation, and if the scriptural idea of the church were held to, this would not exist.

Third, Pendleton stated, "A practical abandonment of the Scriptural meaning of the word church has affected the question of church membership very injuriously."[55] He specifically referred to the lack of New Testament warrant for infant membership and the New Testament teaching that the church should be a body of believers. The church should not admit unsaved people into membership. If a church by mistake admitted a non-regenerate member, then the actions

---

[52]Pendleton, "The Scriptural Meaning of the Term Church," 80. Another reason for rejecting the union of church and state, though not noted by Pendleton, is that the union of church and state has at times jeopardized religious liberty. Donald Durnbaugh stated that the first claim for freedom of religion published in the English language was by Thomas Helwys in 1612 titled *A Short Declaration of the Mistery of Iniquity*. This document has been published as Thomas Helwys, *The Mistery of Iniquity* (London: Kingsgate Press, 1935) or for more information see Donald F. Durnbaugh, *The Believers' Church* (Scottdale: Herald Press, 1968), 97.

[53]Pendleton, "The Scriptural Meaning of the Term Church," 80. Strong, *Systematic Theology*, vol. 3, 912–3, agreed with Pendleton and gave five reasons for refuting this view.

[54]Pendleton, "The Scriptural Meaning of the Term Church," 80. Strong, *Systematic Theology*, vol. 3, 913, wrote that this type of church logically leads to the theory of Romanism when two areas need a superior authority to settle their differences.

[55]Pendleton, "The Scriptural Meaning of the Term Church," 81.

of that member would demonstrate such and church discipline should be practiced to insure that, as much as possible, the church was a body of gathered believers.[56]

In addition to the proper understanding of the scriptural sense of the word "church," Pendleton claimed that only Baptists fully understand the church as the "kingdom of Christ."[57] This phrase implied that Christ is "King—he is Monarch." Thus, the churches of Christ were invested with judicial and executive power, but they have no legislative power.[58] Christ is the head of each local church and each local church answers only to Christ.

Rejection of Episcopalian Church Government

The bishop is an essential office in the Episcopalian system of government, and their understanding of the role of the bishop distinguishes their system of government from

---

[56]This issue has been debated throughout history going back to the controversy between Augustine and the Donatist over the idea of a "pure church" or a "mixed church." Robert Markus, "Donatism," *Augustine Through the Ages*, ed. Allan Fitzgerald (Grand Rapids: William B. Eerdmans, 1999), 286, wrote, "The issue between Augustine and the Donatists concerned, at bottom, the nature of the church and of the relation between it and the world. Central to Augustine's position was the insistence . . . that the church was a mixed body containing overt sinners." Furthermore, Leonard Verduin, *The Reformers and Their Stepchildren* (Sarasota: Christian Hymnary, 2000), 40, linked the Donatist and the Anabaptist as possessing similar visions of a pure church. See also H. Leon McBeth, *The Baptist Heritage* (Nashville: Broadman Press, 1987), 75–6.

[57]Pendleton, *Three Reasons Why I Am a Baptist, with a Fourth Reason Added, on Communion*, 151. Current theologians differ concerning the connection between the church and the kingdom. For a discussion of this, see Edmund Clowney, *The Church* (Downers Grove: InterVarsity, 1995), 41; Veli-Matti Kärkkäinen, *An Introduction to Ecclesiology: Ecumenical, Historical & Global Perspectives* (Downers Grove: InterVarsity, 2002), 206–7; Avery Dulles, *Models of the Church* (New York: Doubleday, 2002), 96; and Craig Blaising and Darrell Bock, *Progressive Dispensationalism* (Wheaton: Victor Books, 1993), 255–70.

[58]Pendleton, Distinctive Principles of Baptists, 187.

Baptists.[59] In addition to bishops, this system recognizes the officers of deacon and elder.[60] Richard Hooker, a well-known Anglican theologian said, "A thousand five hundred years and upward the Church of Christ has now continued under the sacred regiment of bishops."[61] The duty of the bishops was well described by Hooker. He wrote:

> A Bishop is a minister of God, unto whom with permanent continuance there is given not only power of administering the Word and Sacraments, which power other Presbyters have; but also a further power to ordain ecclesiastical persons, and a power of cheifty in government over Presbyters as well as Laymen, a power to be by way of jurisdiction a Pastor even to Pastors themselves.[62]

Since the bishops could not govern over all the members of the church, the presbyter exercised this duty as a representative of the bishops. Additionally another level of service was found in the deacons.

Pendleton specifically rejected the office of bishop by writing, "The modern application of the term bishop to a man who has under his charge a district of country, is very

---

[59]Joseph Buchanan Bernardin, *An Introduction to the Episcopal Church* (New York: Morehouse-Barlow, 1957), 15. For discussion of the various forms of government see, Edward LeRoy Long, Jr. *Patterns of Polity* (Cleveland: Pilgrim Press, 2001); A. S. McGrade, "Introduction," *Of the Laws of Ecclesiastical Polity*, abridged ed., eds. McGrade and Brian Vickers (New York: St. Martin's, 1975); Paul F. M. Zahl, "The Bishop-Led Church," in *Perspectives on Church Government*, eds. Chad Brand and R. Stanton Norman (Nashville: Broadman & Holman, 2004); and Peter Toon, "Episcopalianism," in *Who Runs the Church?*, eds. Paul Engle and Steven Cowan (Grand Rapids: Zondervan, 2004).

[60]This view goes back to Ignatius and can be found in his, "Letter to the Ephesians," in *Ante-Nicene Fathers*, ed. Philip Schaff, vol. 1 (Peabody: Hendrickson, 1999), 51. He said, "Do ye, beloved, be careful to be subject to the bishop, and the presbyters and the deacons."

[61]Richard Hooker, *Of the Laws of Ecclesiastical Polity*, abridged ed., eds. McGrade and Brian Vickers (New York: St. Martin's Press, 1975), 311.

[62]Hooker, Of the Laws of Ecclesiastical Polity, 312.

objectionable. It has almost banished from Christendom the idea originally attached to the term."[63] Pendleton believed that the terms bishop, pastor, and elder described the same office.[64] Additionally, he believed that Baptist church independence placed the Baptist and Episcopalian structure in direct opposition. He stated:

> Independency is in irreconcilable conflict with Episcopacy and Presbyterianism, and distinctly affirms these three truths: 1) That the governmental power is in the hands of the members of a church; 2) The right of a majority of the members of a church to rule in accordance with the law of Christ; and 3) That the power of a church cannot be transferred or alienated, and that church action is final.[65]

An additional reason used in support of a bishop led system of government was its equity and efficiency. Pendleton responded by writing, "If it is 'wise' to exclude the laity from the Annual and General Conferences, there is wisdom in the Methodist government. If it is 'equitable' for the people not to be allowed to say who shall preach for them, there is equity in it."[66] He continued, "In short, if it is wise, equitable and efficient to adopt a system of government in direct opposition to the letter and spirit of the New Testament, I know of none 'wiser, more equitable, and more efficient' than the

---

[63]Pendleton, *Baptist Church Manual*, 100.

[64]Pendleton, *Three Reasons Why I Am a Baptist, with a Fourth Reason Added, on Communion*, 148. This was the typical Baptist position. Anderson, "The Ecclesiology of Ante-Bellum Baptist Churches in the South," 66, stated about this period of time, "Baptists recognized two divinely designated officers emanating from the New Testament. These two officers were the Bishop, occasionally called elder, shepherd, overseer, brother, or with increasing frequency in the later sources minister or pastor, and the Deacon."

[65]Pendleton, *Christian Doctrines*, 338.

[66]James Madison Pendleton, "Methodist Church Government," *Tennessee Baptist* (June 16, 1855). This was in response to John McFerrin, "Methodist Church Government," *Christian Advocate* (May 31, 1855). McFerrin edited that publication but was best known for his *History of Methodism*. He also preached and served as a confederate chaplain.

Methodist system."67 Pendleton based his formulation of church government primarily on his interpretation of biblical revelation and not pragmatic or historical evidence.

One Methodist retorted that their system of government was more like a republican government and was based on the council at Jerusalem.68 To this Pendleton argued that the representatives of the Methodist church are not elected by the members. He questioned, "'Representatives of the people?' 'Elected by the members?' How are they elected by the members?" and responded that "the people do not elect the members of those Conferences and the Conferences are not responsible to the people."69 Thus, Pendleton rejected the bishop led church.

Rejection of the Presbyterian System of Government

Charles Hodge stated, "Presbyterianism is a mode of church government as definite and as well understood as any other form of ecclesiastical polity. Its fundamental principle is, that the government of the church rests upon the Presbyteries; that is, the clerical and lay elders."70 In this system of government, the authority rests in the presbytery. The presbytery retains the power to dismiss pastors "with or

---

67James Madison Pendleton, "Methodist Church Government," *Tennessee Baptist* (September 15, 1855).

68The Jerusalem council can be found in Acts 15. This reason was put forth by James L. Chapman, "Defense of the Scriptural and Republican Character of the M. Church Government," *Christian Advocate* (May 31, 1855); and James L. Chapman, "Defense of the Scriptural and Republican Character of the M. Church Government," *Christian Advocate* (June 7, 1855). These articles resulted from a debate with J. R. Graves. For more information, see James L. Chapman and J. R. Graves, *Defence of the Government of the Methodist Episcopal Church: in His Debate with the Rev. J. R. Graves, at Canton, Miss., May, 1855* (Nashville: Southern Methodist Publishing House, 1860).

69James Madison Pendleton, "Chapman on Church Government," *Tennessee Baptist* (June 23, 1855).

70Charles Hodge, The Constitutional History of the Presbyterian Church in the United States of America (Philadelphia: Presbyterian Board of Publication, 1863), 92.

without their consent" and the power of "erecting new churches; dividing congregations; appointing supplies...."[71]

The Presbyterian's system of church government conflicted with Pendleton's view in three distinct areas. The first area of difference was the connectedness of churches which rejected the principle of independence. Pendleton wrote of the Presbyterian system, "The pastor and ruling elders of a congregation constitute what is called the 'session of the church.'"[72] The session was responsible for receiving, dismissing, and excluding members. Above the session, "there is an appeal to Presbytery [synod], which is composed of preaching and ruling elders" and above the synod came an appeal to a General Assembly, which has the final say.[73] Pendleton questioned the scriptural basis for such an elaborate form of government, much less the splitting of the office of elder. He also spoke against the claim that local church independence would destroy the vary nature of a church and that a church's existence relied upon other churches. Hodge said concerning church independence:

> This theory, however, is thoroughly opposed to the common faith of the Church, and, as we think, to the plain teachings of the New Testament. It owes its origin to the desire to make the phenomenal agree with the real, the visible with the invisible Church. This can never be realized in this world, and it never was designed that men should accomplish this desirable end. Men cannot

---

[71]Ibid., 98, 101.

[72]Pendleton, *Baptist Church Manual*, 101. Joan S. Gray and Joyce C. Tucker, *Presbyterian Polity for Church Officers* (Louisville: Geneva, 1999), 60–74, discusses the session of a church.

[73]Pendleton, *Three Reasons Why I Am a Baptist, with a Fourth Reason Added, on Communion*, 149. Gray, *Presbyterian Polity for Church Officers*, 109–25. Gray states that the first Presbyterian General Assembly met in 1789 in Philadelphia, Pennsylvania (120).

read the heart. They cannot discriminate between the growing wheat and tares.[74]

Pendleton replied to Hodge, "To this I must object, and insist that the vitality of a church depends on its union with Jesus Christ."[75] However, the quote from Hodge revealed a second difference between the Presbyterian system and the Baptist system.

Second, the Presbyterians did not believe in a regenerate church membership but held to a mixed church membership. Hodge offered several reasons for supporting a mixed church, such as a pure church is not possible in a society governed by men, all professing believers are not truly regenerate, Christ admitted Judas to the twelve, and all attempts have failed. One additional area Hodge cited was Christ's comments on the wheat and the tares. He said, "He charged his disciples not to undertake to separate them, because they could not, in all cases, distinguish the one from the other. Both were to be allowed to grow together until the harvest."[76] In this, Hodge followed Calvin who wrote, "The church is at the same time mingled of good men and bad."[77] Thus, the church, in their opinion, should contain both regenerate and unregenerate until the time of Christ.

A third area of difference from most Baptists was the splitting of the office of elder into two separate offices.[78]

---

[74]Charles Hodge, *Discussions in Church Polity* (New York: Charles Scribner's Sons, 1878), 246.

[75]James Madison Pendleton, "Presbyterian High-Churchism," *Tennessee Baptist* (June 30, 1855).

[76]Charles Hodge, *Systematic Theology*, vol. 3 (Peabody: Hendrickson, 2001), 548.

[77]Calvin, *Institutes of the Christian Religion*, 1027. He appealed to Christ comparing the church to a net which catches all kind of fish that are not sorted until the end in Matt 13:47–58; to the parable of the sower in Matt 13:24–30; and to the grain on the threshing floor in Matt 3:12. All these references appealed to a mixed congregation that would not be sorted out until the judgment of Christ.

[78]In contrast to the majority view, W. B. Johnson argued for a third office. See W. B. Johnson, "The Gospel Developed (1846)," in *Polity:*

Presbyterians believed that Scripture warrants the division of the office into teaching elder and ruling elder.[79] Pendleton specifically disagreed with the office of ruling elder saying, "Presbyterians properly use the term Bishop as synonymous with Pastor, but the office of Ruling Elder is without sufficient Scriptural warrant. The arguments in favor of it are not satisfactory."[80] Pendleton further commented, "While presbyterians, therefore, talk and write about the *expediency* of their form of government, they ought to say nothing of its *scripturalness*."[81]

Thus, Pendleton rejected both the Presbyterian and the Episcopalian systems of church government. He affirmed the independence of the local church which separated his beliefs from those who held to collective groups governing multiple churches. Pendleton also supported the congregational form

---

Biblical Arguments on How to Conduct Church Life, ed. Mark Dever (Washington: Center for Church Reform, 2001), 191. Additionally, Samuel Jones gave arguments on both sides. Samuel Jones, "Treatise of Church Discipline (1805)," in *Polity: Biblical Arguments on How to Conduct Church Life*, ed. Mark Dever (Washington: Center for Church Reform, 2001). Greg Wills indicates that the distinction between ruling and teaching elder had dropped out of practice by 1820 among Baptists but can be seen occurring sporadically since that time. See Greg Wills, "The Church," in *Polity: Biblical Arguments on How to Conduct Church Life*, ed. Mark Dever (Washington: Center for Church Reform, 2001), 34. Also, Benjamin Griffith's "A Short Treatise (1743)" includes a section on ruling elders. See *Polity: Biblical Arguments on How to Conduct Church Life*, 95–112.

[79]The primary verse used to create the distinction between ruling elders and teaching elders is 1 Tim 5:17 which says, "Let the elders who rule well be counted worthy of double honor, especially those who labor in the word and doctrine." For a recent presentation of the arguments for ruling elders, see L. Roy Taylor, "Presbyterianism," in *Who Runs the Church? 4 Views on Church Government*, eds. Paul Engle and Steven Cowan (Grand Rapids: Zondervan, 2004), 71–130; and Robert Reymond, "The Presbytery-Led Church: Presbyterian Church Government," in *Perspectives on Church Government*, eds. Chad Brand and R. Stanton Norman (Nashville: Broadman & Holman, 2004), 87–156.

[80]Pendleton, "The Scriptural Meaning of the Term Church," 77.

[81]Pendleton, Distinctive Principles of Baptists, 184.

of church government which distinguished him from those who place power in a selected group. Finally, Pendleton believed that there were only two offices in the New Testament, which separated his view from those who held to three offices, or separated the office of elder into ruling elder and teaching elder.

THE GRAVES-HOWELL CONTROVERSY

The Graves-Howell controversy deserves special attention as a case study in Baptist polity. Howell and the First Baptist Church of Nashville, Tennessee placed Graves under disciplinary action. Graves felt the case was not properly handled so he and other former members appealed to the local association and national convention claiming to be to true First Baptist Church of Nashville.[82] This predicament put Pendleton in a difficult position. Although Pendleton attempted to word his position in such a way as to support his friend Graves without compromising his ecclesiological principles, this case study will demonstrate that personal matters affected Pendleton's position on the issue. Throughout his life, Pendleton continued to support local church independence and congregational church polity, but this situation tested both of those beliefs not only for Pendleton but for Southern Baptists.

The matter of Graves's discipline could not be appealed as the church has the final authority in discipline; however, Graves held that the church did not conduct itself according to Scripture in executing church discipline and thus, was no longer a church. Graves, along with several other excluded members, asked the association and national convention to decide who was the true church. This bitter and personal

---

[82]For a complete study, see Weatherford, "The Graves-Howell Controversy." A short summary is also in Wardin, *Tennessee Baptists: A Comprehensive History 1779–1999*; and James E. Tull, *High-Church Baptists in the South* (Macon: Mercer Press, 2000), 85–92. For Howell's article and Graves's response, see *Tennessee Baptist*, February 28, 1858. For Howell's viewpoint, see R. B. C. Howell et al., *Both Sides*.

controversy ended by establishing the precedent that the national convention would not interfere with local church matters. Despite the final decision, Pendleton found himself answering questions concerning his beliefs over local church autonomy.

In one article, Pendleton responded to allegations against him. Pendleton stated the allegation as follows, "I believed in the right of a majority in a Church to govern, but that I have now changed my ground that I may defend my friend Graves."[83] Pendleton defended his position by asserting that if a church acts at variance with the New Testament, the church's actions are not binding.[84] He further stated, "Entertaining the opinion that Elder Howell's party in Nashville, in the proceedings against Elder Graves, violated the law of Christ, I have no more regard for its decisions, than I would have for those of a Masonic Lodge, should a Lodge so far transcend the limits of its jurisdiction, as to act upon ecclesiastical matters."[85]

This controversy would come to a head at the Southern Baptist Convention of 1859. Pendleton had suggested that neither Graves nor Howell run for president of the convention.[86] Despite this apparent act of peace, Pendleton offered the resolution asking that the messengers of the First Baptist Church of Nashville not be seated. Tull stated, "This bold bid would have made the Southern Baptist Convention an appellate court. The resolution was set aside by the

---

[83]James Madison Pendleton, "Probably Too Fast," *Tennessee Baptist* (April 9, 1859).
[84]Ibid.
[85]Ibid. It is doubtful that Pendleton randomly chose to compare the church to a Masonic lodge since Graves's opponent, Howell, was a Mason. Pendleton had previously written against such "secret societies." Pendleton, "Query—Secret Societies."
[86]Pendleton, "A Good Thing."

Convention which approved J.E. Dawson's motion to lay it on the table."[87]

In evaluating Pendleton's actions with his theological formulation, this author concludes that his personal relationship with Graves did affect his actions during this time frame. Whether Graves deserved the discipline he received is a matter for others to decide. The issue at question is Pendleton's participation. Pendleton's theological formulation allowed a person or a minority of members to withdraw from the church should they feel that the church acted contrary to the New Testament. However, establishing another church by the same name and asking the association and national convention not to seat the First Baptist Church of Nashville was wrong. This author has reached this conclusion based on Pendleton's own comments concerning church independence and his comments concerning the American system of government.[88] Pendleton stated that it was the right of the majority to rule, and thus the majority has no need to revolt. Conversely, the minority has no right to rule or revolt as they have willingly conceded power to the majority. By this logic, the minority in the First Baptist Church of Nashville had no recourse other than to withdraw from the church if they felt its actions were unscriptural. Furthermore, since they had conceded power, they had no right to challenge them as the true First Baptist Church. Pendleton said himself, "It results of necessity from church independence that a majority must rule, that the power of a church cannot be transferred or alienated, and that church

---

[87]Tull, *High-Church Baptists in the South*, 91. Howell would eventually win the election and immediately resign. Howell said in his resignation, "I have seen a disposition to convert this convention into an ecclesiastical court—to the subversion of those great principles which have existed ever since the foundation of the church." See Tull, *High-Church Baptists in the South*, 92. Also published in the *Tennessee Baptist* (June 11, 1859).

[88]James Madison Pendleton, *Reminiscences of a Long Life* (Louisville, KY: Baptist Book Concern, 1891), 121.

action is final."⁸⁹ Pendleton's response was that since the First Baptist Church of Nashville acted outside of Scripture, they were no longer a church. Thus, it was consistent for Graves and company to question them. No matter the conclusion, this controversy forced Pendleton to walk a fine line in order not to compromise his views of local church independence while supporting his friend Graves.

PENDLETON AMONG HIS CONTEMPORARIES

In order to understand Pendleton's place in Baptist history, a study of his contemporaries is necessary. This survey will examine some major Baptist theologians during this time frame and their position on the issue of church polity. This section will be broken down into three topics. First, this author will address church independence among Baptist contemporaries, and second, this author will discuss the congregational form of church government among Baptists. Both church independence and congregational government are widely supported by Baptists. The third area will address the officers of the church. This section will reveal that there were certain Baptists who held to more than two officers by dividing the office of elder into ruling elder and teaching elder. The end result will show that Pendleton supported the majority opinion among Baptists concerning the issues of church government.

The Independence of the Local Church

Pendleton was not alone in his belief that Baptist churches were autonomous. In fact, Henry Lee Anderson speaking of the autonomy of ante-bellum Baptist churches in the South wrote, "Baptists of this period not only valiantly supported this autonomy, but they also claimed that it was explicitly

---

⁸⁹Pendleton, Distinctive Principles of Baptists, 188. Almost the exact wording was contained in *Three Reasons Why I Am a Baptist with a Fourth Added on Communion*, 153.

taught in Scripture."⁹⁰ This view was so widely held by the Baptists that this author has yet to find any Baptist writer who supported another position. Additionally, the interaction between the denominations on this issue was minimal.⁹¹ For Baptists, the defense of church independence received less attention because it did not receive the same challenge as baptism did.⁹² A great majority of Baptists believed in the independence of the local church.⁹³

On this issue Pendleton, Dagg, and Hiscox all agreed completely. Dagg wrote, "Each church, as a distinct

---

⁹⁰Anderson, "The Ecclesiology of Ante-Bellum Baptist Churches in the South," 37.

⁹¹There was some interaction. See, for instance, James Henley Thornwell, *The Elder Question: Extracted from the Southern Presbyterian Review* (np, privately published). This is a response to Robert Breckinridge (1800–1871) who was professor of theology at the Presbyterian seminary in Danville, Kentucky, and who wrote *The Knowledge of God, Subjectively Considered* (New York: R. Carter, 1859); and *The Knowledge of God, Objectively Considered* (New York: R. Carter, 1858).

⁹²Other denominations supported their respective views. See Board of Publication of the Reformed Protestant Dutch Church, *A Message to Ruling Elders; Their Office and Their Duties* (New York: Board of Publication of the Reformed Protestant Dutch Church, 1859); and Robert Breckinridge, *The Christian Pastor, One of the Ascension Gifts of Christ. To Which Are Added by Way of Appendix, Presbyterian Government Not a Hierarch, but a Commonwealth; and Presbyterian Ordination Not a Charm, but an Act of Government* (Baltimore: by the author, 1845).

⁹³This can be seen in the confessions. Local church autonomy was affirmed in the London Confession of 1644, article thirty-six; the Second London Confession of 1677, chapter twenty-six, section fifteen; and carried over to the Philadelphia Confession of Faith (1742), chapter twenty-seven, section fifteen. This non-comprehensive list includes works supporting church independence: Wayland, *Notes on the Principles and Practices of Baptist Churches*; Hezekiah Harvey, *The Church: Its Polity and Ordinances* (Philadelphia: American Baptist Publication Society, 1879); J. L. Reynolds, *Church Polity: or The Kingdom of Christ, in Its Internal and External Development* (Richmond: Harrold & Murray, 1849); P. H. Mell, *Corrective Church Discipline* (Charleston: Southern Baptist Publication Society, 1860); William Williams, *Apostolic Church Polity* (Philadelphia: American Baptist Publication Society, 1874); and W. B. Johnson, *The Gospel Developed Through the Government and Order of the Churches of Jesus Christ* (Richmond: H. K. Ellyson, 1846).

organization, was independent of every other church. No intimation is anywhere given that the acts of one church were supervised by another church, or by any ecclesiastical judicatory established by a combination of churches."[94] Hiscox made a bold assertion concerning not only his view but the view of all Baptists by saying, "That independency is the true form of Church government, as opposed to Prelacy and Presbyterianism, will not now be argued, but is assumed, as accepted by all Baptists, taught in the New Testament, verified by history, and justified by the genius of the gospel itself."[95] Although the majority of Baptists believed in the independence of the local church, the Landmark movement focused on it more than some.

Some Baptists coupled local autonomy with the importance of association with other churches. For example the *Philadelphia Confession* stated in chapter twenty-seven section fifteen, "It is according to the mind of Christ, that many churches holding communion together, do by their messengers meet to consider and give their advice in or about that matter in difference, to be reported to all the Churches concerned."[96] Additionally, an essay drafted by Benjamin Griffith and adopted by the Philadelphia Baptist Association further demonstrates the combination of autonomy with the importance of association. Griffith wrote, "Such churches there must be—agreeing in doctrine and practice, and independent in their authority and church power—before they can enter into a confederation and choose delegates or representatives to associate together; and thus the several independent churches being the constituents, the association. . . ."[97] Pendleton never minimized the importance of the association and attended meetings regularly. In fact,

---

[94]Dagg, Manual of Church Order, 83.
[95]Hiscox, The New Directory for Baptist Churches, 145.
[96]Timothy George and Denise George, eds., *Baptist Confessions, Covenants, and Catechisms* (Tennessee: Broadman & Holman, 1966), 87.
[97]Winthrop Hudson, "Documents on the Associations of Churches," *Foundations* 4 (1961): 335.

Pendleton met his wife on the way to the Russell Creek Association meeting in 1837.[98] Also, he was called as pastor of Upland Baptist Church on his way to the Philadelphia Association meeting in 1865.[99] Unlike Graves, who has been credited with attacking the Southern Baptist Convention and encouraging the formation of new convention, Pendleton's actions demonstrated an understanding of the importance of associations.[100]

Congregational form of Church Government

The congregational form of church government which Pendleton supported was also widely held by Baptists. Anderson referred to the congregational form of government and the responsibility of the local church to administer its own discipline as a "basic Baptist ecclesiological tenet" which could be found in the associational records of churches throughout the South.[101] Anderson's description of antebellum Baptists in the South did not change throughout the nineteenth century. Baptist literature overwhelmingly favored the congregational form of church government. Typically the defense of this position included scriptural support for the right to determine membership whether that be by exclusion through discipline or reinstatement and the

---

[98]Pendleton, Reminiscences of a Long Life, 52.
[99]Ibid., 139.
[100]For information on Graves's attack on the Southern Baptist Convention and encouragement of forming a new convention, see David O. Moore, "The Landmark Baptists and Their Attack Upon the Southern Baptist Convention Historically Analyzed" (Ph.D. diss., Southern Baptist Theological Seminary, 1950). For more information on the role of the association in Baptist life, see Moore, "Crazy Quilt: Southern Baptist Patterns of the Church;" Shurden, *Associationalism Among Baptist in America 1707–1814*; Hudson, "Documents on the Associations of Churches;" and Maring and Hudson, *A Baptist Manual of Polity and Practice*.
[101]Anderson, "The Ecclesiology of Ante-Bellum Baptist Churches in the South," 143.

right to select the officers of the church.[102] From this, most Baptist writers inferred that the congregation had authority in all matters not discussed by Scripture. In addition to specific passages of Scripture, this form of church government has often been supported by appealing to the priesthood of the believers in a church containing a regenerate church membership;[103] however, Pendleton never appealed to the priesthood of the believer. In Baptist life, autonomy and congregationalism were seen as connected and both were overwhelmingly supported.

The Officers of the New Testament Church

Most Baptists held that the New Testament established only two officers in the local church. Anderson stated concerning the beliefs of the ante-bellum period, "Baptists recognized two divinely designated officers emanating from the New Testament."[104] Robert Wring has written that "the consistent polity practice of Baptist Churches, since the formation of the Southern Baptist Convention in 1845, has been the two-officer model of leadership which is expressed in the pastor and deacons pattern of local church government."[105]

---

[102]This scriptural support would come from Matthew 18 for discipline, from Act 6 for election of deacons, from 1 Corinthians for exclusion of membership, and from 2 Corinthians for inclusion of excluded member or acceptance of membership.

[103]Daniel Akin, "The Single-Elder-Led Church," in *Perspectives on Church Government*, eds. Chad Brand and R. Stanton Norman (Nashville: Broadman & Holman, 2004), 35, wrote, "Theologically, this [priesthood of all believers] is one of the more important defenses for Congregational polity." See also James Leo Garrett Jr., "The Congregational-Led Church," in *Perspectives on Church Government*, eds. Chad Brand and R. Stanton Norman (Nashville: Broadman & Holman, 2004), 185; Paige Patterson, "Single-Elder Congregationalism," in *Who Runs the Church?* eds. Paul Engle and Steven Cowan (Grand Rapids: Zondervan, 2004), 139; and Grenz, *The Baptist Congregation*, 56.

[104]Anderson, "The Ecclesiology of Ante-Bellum Baptist Churches in the South," 66.

[105] Robert Wring, "An Examination of the Practice of Elder Rule in Selected Southern Baptist Churches in Light of the New Testament

However, that assertion is questioned by the office of ruling elder, specifically when authority to accept members, dismiss members, or decide on matters of discipline fell to those holding this office.

Most Baptists responded to the office of ruling elder by stressing that only two offices were appointed by the New Testament. In contrast to the majority view, the work of W. B. Johnson provided for a third office or at least a division of duty within the office of elder. He stated, "Whilst all were rulers, some, in addition to the authority of office, *labored in the word and doctrine*, that is, *preached the gospel of Christ*."[106] Additionally, Samuel Jones wrote in favor of the office of ruling elder.[107] Greg Wills indicated that the minority position of a distinction between ruling and teaching elder declined even farther by 1820 and could only be found sporadically after that time.[108]

Harvey summarized the office of ruling elder well by writing, "The 'ruling elders' in the presbyterian Church are a body of laymen, presided over by the pastor, to whom are committed the admission and discipline of members and the spiritual oversight of the church."[109] He concluded, "Plainly, also, a ruling eldership . . . which assumes authority to admit and discipline and exclude members, is disproved by all those passages, heretofore cited, which show that these functions belong only to the church assembled as congregation."[110] Hiscox discussed those who have three offices and then wrote, "But if the Scriptures be appealed to, and primitive churches be accepted as examples, it would seem to be a

---

Teaching" (Ph.D. diss., Mid-America Baptist Theological Seminary, 2002), 211.

[106]Johnson, "The Gospel Developed (1846)," 191.

[107]Jones, "Treatise of Church Discipline (1805)," 145.

[108]Wills, "The Church," 34. Griffith's "A Short Treatise (1743)," 95–112, also included a section on ruling elders.

[109]Harvey, *The Church*, 77.

[110]Ibid., 79.

question settled, that in apostolic times, and for many years after, pastors and deacons only were known as permanent Church officers."[111]

The support for the office of ruling elder came primarily from 1 Tim 5:17. Dagg wrote concerning 1 Tim 5:17, "The text furnishes no authority for Presbyterian lay elders; and no argument for supposing that deacons are called elders."[112] Reynolds wrote concerning support for the office of ruling elder:

> For the support of this distinction, the passages of Scripture principally relied on are 1 Tim 5:17; 1 Cor 12:28. The latter passage is too indefinite in its phraseology to establish the distinction, and would probably never have been supposed to contain it, had not an erroneous interpretation of the former passage previously led to the belief that such a distinction really existed.[113]

Concerning the same passage William Williams, who was an original member of the faculty of Southern Seminary wrote:

> The distinction of preaching elder and ruling elder, made by the Presbyterians, rests upon a single passage of Scripture, 1 Tim 5:17. (The passage in 1 Cor 12:28, and that in Rom 12:8, are so indefinite as to the import of the terms used, and therefore susceptible of such a variety of interpretations, that they would surely have never been thought of in this connection, if it had not been for the one in First Timothy.)[114]

Williams went on to write that 1 Tim 5:17 does not warrant two offices. Thus, the majority of Baptists during Pendleton's day affirmed only two offices and rejected the office of ruling

---

[111]Hiscox, The New Directory for Baptist Churches, 84.
[112]Dagg, Manual of Church Order, 267.
[113]Reynolds, *Church Polity*, 114.
[114]Williams, "Apostolic Church Polity," 533.

elder specifically. Pendleton contributed to popularizing this view through his *Church Manual* and *Three Reason Why I Am a Baptist*.

PENDLETON'S UNIQUE CONTRIBUTION

In the area of polity, Pendleton has two unique contributions. The first came through his focus on the visible church. By focusing on the local, visible church in his *Church Manual* and *Three Reasons Why I Am a Baptist*, Pendleton and other Landmarkers formed a stream of thought in Baptist life which Moore identifies as the localist strand.[115] Pendleton's emphasis on the local, visible church and the qualifications in order to be a visible church resulted in less emphasis on the connectedness of believers as spiritual children of God and restricted cooperation to only those with whom he agreed, and led to a greater elaboration of the issues of church government and a popularization of the Baptist position.

Second, congregational church government, local church autonomy, and two scriptural offices established by the New Testament became staples in works on Baptist distinctives. As one of the most popular Baptist writers of the nineteenth century, Pendleton uniquely contributed to the popularization of Baptist polity and did his part to insure that discussions of Baptist distinctives in future generations would include a discussion of church polity. Part of his lasting influence can be demonstrated by looking at the current academic works on Baptist polity.

---

[115]Moore called this strand of Baptist thought the "localist" view as opposed to the "connectional" or the "individualist" strand. See Moore, "Crazy Quilt: Southern Baptist Patterns of the Church," 12.

CURRENT DISCUSSIONS ON CHURCH POLITY

The issue of church polity has experienced a renaissance with many books being written on Baptist church polity.[116] Two dissertations written in this area are worthy of note. One dissertation written by Robert Wring is titled "An Examination of the Practice of Elder Rule in Selected Southern Baptist Churches in the Light of New Testament Teaching."[117] This work finds value in that it summarizes the historical position and provides current research through personal interviews with some of the more prominent Southern Baptist leaders. Another dissertation written by David Crosby titled "Church Government in the Church Growth Movement: Critique from a Historic Baptist Perspective" discusses the affects of pragmatic church growth techniques on the theological formulation of church government.[118] He concluded that some principles supported by the church growth movement have been harmful to a proper practice of traditional Baptist polity. These two works provide valuable insight and resources to the discussion of church polity.[119]

The Independence of the Local Church

The issue of local church independence in recent discussions has been important to some Baptists who may disagree with

---

[116]Two of the newest book published on this issue are Chad Brand and R. Stanton Norman, eds., *Perspectives on Church Government* (Nashville: Broadman & Holman, 2004), and Paul Engle and Steve Cowan, eds., *Who Runs the Church? 4 Views on Church Government* (Grand Rapids: Zondervan, 2004).

[117]Robert Wring, "An Examination of the Practice of Elder Rule in Selected Southern Baptist Churches in Light of the New Testament Teaching" (Ph.D. diss., Mid-America Baptist Theological Seminary, 2002).

[118]David Eldon Crosby, "Church Government in the Church Growth Movement" (Ph.D. diss., Baylor University, 1989).

[119]Another dissertation which is somewhat related is R. Stanton Norman, "A Critical Analysis of the Intentional Efforts of Baptists to Distinguish Themselves Theologically from Other Christian Denominations" (Ph.D. diss., Southwestern Baptist Theological Seminary, 1997).

the conservative resurgence in the Southern Baptist Convention as they believe that local churches are being coerced by the state or national convention. This can be seen in *Defining Baptist Convictions: Guidelines for the Twenty-First Century* where Rosalie Beck wrote a chapter titled "The Church is Free to Make Its Own Decisions under the Lordship of Christ." In this chapter, she appealed to the priesthood of the believer, soul competency, and "theo-democracy" in the local church to defend independence.[120]

Congregational form of Church Government

The literature discussing church government has been varied with books supporting elder rule in the local church from Presbyterians. One book read by many Baptists supporting elder rule and specifically denying the right of the congregation to appoint elders is that of Alexander Strauch. He opposes congregationalism saying, "Why, for example, should a member who attends church four or five times a year have a vote equal to that of a wise, experienced elder who knows the facts and wants only God's best for the church?"[121] Another prominent pastor who supports elder rule is John MacArthur. Wring writes, "MacArthur is a strong advocate of ruling elders."[122] MacArthur himself writes, "Scripture implies that anyone at a lower level of leadership involved in decision making as it relates to church

---

[120]Rosalie Beck, "The Church is Free to Make Its Own Decisions under the Lordship of Christ," in *Defining Baptist Convictions: Guidelines for the Twenty-First Century*, ed. Charles Deweese (Franklin: Providence, 1999), 137, stated, "The doctrine of autonomy demands a high degree of respect for differences among Baptists." Additionally, she believes that Baptists must be aware of coercion from associations, state or national conventions. She wrote, "Each has the right before God to chart its own course within the broad sweep of Baptist life; yet, this diversity unsettles some Baptists, and they respond by trying to coerce conformity. If autonomy truly is part of the Baptist faith, then coercion has no place" (136–7).

[121]Alexander Strauch, *Biblical Eldership* (Littleton: Lewis & Roth, 1988), 118.

[122]Wring, "An Examination of the Practice of Elder Rule in Selected Southern Baptist Churches in the Light of New Testament Teaching," 154.

polity or doctrine should be under the elders' authority."[123] Additionally, the Grace Community Church by-laws state that all authority is vested in the Board of Elders.[124]

Meanwhile, several current Baptist theologians believe that the New Testament supports the traditional Baptist position.[125] Among these two deserve notation. Norman includes a chapter titled "Distinctive Polity" in his work *More Than Just a Name*.[126] He states, "Baptist distinctives conclude that the only form of church government taught in the New Testament is Congregationalism."[127] In addition to Norman, Gerald Cowen's *Who Rules The Church?* supports the traditional Baptist position. He writes, "The democratic structure of congregational government is supported by a number of New Testament principles."[128]

The Officers in the New Testament Church

Current discussion over the officers in the New Testament church center on whether a plurality of elders or a primary elder is the best model. John Piper and Mark Dever support a plurality of elders.[129] However, this discussion can best be

---

[123]John MacArthur Jr., *Answering the Key Questions about Elders* (Panorama City: Grace to You, 1984), 30.

[124]Grace Community Church, Sun Valley, CA: "By-laws of Grace Community Church," (Sun Valley, CA: Grace Community Church, 1999). See article 4.

[125]Wring, "An Examination of the Practice of Elder Rule in Selected Southern Baptist Churches in the Light of New Testament Teaching," lists the following as some of those supporting congregation rule and two officers in the church: (1) Beverly Gray Allison, (2) Paige Patterson, (3) James T. Draper Jr., (4) Daniel Akin, (5) James Leo Garrett Jr., (6) Adrian Rogers, (7) Gerald Cowen, and (8) David Dockery. One additional name, Stan Norman, will be discussed since he has written on this issue.

[126]Norman, *More Than Just a Name*, 118–34.

[127]Ibid., 119. He also states, "Baptists believe that each church is independent of every other church."

[128]Cowen, Who Rules the Church? Examining Congregational Leadership and Church Government, 85.

[129]See Mark Dever, *A Display of God's Glory* (Washington: Center for Church Reform, 2001); and John Piper, *Biblical Eldership* (Minneapolis: Desiring God Ministries, 1999).

seen in two previously noted books. In the first, *Who Runs the Church? 4 Views on Church Government*, Samuel Waldron presents a case for "Plural-Elder Congregationalism" and Paige Patterson supports a "Single-Elder Congregationalism." The second book, *Perspectives on Church Government*, contains a chapter by Daniel Akin, "The Single-Elder-Led Church" and a chapter by James R. White, "The Plural-Elder-Led Church." These two books best demonstrate the difference between those supporting a plurality of elders and those supporting the primary elder position.

PENDLETON'S LASTING INFLUENCE

Although local church autonomy, congregational government, and two officers in the local church were not created by James Madison Pendleton, his lasting legacy includes the popularization of these views. Pendleton and the Landmark movement emphasized the local church and clearly articulated the Baptist position on local church issues. His lasting influence can be demonstrated by the continued use of his *Church Manual*,[130] and by his influence on important current Baptist leaders today. James Leo Garrett notes Pendleton multiple times in his defense for a congregation-led church.[131] Furthermore, Paige Patterson notes Pendleton

---

[130]F. M. McConnell reworked Pendleton manual in 1900. See F. M. McConnell, *Pendleton's Church Manual: Designed for the Use of Baptist Churches* (Dallas: B. J. Robert Book Company, 1900). Also J. E. Cobb wrote his *Baptist Church Manual* in 1941 and said in his preface, "The author of this manual recognizes that the manual most generally used among our particular group of Baptists is that of Dr. J. M. Pendleton." Pendleton's *Church Manual* continues to be in circulation. In 1955 a new publication of Pendleton's *Church Manual* was released by Judson Press, and in 1966 another new publication was released by Broadman Press. See James Madison Pendleton, *Church Manual* (Philadelphia: Judson Press, 1955); and James Madison Pendleton, *Baptist Church Manual* (Tennessee: Broadman Press 1966).

[131]Garrett, "The Congregation-Led Church: Congregational Polity," 178, 182.

in defense of single-elder congregationalism.[132] Thus, in two works both written in 2004, Pendleton's work continued to be noted. One must conclude that Pendleton's lasting contribution came through his focus on the local church with a defense of the Baptist position which stressed local church autonomy, congregational polity, and two officers—a position which Pendleton helped popularize.

---

[132]Patterson, "Single-Elder Congregationalism," 145.

CHAPTER 4

THE LORD'S SUPPER: WITH WHOM SHOULD WE COMMUNE?

Introduction

Although Pendleton never wrote a book specifically addressing the Lord's Supper, he discussed the different aspects of the ordinance in various works. A clear yet comprehensive analysis of Pendleton's writings on this topic must be divided into several headings. The headings utilized by this author will include: the institution of the Lord's Supper, the participants of the Lord's Supper, the elements of the Lord's Supper, the symbolism of the Lord's Supper, and the frequency of the Lord's Supper. Through these divisions, the author will attempt to summarize Pendleton's theological formulation while laying the proper foundation for evaluation of his work and comparison to other theologians.

After presenting Pendleton's thought, a noteworthy disagreement between Pendleton and Graves will occupy the author's attention. This disagreement involved two separate issues. First, Pendleton and Graves disagreed over the appropriateness of denominational communion. Pendleton saw no harm in the practice while Graves supported the strictest form of close communion. The second issue concerned whether close communion was part of Landmarkism. Pendleton held that Landmarkism centered on the refusal to recognize Pedobaptist ministers as Gospel ministers. Graves, however, included close communion as a tenet of Landmarkism. This discussion will hopefully clarify any existing misinformation concerning Pendleton's position on communion and create a reconsideration of whether close communion is a tenet of Landmarkism.

PENDLETON'S THEOLOGY OF THE LORD'S SUPPER

The Institution of the Lord's Supper

A complete understanding of the Lord's Supper must look not only in the New Testament, but also at the connection to the Old Testament institution of the Passover. Pendleton, using Paul's words to the Corinthians, "Christ our Passover is sacrificed for us," linked the Lord's Supper to the Passover.[1] The Jewish people celebrate the Passover once a year to commemorate the deliverance from Egypt which included the passing over of the angel from killing the firstborn son at the sight of blood on the doorpost. Christians partake of a similar supper which commemorates God's firstborn son who shed His blood through the death of the cross to deliver mankind from the consequences of sin.

This ordinance has been called many names. Some call it "the Lord's Supper because it was instituted in the evening—the Passover supper had just closed, when Jesus took bread and gave thanks."[2] It has also been known as "communion," "breaking of bread," and "feast." Pendleton specifically noted the term "eucharist" from the Greek word meaning to give thanks and the term "sacrament" from the Latin *sacramentum* meaning "an oath" which is taken to the Lord.[3]

The New Testament contains multiple and similar accounts of the Lord's Supper and indicates that its practice should be continued.[4] Pendleton noted one additional command to

---

[1] James Madison Pendleton, "Thoughts on the Lord's Supper: Number 1," *Tennessee Baptist* (October 29, 1859).
[2] James Madison Pendleton, "Thoughts on the Lord's Supper: Number 2," *Tennessee Baptist* (November 5, 1859).
[3] Ibid.
[4] James Madison Pendleton, "[Thoughts on] the Lord's Supper: Number 3," *Tennessee Baptist* (November 12, 1859). The Gospel accounts of the Lord's Supper can be found in Matt 26:26–30; Mark: 22–26; and Luke

partake of the Lord's Supper which he found in the great commission. He wrote, "The reference to the Lord's Supper is to be found in the third injunction of the commission—'teaching them to observe all things whatsoever I have commanded you.' Among these 'all things' were the Savior's directions in relation to communion at his table."[5] From Christ's command to celebrate the Lord's Supper, Pendleton concluded that any true church must properly administer the ordinance.

The Participants of the Lord's Supper

Two categories of participants exist in the ordinance of the Lord's Supper—the administrator and the recipient. Of these two, the administrator will be discussed first. Pendleton believed that the proper administrator of the Lord's Supper must be a properly ordained minister. For a person to be properly ordained, the person must qualify for ordination by being a Christian and having received proper baptism by a true church. Although people of other denominations would not agree with Pendleton's marks for a true church, some did believe that the administrator of the Supper should be properly ordained.[6] For example, Rosser stated, "The proper administrator is the man who has believed in the Lord Jesus Christ, been born again, called by the Holy Ghost to preach the gospel, and has been solemnly set apart by the church, according to its form of ordination, to dispense the word of God and to administer the holy sacraments."[7] Pendleton believed that the ordinances were to be governed by the

---

22:17–20. 1 Cor 11:26 indicates that the ordinance should be continued when it states, "as often as you eat this bread and drink this cup, you proclaim the Lord's death till He comes."

[5]James Madison Pendleton, "The Scriptural Meaning of the Term Church," *The Southern Baptist Review* 1 (February–March 1855): 66–7.

[6]James Madison Pendleton, "Old Landmark Methodists," *Tennessee Baptist* (December 13, 1856).

[7]Leonidas Rosser, *Baptism: Its Nature, Obligation, Mode, Subjects, and Benefits* (Richmond: By the author, 1853), 26.

church and administered by the person whom the church set aside for such duties.

In addition to having a proper administrator, the Lord's Supper must be administered to proper recipients. Pendleton believed that a person must meet two requirements before being a proper recipient. The spiritual requirement was salvation and the ritual requirement was baptism. Both of these requirements come from the fact that the Lord's Supper is a ordinance administered by the local church and members of the local church should be baptized Christians.

Pendleton limited the ordinance to believers and stated that it was a church ordinance. He wrote, "Almost all concede that the Lord's Supper is a church ordinance, and that its observance should be restricted to church members."[8] In addition to affirming that the Lord's Supper is a church ordinance, he condemned the administration of the ordinance outside the local church. He said, "We introduce this topic not to enlarge on it, but to take occasion to condemn the practice of administering the 'communion' to sick and dying persons at their homes. It is decidedly improper. Individuals as such have no right to the Lord's Supper. They must partake of it as a church—in no other way."[9] Again in another location he commented, "A few members of a Church, casually thrown together in a sick room, are not the Church. They cannot, therefore, truly celebrate the Lord's Supper."[10] Pendleton's emphasis on the local church can be seen clearly in this discussion.

In addition to the spiritual qualification for the Lord's Supper, there exists a ritual qualification—baptism. Pendleton claimed, "As to the relation of the ordinances to each other it is proper to say that Baptism precedes the Lord's Supper."[11] Because Pendleton contended that valid

---

[8]Pendleton, "The Scriptural Meaning of the Term Church," 67.
[9]Ibid., 70.
[10]James Madison Pendleton, "Query," *Tennessee Baptist* (June 25, 1859).
[11]Pendleton, "The Scriptural Meaning of the Term Church," 66.

baptism consisted of immersion of believers, this qualification met with objection. Allowing those from other denominations, including those baptized as infants, to participate in the Lord's Supper is commonly referred to as open communion. Pendleton disagreed with this practice.

Pendleton felt that Pedobaptists should not be allowed to commune with Baptists because they have never properly been baptized. "A refusal on the part of Baptists to unite in the Lord's Supper with Pedobaptists grows out of the fact that the latter have ever been considered by the former as unbaptized, and consequently without a scriptural church membership."[12] Pendleton continued, "Pedobaptists concede the precedence of baptism to the Lord's Supper. Indeed, their practice of infant baptism extorts the concession from them."[13] He also found support from William Wall of the Church of England who wrote, "Among all the absurdities

---

[12]James Madison Pendleton, *Christian Doctrines: A Compendium of Theology* (Philadelphia: American Baptist Publication Society, 1906), 361. All Baptists have not restricted Pedobaptists from communion. The most celebrated controversy was between William Kiffin and John Bunyan. Kiffin firmly stood for close communion while Bunyan argued that proper baptism was not a requirement for communion. In 1672 Bunyan wrote "A Confession of My Faith" to which Kiffin responded in 1673 with his work *Serious Reflections*. The debate continued as Bunyan answered in *Differences in Judgement Concerning Water Baptism No Bar to Communion* in 1673. Kiffin's final response came in *A Sober Discourse of Right to Church Communion* published in 1681. For Bunyan's two works, see John Bunyan, *The Miscellaneous Works of John Bunyan*, vol. 4, ed. T. L. Underwood (Clarendon Press: Oxford, 1989), 131–88, 189–264. For Kiffin's work, see William Kiffin, *Some Serious Reflections on that Part of Mr. Bunyan's Confession of Faith Touching Church Communion with Unbaptized Persons* (London: Printed for Francis Smith, 1673); and William Kiffin, *A Sober Discourse of Right to Church Communion* (London: Geo. Larkin, 1681). For a discussion of the controversy, see McBeth, *The Baptist Heritage*, 81–3. Timothy George, "Controversy and Communion: The Limits of Baptist Fellowship from Bunyan to Spurgeon," in *The Gospel in the World*, ed. D. W. Bebbington (Waynesboro: Paternoster, 2002): 38–58, noted John Bunyan, Robert Hall, and Charles Spurgeon as three main proponents for open communion in Baptist life.

[13]Pendleton, *Christian Doctrines*, 364.

that ever were held, none ever maintained that any person should partake of communion before he was baptised."[14]

Continuing to substantiate the claim that baptism should come before partaking of the Lord's Supper, Pendleton referred to Matt 28:18–19. This commission demonstrates the fact that discipleship should be followed by baptism which is the first outward manifestation of the internal relationship. In Pendleton's words, "Now, according to this commission, it is evident that the process of discipleship is to be followed so immediately by the administration of baptism as to leave no room for an observance of the Lord's Supper to intervene. Baptism is the first thing after a person is discipled to Christ."[15] He wrote elsewhere, "Where is there room for communion between faith and baptism, when baptism is the divinely appointed method of professing faith?"[16] Pendleton then discussed several conversion stories in Acts demonstrating a high probability that the Lord's Supper was not observed between the profession of faith and the act of baptism. He concluded, "The whole tenor of the New Testament indicates that the priority of baptism to communion is not an accidental but a divinely established priority. This cannot be successfully denied."[17] Additionally Pendleton argued for the priority of baptism because, "The meeting of a *church* is indispensable to a scriptural observance of the solemn rite."[18] Since baptism is prerequisite to membership in the visible church, none but baptized believers can partake of the Lord's Supper.

---

[14]William Wall, *The History of Infant Baptism*, vol. 2 (Oxford: Oxford University Press, 1862), 259. Pendleton quoted him in *Christian Doctrines*, 364–5.
[15]Pendleton, *Christian Doctrines*, 363.
[16]James Madison Pendleton, "[Thoughts on] the Lord's Supper: Number 21," *Tennessee Baptist* (February 9, 1861).
[17]Ibid.
[18]Pendleton, *Christian Doctrines*, 360.

The Elements of the Lord's Supper

Throughout history there have been at least three views on what happens to the elements during the Lord's Supper—transubstantiation, consubstantiation, and no change. Pendleton understood that the proper elements were unleavened bread and wine or juice from the fruit of the vine. This was not debated; however, whether the elements underwent a change had been debated for centuries.[19]

Pendleton first discussed the doctrine of transubstantiation. He summarized its teaching by writing, "In view of this decree it is plain that Romanists believe the soul and divinity of Christ as well as his body and blood to be in the sacrament of the Eucharist."[20] While discussing the change, Thomas Aquinas stated, "This is done by divine power in this sacrament; for the whole substance of the bread and wine is changed into the whole substance of the body and blood of Christ. Hence this is not a formal but a substantial conversion which is not due to any natural movement; it therefore merits a name of its own, and may be called *transubstantiation*."[21] Pendleton responded by saying that if these elements truly contain the divinity of Christ, they should be worshiped; however, Pendleton believed the elements did not contain such divinity and that the Papists may be guilty of idolatry. This view results from a strictly

---

[19] For a good discussion of the debate, see Gary Macy, *The Theologies of the Eucharist in the Early Scholastic Period* (Oxford: Clarendon Press, 1984), 18–43.

[20] James Madison Pendleton, "Thoughts on the Lord's Supper: Number 4," *Tennessee Baptist* (November 26, 1859). J. H. Srawley, "Introduction," in *St. Ambrose "On the Mysteries" and the Treatise on the Sacraments by an Unknown Author*, trans. T. Thompson, ed. J. H. Srawley (New York: Macmillan, 1919), 34–5, stated, "The conception of a 'conversion' of the elements into the body and blood of Christ was probably derived by Ambrose . . . from Greek sources. It appears for the first time in the *Catecheses* of Cyril of Jerusalem, and was elaborated with a special theory of his own by Gregory of Nyssa."

[21] Thomas Aquinas, *The Blessed Sacrament and the Mass*, trans. Rev. F. O'Neill (Maryland: Newman Press, 1955), 20.

literal interpretation of "this is my body," whereas Pendleton attempted to demonstrate that in many places the Lord used metaphorical language. After citing "I am the door," "I am the way," "I am the true vine," "I am the light of the world," and others, he said, "The verb *to be* is often used by Christ to signify *represents*."[22] Thus, the bread represents the body, and the wine represents the blood.[23]

In introducing the view expressed by Martin Luther of consubstantiation, Pendleton stated, "Often one error leads to another, and sometimes the renunciation of one leads to the adoption of another."[24] Luther did not believe with the Romanists that the bread and the wine are transformed and become the body and blood of our Lord. However, Luther continued to maintain that Christ's body and blood were present. Luther rejected the Catholic doctrine when he wrote concerning transubstantiation, "When I learned later what church it was that had decreed this, namely the Thomistic—that is, the Aristotelian church—I grew bolder, and after floating in a sea of doubt, I at last found rest for my conscience in the above view, namely, that it is real bread and real wine, in which Christ's real flesh and real blood are

---

[22]Pendleton, "Thoughts on the Lord's Supper: Number 4." This was also the first of Zwingli's two main objections to the doctrine. He wrote that the "sacrament is the sign of a holy thing" and that "the sign and the thing signified cannot be one and the same." See Zwingli, "On the Lord's Supper," in *Zwingli and Bullinger: Library of Christian Classics*, vol. 14, trans. G. W. Bromiley (Philadelphia: Westminster Press, 1953), 188. Zwingli concluded that "this is my body" is "not literal but figurative and symbolical" (199).

[23]This debate can be traced back to Ratramnus and Radbertus. Radbertus wrote first supporting the traditional view of transubstantiation. Shortly after, Ratramnus responded in A. D. 843 at the request of Charles the Bald, King of the Franks, and refuted the claim that the elements changed substantively. See Pascasius Radbertus, *De Corpore et Sanguine Domini* (Turnholti: Typographi Brepols, 1969); and Ratramnus, *De Corpore et Sanguine Domini* (London: North-Holland, 1974).

[24]James Madison Pendleton, "[Thoughts on] the Lord's Supper: Number 5," *Tennessee Baptist* (December 10, 1859).

present in no other way and to no less a degree than the others assert them to be under their accidents."[25] Concerning the change, Luther said, "the bread is changed into his true natural body and the wine into his natural true blood."[26] He addressed Zwingli and others who opposed his view by writing, "Let them go, therefore, and let us adhere to the words as they read: that the body of Christ is present in the bread and that his blood is truly present in the wine. This does not mean that he is not present in other places also with his body and blood, for in believing hearts he is completely present with his body and blood."[27] From this quote, it is evident that Luther attributed the quality of ubiquity to the body and blood of Christ in conjunction with his understanding of "this is my body."

Pendleton listed many of the same objections against Consubstantiation which he listed against Transubstantiation. He stated, "Both doctrines presuppose the presence of the Savior's body in different places at the same time—a notion in conflict with our fundamental conception of material substances."[28] He continued to say that Consubstantiation represents a poorer interpretation than Transubstantiation. Transubstantiation takes a literal interpretation, memorial a symbolic, but Consubstantiation

---

[25]Martin Luther, "The Babylonian Captivity of the Church," in *Martin Luther's Basic Theological Writings*, ed. Timothy Lull (Minneapolis: Fortress Press, 1989), 285.

[26]Martin Luther, "The Sacrament of the Body and Blood of Christ," in *Martin Luther's Basic Theological Writings*, ed. Timothy Lull (Minneapolis: Fortress Press, 1989), 252.

[27]Martin Luther, "The Sacrament of the Body and Blood—Against the Fanatics," in *Martin Luther's Basic Theological Writings*, ed. Timothy Lull (Minneapolis: Fortress Press, 1989), 325. For a discussion of the debate between Luther and Zwingli over this issue, see Timothy George, *Theology of the Reformers* (Nashville: Broadman & Holman, 1988), 144–58.

[28]Pendleton, "[Thoughts on] the Lord's Supper: Number 5." This was the second of Zwingli's two main arguments. He believed that the ascension of Christ did away with the possibility of a literal presence of Christ's body in the elements. Zwingli attributed omnipresence only to the divine nature of Christ and not the human. See, Zwingli, "On the Lord's Supper," 213.

takes a third interpretation, that Christ meant to say, "This contains my body."[29]

Pendleton believed that the bread and the wine in the Lord's Supper are a representation of the body and blood of Christ. In partaking, Christians do nothing more than commemorate the broken body and shed blood of the Lord Jesus. In distinguishing Baptist identity from others, he stated:

> In their views of the two ordinances of the gospel, I believe Baptists stand alone. They are the only people in the world who insist that those, and those alone, who by faith in Christ have been brought into a state of justification have anything to do with either baptism or the Lord's Supper. They deny to these ordinances all saving efficacy, and attribute to them only a symbolic significance. This is the scriptural view of the matter.[30]

He further commented, "By a figure we may be said to eat his flesh in eating the bread, and to drink his blood in drinking the wine. Literally and truly we partake of bread and wine as memorials of his body and blood . . . ."[31] This we do "in remembrance" of Christ. Lastly, Pendleton noted Paul's teaching that "a discernment of the body and blood of the Lord Jesus is indispensable to a proper celebration of the

---

[29]Pendleton, "[Thoughts on] the Lord's Supper: Number 5."

[30]Ibid. This would not be the view of all Baptists. Some Baptists would include a spiritual presence. The Second London Confession includes in Chapter 30, article 7, "Worthy receivers, outwardly partaking of the visible Elements in this Ordinance, do then also inwardly by faith, really and indeed, yet not carnally, and corporally, but spiritually receive, and feed upon Christ crucified & all the benefits of his death: the Body and Blood of *Christ*, being then not corporally, or carnally, but spiritually present to the faith of Believers, in that Ordinance, as the Elements themselves are to their outward senses."

[31]James Madison Pendleton, "[Thoughts on] the Lord's Supper: Number 6," *Tennessee Baptist* (December 17, 1859).

sacred Supper," and that includes the ability "to perceive his body and blood as represented by the bread and wine."[32]

To summarize, Pendleton, believing that the Lord's Supper is a memorial, focused primarily on remembrance of Christ. He wrote, "The Lord's Supper is a memorial of the death of Christ. The bread broken represents his body crucified—the wine poured forth represents the blood shed on Calvary."[33] This view centered on two beliefs. First, Christ's human body and blood could not be present in multiple locations at one time. Second, "this is my body" should be taken figuratively and emphasis placed on "this do in remembrance."

The Symbolism of the Lord's Supper

Pendleton stressed the symbolism present in the Lord's Supper believing that a complete understanding would make the ordinance more meaningful. For example, the Lord's Supper should bring forth mental images such as beholding the redeemer's death.[34] He commented, "If ever the tragedy of Calvary should engross the thoughts of the Christian to the exclusion of every other topic, it is when he sits at the table of the Lord. Then the death of his Lord should monopolize all the power of memory."[35] A complete understanding recognized that the Lord's Supper also symbolized: (1) the amazing love of God, (2) the justice of God, (3) the holiness of the divine character, (4) the wisdom of God, and (5) the evil of sin.[36] Pendleton believed that by

---

[32] James Madison Pendleton, "Thoughts on the Lord's Supper: Number 7," *Tennessee Baptist* (January 7, 1960).

[33] Pendleton, "The Scriptural Meaning of the Term Church," 66.

[34] James Madison Pendleton, "Thoughts on the Lord's Supper: Number 8," *Tennessee Baptist* (January 21, 1860).

[35] James Madison Pendleton, *Baptist Church Manual* (Nashville: Broadman & Holman, 1966), 89.

[36] For theses emphasis, see the following articles in corresponding order. James Madison Pendleton, "[Thoughts on] the Lord's Supper: Number 10," *Tennessee Baptist* (March 3, 1860). James Madison Pendleton, "[Thoughts on] the Lord's Supper: Number 11," *Tennessee Baptist* (March 31, 1860). James Madison Pendleton, "[Thoughts on] the Lord's Supper: Number 12,"

focusing on the symbolism present in the Lord's Supper, the event could be more meaningful.

The Frequency of the Lord's Supper

When asked about the frequency of the Lord's Supper, Pendleton responded that the Bible does not dictate how often one should partake. He went on to say, "If the Scriptures do not inform us how often we are to come to the Table of the Lord, every Church must exercise its own best judgment in the matter."[37] However, he warns that the greatest danger in frequency is partaking of the supper too seldom.[38] Additionally, Pendleton believed that Scripture did not comment on the proper day for partaking of the Lord's Supper. He wrote, "The ordinance was not instituted on the first day of the week, and there is nothing wrong in its observance any day of the week. Still, the first day of the week, being set apart for religious worship, is doubtless the most appropriate day."[39]

DISAGREEMENT WITH GRAVES OVER DENOMINATIONAL COMMUNION

In order to discuss the disagreement between Graves and Pendleton on the issue of communion, this author will first discuss their individual positions and then their debate. They specifically disagreed over denominational communion—the

---

Tennessee Baptist (April 7, 1860). James Madison Pendleton, "[Thoughts on] the Lord's Supper: Number 13," *Tennessee Baptist* (April 28, 1860). James Madison Pendleton, "[Thoughts on] the Lord's Supper: Number 14," *Tennessee Baptist* (May 12, 1860).

[37]James Madison Pendleton, "Queries and Answers," *Tennessee Baptist* (July 3, 1858).

[38]Pendleton's work did not address the concern that the Lord's Supper might become too common and ritualistic. He apparently felt that the Baptist tendency was not to practice the Lord's Supper often enough.

[39]James Madison Pendleton, "Queries and Answers," *Tennessee Baptist* (July 3, 1858).

intercommunion of Baptists.[40] First, Graves's close communion position which stated that Baptists should not commune with other Baptists will be presented. Second, Pendleton's allowance of denominational communion which meant that each individual Baptist church may invite other Baptists to join in communion as a matter of courtesy will be discussed. Third, this author will demonstrate that Pendleton recognized the differences and addressed them. In conclusion, this section will evaluate both positions.

Graves's Position

Graves developed his position over a period of time moving from the acceptance of denominational communion outside of the local church to a strict view of close communion.[41] When he first arrived in Kentucky, Graves participated in the observance of communion at an associational meeting.[42] Graves would soon come to believe that the Lord's Supper was a church ordinance and should not be practiced at associational meetings. He maintained that Baptist churches could invite members of other Baptist churches to communion if the church desired to do so. He said, "The members of one church (though of the same faith and order) can come to the communion of another only by an act of courtesy and not by *right*, for each church is independent."[43] By 1855, Graves would modify his view no longer supporting the celebrating of communion at associational meetings.[44]

---

[40]For the definition of the terms used relating to communion, see "Terms of Communion" in the introduction of this dissertation.

[41]James E. Taulman, "Baptism and the Lord's Supper: As Viewed by A. C. Dayton, J. M. Pendleton, and J. R. Graves," *The Quarterly Review* (April 1975): 67.

[42]O. L. Hailey, *J. R. Graves: Life, Times and Teachings* (Nashville: O. L. Hailey, 1929), 50.

[43]J. R. Graves, "Beliefs," *Tennessee Baptist* (February 8, 1867).

[44]See T. A. Patterson, "The Theology of J. R. Graves, and Its Influences on Southern Baptist Life" (Th.D. diss., Southwestern Baptist Theological Seminary, 1944), 222; James E. Tull, *High-Church Baptists in the South* (Macon: Mercer Press, 2000), 35; and James E. Taulman, "Baptism and the

By April 24, 1875, Graves modified his view to a more stringent position. He no longer allowed denominational communion. He wrote, "No Church is any more warranted to extend an invitation to the members of other churches to commune with her, than to vote in her church meetings, since each act is purely a local church act."[45] In addition to this publication, Graves speaking in 1880 stated that he had settled his mind on the issue of communion and had decided that only the members of the local congregation should participate.[46] Graves later said of his participation in communion at an associational meeting:

> We came into the state from Kentucky in 1845, and this was the second meeting of the Association we had attended. We knew no better. We deferred without a question to the opinions of our grave and reverend seigniors. But this very act awakened investigation and the columns of our paper abundantly show that we openly opposed this associational communion and declared for its observance as a church ordinance. . . .[47]

This article demonstrates Graves's disapproval of communion at associational meetings.

Graves clearly articulated his mature thought in his book *Intercommunion: Inconsistent, Unscriptural and Productive of Evil* written in 1881.[48] In fact, this work contains a

---

Lord's Supper: As Viewed by A. C. Dayton, J. M. Pendleton, and J. R. Graves," *The Quarterly Review* (April 1975): 68.

[45]J. R. Graves, "Beliefs," *Tennessee Baptist* (April 24, 1875).

[46]As in J. J. D. Renfroe, *Vindication of the Communion of Baptist Churches* (Selma: John West, 1882), 13–14.

[47]J. R. Graves, "Reply to S. H. Ford," *Tennessee Baptist* (June 16, 1883).

[48]Graves wrote at least three books on the Lord's Supper. His most detailed work is *Intercommunion: Inconsistent, Unscriptural, and Productive of Evil* (Memphis: Baptist Book House, 1881). His other works include: *The Lord's Supper: A Church Ordinance, and So Observed by the Apostolic Churches* (Texarkana: Baptist Sunday School Committee, 1881)

chapter entitled, "The Inconsistencies, and the Evils of Intercommunion Among Baptists."[49] Graves provided two chapters specifically addressing denominational communion. First, he discussed the evils of intercommunion among Baptists by providing four inconsistencies and nine evils associated with intercommunion among Baptists. Second, Graves addressed certain objections to his position. One of the objections he chose to address was from Pendleton.

Graves's central objection to denominational communion rested in the fact that it reached outside of the local assembly. The inclusion of those not members of that particular local assembly moves the ordinance from a local church ordinance to a denominational ordinance which results in the local assembly having no ordinance of its own.[50] Additionally, the inclusion of members outside the local assembly removes the ability of the local church to govern properly the ordinance.[51] Most of the evils of denominational communion which Graves noted related to the proper practice of church discipline. For example, if one church placed a member under discipline and another church allowed the member to partake in communion, then not only has church discipline suffered, but according to Graves, the local church's authority in discipline and the cooperation between the two churches has been injured.

In another chapter, entitled "Objections to Church Communion Reviewed," Graves set out to address three objections. He stated those objections as: "(1) Paul and his eight companions, belonging to different churches, communed with the church at Troas; (2) a local church has the RIGHT to invite members of other churches to her table; and (3) it tends to destroy fellowship between the churches,

---

and *What Is It to Eat and Drink Unworthily?* (Texarkana: Baptist Sunday School Board, 1881).

[49]Graves, *Intercommunion*, 307–23.
[50]Ibid., 308.
[51]Ibid., 309.

and creates an extreme independency."[52] Graves attempted to refute the first objection, but when coming to Pendleton's objection, Graves changed the issue. In the text under his second heading, he only addressed part of Pendleton's argument. Graves worded the objection as follows: "It is objected that should the Supper be observed as a church ordinance, a majority of our preachers could not commune with the churches they preach to, since they serve three, four, and sometimes five."[53] To this one part Graves responded that one pastor serving several churches is a departure from the apostolic practice. Graves spent less than one page dealing with this objection. Thus, Graves never refuted Pendleton's complete argument but only one application of his argument. The reason for this may lie in the fact that a complete rebuttal of Pendleton's view could be seen as diminishing the autonomy of the local church by taking away the "right" of a church to invite to the Lord's Supper those who are scripturally eligible. Graves's most persuasive argument focused on close communion being necessary for the proper practice of church discipline.

Pendleton's Position

As Pendleton's doctrine of the Lord's Supper has already been summarily presented, this section will focus solely on his views pertaining to intercommunion among Baptists. It will be demonstrated that Pendleton believed a Baptist church may invite a member of another Baptist church to partake of Communion. He did this while still maintaining that Communion is a church ordinance and not a denominational ordinance. He stated, "The doctrine of

---

[52]Ibid., 340.
[53]Ibid., 348–9. Pendleton could have developed this objection because he served multiple churches in the early part of his ministry. The arrangement with these churches was that he would preach one Saturday and two Sundays in the month to each of the Hopkinsville and Bethel churches. See Spencer, *A History of Kentucky Baptists*, 524.

Baptists has ever been, that the Lord's Supper is a Church ordinance...."⁵⁴

Pendleton's focus on the church as the guardian of the ordinance and his focus on church independence impacts his formulation of denominational communion. He began by stating, "No member of a Baptist church can claim it as a right, to commune with any other Baptist Church."⁵⁵ This proposition rests on two facts. First, the church is guardian of the purity of the ordinances, and second, "every church is an independent body—a democratic sovereignty under Christ."⁵⁶ Pendleton believed the purity of the church as well as of the Lord's Supper was to be preserved by a regenerate church membership. He acknowledged that sometimes mistakes are made since church members cannot know the heart of a person. Thus, a church must practice church discipline in order to maintain a regenerate membership. Because the church must practice church discipline, Pendleton stated, "The truth is, no church can of right be required to invite to its communion those over whom it has no power of discipline."⁵⁷ Thus, church governance and independence control the administration of the Lord's Supper.

---

⁵⁴James Madison Pendleton, *Three Reasons Why I Am a Baptist with a Fourth Reason Added on Communion* (St. Louis: National Baptist Publishing, 1856), 177.

⁵⁵Ibid., 206. This discussion is omitted from Pendleton's later revision of this work, and has been misunderstood by some historians. For example, William Brackney, *The Baptists* (New York: Greenwood Press, 1988), 65, quoted from this section in *Three Reasons* to support Graves's position of closed communion and rejection of denominational communion. The context of Brackney's discussion gives the impression that Pendleton also rejected denominational communion which is not true. Pendleton in these statements merely supported the local authority of the church and the fact that no other church could impose rules or make demands on a local assembly.

⁵⁶Pendleton, Three Reasons Why I Am a Baptist with a Fourth Added on Communion, 206.

⁵⁷Ibid., 209.

While no person can claim denominational communion as a right, Pendleton did support it as a matter of courtesy. On inviting members of other Baptist churches he wrote, "It [the church] may do so, and ought to do so as a matter of *courtesy*, but only as a matter of courtesy."[58] Again emphasizing the church's authority, Pendleton added that a church may extend the invitation through courtesy on one occasion and withhold the invitation on another. The decision belongs to the church. Additionally, church independence means that no church may force another church to accept its membership. Despite the emphasis on church authority, Pendleton implied that intercommunion among Baptists was a common practice. He commented:

> This love prompts the exercise of the Christian courtesy already referred to, and makes it delightful to sit down with our fellow-Christians at the table of the Lord. And while we deny to members of Baptist Churches of the same faith and order with ourselves the *right* to claim admittance to the Lord's Table in any church except that to which they belong, nothing is more common than cordial invitations by courtesy.[59]

Thus, Pendleton allowed for denominational communion while upholding the autonomy of the local church and the importance of church discipline.

Pendleton omitted the discussion of intercommunion among Baptists from his *Distinctive Principles of Baptists*. Probably, his omission resulted from the publication of Graves's view in 1881—just one year before Pendleton's book was printed. After the debate, Pendleton may have concluded that his view on denominational communion was not a Baptist distinctive. However, this omission should not be seen as a change in his view. Pendleton made it clear in a letter to J. J. D. Renfroe that he continued to hold the same position and

---

[58]Ibid.
[59]Ibid., 210–11.

that he disagreed with Graves over the issue.[60] Pendleton wrote this letter in the same year that he published his *Distinctive Principles of Baptists*. This author will now discuss that letter and the disagreement with Graves.

The Disagreement Discussed

A two-fold disagreement with Graves existed. First, Pendleton held that denominational communion among Baptists was not detrimental. Second, Pendleton believed that this issue was not part of the Landmark question.[61] The Landmark question centered on the recognition of Pedobaptist preachers as gospel ministers. This disagreement can be seen in a letter written to J. J. D. Renfroe. Pendleton made several assertions which demonstrated disagreement with Graves.

This letter demonstrates four important facts concerning Pendleton. First, he disagreed with Graves over the question of denominational communion. Pendleton stated, "The evils which Bro. Graves thinks results from intercommunion among Baptists, I have never seen. True, I have not been a Baptist so long as some others, for it is only fifty-three years this month since I was baptized."[62] Pendleton did not recognize the evils to which Graves alluded concerning denominational communion.

Second, Pendleton's main argument for his position came from the ordination of preachers. He stated:

---

[60]James Madison Pendleton, "Introduction," in *Vindication of the Communion of Baptist Churches*, by J. J. D. Renfroe (Selma: John L. West, 1882).

[61]James Tull states concerning the difference between Pendleton and Graves, "J. M. Pendleton always stood closer to the commonly held Baptist views of his time than either Graves or Dayton." One of the areas Tull noted was denominational communion. See Tull, *High-Church Baptists in the South*, 44.

[62]Pendleton, "Introduction," in Vindication of the Communion of Baptist Churches, 6.

> Bro. Graves was ordained by a church in Jessamine County, Kentucky. I should like to know how he has been recognized as a preacher by a thousand other Baptist churches except through the courtesy accorded to the action of the ordaining church. . . . There is much force in the courtesy argument, and without it ordinations, through their frequency, would become insufferably burdensome.⁶³

From the argument for courtesy, Pendleton drew his conclusions about denominational communion.

Third, Pendleton disagreed with Graves over the extent of Landmarkism. He stated, "I cannot close it without saying that I deeply regret the effort made by many to make this non-intercommunion theory a part of the 'old landmark' question. It has no legitimate connection with it. You will permit me to say that a non-recognition of Pedobaptist preachers as gospel ministers is the leading idea in Landmarkism. I certainly ought to know this. . . ."⁶⁴ As one of the leading supporters of Landmarkism, Pendleton felt that he knew its main tenets.

Fourth, Pendleton confirmed that he never abandoned Landmarkism. He wrote, "I adhere, as in other years, to the Landmark doctrine. I do not believe that Baptists can consistently recognize Pedo-Baptist preachers by pulpit exchanges, etc. Nor can they ever give full force to their protest against the errors of Pedobaptism while such recognition is given. This seems to me as clear as the light of day."⁶⁵ Thus, Pendleton never relinquished his belief in Landmarkism.

This author has been unable to find any response by Graves to Pendleton's letter or to the book by J. J. D. Renfroe. However, Pendleton's letter and Graves's earlier book clearly

---

⁶³Ibid., 6–7.
⁶⁴Ibid., 7–8.
⁶⁵Ibid., 8.

establish the acknowledgment by both sides of a difference of opinion on this issue. In evaluation of this disagreement, both Graves and Pendleton felt that they were supporting the biblical position. Graves's emphasis on the local church and focus on church discipline provided good reasons for holding to close communion. Similarly, Pendleton emphasized the autonomy of the local church to make the decision on who could participate so long the participant met the scriptural qualifications. Pendleton's secondary emphasis was that Christian courtesy should be extended. This disagreement becomes an important disagreement primarily because close communion in recent publications has been seen as a Landmark tenet.[66] However, this disagreement should cause the association of close communion and Landmarkism to be reexamined.

PENDLETON AMONG HIS CONTEMPORARIES

Pendleton understood that his position met with mixed reviews. He would encounter opposition from Pedobaptists who did not like the implication that their baptisms were not valid. He would encounter opposition from Baptists who either accepted other forms of baptism as valid or did not see valid baptism as a prerequisite to communion. As proper baptism has already been discussed, this chapter will focus on those who denied proper baptism as a prerequisite to communion. Additionally, the issue of denominational communion will be addressed demonstrating that Baptists did not have a unified position.

---

[66]Bill Leonard, *Baptist Ways: A History* (Valley Forge: Judson Press, 2003), 183–4, claims that closed communion is part of the basic beliefs of Landmarkism. Additionally, William Brackney, *The Baptists* (New York: Greenwood Press, 1988), 65, included a Pendleton quote in a section supporting Graves's view of close communion which implies Pendleton's agreement. Lastly, H. Leon McBeth, *The Baptist Heritage* (Nashville: Broadman Press, 1987), 449, stated, "Pendleton's [*Church*] *Manual* advances Landmark views of Baptist life on closed communion, alien immersion, and Baptist successionism."

Pendleton's Interaction with Other Baptist Contemporaries

Pendleton experienced two separate disagreements with Baptists over communion. The first difference came over denominational communion and the second over open communion. Pendleton spent little time debating denominational communion and his arguments have already been summarized in his debate with Graves over the issue. One other person with whom Pendleton disagreed on this issue was W. W. Gardner. In his work *Church Communion, As Practiced by the Baptists, Explained and Defended*, Gardner wrote, "Now, as church fellowship grows out of mutual church relations, and hence is restricted to the members of each particular church, so *Church Communion* grows out of church fellowship, and is necessarily *limited* to those *church acts and privileges* which belong to the members of the same particular church."[67] Thus, Gardner supported Graves's position. Graves was well aware of this fact, and included a letter from Gardner in his work on communion.[68]

However, Pendleton's efforts centered on convincing Baptists that open communion was not right. He said, "It is not, however, my purpose to refer in this connection so much to Pedobaptists as to those Baptists who deny the precedence of baptism to the Lord's Supper."[69] One person to whom he was referring was Robert Hall and his work *On Terms of Communion*.[70] He commented concerning Hall, "But while Mr. Hall considered Pedobaptists unbaptized, he insisted on their right as *unbaptized* persons to come to the Lord's Table. He did not admit baptism to be a prerequisite to the Lord's

---

[67]W. W. Gardner, Church Communion, As Practiced by the Baptists, Explained and Defended (Cincinnati: George E. Stevens, 1873), 17–8.

[68]Graves, *Intercommunion*, 352.

[69]James Madison Pendleton, "[Thoughts on] the Lord's Supper: Number 19," *Tennessee Baptist* (October 27, 1860).

[70]Robert Hall, On Terms of Communion: with a Particular View to the Case of the Baptists and Pedobaptists (np: G. J. Loomis, 1816).

Table."[71] Hall argued that John's baptism was different than that instituted by Christ and that modern day baptism did not occur until after the first Lord's Supper had been celebrated.[72] Hall concluded "that baptism, considered as a christian institution, had no existence during the personal ministry of our Saviour. . . ." and thus the original participants of the Lord's Supper were unbaptized.[73] Pendleton replied, "To demolish all that Robert Hall ever wrote in favor of 'Mixed Communion,' it is only necessary to show the scriptural priority of baptism to the Lord's Supper."[74] Pendleton's attempt to establish the precedence of baptism has been discussed and will be briefly revisited later.

Wriothesley Noel in his *Essay on Christian Baptism* also argued that infant baptism was wrong but did not grant the necessity of proper baptism for communion. Noel believed that many Pedobaptists were good servants of Christ and as such should be admitted to the Lord's table.[75] He commented, "We are called to receive all Christ's disciples, notwithstanding their errors, as Christ has received us, notwithstanding ours."[76] Thus, Noel rejected the necessity of baptism to participation in the Lord's Supper.

Perhaps Pendleton's most famous opposition came from Charles Spurgeon. Pendleton quoted Spurgeon as writing, "We believe restricted fellowship to be impossible among the saints of God. With all the church we do and must

---

[71]Pendleton, *Christian Doctrines*, 361.
[72]Robert Hall, *The Works of Robert Hall*, ed. Olinthus Gregory, vol. 3 (London: George Routledge and Sons, 1866), 15.
[73]Ibid., 31.
[74]Pendleton, Baptist Church Manual, 92.
[75]Wriothesley Noel, *Essay on Christian Baptism* (New York: Harper & Brothers, 1850), 288. Noel left the church of England in 1848 to become a Baptist minister. He was pastor of St. John's Street Chapel, Bedford Row until 1868.
[76]Ibid., 289.

commune."⁷⁷ In another sermon, Spurgeon stated, "Certain brethren restrict their communion in the outward ordinance, and they think they have good reasons for doing so; but I am unable to see the force of their reasoning."⁷⁸ Spurgeon allowed all Christians to participate in the Lord's Supper.

Pendleton fought vehemently against such views, and others fought with him. Pendleton took every opportunity to recognize those with whom he agreed.⁷⁹ In support of his position, he discussed the baptism of the disciples before the institution of the Lord's supper. He wrote, "Baptism was administered by the direction and under the observation of Christ during his personal ministry *before* he instituted the sacred supper. Why before? Was it not because the Savior intended to establish the priority of baptism to communion? To what other conclusion can we come?"⁸⁰ Additionally, Pendleton referred to the commission of Christ to establish the precedence of baptism.⁸¹ Pendleton was not alone in his opposition to open communion and support of denominational communion.

Of the many works which agreed with Pendleton's position, John Dagg is perhaps the most prominent. Dagg in his book *Manual of Church Order* stated that a person must be baptized in order to commune. He wrote, "Why should baptism be trodden under foot, to open the way of access to

---

⁷⁷James Madison Pendleton, "Spurgeon's Views of Communion," *Tennessee Baptist* (December 24, 1859). The quote from Spurgeon came from a letter he sent in response to inquiries over his view of communion. This letter was reprinted in what appears to be its entirety in Pendleton's article.

⁷⁸Charles Spurgeon, *12 Sermons on the Lord's Supper* (Grand Rapids: Baker Book House, 1980), 15–6.

⁷⁹James Madison Pendleton, "Open Communion Shown to be Unscriptural and Deleterious by John L. Waller: a Review," *Tennessee Baptist* (July 30, 1859).

⁸⁰James Madison Pendleton, "[Thoughts on] the Lord's Supper: Number 20," *Tennessee Baptist* (January 12, 1861).

⁸¹Pendleton, "The Scriptural Meaning of the Term Church," 66–7.

the eucharist?"[82] Additionally, Dagg held a similar position on denominational communion by stating, "This transient communion is now practised. The Lord's supper is properly a church ordinance; but an individual, duly qualified to be admitted to membership in a church, may be admitted for the time as a member, and received to transient communion, without any departure from the design of the institution."[83] Thus, Dagg and Pendleton were in complete agreement on this issue.

Hiscox in his *New Directory for Baptist Churches* agreed with Pendleton by supporting that Baptist should not commune with Pedobaptists.[84] In addition, Hiscox also supported the argument from courtesy. He wrote, "If the members of sister churches are invited to partake, it is an act of courtesy proffered, and not a right allowed."[85] He further emphasized that the autonomy of the church required that each church make the decision which should be carried out by the administrator. Thus, Pendleton and Hiscox agreed on the issue.

Pendleton's Interaction with Non-Baptist Contemporaries

Pendleton's major point of interaction with non-Baptists came by trying to establish that baptism must come before the Lord's Supper. If Pendleton could establish that baptism must come before the Lord's Supper, then he could defend that Baptists should not commune with Pedobaptists because Pedobaptists have never been properly baptized. Thus, Pendleton quoted Doddridge who said, "It is certain that Christians in general have always been spoken of, by the most ancient Fathers, as baptized persons. And it is also

---

[82]John Dagg, *Manual of Church Order* (Charleston: Southern Baptist Publication Society, 1858; reprint, Harrisonburg: Gano Books, 1990), 225.

[83]Ibid., 214.

[84]Edward Hiscox, *The New Directory for Baptist Churches* (Philadelphia: Judson Press, 1894), 445–68.

[85]Ibid., 140.

certain that, as far as our knowledge of primitive antiquity extends, no unbaptized person received the Lord's Supper."[86]

He further quoted from Hibbard, a Methodist author that wrote *Christian Baptism*. Pendleton included the following quote in multiple works:

> It is but just to remark, that in one principle the Baptist and Pedobaptist churches agree. They both agree in rejecting from Communion at the table of the Lord, and in denying the rights of church fellowship to all, who have not been baptized. Valid baptism they consider as essential to constitute visible church membership. This, also, we hold. The only question then that here divides us is, what is essential to valid baptism?[87]

Thus, Pendleton's interaction with non-Baptists over communion centered around his attempt to establish the priority of proper baptism to participation in the Lord's Supper.

PENDLETON'S UNIQUE CONTRIBUTION

Pendleton's formulation of the doctrine of the Lord's Supper provided nothing new. He did not create a new doctrine or a new way of expressing the doctrine. He held to the traditional memorial view of the Lord's Supper and formulated his position in the same way many Baptists of his day did. However, Pendleton did have two unique contributions.

First, Pendleton was the only member of the "Landmark Triumvirate" to allow for denominational communion. While

---

[86]Philip Doddridge, *Miscellaneous Works* (London: William Ball, 1839), 510. As in Pendleton, *Baptist Church Manual*, 96–7. Philip Doddridge (1702–1751) was born in London and eventually became pastor and head of the academy at Northampton.

[87]Freeborn G. Hibbard, Christian Baptism: Mode, Obligation, Import and Relative Order (New York: Carlton & Lanahan, 1841), 174. As in Pendleton, Three Reasons Why I Am a Baptist with a Fourth Added on Communion, 189–91. Also in Baptist Church Manual, 97.

Dayton had passed away before the debate heated up, Graves opposed Pendleton on this issue. In addition to allowing for denominational communion, Pendleton also restricted Landmarkism to a rejection of Pedobaptist ministers as Gospel ministers.

This author believes that in Pendleton's day, he won the argument; however, Graves's successfully tied the issue to Landmarkism for future generations. The fact that Pendleton won the day is supported by the majority of literature of his time. Influential contemporary theologians like Dagg and Hiscox, who have already been discussed, held a similar position as Pendleton. Additionally, people like J. B. Moody, writing shortly after Pendleton, agreed with his position. Moody wrote referring to Graves, "I think he erred by introducing church communion, as that does not involve other denominations. Indeed, I know many Landmark Baptists who discard church communion, and many church communionists who discard Landmarkism. Let each question stand on its own merits, as one does not involve the other."[88] Jeremiah Jeter said, "We have endeavored to show that the supper is a feast within, and not without, a church, designed for all its members, and only for its members, or for members of other churches maintaining the same terms of communion."[88] Charles Jenkens wrote that "there can be no consistent intercommunion except between those churches whose views of divine truth are so accordant that membership in the one may justly entitle an individual to membership in the other."[89] He also agreed with Pendleton when he stated, "No church can *demand* anything of her

---

[88]J. B. Moody, "Introduction to the Third Edition," in *Landmarkism, Liberalism and the Invisible Church* (Fulton: National Baptist Publishing House, 1899), 8.

[88]Jeremiah Jeter, Baptist Principles Reset: Consisting of a Series of Articles on Distinctive Baptist Principles (Richmond: Religious Herald, 1902), 113.

[89]Charles Jenkens, *Baptist Doctrines* (St. Louis: Chancy R. Barns, 1881), 192.

sister churches, not even communion."[90] Pendleton's view had many supporters.

Despite having support in his time, most modern works connect close communion with Landmarkism and by association with Pendleton. Some of these works have already been discussed and others will be discussed in the next section.[91] These works demonstrate that Graves successfully attached this issue to Landmarkism despite Pendleton's objections. Pendleton may have won the battle, but Graves has left the longer legacy.

Pendleton's second unique contribution was connecting pulpit affiliation and communion. Pendleton held that Baptists could not consistently allow Pedobaptists to preach in their pulpits and not allow them to commune at the Lord's Supper. Thus, Pendleton put forth the position that Baptist should not allow Pedobaptists to preach in Baptist pulpits. This, to Pendleton, was the only consistent position. If Pendleton did not originate this position, he certainly popularized it.

CURRENT DISCUSSIONS ON THE LORD'S SUPPER

In 1983, Michael James Lovett wrote a dissertation entitled, "An Inquiry into the Theological Development of Southern Baptist Communion Thought." In this work, he marks the Landmark Movement as "the third, and perhaps most significant, factor which altered Southern Baptist Communion thought. . . ."[92] Thus, Landmarkism changed, in Lovett's view, the Southern Baptist position on communion. In his thesis, Lovett pointed out one area of consistency among Graves and Pendleton. He stated, "The Landmark

---

[90]Charles Jenkens, *What Made Me a Baptist* (Richmond: Virginia Baptist Historical Society, 1901), 90.

[91]For the works already discussed, see the discussion of Landmarkism on pages 6–13 of this dissertation.

[92]Michael James Lovett, "An Inquiry into the Theological Development of Southern Baptist Communion Thought" (Th.M. thesis, Southeastern Baptist Theological Seminary, 1983), 96.

interpretation of the Lord's Supper subordinates and contextualizes all value and meaning of Communion to focus on autonomy, authority, obedience and individualism. . . . The local autonomy of the church is stressed."[93] Graves and Pendleton both stressed the governance of the church over the ordinance. However, Lovett did not accurately describe Pendleton's view when he said concerning both Pendleton and Graves, "Only those belonging to the immediate congregation may participate in the Communion event."[94] This provides a classic example of Graves speaking for the entire movement. While Graves held to this view, Pendleton did not.

In addition to those who do not fully understand Pendleton's position, there are current Baptists who strongly disagree with close communion and the influence of Landmarkism. For example John Finley wrote, "In America, the heresy of Landmarkism produced too many suspicious children who despised an ecumenical spirit and forbade any observance of the ordinance beyond the local church."[95] As strongly as Finley may disagree, he acknowledged the influence of Landmarkism.

Finley was not alone. Thomas Halbrooks also criticized Landmarkism and what he believed was its position on communion. He wrote, "With a biblical literalism and legalism, Landmarkers taught that the important thing about the ordinances was to do them correctly, just as Christ had ordained that we do them. It seemed to matter little what they meant. Landmarkers expressed no concern for any mystery beyond the action."[96] Halbrooks did not believe proper baptism was a necessity to the Lord's Supper.

---

[93]Ibid. 99.
[94]Ibid.
[95]John M. Finley, "Worship Culminates in the Lord's Supper," in *Defining Baptist Convictions*, ed. Charles W. Deweese (Franklin: Providence House, 1996), 119.
[96]G. Thomas Halbrooks, "Communion," in *A Baptist's Theology*, ed. R. Wayne Stacy (Macon: Smyth & Helwys, 1999), 184.

Concerning those who can administer the Lord's Supper, Halbrooks commented, "Anyone who is designated by a body of believers can celebrate communion."[97] Fisher Humphreys commented, "This is the supper of the Lord; he has commanded us to take it, but he has not authorized us to exclude from it anyone who is a member of his body."[98] Thomas Clifton added additional support by stating that although Kiffin and closed communion won the debate, Bunyan and open communion "prevails in our time."[99] He believed that all should be allowed to participate. Clifton continued, "The Lord's Table does not need our fences. We cannot defile what Christ has made clean. The one who was made sin welcomes sinners. Is there, then, anyone left to fence out?"[100] Although several of these quotes support open communion, the Baptist Faith and Message continues to support or at the very least imply close communion. It states in article seven, "The Lord's Supper is a symbolic act of obedience whereby members of the church, through partaking of the bread and the fruit of the vine, memorialize the death of the Redeemer and anticipate His second coming." Thus, the only consistency is that various opinions on the matter continue to exist.

PENDLETON'S LASTING INFLUENCE

Although Finley and Halbrooks attributed the practice of close communion to the Landmark movement, this author does not believe the connection of close communion and Landmarkism should continue for three reasons. First, Bunyan and Kiffin clearly laid out the arguments on both sides of the debate before Landmarkism gained influence.

---

[97]Ibid., 189.

[98]Fisher Humphreys, "A Baptist Theology of the Lord's Supper," in *Proclaiming the Baptist Vision: Baptism and the Lord's Supper*, ed. Walter Shurden (Macon: Smyth & Helwys, 1999), 124.

[99]Thomas Clifton, "Fencing the Table," in *Proclaiming the Baptist Vision: Baptism and the Lord's Supper*, ed. Walter Shurden (Macon: Smyth & Helwys, 1999), 70.

[100]Ibid., 71.

Second, some Baptists who would not agree with Landmarkism held to close communion and some who agreed with Landmarkism did not hold to close communion. Third, Graves and Pendleton never agreed completely on the issue of communion. Thus, although close communion has been attached to the Landmark movement, it did not form one of its original tenets or originate from the movement. More accurately, there have always been differing opinions within Baptist life on the issue of close communion. However, due to the widespread misconception about Pendleton supporting the same view as Graves, it appears that Pendleton has little lasting contribution in the discussion of close communion or denominational communion. Perhaps a proper understanding of his position will clear up any misconceptions concerning Landmarkism and close communion.

However, Pendleton has had two lasting contributions which some will see as positive and others would see as negative. Through his and Landmarkism's emphasis on the local church, communion is no longer practiced at associational or denominational meetings. Finley wrote concerning Landmarkism's lasting influence, "The fact that many Baptists today are still reluctant to share the Lord's Supper within the setting of a seminary chapel service, youth retreat, or denominational gathering is evidence enough that a limited view is still with us."[101] One additional lasting influence comes in Pendleton's denial of anything more than a memorial meaning to the Lord's Supper. Although Pendleton perhaps underemphasized the possibility of a spiritual presence, the memorial view seems to be the majority position among current Baptists.[102]

---

[101]Finley, "Worship Culminates in the Lord's Supper," 119.
[102]See Lovett's Th.M. thesis, "An Inquiry into the Theological Development of Southern Baptist Communion Thought" for evidence of this.

CHAPTER 5

CONCLUSION: EVALUATION OF JAMES MADISON PENDLETON

Purpose of the Dissertation

This dissertation from the outset intended to investigate the life and literary works of James Madison Pendleton specifically looking for his contributions to Baptist ecclesiology. The lack of a dissertation devoted specifically to Pendleton combined with Pendleton's involvement in the Landmark movement provided hope that a significant contribution could be made by further clarifying Pendleton's beliefs or by identifying his unique contributions. Additionally, the dissertation hoped to determine if Pendleton had left a lasting legacy and if so to identify what that legacy included. The findings of this dissertation will be succinctly presented in the following pages.

EVALUATION OF PENDLETON'S UNIQUE CONTRIBUTIONS TO BAPTIST ECCLESIOLOGY

Pendleton left three notable unique contributions to Baptist ecclesiology. First, Pendleton developed the logical argument for the denial of Pedobaptist ministers as Gospel ministers. Second, Pendleton supported a restricted view of Landmarkism which identified more with mainstream Baptists. Third, Pendleton popularized if not began a new genre of Baptist literature. Each of these contributions will be briefly discussed elaborating on Pendleton's contribution.

First, Pendleton developed the logical argument for the denial of Pedobaptist ministers as Gospel ministers. Through the four articles which would later be published as a pamphlet under the popular name *An Old Landmark Re-set*, Pendleton published a systematic apology for the non-recognition of Pedobaptist ministers as Gospel ministers. In this apology, Pendleton noted proper baptism as the line of demarcation between a true church and a religious society— as a mark of the *being* of a church and not the *well being* of a church. This distinction caused those who followed him to re-examine the necessary elements for the *being* of a church. If nothing but the immersion of believers is proper baptism, and proper baptism is required for the *being* of a church, then many religious groups do not possess churches. Recognizing Pendleton's implications, some definitions of the *being* of a church avoid including in that definition the ordinances "rightly" administered.[1] This definition allows for less division between the denominations.

Second, Pendleton identified more with mainstream Baptists than other Landmarkers because of his restricted view of Landmarkism.[2] Pendleton's restricted view of Landmarkism did not include support of church succession, advocacy of close communion, or a denial of universal church. He differed in these three tenets often associated with Landmarkism and specifically with Graves and Dayton. A study of Pendleton allows one to pinpoint the central aspect of Landmarkism as the rejection of Pedobaptist ministers as Gospel ministers. In

---

[1] A. H. Strong, *Systematic Theology*, vol. 3 (Philadelphia: Judson Press, 1909), 890, specifically said, "We do not define the church as a body of 'baptized believers,' because baptism is but one of 'Christ's laws.'"

[2] Tull states concerning the difference between Pendleton and Graves, "J. M. Pendleton always stood closer to the commonly held Baptist views of his time than either Graves or Dayton." One of the areas Tull noted was denominational communion. See James E. Tull, *High-Church Baptists in the South* (Macon: Mercer Press, 2000), 44.

addition, Pendleton's recognition of the universal church helped Southern Baptists prevent a potential controversy.[3]

Third, Pendleton's unique and perhaps most lasting contribution comes from the fact that he popularized if not began a new genre of writing which focused on Baptist identity. Three types of books exists in this area of writing. First, early works from authors like Booth and Ryland demonstrate a defense of only one or two doctrines.[4] For example, both Ryland and Booth focused on baptism, refuted infant baptism, and discussed communion only as it related to baptism. R. Stanton Norman discussed these as precursors to works on Baptist distinctives.[5]

The second category are those works which give Baptist views as a confession of faith. These works focus on what Baptists believe and not necessarily what distinguishes them from other religious societies. Thus, one would find the

---

[3]The clause "redeemed in the aggregate" would be significant not only for Pendleton's time but in Kansas City in 1963, when the Baptist Faith and Message was being voted upon. The proposed Baptist Faith and Message contained new wording on the church, "which includes all of the redeemed of all ages." This reference to the universal church was objected to by many with Landmark sentiments. However, "Hobbs, with Albert McClellan's coaching, called the group's attention to a J. M. Pendleton quotation acknowledging New Testament use of *church* to mean the redeemed in aggregate. Since Pendleton had been a leader of the Landmark movement, that settled matters."Jesse Fletcher, *The Southern Baptist Convention: A Sesquicentennial History* (Nashville: Broadman & Holman, 1994), 209.

[4]Abraham Booth, *Vindication of the Baptists from the Charge of Bigotry, in Refusing Communion at the Lord's Table to Pedobaptists* (Philadelphia: American Baptist Publication Society, 1778); Theophilus [pseud.], *An Appeal to Baptists in Their Necessity and Importance of the Maintenance of Their Denominational Principles as Essential to the Establishment of Their Kingdom of God Upon Earth* (London: G. B. Dyer, 1841); and John Ryland, *A Candid Statement of the Reasons which Induce the Baptists to Differ in Opinion and Practice from So Many of Their Christian Brethren* (Philadelphia: Anderson and Meehan, 1820).

[5]R. Stanton Norman, "A Critical Analysis of the Intentional Efforts of Baptists to Distinguish Themselves Theologically from Other Christian Denominations" (Ph.D. diss., Southwestern Baptist Theological Seminary, 1997), 26.

Baptist belief on the doctrine of the trinity, the doctrine of soteriology, and others. This type work existed before Pendleton and has continued after him.[6]

Pendleton represented the shift to the third type of literature which moves from a defense of proper baptism to the inclusion of other doctrines. He added congregational polity in 1853 with *Three Reasons Why I Am a Baptist* and the proper view of the Lord's Supper with *Three Reasons Why I Am a Baptist with a Fourth Added on Communion* in 1856. In his discussion of the Lord's Supper, he expanded the topic to include transubstantiation, consubstantiation, and the memorial view rather than merely justifying the exclusion of Pedobaptists because of their lack of proper baptism. This type work falls within the category of Baptist works which focus on distinctive Baptist principles and not doctrines that are held in common by multiple denominations like the trinity, scripture, and justification by faith. Pendleton either founded or encouraged the transition in this genre through his three efforts including *Distinctive Principles of Baptists*. By writing *Three Reasons Why I Am a Baptist* in 1853, Pendleton began or popularized a genre of literature that now contains many books.[7]

---

[6]Examples of this type literature would be the 1644 London Confession of Faith, the Philadelphia Confession of Faith (1742), the New Hampshire Confession (1833), the Baptist Faith and Message (1925), the Baptist Faith and Message (1963), and the Baptist Faith and Message (2000). Most of these confessions can be found in William Lumpkin, *Baptist Confessions of Faith* (Valley Forge: Judson Press, 1969) or in Timothy George and Denise George, eds., *Baptist Confessions, Covenants, and Catechisms* (Tennessee: Broadman & Holman, 1966).

[7]The following list represents some works which could be placed in this tradition. William Cecil Duncan, *A Brief History of the Baptists and Their Distinctive Principles and Practices* (New York: Edward H. Fletcher, 1855); Francis Wayland, *Notes on the Principles and Practices of Baptist Churches* (New York: Sheldon & Co., 1857); J. L. Burrows, *What Baptists Believe* (Baltimore: H. M. Wharton & Company, 1887); T. T. Eaton, *The Faith of Baptists* (Louisville: Baptist Book Concern, 1898); J. M. Frost, *Baptist: Why and Why Not* (Nashville: Sunday School Board of the Southern Baptist Convention, 1900); C. A. Jenkens, *What Made Me a*

THOMAS WHITE

EVALUATION OF PENDLETON'S LASTING INFLUENCE ON BAPTIST ECCLESIOLOGY

Baptist (Richmond: Virginia Baptist Historical Society, 1901); Jeremiah Jeter, *Baptist Principles Reset: Consisting of a Series of Articles on Distinctive Baptist Principles* (Richmond: Religious Herald, 1902); J. F. Love, *The Baptist Position and the Position for a Baptist* (Nashville: Sunday School Board, 1903); Philip Jones, *A Restatement of Baptist Principles* (Philadelphia: Griffith & Rowland, 1909); Louie D. Newton, *Why I am a Baptist* (New York: Thomas Nelson, 1957); H. Wheeler Robinson, *Baptist Principles* (London: Carey Kingsgate, 1960); Joe T. Odle, ed., Why I am a Baptist (Nashville: Broadman, 1972); Walter Shurden, *The Baptist Identity: Four Fragile Freedoms* (Macon: Smyth & Helwys, 1993); Charles W. Deweese, ed., *Defining Baptist Convictions: Guidelines for the Twenty-First Century* (Franklin: Providence House, 1996); Cecil Staton, Jr., *Why I Am a Baptist: Reflections on Being Baptist in the 21st Century* (Macon: Smyth and Helwys, 1999); Thomas Nettles and Russell Moore, eds., *Why I Am a Baptist* (Nashville: Broadman & Holman, 2001); and R. Stanton Norman, *More Than Just a Name* (Nashville: Broadman & Holman, 2001).

Determining someone's lasting contribution is a difficult task. Many factors must be taken into account especially when addressing Pendleton's lasting influence. Pendleton could have been neglected, omitted, or consulted for several reasons which do not relate to the quality of his work. Those reasons include the following: (1) he did not agree with slavery, (2) he moved North leaving the Southern Baptist Convention and helping the American Baptist Publication Society, and (3) he is identified with Landmarkism. While acknowledging that these external factors play a role and that identifying lasting influence is a difficult task, one measure of Pendleton's lasting influence can be found by consulting other printed works. By consulting these works, this dissertation will demonstrate that although Pendleton's popularity has waned since his death and with the diminishing influence of Landmarkism, his work is still utilized and his influence is still mildly present in certain circles.

Pendleton's influence during his time was substantial. Joseph Borum stated in 1877, "No publications are more sought for, than those which issue from his pen, by Baptists."[8] Spencer, writing in 1886 stated, "From 1838, to the present time, he has probably written more for the periodical press than any other man who has regularly filled the pastoral office; and, yet he has never published an articles that did not evince calm thought and mature deliberation."[9] One modern writer, Rufus Spain, notes that Pendleton's works *Christian Doctrines: A Compendium of Theology*, and *Church Manual: Designed for the Use of Baptist Churches* best represent Baptist theology in the latter half of the nineteenth century.[10] These three notations

---

[8]Joseph H. Borum, *Biographical Sketches of Tennessee Baptist Ministers* (Memphis: Rogers and Co., 1880), 513. On this page Borum indicated that he was writing the part on Pendleton in 1877.

[9]J. H. Spencer, *A History of Kentucky Baptists* (Cincinnati: J. H. Spencer, 1885), 524.

[10]Rufus B. Spain and Samuel S. Hill, *At Ease in Zion: Social History of Southern Baptists 1865–1900* (Tuscaloosa: University of Alabama, 2003), 2.

clearly demonstrate that his work had influence at least among Baptists during his lifetime.

Additionally, Pendleton's influence carried over into the early 1900s. Burnett writing in 1919 stated the following about Pendleton:

> The writer has read most of Dr. Pendleton's published works, and with interest and profit, and so has many another preacher and layman in Tennessee and the Southland. His *Church Manual* is a standard among our churches. His "Notes" on the New Testament are found in the libraries of many of our preachers and Sunday school teachers. His ablest work, I dare say, is his "Christian Doctrines," a work that will never perish, "concise, yet comprehensive, simple, lucid, logical, Scriptural," supplying a long-felt want in the curriculum of theological education and in the libraries of Christian households.[11]

In addition to these comments, Pendleton also had his works translated into other languages. His *Church Manual* was translated into German in the early 1900's, and his *Christian Doctrines* was translated into Spanish by 1928.[12] His works were already being revised and republished by 1900.[13] He was noted in other works such as Dargan's *Ecclesiology*, published in 1897.[14]

---

[11]J. J. Burnett, *Sketches of Tennessee's Pioneer Baptist Preachers* (Nashville: Marshall & Bruce, 1919), 405.

[12]James Madison Pendleton, *Handbuch fur gemeindeglieder*, Translator not given (Cleveland: Publickations-Verein des Deutschen, [n.d.]), and James Madison Pendleton, *Compendio de teologia cristiana,* Translated by Alejandro Trevino (El Paso: Casa Bautists de Publicaciones, 1928).

[13]F. M. McConnell, *Pendleton's Church Manual: Designed for the Use of Baptist Churches* (Dallas: B. J. Robert Book Company, 1900).

[14]Edwin C. Dargan, *Ecclesiology: A Study of the Churches* (Louisville: Chas. T. Dearing, 1897), 216. He mentions Pendleton only once but states in the preface that "the bibliography at the end of the book will show the principal sources from which help has been derived." Pendleton is included in that bibliography.

Although Pendleton's work would not continue to be the standard, his influence has lasted into modern times with varying importance. For certain organizations such as the Baptist Missionary Association of America, Pendleton continues to be a major influence. One such example of this influence comes in J. E. Cobb's *Baptist Church Manual*. This work states in the preface, "The author of this manual recognizes that the manual most generally used among our particular group of Baptists is that of Dr. J. M. Pendleton."[15] Another example is Moser's work based on Pendleton's *Church Manual*.[16] McBeth in his *The Baptist Heritage* says, "Pendleton's major influence came through his popular *Church Manual*, first published in 1867 and still available.... Through this manual, generations of Southern Baptist pastors have absorbed Landmarkism, often without knowing it."[17] Another example of his importance comes by his inclusion in the book *Baptist Theologians*.[18] In addition Pendleton is mentioned in many modern works and particularly in two recent books comparing views of church government.[19] Thus, Pendleton's lasting influence has come primarily from his *Church Manual* and *Christian Doctrines*.

---

[15]J. E. Cobb, *Baptist Church Manual* (Little Rock: Baptist Publishing House, 1941), i. It goes on to say, "That manual [Pendleton's] is excellent in some respects, but from the author's viewpoint it is also seriously lacking in others. Dr. Pendleton's "church in the aggregate" idea and his postmillenialism are especially objectionable to the writer of this little volume. . . . The order of arrangement in this manual is quite similar to that of Dr. Pendleton and also that of Dr. Hiscox."

[16]N. S. Moser Sr., *Baptist Doctrine in One Year: Based on Pendleton's Church Manual* (Little Rock: Central Baptist Church Publications, 1960).

[17]H. Leon McBeth, *The Baptist Heritage* (Nashville: Broadman Press, 1987), 449.

[18]Timothy George and David Dockery, eds., *Baptist Theologians* (Nashville: Broadman Press, 1990). He was one of thirty-three theologians included in this work.

[19]Paige Patterson, "Single-Elder Congregationalism," in *Who Runs the Church?* eds. Paul Engle and Steven Cowan (Grand Rapids: Zondervan, 2004), 145; James Leo Garrett Jr., "The Congregational-Led Church," in *Perspectives on Church Government*, eds. Chad Brand and R. Stanton Norman (Nashville: Broadman & Holman, 2004), 178, 182. See also

Pendleton could be said to have other lasting contributions to Baptist ecclesiology which would not be exclusive to him. Current definitions of the *being* of a church recognize the implications pointed out by Pendleton and often avoid including the "right" practice of the ordinances in that definition or use a different interpretation of what "right" practice of the ordinances mean.[20] Other factors have also influenced the current definitions of a church. Additionally, the genre of literature which Pendleton popularized continues to be propagated.[21] Any other influence has diminished with the waning influence of Landmarkism.

Pendleton's contribution to Baptist theology through his focus on ecclesiology and propagation of Landmarkism will be remembered. He left a legacy of godliness and of

---

William Brackney, *The Baptists* (New York: Greenwood Press, 1988), 41, 65. This work notes Pendleton's *Church Manual* and his views on communion.

[20]Thomas Oden, *Life in the Spirit* (Peabody: Prince, 2001), 272, stated the following as the definition of a church: "The Christian church is the community through whom the Holy Spirit administers redemption and distributes gifts, the means in and by which God makes his reconciling work in Christ present to humanity." From the Baptist perspective, Wayne Grudem, *Systematic Theology* (Grand Rapids: Zondervan, 1994), 853, gave the following as the definition of a church: "The church is the community of all true believers for all time." Grudem went further discussing the marks of a church and the "right" practice of the ordinances, noting that the proper interpretation of "right" practice has to do with salvation. If the ordinances are administered in a detrimental way to salvation by grace through faith, then they are not "rightly" administered. He stated that when "participation in the sacraments is seen as a 'work' that can earn merit with God. Such a group of people is not a true Christian church" (866).

[21]The following works could be included in the genre of defining Baptist distinctives. Charles W. Deweese, ed., *Defining Baptist Convictions: Guidelines for the Twenty-First Century* (Franklin: Providence House, 1996); Cecil Staton, Jr., *Why I Am a Baptist: Reflections on Being Baptist in the 21st Century* (Macon: Smyth and Helwys, 1999); Thomas Nettles and Russell Moore, eds., *Why I Am a Baptist* (Nashville: Broadman & Holman, 2001); and R. Stanton Norman, *More Than Just a Name* (Nashville: Broadman & Holman, 2001).

conviction rooted in theological conservatism. He spent his life preaching, teaching, and writing about God's word. He stood firmly for what he believed was right, even if it meant arguing against slavery while living in the South. His commitment to Scripture and his love for God are unquestionable. At the completion of this study, this author recognizes that Pendleton was human and made mistakes, but most of all, this author has a profound respect for the pastor and theologian known as James Madison Pendleton.

BIBLIOGRAPHY OF RELEVANT SOURCES
Pendleton's Works

BOOKS

Pendleton, James Madison. *The Atonement of Christ*. Philadelphia: American Baptist Publication Society, 1885.

—*Baptist Church Manual*. Yokohama: American Baptist Missionary Union, 1893.

—*Baptist Church Manual*. Nashville: Broadman & Holman, 1966.

—*Brief Notes on the New Testament*. Philadelphia: American Baptist Publication Society, 1884.

—*Christian Doctrines: A Compendium of Theology*. Philadelphia: American Baptist Publication Society, 1906.

—*Christianity Susceptible of Legal Proof*. Nashville: Southwestern Publishing House, 1858.

—*Church Manual: Designed for the Use of Baptist Churches*. Philadelphia: American Baptist Publication Society, 1867.

—*Church Manual: Designed for the Use of Baptist Churches*. Nashville: Executive Board, Tennessee Baptist Convention, 1867.

—*Church Manual: Designed for the Use of Baptist Churches*. Philadelphia: American Baptist Publication Society, 1912.

—*Church Manual: Designed for the Use of Baptist Churches.* Philadelphia: Judson Press, 1943.

—*Church Manual: Designed for the Use of Baptist Churches.* Philadelphia: Judson Press, 1945.

—*Church Manual: Designed for the Use of Baptist Churches.* Nashville: Broadman Press, 1946.

—*Church Manual: Designed for the Use of Baptist Churches.* Philadelphia: Judson Press, 1949.

—*Church Manual: Designed for the Use of Baptist Churches.* Nashville: Broadman Press, 1953.

—*Church Manual: Designed for the Use of Baptist Churches.* Philadelphia: Judson Press, 1955.

—*Church Manual: Designed for the Use of Baptist Churches.* Nashville: Convention Press, 1955.

—*Church Manual: Designed for the Use of Baptist Churches.* Philadelphia: Judson Press, 1958.

—*Church Manual: Designed for the Use of Baptist Churches.* Philadelphia: American Baptist Publication Society, 1978.

—*Compendio de teologia cristiana.* Translated by Alejandro Trevino. El Paso: Casa Bautists de Publicaciones, 1928.

—*Distinctive Principles of Baptists.* Philadelphia: American Baptist Publication Society, 1882.

—*Handbuch fur gemeindeglieder.* Translator not given. Cleveland: Publickations- Verein des Deutschen, [n.d.].

—*Journal of James Madison Pendleton.* privately published, 1844.

—*Notes of Sermons.* Philadelphia: American Baptist Publication Society, 1886.

—*An Old Landmark Re-set: or Ought Baptists Invite Pedobaptists to Preach in Their Pulpits?* Nashville: Graves & Marks, 1854.

—*Questions to the Impenitent.* St. Louis: St. Louis Baptist Publishing, 1857.

—*Reminiscences of a Long Life.* Louisville: Baptist Book Concern, 1891.

—*Short Sermons on Important Subjects.* St. Louis: National Baptist Publishing, 1859.

—*Sermon on the Death of J. H. Eaton,* Nashville: Southwestern Publishing House, 1859.

—*Thoughts on Christian Duty.* Nashville: Southwestern Publishing House, 1857.

—*Three Reasons Why I Am a Baptist.* Cincinnati: Moore, Anderson & Company, 1853.

—*Three Reasons Why I Am a Baptist with a Fourth Reason Added on Communion.* St. Louis: National Baptist Publishing, 1856.

Pendleton, James Madison, et al. *Landmarkism, Liberalism and the Invisible Church.* Fulton: National Baptist Publishing House, 1899.

JOURNAL ARTICLES CITED

Pendleton, James Madison. "The Atonement of Christ." *The Southern Baptist Review* 2 (January–February 1856): 41–61.

—"Campbellism Examined." *The Southern Baptist Review* (February 1855): 84–142.

—"Extemporaneous Preaching." *The Southern Baptist Review* 1 (April–May 1855): 261–75.

—"Justification." *The Southern Baptist Review* 2 (January–February 1856): 149–163.

—"Peter Edwards on Baptism." *The Southern Baptist Review* 4 (June 1858): 419–34.

—"Plea for Thorough Female Education." *The Southern Baptist Review* 2 (July–August 1856): 369–84.

—"Review of Dagg's *Church Order.*" *The Southern Baptist Review* 5 (January 1859): 36–55.

—"Review of Dr. Summers on Baptism." *The Southern Baptist Review* 1 (October–December 1855): 575–607.

—"A Review of Principles and Practices of Baptists." *The Southern Baptist Review* 3 (January 1857): 51–73.

—"The Scriptural Meaning of the Term Church." *The Southern Baptist Review* 1 (January 1855): 6–17.

—"The Scriptural Meaning of the Term Church." *The Southern Baptist Review* 1 (February–March 1855): 65–83.

JOURNAL ARTICLES NOT CITED

Pendleton, James Madison. "Able Ministry." *The Southern Baptist Review* 5 (June 1859): 321–32.

—"Astronomy and Redemption." *The Southern Baptist Review* 1 (July–August 1855): 449–57.

—"Breckinridge on Baptism." *The Southern Baptist Review* 5 (April 1859): 530–59.

—"Breckinridge on Baptism." *The Southern Baptist Review* 6 (January 1860): 61–82.

—"Breckinridge's Theology." *The Southern Baptist Review* 4 (April 1858): 300–14.

—"Christianity Susceptible of Legal Proof." *The Southern Baptist Review* 4 (January 1858): 14–33.

—"Dr. Alexander's Doubts on the Propriety of Infant Baptism." *The Southern Baptist Review* 1 (January 1855): 31–39.

—"Faith—Justification by Faith." *The Southern Baptist Review* 2 (March–April 1856): 149–63.

—"Fuller's Sermons." *The Southern Baptist Review* 6 (June 1860): 263–78.

—"Fuller's Sermons." *The Southern Baptist Review* 6 (October 1860): 554–69.

—"A Good Minister of Christ." *The Southern Baptist Review* 3 (October 1857): 573–89.

—"Importance of Ministerial Piety." *The Southern Baptist Review* 2 (September–October 1856): 497–507.

—"In Obeying the Dictates of Conscience, Do We Necessarily Do Right?" *The Southern Baptist Review* 2 (May–June 1856): 290–303.

—"Infant Baptism—a Review of Summers on Infant Baptism." *The Southern Baptist Review* 2 (January–February 1856): 1–20.

—"Life and Times of Elder Reuben Ross." *The Southern Baptist Review* 6 (September 1860): 395–419.

—"The Life of Spencer H. Cone." *The Southern Baptist Review* 2 (May–June 1856): 304–19.

—"Review of African Missions." *The Southern Baptist Review* 3 (February 1857): 230–46.

—"Review of Burmah's Great Missionary." *The Southern Baptist Review* 1 (July–August 1855): 322–37.

—"Review of Surgeon's Sermons." *The Southern Baptist Review* 2 (November–December 1856): 721–35.

Newspaper Articles Cited

Pendleton, James Madison. "An Able Ministry," *Western Recorder*, June 11, 1851.

—"Another False Impression," *Tennessee Baptist*, May 26, 1860.

—"Are the Heathen Saved Without the Gospel," *Tennessee Baptist*, November 26, 1859.

—"The Baptism of a Methodist Minister," *Tennessee Baptist*, November 8, 1856.

—"Bro. Hendren's Letter," *Tennessee Baptist*, November 27, 1858.

—"Brother Manly on Immersions of Pedobaptists," *Tennessee Baptist*, June 27, 1857.

—"Chapman on Church Government," *Tennessee Baptist*, June 23, 1855.

—"The Charges Against J. R. Graves," *Tennessee Baptist*, September 18, 1858.

—"Church Democracy," *Tennessee Baptist*, July 19, 1856.

—"Church Independence," *Tennessee Baptist*, July 30, 1859.

—"Church Independence," *Tennessee Baptist*, October 6, 1860.

—"Close Communion Once More," *Tennessee Baptist*, November 27, 1858.

—"Communion in the Lord's Supper," *Tennessee Baptist*, April 3, 1858.

—"The Communion Question," *Tennessee Baptist*, March 27, 1858.

—"Conant's Revision of Matthew: Number 1," *Tennessee Baptist*, January 26, 1861.

—"The Constitution of Churches," *Tennessee Baptist*, February 18, 1860.

—"Conversations on the Acts of the Apostles: Number 1," *Tennessee Baptist*, August 23, 1856.

—"Corrections," *Baptist Banner,* October 3, 1849.

—"The Council," *Tennessee Baptist*, March 12, 1859.

—"Dr. Hill on Baptism," *Tennessee Baptist*, February 2, 1856.

—"Dr. N. L. Rice and Immersion," *Tennessee Baptist*, August 18, 1855.

—"Enemies at Work," *Tennessee Baptist*, March 24, 1860.

—"A False Impression Made," *Tennessee Baptist*, April 23, 1859.

—"A Few Parting Words," *Tennessee Baptist*, July 13, 1861.

—"A Good Thing," *Tennessee Baptist*, April 30, 1859.

—"The Hand of Fellowship," *Tennessee Baptist*, October 20, 1860.

—"How Mr. Graves Stands at Home," *Tennessee Baptist*, July 23, 1859.

—"How Unreasonable," *Tennessee Baptist*, December 11, 1858.

—"On Howell's Election Again," *Tennessee Baptist*, July 23, 1859.

—"Inconsistency," *Tennessee Baptist*, February 12, 1859.

—"Infant Baptism," *Tennessee Baptist*, February 12, 1859.

—"The Interview Sought, and Avoided," *Tennessee Baptist*, June 4, 1859.

—"J. R. Graves on Slavery," *Tennessee Baptist*, May 8, 1858.

—"The Last Charge Against J. R. Graves," *Tennessee Baptist*, June 11, 1859.

—"Leaving Kentucky," *Tennessee Baptist*, January 10, 1857.

—"Letter Entitled, 'Mary Sharpe College, Winchester, Tennessee,'" *Tennessee Baptist*, April 1, 1854.

—"Letter to Brother Graves," *Tennessee Baptist*, March 27, 1852.

—"Letter to Brother Graves," *Tennessee Baptist*, June 5, 1852.

—"Letter to Brother Graves," *Tennessee Baptist*, October 3, 1857.

—"Letter to the Church in Murfreesboro," *Tennessee Baptist*, January 22, 1859.

—"Letters to Young Preachers: Number 1," *Tennessee Baptist*, April 14, 1860.

—"Look Here," *Tennessee Baptist*, April 9, 1859.

—"Methodist Church Government," *Tennessee Baptist*, June 16, 1855.

—"Methodist Church Government," *Tennessee Baptist*, September 15, 1855.

—"Methodists Getting Right," *Tennessee Baptist*, February 9, 1856.

—"The 'Mississippian,'" *Tennessee Baptist*, April 21, 1860.

—"Mistakes Corrected," *Western Recorder*, September 30, 1865.

—"More About Slavery," *Tennessee Baptist*, June 9, 1860.

—"New Relation," *Tennessee Baptist*, May 15, 1858.

—"Old Landmark Methodists," *Tennessee Baptist*, December 13, 1856.

—"An Old Landmark Re-set," *Tennessee Baptist*, January 17, 1855.

—"Open Communion Shown to Be Unscriptural and Deleterious by John L. Waller: a Review," *Tennessee Baptist*, July 30, 1859.

—"Ordination," *Tennessee Baptist*, June 30, 1860.

—"Ought Baptists to Recognize Pedobaptist Preachers as Gospel Ministers?," *Tennessee Baptist*, July 22, 1854.

—"Ought Baptists to Recognize Pedobaptist Preachers as Gospel Ministers? Number Two," *Tennessee Baptist*, August 5, 1854.

—"Ought Baptists to Recognize Pedobaptist Preachers as Gospel Ministers? Number Three," *Tennessee Baptist*, August 12, 1854.

—"Ought Baptists to Recognize Pedobaptist Preachers as Gospel Preachers?" *Tennessee Baptist*, December 16, 1854.

—"Pedobaptist Immersions," *Tennessee Baptist*, May 1, 1858.

—"Please Spare Me," *Tennessee Baptist*, May 19, 1860.

—"Presbyterian High-Churchism," *Tennessee Baptist*, June 30, 1855.

—"Proceedings of the First Baptist Church at Its Meeting of the Night of the 12th of Oct. 1858," *Tennessee Baptist*, October 23, 1858.

—"Probably Too Fast," *Tennessee Baptist*, April 9, 1859.

—"Prof. J. M. Pendleton," *Tennessee Baptist*, June 2, 1860.

—"Queries and Answers," *Tennessee Baptist*, July 3, 1858.

—"Query," *Tennessee Baptist*, June 25, 1859.

—"Query—Secret Societies," *Tennessee Baptist*, August 8, 1857.

—"Read This All Ye People," *Tennessee Baptist*, February 26, 1859.

—"Reprint of Letter of J. M. Pendleton to Dr. Hill, Editor of Presbyterian Herald," *Tennessee Baptist*, September 2, 1854.

—"Revival Intelligence," *Western Recorder*, March 17, 1852.

—"Short Sermons Number 1: The Piety of the Thessalonian Church," *Tennessee Baptist*, February 5, 1853.

—"Slavery Again," *Tennessee Baptist*, August 11, 1860.

—"The Slavery Question," *Tennessee Baptist*, March 3, 1860.

—"The South Western Baptist," *Tennessee Baptist*, March 20, 1858.

—"Southern Baptist Convention," *Tennessee Baptist*, April 9, 1859.

—"Southern Baptist Convention," *Tennessee Baptist*, May 21, 1859.

—"Sovereignty of Churches," *Tennessee Baptist*, November 12, 1859.

—"Spurgeon on Baptism," *Tennessee Baptist*, October 10, 1857.

—"Spurgeon's Views of Communion," *Tennessee Baptist*, December 24, 1859.

—"Startling Disclosures," *Tennessee Baptist*, March 27, 1858.

—"Strange Injustice," *Tennessee Baptist*, October 23, 1858.

—"Sunday Morning Thoughts," *Tennessee Baptist*, May 15, 1858.

—"That Correspondence," *Tennessee Baptist*, October 9, 1858.

—"There Is No Danger," *Tennessee Baptist*, June 5, 1858.

—"Thoughts on Christian Duty Number 1: The Christian Profession," *Tennessee Baptist*, May 6, 1854.

—"Thoughts on Giving: Number 1," *Tennessee Baptist*, November 26, 1859.

—"Thoughts on Jewelry," *Tennessee Baptist*, August 22, 1857.

—"Thoughts on the Lord's Supper: Number 1," *Tennessee Baptist*, October 29, 1859.

—"Thoughts on the Lord's Supper: Number 2," *Tennessee Baptist*, November 5, 1859.

—"[Thoughts on] the Lord's Supper: Number 3," *Tennessee Baptist*, November 12, 1859.

—"Thoughts on the Lord's Supper: Number 4," *Tennessee Baptist*, November 26, 1859.

—"[Thoughts on] the Lord's Supper: Number 5," *Tennessee Baptist*, December 10, 1859.

—"[Thoughts on] the Lord's Supper: Number 6," *Tennessee Baptist*, December 17, 1859.

—"Thoughts on the Lord's Supper: Number 7," *Tennessee Baptist*, January 7, 1960.

—"Thoughts on the Lord's Supper: Number 8," *Tennessee Baptist*, January 21, 1860.

—"Thoughts on the Lord's Supper: Number 9," *Tennessee Baptist*, February 4, 1860.

—"[Thoughts on] the Lord's Supper: Number 10," *Tennessee Baptist*, March 3, 1860.

—"[Thoughts on] the Lord's Supper: Number 11," *Tennessee Baptist*, March 31, 1860.

—"[Thoughts on] the Lord's Supper: Number 12," *Tennessee Baptist*, April 7, 1860.

—"[Thoughts on] the Lord's Supper: Number 13," *Tennessee Baptist*, April 28, 1860.

—"[Thoughts on] the Lord's Supper: Number 14," *Tennessee Baptist*, May 12, 1860.

—"[Thoughts on] the Lord's Supper: Number 15," *Tennessee Baptist*, June 2, 1860.

—"[Thoughts on] the Lord's Supper: Number 16," *Tennessee Baptist*, September, 1, 1860.

—"[Thoughts on] the Lord's Supper: Number 17," *Tennessee Baptist*, September 15, 1860.

—"[Thoughts on] the Lord's Supper: Number 18," *Tennessee Baptist*, October 6, 1860.

—"[Thoughts on] the Lord's Supper: Number 19," *Tennessee Baptist*, October 27, 1860.

—"[Thoughts on] the Lord's Supper: Number 20," *Tennessee Baptist*, January 12, 1861.

—"[Thoughts on] the Lord's Supper: Number 21," *Tennessee Baptist*, February 9, 1861.

—"To the Public," *Western Recorder*, May 26, 1852.

—"Union University," *Tennessee Baptist*, August 15, 1857.

—"The Validity of Baptism Administered by an Unbaptized Evangelist," *Tennessee Baptist*, June 21, 1856.

—"What Is an Abolitionist?," *Tennessee Baptist*, August 14, 1858.

—"Where Is the Danger," *Tennessee Baptist*, October 1, 1859.

—"Who Will Accept the Challenge?," *Tennessee Baptist*, July 22, 1854.

—"Why Infant Baptism Is Neglected," *Tennessee Baptist*, April 13, 1861.

Newspaper Articles Not Cited

Pendleton, James Madison. "1 and 2 Thessalonians," *Tennessee Baptist*, July 26, 1856.

—"$2,000 Wanted," *Tennessee Baptist*, August 13, 1859.

—"An Able Ministry Continued," *Western Recorder*, June 18, 1851.

—"Absence from Home," *Tennessee Baptist*, July 21, 1860.

—"A. C. Dayton," *Tennessee Baptist*, June 30, 1860.

—"An Address by Elder J. M. Pendleton, Delivered at the Opening of the Bethel High School Russellville, Kentucky," *Tennessee Baptist*, May 13, 1854.

—"American Baptist Publication Society," *Tennessee Baptist*, December 6, 1856.

—"American Bible Society," *Tennessee Baptist*, August 22, 1857.

—"The American Messenger," *Tennessee Baptist*, February 25, 1860.

—"The American Tract Society," *Tennessee Baptist*, August 22, 1857.

—"The Amiableness of Mr. McFerrin," *Tennessee Baptist*, February 14, 1857.

—"Amusing," *Tennessee Baptist*, July 17, 1858.

—"Another Convention," *Tennessee Baptist*, February 27, 1858.

—"Another Extract on Revision," *Tennessee Baptist*, April 12, 1856.

—"Another Mob in Louisville," *Tennessee Baptist*, June 20, 1857.

—"The Anrora," *Tennessee Baptist*, March 24, 1860.

—"Answer," *Tennessee Baptist*, August 2, 1856.

—"Answer to 'Inquirer'," *Tennessee Baptist*, December 18, 1858.

—"The Appearing of Christ." *Tennessee Baptist*, August 22, 1857.

—"The Arkansas Baptist," *Tennessee Baptist*, November 10, 1860.

—"Baptismal Demonstrations," *Tennessee Baptist*, January 10, 1857.

—"Baptist Churches in Memphis," *Tennessee Baptist*, November 26, 1859.

—"Baptist Female Institute," *Tennessee Baptist*, October 2, 1858.

—"Beneficiary Fund," *Tennessee Baptist*, March 24, 1860.

—"Bethel Association," *Tennessee Baptist*, October 22, 1859.

—"Bethel Church, Christian County, KY.," *Tennessee Baptist*, November 20, 1858.

—"Bethel Church, Christian Co., Ky," *Tennessee Baptist*, September 15, 1860.

—"Bethel High School, Russellville, KY.," *Tennessee Baptist*, January 5, 1856.

—"A Bold Advance!—Infant Baptism Declared by a Presbyterian Synod Not to Be a Divine Ordinance!!! Trouble Ahead," *Tennessee Baptist*, August 28, 1858.

—"Book Burning," *Tennessee Baptist*, March 17, 1860.

—"Book Notice," *Tennessee Baptist*, January 8, 1859.

—"The Book of Job by Prof. Conner," *Tennessee Baptist*, December 13, 1856.

—"Born of Water," *Tennessee Baptist*, April 17, 1858.

—"Bowling Green, KY," *Tennessee Baptist*, September 3, 1859.

—"Brethren, Help," *Tennessee Baptist*, January 8, 1859.

—"Brethren Kendrick and Bester on the Landmark," *Tennessee Baptist*, October 10, 1857.

—"Brethren You Must Help," *Tennessee Baptist*, October 22, 1859.

—"Bro. Fish," *Tennessee Baptist*, August 6, 1859.

—"Bro. Hillsman," *Tennessee Baptist*, December 11, 1858.

—"Bro. Mell's Article," *Tennessee Baptist*, June 16, 1860.

—"Bro. Walker's Request," *Tennessee Baptist*, June 12, 1858.

—"Bro. Waltons–Explanation," *Tennessee Baptist*, July 10, 1858.

—"Brother Adiel Sherwood," *Tennessee Baptist*, October 25, 1856.

—"Brother Bowen's Notice of Theodosia 2d.," *Tennessee Baptist*, April 18, 1857.

—"Brother Coleman and the Landmark," *Tennessee Baptist*, March 1, 1856.

—"Brother Tichnor's Letter," *Tennessee Baptist*, August 21, 1858.

—"Brownlow Right For Once," *Tennessee Baptist*, August 2, 1856.

—"Butler's Series of School Books," *Tennessee Baptist*, March 5, 1859.

—"Call on God in Prayer," *Tennessee Baptist*, May 11, 1861.

—"Can a Woman Divorce a Man for Any Cause?," *Tennessee Baptist*, December 8, 1860.

—"Can it be so," *Tennessee Baptist*, March 10, 1860.

—"A Card," *Tennessee Baptist*, January 15, 1859.

—"Central Female Institute, Clinton Miss.," *Tennessee Baptist*, September 27, 1856.

—"A Challenge," *Tennessee Baptist*, April 19, 1856.

—"Christian Beneficence," *Tennessee Baptist*, June 2, 1860.

—"The Christian Character of Paul," *Tennessee Baptist*, December 19, 1857.

—"The Christian Chronicle," *Tennessee Baptist*, May 12, 1855.

—"The Christian Chronicle," *Tennessee Baptist*, January 8, 1859.

—"The Christian Chronicle Corrected," *Tennessee Baptist*, April 19, 1856.

—"The 'Christian Observer' on Church Discipline," *Tennessee Baptist*, May 29, 1890.

—"Christian Repository," *Tennessee Baptist*, June 30, 1855.

—"The Christian's First Love," *Tennessee Baptist*, November 11, 1857.

—"A Christian's Hope," *Tennessee Baptist*, March 21, 1857.

—"Christians Often Lose Their First Blessedness," *Tennessee Baptist*, October 13, 1860.

—"Christians Should Seek to Regain Their First Blessedness," *Tennessee Baptist*, October 20, 1860.

—"A College Endowed," *Tennessee Baptist*, May 2, 1857.

—"The Colportage Work," *Tennessee Baptist*, October 6, 1860.

—"Commencement of Union University," *Tennessee Baptist*, July 29, 1854.

—"The Commission Thus Notices the Last Southern Baptist Review," *Tennessee Baptist*, September 18, 1858.

—"Conant's Revision of Matthew: Number 2," *Tennessee Baptist*, February 2, 1861.

—"Conant's Revision of Matthew: Number 3," *Tennessee Baptist*, February 16, 1861.

—"Conant's Revision of Matthew: Number 4," *Tennessee Baptist*, March 9, 1861.

—"Conant's Revision of Matthew: Number 5," *Tennessee Baptist*, March 16, 1861.

—"Conant's Revision of Matthew: Number 6," *Tennessee Baptist*, March 23, 1861.

—"Conant's Revision of Matthew: Number 7," *Tennessee Baptist*, April 6, 1861.

—"Conant's Revision of Matthew: Number 8," *Tennessee Baptist*, April 20, 1861.

—"Conant's Revision of Matthew: Number 9," *Tennessee Baptist*, April 27, 1861.

—"Conant's Revision of Matthew: Number 10," *Tennessee Baptist*, May 25, 1861.

—"Conant's Revision of Matthew: Number 11," *Tennessee Baptist*, July 13, 1861.

—"The Concord Association," *Tennessee Baptist*, September 17, 1859.

—"Concord Association," *Tennessee Baptist*, December 1, 1860.

—"The Constraining Love of Christ," *Tennessee Baptist*, August 9, 1856.

—"Conversations on the Acts of the Apostles: Number 2," *Tennessee Baptist*, September 6, 1856.

—"Conversations on the Acts of the Apostles: Number 3," *Tennessee Baptist*, September 13, 1856.

—"Conversations on the Acts of the Apostles: Number 4," *Tennessee Baptist*, September 20, 1856.

—"Conversations on the Acts of the Apostles: Number 5," *Tennessee Baptist*, October 11, 1856.

—"Conversations on the Acts of the Apostles: Number 9," *Tennessee Baptist*, January 10, 1857.

—"Conversations on the Acts of the Apostles: Number 10," *Tennessee Baptist*, February 14, 1857.

—"Conversations on the Acts of the Apostles: Number 11," *Tennessee Baptist*, April 11, 1857.

—"Conversations on the Acts of the Apostles: Number 12," *Tennessee Baptist*, June 6, 1857.

—"Conversations on the Acts of the Apostles: Number 13," *Tennessee Baptist*, June 20, 1857.

—"Conversations on the Acts of the Apostles: Number 14," *Tennessee Baptist*, August 8, 1857.

—"Conversations on the Acts of the Apostles: Number 15," *Tennessee Baptist*, August 22, 1857.

—"Conversations on the Acts of the Apostles: Number 16," *Tennessee Baptist*, October 3, 1857.

—"Conversations on the Acts of the Apostles: Number 17," *Tennessee Baptist*, November 28, 1857.

—"Conversations on the Acts of the Apostles: Number 19," *Tennessee Baptist*, May 29, 1858.

—"Conversations on the Acts of the Apostles: Number 20," *Tennessee Baptist*, July 24, 1858.

—"Conversations on the Acts of the Apostles: Number 21," *Tennessee Baptist*, September 18, 1858.

—"Correction," *Tennessee Baptist*, March 26, 1859.

—"Correction," *Tennessee Baptist*, January 14, 1860.

—"Corrections," *Tennessee Baptist*, December 22, 1855.

—"To Correspondents," *Tennessee Baptist*, April 28, 1860.

—"Courbeare & Hawson's Life and Epistles of Paul." *Tennessee Baptist*, February 17, 1855.

—"Cumberland University," *Tennessee Baptist*, June 5, 1858.

—"Curious Items," *Tennessee Baptist*, January 23, 1858.

—"Dagg's Theology," *Tennessee Baptist*, April 3, 1858.

—"Daniel Boone," *Tennessee Baptist*, May 19, 1860.

—"The Dark Cloud," *Tennessee Baptist*, November 10, 1860.

—"Dayton's Baptist Monthly," *Tennessee Baptist*, July 21, 1860.

—"Dear Bro. Jones," *Tennessee Baptist*, April 28, 1860.

—"The Death of John Harris," *Tennessee Baptist*, February 28, 1857.

—"The Death of President Eaton," *Tennessee Baptist*, January 22, 1859.

—"The Death of Those We Love," *Tennessee Baptist*, January 23, 1858.

—"Decrease in Baptist Papers," *Tennessee Baptist*, February 16, 1856.

—"Did the Godhead Suffer on the Cross?," *Tennessee Baptist*, February 28, 1857.

—"A Distinction Without a Difference," *Western Recorder*, January 16, 1890.

—"Divine Purpose and Free Agency," *Tennessee Baptist*, November 5, 1859.

—"Do Not Tell Me," *Tennessee Baptist*, August 14, 1858.

—"Don't Know," *Tennessee Baptist*, October 22, 1859.

—"Doulos, Again," *Tennessee Baptist*, May 25, 1861.

—"'Doulos' Once More," *Tennessee Baptist*, June 29, 1861.

—"Downer's Strawberry," *Tennessee Baptist*, August 20, 1859.

—"Dr. F. R. Cossett," *Tennessee Baptist*, July 14, 1855.

—"Dr. Hill," *Tennessee Baptist*, September 2, 1854.

—"Dr. Lynd and Campbellism," *Tennessee Baptist*, December 8, 1855.

—"Dr. Lynd and the Editor of the Tennessee Baptist," *Tennessee Baptist*, July 14, 1855.

—"Drouth Physical and Spiritual," *Tennessee Baptist*, August 16, 1856.

—"Dr. Parsons and the Christian Advocate," *Tennessee Baptist*, December 16, 1854.

—"Dr. Rice and Theodosia Ernest," *Tennessee Baptist*, December 20, 1856.

—"Dr. Rice—Injustice Perhaps," *Tennessee Baptist*, June 16, 1855.

—"Drs. Achill and Hill," *Tennessee Baptist*, February 10, 1855.

—"Duties of the Rich," *Tennessee Baptist*, May 21, 1859.

—"The Editor of the Presbyterian Herald," *Tennessee Baptist*, March 10, 1855.

—"Eld. L. W. Allen's Letter," *Tennessee Baptist*, December 8, 1860.

—"Eld. R. T. Gardner," *Tennessee Baptist*, February 4, 1860.

—"Elder A. C. Dayton," *Tennessee Baptist*, January 22, 1859.

—"Elder A. C. Dayton," *Tennessee Baptist*, April 2, 1859.

—"Elder A. M. Poindexter," *Tennessee Baptist*, March 27, 1858.

—"Elder Alfred Taylor," *Tennessee Baptist*, April 18, 1857.

—"Elder B. Manly," *Tennessee Baptist*, March 12, 1859.

—"Elder Banvard's Letter," *Tennessee Baptist*, April 24, 1858.

—"Elder D. R. Campbell," *Tennessee Baptist*, October 29, 1859.

—"Elder G. H. Martin, of Macon," *Tennessee Baptist*, July 25, 1857.

—"Elder H. F. Buckner," *Tennessee Baptist*, June 30, 1855.

—"Elder I. J. Roberts," *Tennessee Baptist*, September 29, 1855.

—"Elder J. H. Vinton," *Tennessee Baptist*, July 3, 1858.

—"Elder J. M. Bennett," *Tennessee Baptist*, September 24, 1859.

—"Elder J. M. Pendleton," *Western Recorder*, July 24, 1865.

—"Elder J. R. Kendrick," *Tennessee Baptist*, October 24, 1857.

—"Elder Joseph H. Eaton," *Tennessee Baptist*, February 5, 1859.

—"Elder Leonard Fletcher," *Tennessee Baptist*, September 24, 1859.

—"Elder Matt Hillsman," *Tennessee Baptist*, October 2, 1858.

—"Elder Reuben Ross," *Tennessee Baptist*, August 6, 1859.

—"Elder Reuben Ross," *Tennessee Baptist*, February 11, 1860.

—"Elder S. Henderson," *Tennessee Baptist*, April 24, 1858.

—"Elder Samuel Baker," *Tennessee Baptist*, March 27, 1858.

—"Elders Lynd and Seats vs The Tennessee Baptist," *Tennessee Baptist*, September 15, 1855.

—"Elder W. C. Buck," *Tennessee Baptist*, December 24, 1859.

—"Encouraging," *Tennessee Baptist*, March 12, 1859.

—"Enemies of the Cross," *Tennessee Baptist*, January 14, 1860.

—"Ethics for Editors: Truth," *Tennessee Baptist*, September 13, 1856.

—"Explanation," *Tennessee Baptist*, January 16, 1858.

—"Explanation," *Tennessee Baptist*, May 15, 1858.

—"Explanation," *Tennessee Baptist*, June 4, 1859.

—"Explanation," *Tennessee Baptist*, November 12, 1859.

—"Explanation," *Tennessee Baptist*, December 1, 1860.

—"Explanatory," *Tennessee Baptist*, January 21, 1860.

—"Extracts from Methodist Books," *Tennessee Baptist*, August 5, 1854.

—"A Fabrication," *Tennessee Baptist*, September 15, 1855.

—"The Fact Explained at Last," *Tennessee Baptist*, July 14, 1860.

—"The Faithful Centurion: Review," *Tennessee Baptist*, July 24, 1858.

—"Families," *Tennessee Baptist*, May 2, 1857.

—"The Fathers, Where Are They?," *Tennessee Baptist*, March 16, 1861.

—"First Church Nashville," *Tennessee Baptist*, October 9, 1858.

—"A Flagrant Outrage: A. Campbell," *Tennessee Baptist*, June 2, 1855.

—"For the Western Recorder," *Western Recorder*, January 31, 1855.

—"Forgiving Offenses," *Tennessee Baptist*, March 27, 1858.

—"The General Association," *Tennessee Baptist*, October 2, 1858.

—"The General Association," *Tennessee Baptist*, October 13, 1860.

—"George Washing a Praying Man," *Tennessee Baptist*, October 25, 1856.

—"Glasgow Female Seminary," *Tennessee Baptist*, August 11, 1855.

—"Glorifying God in Death," *Tennessee Baptist*, January 7, 1960.

—"The Good Fight of Faith," *Tennessee Baptist*, August 1, 1857.

—"Good News from New York," *Tennessee Baptist*, May 12, 1855.

—"Goshen Association Once More," *Tennessee Baptist*, September 22, 1860.

—"Goshen Association, VA.," *Tennessee Baptist*, November 5, 1859.

—"Goshen Association, Va.," *Tennessee Baptist*, December 8, 1860.

—"Gratitude to Some Unknown One." *Tennessee Baptist*, March 12, 1859.

—"The Great Want of the Age," *Tennessee Baptist*, June 25, 1859.

—"The Greatness of Salvation," *Tennessee Baptist*, November 19, 1859.

—"Has the Denomination Decided?," *Tennessee Baptist*, May 1, 1858.

—"Heirs of God," *Tennessee Baptist*, August 8, 1857.

—"High Churchism Going to Seed," *Tennessee Baptist*, December 22, 1855.

—"His Last Composition," *Tennessee Baptist*, March 31, 1860.

—"The Holy Spirit of God Grieved," *The Baptist*, May 7, 1881.

—"Home and Foreign Journal," *Tennessee Baptist*, April 19, 1856.

—"Hon. Stephen A. Douglas," *Tennessee Baptist*, December 11, 1858.

—"Honor to Whom Honor Is Due," *Tennessee Baptist*, March 24, 1860.

—"How Extremes Meet," *Tennessee Baptist*, April 6, 1861.

—"How Is This?," *Tennessee Baptist*, March 16, 1861.

—"How Is It, Bro. Otis?," *Tennessee Baptist*, April 23, 1859.

—"Immersion Not Baptism—A Review," *Tennessee Baptist*, December 11, 1858.

—"An Impartial Editor," *Tennessee Baptist*, September 29, 1860.

—"An Impostor," *Tennessee Baptist*, February 17, 1855.

—"Injustice to Bro. Bayless," *Tennessee Baptist*, March 27, 1858.

—"Injustice to the Dead—Brother Cone," *Tennessee Baptist*, April 19, 1856.

—"Interesting Items," *Tennessee Baptist*, September 19, 1857.

—"Is God Reconciled to Men?," *Tennessee Baptist*, September 27, 1856.

—"It Cannot Be," *Tennessee Baptist*, May 28, 1859.

—"Items," *Tennessee Baptist*, July 19, 1856.

—"Items of News," *Tennessee Baptist*, September 1, 1855.

—"Items of News," *Tennessee Baptist*, October 27, 1855.

—"'J.' of the Advocate Again," *Tennessee Baptist*, April 4, 1856.

—"'J.' Once More," *Tennessee Baptist*, July 19, 1856.

—"J. H. Brown, ESQ.," *Tennessee Baptist*, October 1, 1859.

—"Jesus Christ Did Not Admit Infants to Membership or Baptism in the Christian Church," *Tennessee Baptist*, August, 1, 1857.

—"Job's Patience," *Tennessee Baptist*, April 3, 1858.

—"John Angell James," *Tennessee Baptist*, November 26, 1859.

—"Joseph Addison Alexander," *Tennessee Baptist*, February 18, 1860.

—"Justice to Mr. McFerrin," *Tennessee Baptist*, August 15, 1857.

—"Kentucky Baptist Association," *Tennessee Baptist*, May 12, 1860.

—"King James' Translators," *Tennessee Baptist*, July 26 1856.

—"The Landmark and Parlor Visitor," *Tennessee Baptist*, September 20, 1856.

—"Landmark Banner and Cherokee Baptist," *Tennessee Baptist*, October 22, 1859.

—"The Landmark Controversy," *Western Recorder*, July 8, 1857.

—"The Landmark Controversy," *Tennessee Baptist*, July 25, 1857.

—"The Last Charge Against J. R. Graves," *Tennessee Baptist*, May 19, 1860.

—"Layman," *Tennessee Baptist*, April 23, 1859.

—"Lectures on Theology," *Tennessee Baptist*, October 10, 1857.

—"Lectures on Theology," *Tennessee Baptist*, November 28, 1857.

—"Lectures on Theology," *Tennessee Baptist*, January 9, 1858.

—"Lectures on Theology," *Tennessee Baptist*, January 23, 1858.

—"Letter to Brother Editor," *Tennessee Baptist*, November 12, 1853.

—"Letter to Brother Graves," *Tennessee Baptist*, November 12, 1853.

—"A Letter to Brother S. H. Ford," *Western Recorder*, January 31, 1855.

—"Letter to S. W. Lynd," *Western Recorder*, May 9, 1855.

—"Letter to the Editor," *Baptist Banner*, September 25, 1850.

—"Letter to the Editor of the Presbyterian Herald," *Tennessee Baptist*, March 10, 1855.

—"Letters to Young Preachers: Number 2," *Tennessee Baptist*, April 28, 1860.

—"Letters to Young Preachers: Number 3," *Tennessee Baptist*, May 5, 1860.

—"Letters to Young Preachers: Number 4," *Tennessee Baptist*, May 12, 1860.

—"Letters to Young Preachers: Number 5," *Tennessee Baptist*, May 26, 1860.

—"Letters to Young Preachers: Number 6," *Tennessee Baptist*, June 9, 1860.

—"Letters to Young Preachers: Number 7," *Tennessee Baptist*, June 23, 1860.

—"Letters to Young Preachers: Number 8," *Tennessee Baptist*, July 28, 1860.

—"Letters to Young Preachers: Number 9," *Tennessee Baptist*, August 18, 1860.

—"Letters to Young Preachers: Number 10," *Tennessee Baptist*, October 6, 1860.

—"Letters to Young Preachers: Number 11," *Tennessee Baptist*, October 20, 1860.

—"Letters to Young Preachers: Number 12," *Tennessee Baptist*, November 17, 1860.

—"Letters to Young Preachers: Number 13," *Tennessee Baptist*, January 12, 1861.

—"Letters to Young Preachers: Number 14," *Tennessee Baptist*, January 19, 1861.

—"Letters to Young Preachers: Number 15," *Tennessee Baptist*, February 16, 1861.

—"Lewisburg University, PA.," *Tennessee Baptist*, August 9, 1856.

—"A Little Amusing," *Tennessee Baptist*, February 13, 1858.

—"A Little Thing for a Great Man," *Tennessee Baptist*, September 15, 1855.

—"Living to Christ," *Tennessee Baptist*, August 6, 1859.

—"Madison University, New York," *Tennessee Baptist*, September 13, 1856.

—"Marriage and the Married Life," *Tennessee Baptist*, October 1, 1859.

—"The Marietta Church Letters," *Tennessee Baptist*, October 8, 1859.

—"Marvelous Ignorance," *Tennessee Baptist*, August 1, 1857.

—"Mary C. Coleman," *Tennessee Baptist*, January 5, 1861.

—"Mary Sharp College," *Tennessee Baptist*, September 20, 1856.

—"Meeting in Murfreesboro," *Tennessee Baptist*, December 8, 1860.

—"Meeting in Murfreesboro," *Tennessee Baptist*, December 22, 1860.

—"Mental Hallucination," *Tennessee Baptist*, May 12, 1855.

—"Messrs. Poindexter and Taylor," *Tennessee Baptist*, September 17, 1859.

—"The Methodist General Conference South on Slavery," *Tennessee Baptist*, August 5, 1854.

—"The Methodist General Conference: Number 1," *Tennessee Baptist*, May 29, 1858.

—"The Methodist General Conference: Number 2," *Tennessee Baptist*, June 19, 1858.

—"A Methodist Preacher on Revision," *Tennessee Baptist*, February 2, 1856.

—"Methodists in Holland," *Tennessee Baptist*, September 13, 1856.

—"Methodists in Trouble," *Tennessee Baptist*, May 17, 1856.

—"Ministerial Compensation," *Tennessee Baptist*, June 2, 1860.

—"Miscellaneous Essays and Reviews. By Albert Barnes In Two Volumes," *Tennessee Baptist*, April 5, 1856.

—"A Mischief-Maker," *Tennessee Baptist*, December 3, 1859.

—"Misrepresentation Corrected," *Tennessee Baptist*, November 27, 1858.

—"Mississippi Baptist," *Tennessee Baptist*, August 21, 1858.

—"Mississippi Baptist," *Tennessee Baptist*, April 21, 1860.

—"The Mississippi Baptist," *Tennessee Baptist*, October 20, 1860.

—"Mississippi College Clinton," *Tennessee Baptist*, September 27, 1856.

—"The Mode of Baptism," *Tennessee Baptist*, March 8, 1856.

—"Mr. Summers on Immersion," *Tennessee Baptist*, April 5, 1856.

—"Mr. Walton," *Tennessee Baptist*, July 23, 1859.

—"Mrs. V. J. Jordan," *Tennessee Baptist*, July 10, 1858.

—"Much More Wicked Than Witty," *Tennessee Baptist*, June 13, 1857.

—"My Father's Grave," *Tennessee Baptist*, September 10, 1859.

—"Nancy Ann Valina Cheek," *Tennessee Baptist*, June 16, 1860.

—"Nashville Christian Advocate," *Tennessee Baptist*, August 18, 1855.

—"The Nashville Christian Advocate," *Tennessee Baptist*, June 27, 1857.

—"Nashville Christian Advocate," *Tennessee Baptist*, October 29, 1859.

—"Nashville Female Academy—Dancing," *Tennessee Baptist*, April 3, 1858.

—"Nashville Matters Again," *Tennessee Baptist*, December 3, 1859.

—"Nearly Slanderous," *Tennessee Baptist*, May 5, 1860.

—"The New Year," *Tennessee Baptist*, January 16, 1858.

—"The New York Chronicle and the Landmark," *Tennessee Baptist*, December 5, 1857.

—"News for Brother Buckner," *Tennessee Baptist*, June 27, 1857.

—"The N. Y. Chronicle and Tennessee Baptist," *Tennessee Baptist*, June 13, 1857.

—"The Old Landmark," *Tennessee Baptist*, April 28, 1855.

—"The 'Old Land-Mark' Vindicated," *Tennessee Baptist*, June 2, 1855.

—"Ought They Not to Be Encouraged," *Tennessee Baptist*, July 21, 1860.

—"Our State Mission," *Tennessee Baptist*, August 6, 1859.

—"Our State Mission," *Tennessee Baptist*, May 19, 1860.

—"Our State Missions," *Tennessee Baptist*, May 7, 1859.

—"The Past Year-The New Year," *Tennessee Baptist*, January 7, 1960.

—"Patience," *Tennessee Baptist*, December 10, 1859.

—"Personal Effort for the Salvation of Souls," *Tennessee Baptist*, March 21, 1857.

—"Philemon," *Tennessee Baptist*, May 19, 1860.

—"Physical Exercise," *Tennessee Baptist*, November 12, 1859.

—"The Place of My Birth," *Tennessee Baptist*, January 26, 1861.

—"Please Notice," *Tennessee Baptist*, October 20, 1860.

—"Polygamy," *Tennessee Baptist*, July 31, 1858.

—"The Power of Prejudice," *Tennessee Baptist*, October 6, 1860.

—"Prayer-Books," *Tennessee Baptist*, April 5, 1856.

—"Prayer for Colleges," *Tennessee Baptist*, February 25, 1860.

—"Prayer for the Country," *Tennessee Baptist*, December 22, 1860.

—"To Preachers," *Tennessee Baptist*, November 12, 1859.

—"Preachers and War," *Tennessee Baptist*, June 1, 1861.

—"Prejudice Against Revision," *Tennessee Baptist*, December 22, 1855.

—"The Presbyterian Herald Orthodox," *Tennessee Baptist*, June 2, 1855.

—"Presbyterian Herald—See What It Says," *Tennessee Baptist*, July 31, 1858.

—"A Presbyterian in Difficulty," *Tennessee Baptist*, September 22, 1855.

—"President Selph," *Tennessee Baptist*, July 24, 1858.

—"The Presidential Election," *Tennessee Baptist*, October 25, 1856.

—"Prof. Kendrick on John the Baptist," *Tennessee Baptist*, April 27, 1861.

—"Prof. Worrell's Articles," *Tennessee Baptist*, March 24, 1860.

—"To the Public," *Tennessee Baptist*, January 15, 1859.

—"The Public Ought to Know," *Tennessee Baptist*, May 5, 1860.

—"Pulpit Communion with Pedobaptists," *Western Recorder*, April 1, 1857.

—"Put the Two Together—Revision," *Tennessee Baptist*, February 28, 1857.

—"The Quack Festival or Dance of ------. An Address Delivered (by request) Before the Medical Society of the University of Nashville. By a Western Medical Editor," *Tennessee Baptist*, April 1, 1854.

—"Queries," *Tennessee Baptist*, August 9, 1856.

—"Queries," *Tennessee Baptist*, April 3, 1858.

—"Queries and Answer," *Tennessee Baptist*, August 16, 1856.

—"Queries and Answers," *Tennessee Baptist*, September 6, 1856.

—"Queries and Answers," *Tennessee Baptist*, September 27, 1856.

—"Queries and Answers," *Tennessee Baptist*, April 20, 1859.

—"Queries and Answers," *Tennessee Baptist*, February 18, 1860.

—"Queries and Answers," *Tennessee Baptist*, March 16, 1861.

—"Query," *Tennessee Baptist*, December 15, 1855.

—"The Question of the Age," *Tennessee Baptist*, January 17, 1855.

—"Questions to the Impenitent Number 2: Is Not the Necessity of Repentance Urgent?," *Tennessee Baptist*, June 3, 1854.

—"Questions to the Impenitent Number (illegible)," *Tennessee Baptist*, February 17, 1855.

—"Questions to the Impenitent Number 11: Can You As Sinners Go to Heaven?," *Tennessee Baptist*, March 24, 1855.

—"Questions to the Impenitent Number 12: Are You Morally Insane?," *Tennessee Baptist*, May 5, 1855.

—"Questions to the Impenitent Number 13: Are You Not Without Christ, and Therefore, Wretched?," *Tennessee Baptist*, June 9, 1855.

—"Questions to the Impenitent Number 14: Do You Not Desire Happiness!," *Tennessee Baptist*, December 8, 1855.

—"Questions to the Impenitent Number 16: What Will You Do in a Dying Hour?," *Tennessee Baptist*, May 17, 1856.

—"Questions to the Impenitent Number 17: What Will You Do on the Judgment Day?," *Tennessee Baptist*, July 12, 1856.

—"Questions to the Impenitent Number 18: How Can You Endure Eternal Misery?," *Tennessee Baptist*, July 19, 1856.

—"Questions to the Impenitent Number 20: The Folly of the Impenitent," *Tennessee Baptist*, February 16, 1861.

—"Qualifications of Editors," *Tennessee Baptist*, December 22, 1860.

—"To the Readers of the Western Recorder," *Tennessee Baptist*, June 16, 1855.

—"Re-opening of the Slave Trade," *Tennessee Baptist*, August 27, 1859.

—"Recollections of the Past," *Tennessee Baptist*, October 6, 1855.

—"Remarkable Assurance," *Tennessee Baptist*, May 1, 1858.

—"A Remarkable Town," *Tennessee Baptist*, June 23, 1855.

—"Remarks," *Tennessee Baptist*, April 19, 1856.

—"Remarks," *Tennessee Baptist*, August 2, 1856.

—"Remarks," *Tennessee Baptist*, May 16, 1857.

—"Remarks," *Tennessee Baptist*, September 29, 1860.

—"Remarks on the Foregoing," *Tennessee Baptist*, August 8, 1857.

—"Remarks to Brother Poindexter's Letter," *Tennessee Baptist*, February 11, 1860.

—"Remarks to Self-Defense," *Tennessee Baptist*, September 8, 1860.

—"Remarks to the Presbyterian Herald," *Tennessee Baptist*, July 26, 1856.

—"Reply," *Tennessee Baptist*, August 27, 1859.

—"Reply," *Tennessee Baptist*, October 6, 1860.

—"Reply," *Tennessee Baptist*, December 22, 1860.

—"Reply," *Tennessee Baptist*, March 23, 1861.

—"Reply," *Tennessee Baptist*, March 30, 1861.

—"Reply to a Member of the Bible Board," *Tennessee Baptist*, January 15, 1859.

—"Reply to Costly Clothing," *Tennessee Baptist*, September 8, 1860.

—"Reply to Duties of the Rich," *Tennessee Baptist*, June 4, 1859.

—"Reply to Free Agency," *Tennessee Baptist*, November 26, 1859.

—"Reply to Letter from Elder L. W. Allen," *Tennessee Baptist*, October 27, 1860.

—"Reply to the Foregoing," *Tennessee Baptist*, November 19, 1859.

—"Report of the Committee on the Two Nashville Letters," *Tennessee Baptist*, July 14, 1860.

—"Requisites to a Revival," *Tennessee Baptist*, April 18, 1857.

—"Response," *Tennessee Baptist*, July 28, 1860.

—"Response to M. W. Philips," *Tennessee Baptist*, August 18, 1860.

—"The Resurrection of Christ," *Tennessee Baptist*, August 2, 1856.

—"Revision," *Tennessee Baptist*, October 22, 1859.

—"The Revision of the English Scriptures," *Tennessee Baptist*, March 1, 1856.

—"Revival News," *Tennessee Baptist*, April 4, 1857.

—"The Revival Spirit," *Tennessee Baptist*, October 20, 1860.

—"Revivals," *Tennessee Baptist*, October 6, 1855.

—"Revivals," *Tennessee Baptist*, December 1, 1860.

—"Revivals," *Tennessee Baptist*, March 9, 1861.

—"The Rich Saved with the Greatest Difficulty," *Tennessee Baptist*, January 15, 1859.

—"The Right Kind of Obedience," *Tennessee Baptist*, May 17, 1856.

—"Robinson's History of Baptism," *Tennessee Baptist*, July 21, 1860.

—"Roman Catholic Baptism—A Query," *Tennessee Baptist*, February 28, 1857.

—"Sabbath Morning Thoughts," *Tennessee Baptist*, October 8, 1859.

—"Sabbath Morning Thoughts," *Tennessee Baptist*, October 22, 1859.

—"Sabbath Morning Thoughts," *Tennessee Baptist*, November 12, 1859.

—"Sabbath Morning Thoughts," *Tennessee Baptist*, November 19, 1859.

—"Sabbath Morning Thoughts," *Tennessee Baptist*, December 10, 1859.

—"Sabbath Morning Thoughts: The Indwelling of the Spirit," *Tennessee Baptist*, January 14, 1860.

—"Sabbath Morning Thoughts," *Tennessee Baptist*, January 28, 1860.

—"Sabbath Morning Thoughts," *Tennessee Baptist*, February 18, 1860.

—"Sabbath Morning Thoughts," *Tennessee Baptist*, March 10, 1860.

—"Sabbath Morning Thoughts," *Tennessee Baptist*, April 14, 1860.

—"Sabbath Morning Thoughts," *Tennessee Baptist*, April 21, 1860.

—"Sabbath Morning Thoughts," *Tennessee Baptist*, May 19, 1860.

—"Sabbath Morning Thoughts," *Tennessee Baptist*, June 2, 1860.

—"Sabbath Morning Thoughts," *Tennessee Baptist*, June 23, 1860.

—"Sabbath Morning Thoughts," *Tennessee Baptist*, June 30, 1860.

—"Sabbath Morning Thoughts," *Tennessee Baptist*, September 29, 1860.

—"Sabbath Morning Thoughts," *Tennessee Baptist*, December 1, 1860.

—"Sabbath Morning Thoughts," *Tennessee Baptist*, November 10, 1860.

—"Sabbath Morning Thoughts," *Tennessee Baptist*, January 5, 1861.

—"Sabbath Morning Thoughts," *Tennessee Baptist*, January 19, 1861.

—"Sabbath Morning Thoughts," *Tennessee Baptist*, February 2, 1861.

—"Sabbath Morning Thoughts," *Tennessee Baptist*, February 9, 1861.

—"Sabbath Morning Thoughts," *Tennessee Baptist*, March 2, 1861.

—"Sabbath Morning Thoughts," *Tennessee Baptist*, March 23, 1861.

—"Sabbath Morning Thoughts," *Tennessee Baptist*, April 6, 1861.

—"Sabbath Morning Thoughts," *Tennessee Baptist*, April 13, 1861.

—"Sabbath Morning Thoughts," *Tennessee Baptist*, April 27, 1861.

—"Sabbath Morning Thoughts," *Tennessee Baptist*, May 11, 1861.

—"Sabbath Morning Thoughts," *Tennessee Baptist*, June 22, 1861.

—"Salvation by Grace Through Faith," *Tennessee Baptist*, November 5, 1859.

—"A Select School," *Tennessee Baptist*, October 22, 1859.

—"Self-Culture," *Tennessee Baptist*, August 21, 1858.

—"The Senior Editor's Tour," *Tennessee Baptist*, April 21, 1860.

—"A Severe Thrust at the Committee of the Recorder by Elder Sears," *Tennessee Baptist*, October 20, 1855.

—"A Short Sermon: Rejoicing in God in Calamity," *Tennessee Baptist*, May 4, 1861.

—"Short Sermons Number 1: Religious Perspective of Happiness," *Tennessee Baptist*, May 6, 1854.

—"Short Sermons Number 2: Making Light of Sin," *Tennessee Baptist*, February 19, 1853.

—"Short Sermons Number 2," *Tennessee Baptist*, September 9, 1854.

—"Short Sermons Number 3: The Holiness of God," *Tennessee Baptist*, March 12, 1853.

—"Short Sermons Number 4: Glorifying God in Death," *Tennessee Baptist*, February 10, 1855.

—"Short Sermons Number 5: The Death of Christ a Wonderful Event," *Tennessee Baptist*, July 9, 1853.

—"Short Sermons Number 6: Influence," *Tennessee Baptist*, March 3, 1855.

—"Short Sermons Number 7: The Dying Christian Triumphant," *Tennessee Baptist*, May 12, 1855.

—"Short Sermons Number 8: Those Who Do Love Christ Accursed of God," *Tennessee Baptist*, June 2, 1855.

—"Short Sermons Number 9: The Choice Which Moses Made," *Tennessee Baptist*, June 16, 1855.

—"Short Sermons Number 10: Enmity to the Cross of Christ," *Tennessee Baptist*, July 21, 1855.

—"Short Sermons Number 11: God is Not the Author of Sin," *Tennessee Baptist*, September 1, 1855.

—"Short Sermons Number 11: The Impart of the Name Jesus," *Tennessee Baptist*, September 15, 1855.

—"Short Sermons Number 12: Christians Urged to Glorify God," *Tennessee Baptist*, September 22, 1855.

—"Short Sermons Number 13: No Teacher Like Christ," *Tennessee Baptist*, August 3, 1855.

—"Short Sermons Number 14: Walking with God," *Tennessee Baptist*, October 20, 1855.

—"Short Sermons Number 15: Reasons for Not Loving the World," *Tennessee Baptist*, October 27, 1855.

—"Short Sermons Number 16: Reasons in Favor of Repentance," *Tennessee Baptist*, November 3, 1855.

—"Short Sermons Number 17: Praying Amiss," *Tennessee Baptist*, November 17, 1855.

—"Short Sermons Number 18: God's Method of Pardoning Sin," *Tennessee Baptist*, December 1, 1855.

—"Short Sermons Number 19: Christ the Way, the Truth, and the Life," *Tennessee Baptist*, December 8, 1855.

—"Short Sermons Number 20: Thanksgiving," *Tennessee Baptist*, December 15, 1855.

—"Short Sermons Number 21: A Church of Christ the Temple of God," *Tennessee Baptist*, December 22, 1855.

—"Short Sermons Number 22: The Value and Importance of Time," *Tennessee Baptist*, January 5, 1856.

—"Short Sermons Number 23: Justification," *Tennessee Baptist*, January 12, 1856.

—"Short Sermons Number 24: The Believer Persuaded of Christ's Ability to Save," *Tennessee Baptist*, January 26, 1856.

—"Short Sermons Number 25: Christ's Disciples in the World," *Tennessee Baptist*, February 2, 1856.

—"Short Sermons Number 26: The Lord Reigns," *Tennessee Baptist*, February 16, 1856.

—"Short Sermons Number 27: The Friends of Christ," *Tennessee Baptist*, February 23, 1856.

—"Short Sermons Number 28: Adoption," *Tennessee Baptist*, March 1, 1856.

—"Short Sermons Number 29: Regeneration," *Tennessee Baptist*, April 26, 1856.

—"Short Sermons Number 30: The Nature, Effect, and Necessity of Conversion," *Tennessee Baptist*, May 17, 1856.

—"Short Sermons Number 33: God the Guide of His People," *Tennessee Baptist*, June 21, 1856.

—"Short Sermons Number 34: Faith Overcomes the World," *Tennessee Baptist*, July 12, 1856.

—"Short Sermons Number 35: Accountability to God," *Tennessee Baptist*, August 9, 1856.

—"Short Sermons Number 36: Rest for the People of God," *Tennessee Baptist*, August 16, 1856.

—"Short Sermons Number 37: Godliness in all Respects Profitable," *Tennessee Baptist*, August 23, 1856.

—"Short Sermons Number 38: (illegible)," *Tennessee Baptist*, August 30, 1856.

—"Short Sermons Number 39: The Inspiration and Utility of the Scriptures," *Tennessee Baptist*, September 6, 1856.

—"Short Sermons Number 40: Who Will Not and Who Will Enter Into Heaven," *Tennessee Baptist*, September 27, 1856.

—"Short Sermons Number 41: Christ the Source of Wisdom, Righteousness, Sanctification, and Redemption," *Tennessee Baptist*, October 4, 1856.

—"Short Sermons Number 42: The Results of Apostolic Preaching on Pentecost," *Tennessee Baptist*, October 25, 1856.

—"Short Sermons Number 44: Christians Should Awake Out of Sleep Because Their Salvation Is Near," *Tennessee Baptist*, February 14, 1857.

—"Short Sermons Number 45: The Upright—What God Is to Them and Does for Them," *Tennessee Baptist*, March 21, 1857.

—"Short Sermons Number 46: The Christian Profession," *Tennessee Baptist*, April 18, 1857.

—"Short Sermons Number 47: The Wisdom of God in Redemption," *Tennessee Baptist*, April 25, 1857.

—"Short Sermons Number 48: The Law and the Gospel," *Tennessee Baptist*, July 25, 1857.

—"Short Sermons Number 49: Want of Love to God," *Tennessee Baptist*, August 8, 1857.

—"Some of the Defects of Modern Religion," *Tennessee Baptist*, October 17, 1857.

—"Something for Dr. McFerrin," *Tennessee Baptist*, February 23, 1856.

—"Something Strange," *Tennessee Baptist*, June 11, 1859.

—"The South Western Baptist," *Tennessee Baptist*, November 28, 1857.

—"The South-Western Baptist," *Tennessee Baptist*, July 3, 1858.

—"Southern Baptist Convention," *Tennessee Baptist*, June 15, 1861.

—"Southern Baptist Publication Society," *Tennessee Baptist*, August 8, 1857.

—"Southern Baptist Sabbath School Union," *Tennessee Baptist*, November 12, 1859.

—"Southern Baptist Sabbath School Union," *Tennessee Baptist*, December 1, 1860.

—"Southern Baptist Sunday School Union," *Tennessee Baptist*, August 21, 1858.

—"Specimen of the Revision of the Old Testament," *Tennessee Baptist*, June 23, 1855.

—"Spiritual Drouth," *Tennessee Baptist*, August 18, 1860.

—"Spurgeon's Life and Ministry," *Tennessee Baptist*, April 3, 1858.

—"The State of the Country," *Tennessee Baptist*, November 24, 1860.

—"Statement of Elder J. M. Pendleton," *Tennessee Baptist*, May 21, 1859.

—"The St. Louis Presbyterian," *Tennessee Baptist*, April 12, 1856.

—"Strange Injustice," *Tennessee Baptist*, December 5, 1857.

—"Strike, But Hear Me: A Review," *Tennessee Baptist*, August 21, 1858.

—"The Students of Union University," *Tennessee Baptist*, March 2, 1861.

—"Substitution Again," *Western Recorder*, February 5, 1891.

—"Sunday Morning Thoughts," *Tennessee Baptist*, May 29, 1858.

—"Sunday Morning Thoughts," *Tennessee Baptist*, June 12, 1858.

—"Sunday Morning Thoughts," *Tennessee Baptist*, June 19, 1858.

—"Sunday Morning Thoughts," *Tennessee Baptist*, July 10, 1858.

—"Sunday Morning Thoughts," *Tennessee Baptist*, July 31, 1858.

—"Sunday Morning Thoughts," *Tennessee Baptist*, September 18, 1858.

—"Sunday Morning Thoughts," *Tennessee Baptist*, December 11, 1858.

—"Sunday Morning Thoughts," *Tennessee Baptist*, January 29, 1859.

—"Sunday Morning Thoughts," *Tennessee Baptist*, March 5, 1859.

—"Sunday Morning Thoughts," *Tennessee Baptist*, March 26, 1859.

—"Sunday Morning Thoughts," *Tennessee Baptist*, April 9, 1859.

—"Sunday Morning Thoughts," *Tennessee Baptist*, April 16, 1859.

—"Sunday Morning Thoughts," *Tennessee Baptist*, April 23, 1859.

—"Sunday Morning Thoughts," *Tennessee Baptist*, April 30, 1859.

—"Sunday Morning Thoughts," *Tennessee Baptist*, May 14, 1859.

—"Sunday Morning Thoughts," *Tennessee Baptist*, May 28, 1859.

—"Sunday Morning Thoughts," *Tennessee Baptist*, June 18, 1859.

—"Sunday Morning Thoughts," *Tennessee Baptist*, July 2, 1859.

—"Sunday Morning Thoughts," *Tennessee Baptist*, July 16, 1859.

—"Sunday Morning Thoughts," *Tennessee Baptist*, August 6, 1859.

—"Sunday Morning Thoughts," *Tennessee Baptist*, August 13, 1859.

—"Sunday Morning Thoughts," *Tennessee Baptist*, August 27, 1859.

—"Sunday Morning Thoughts," *Tennessee Baptist*, September 3, 1859.

—"The Sunday School Convention," *Tennessee Baptist*, December 11, 1858.

—"Sunday School Convention," *Tennessee Baptist*, September 12, 1857.

—"The S. Western Baptist and the Old Landmark," *Tennessee Baptist*, August 2, 1856.

—"The Symmetry of Christian Character," *Tennessee Baptist*, May 5, 1860.

—"That Committee Once More," *Tennessee Baptist*, November 3, 1855.

—"That Learned Methodist Preacher," *Tennessee Baptist*, August 23, 1856.

—"That Same Committee," *Tennessee Baptist*, October 27, 1855.

—"That Week of Prayer," *Tennessee Baptist*, July 2, 1859.

—"Theological Endowment," *Tennessee Baptist*, November 12, 1859.

—"Theological Lectures," *Tennessee Baptist*, April 4, 1857.

—"Theological Professorship," *Tennessee Baptist*, January 15, 1859.

—"Theological Schools," *Tennessee Baptist*, September 22, 1860.

—"Theological Schools," *Tennessee Baptist*, October 13, 1860.

—"The Thing Explained," *Tennessee Baptist*, November 20, 1858.

—"Things New and Strange," *Tennessee Baptist*, August 14, 1858.

—"Thoughts for the Times," *Tennessee Baptist*, May 18, 1861.

—"Thoughts on Backsliding Number 3: Criminality," *Tennessee Baptist*, June 21, 1856.

—"Thoughts on Christian Duty Number 2: Holding Fast Our Profession," *Tennessee Baptist*, May 13, 1854.

—"Thoughts on Christian Duty Number 5: Family Worship," *Tennessee Baptist*, July 8, 1854.

—"Thoughts on Christian Duty Number 6: Public Worship," *Tennessee Baptist*, July 29, 1854.

—"Thoughts on Christian Duty Number 7: Prayer Meeting," *Tennessee Baptist*, August 12, 1854.

—"Thoughts on Christian Duty Number 14: Christian Joy," *Tennessee Baptist*, February 24, 1855.

—"Thoughts on Christian Duty Number 17: God's People are His Witnesses," *Tennessee Baptist*, August 11, 1855.

—"Thoughts on Christian Duty Number 18: The Proper Use of Money," *Tennessee Baptist*, October 20, 1855.

—"Thoughts on Christian Duty Number 19: The Endurance of Affliction," *Tennessee Baptist*, February 2, 1856.

—"Thoughts on Giving: Number 2," *Tennessee Baptist*, December 3, 1859.

—"Thoughts on Giving: Number 3," *Tennessee Baptist*, December 10, 1859.

—"Thoughts on Giving: Number 4," *Tennessee Baptist*, December 17, 1859.

—"Thoughts on Giving: Number 5," *Tennessee Baptist*, December 24, 1859.

—"Thoughts on Giving: Number 6," *Tennessee Baptist*, January 14, 1860.

—"Thoughts on Giving: Number 7," *Tennessee Baptist*, January 21, 1860.

—"Thoughts on Giving: Number 8," *Tennessee Baptist*, January 28, 1860.

—"Thoughts on Giving: Number 9," *Tennessee Baptist*, February 25, 1860.

—"Thoughts on Giving: Number 10," *Tennessee Baptist*, March 3, 1860.

—"Thoughts on Giving: Number 11," *Tennessee Baptist*, March 17, 1860.

—"Thoughts on Giving: Number 12," *Tennessee Baptist*, March 24, 1860.

—"Thoughts on Giving: Number 13," *Tennessee Baptist*, March 31, 1860.

—"Thoughts on Giving: Number 14," *Tennessee Baptist*, April 7, 1860.

—"Time is Passing Away," *Tennessee Baptist*, January 5, 1861.

—"The Translation of 'Baptizo'," *Tennessee Baptist*, December 3, 1859.

—"A Tribute of Respect," *Tennessee Baptist*, January 22, 1859.

—"Union Prayer Meeting," *Tennessee Baptist*, January 5, 1861.

—"Union University," *Tennessee Baptist*, November 27, 1858.

—"Union University," *Tennessee Baptist*, December 18, 1858.

—"Union University," *Tennessee Baptist*, March 5, 1859.

—"Union University," *Tennessee Baptist*, August 20, 1859.

—"Union University," *Tennessee Baptist*, January 21, 1860.

—"Union University," *Tennessee Baptist*, March 10, 1860.

—"Union University," *Tennessee Baptist*, September 15, 1860.

—"Union University," *Tennessee Baptist*, December 22, 1860.

—"Union University," *Tennessee Baptist*, April 20, 1861.

—"Union with Pedobaptists," *Tennessee Baptist*, December 15, 1860.

—"The Vicksburg Sun," *Tennessee Baptist*, June 16, 1860.

—"Victory Over Death and the Grave Through Jesus," *Tennessee Baptist*, June 26, 1858.

—"Waiting Sometime for Seats," *Tennessee Baptist*, June 16, 1855.

—"Was Judas at the Lord's Supper?," *Tennessee Baptist*, April 9, 1859.

—"The Western Recorder," *Tennessee Baptist*, April 21, 1860.

—"The Western Recorder," *Tennessee Baptist*, October 13, 1855.

—"The Western Recorder and Presbyterian Herald," *Tennessee Baptist*, February 21, 1857.

—"What Romanists Mean by Liberty of Conscience," *Tennessee Baptist*, August 5, 1854.

—"What a Methodist Says," *Tennessee Baptist*, November 27, 1858.

—"What Is to Be Done in Heaven?," *Tennessee Baptist*, April 18, 1857.

—"What Must Christians Do to Regain Their First Blessedness?," *Tennessee Baptist*, October 27, 1860.

—"What Next?," *Tennessee Baptist*, February 13, 1858.

—"What W. W. Everts Says," *Tennessee Baptist*, June 30, 1860.

—"Where Shall Retrenchment Commence?," *Tennessee Baptist*, November 24, 1860.

—"Which Things the Angels Desire to Look Into," *Tennessee Baptist*, October 17, 1857.

—"Williams on Campbellism," *Tennessee Baptist*, January 12, 1861.

—"Who Are the Daughters?," *Tennessee Baptist*, June 30, 1855.

—"Who Can Explain?," *Tennessee Baptist*, July 24, 1858.

—"Who is Right?," *Tennessee Baptist*, May 1, 1858.

—"Who Will Aid in a Good Work?," *Tennessee Baptist*, April 21, 1860.

—"Why Brother South Left the Methodists," *Tennessee Baptist*, July 25, 1857.

—"Why the Landmark Was Reset," *Tennessee Baptist*, January 14, 1860.

—"Why Was Christ Baptized?," *Tennessee Baptist*, August 9, 1856.

—"Will You Be One to Respond," *Tennessee Baptist*, October 10, 1857.

—"Words of Comfort," *Tennessee Baptist*, August 18, 1860.

—"A Word to Brother Hillsman," *Tennessee Baptist*, December 5, 1857.

—"A Word Used Correctly," *Tennessee Baptist*, December 22, 1855.

—"A Worldly Spirit," *Tennessee Baptist*, August 1, 1857.

—"The Work of a Crazy Man," *Tennessee Baptist*, December 22, 1860.

OTHER SOURCES

Books

Ahern, Dianne. *Today I Was Baptized*. Ann Arbor: Aunt Dee's Attic, 2000.

Amonette, Austin Bennett. "Alexander Campbell Among the Baptists: An Examination of the Beginning, Ambiguity, and Deterioration of Their Relationship, 1812–1830." Ph.D. diss., New Orleans Baptist Theological Seminary, 2002.

Anderson, Henry Lee. "The Ecclesiology of Ante-Bellum Baptist Churches in the South." Th.D. diss., New Orleans Baptist Theological Seminary, 1960.

Aquinas, Thomas. *The Blessed Sacrament and the Mass*. Translated by F. O'Neill. Maryland: Newman Press, 1955.

Arnold, Albert. *Prerequisites to Communion*. Boston: Gould and Lincoln, 1861.

Barnes, Albert. *Notes on the New Testament, Explanatory and Practical: 1 Corinthians*. Grand Rapids: Baker Book House, 1949.

Barth, Karl. *The Teaching of the Church Regarding Baptism*. London: SCM, 1948.

Beasley-Murray, George. *Baptism in the New Testament*. Grand Rapids: Eerdmans, 1973.

Bebbington, David W., ed. *The Gospel in the World*. Waynesboro: Paternoster, 2002.

Belcher, Joseph. *Memorials of Baptist Martyrs*. Philadelphia: American Baptist Publication Society, 1854.

Bell, Marty G. "James Robinson Graves and the Rhetoric of Demagogy: Primitivism and Democracy in Old Landmarkism (Baptist)." Ph.D. diss., Vanderbilt University, 1990.

Benedict, David. *A General History of the Baptist Denomination in America and Other Parts of the World*. New York: Lewis Colby, 1848.

Bernardin, Joseph Buchanan. *An Introduction to the Episcopal Church*. New York: Morehouse-Barlow, 1957.

Blaising, Craig, and Darrell Bock. *Progressive Dispensationalism*. Wheaton: Victor Books, 1993.

Board of Publication of the Reformed Protestant Dutch Church. *A Message to Ruling Elders; Their Office and*

Their Duties. New York: Board of Publication of the Reformed Protestant Dutch Church, 1859.

Bogard, Ben. *Pillars of Orthodoxy, or Defenders of the Faith*. Louisville: Baptist Book Concern, 1900.

Boles, John B. *The Great Revival*. Lexington: University of Kentucky, 1972.

Bone, Michael Henry. "A Study of the Writings of J. R. Graves (1820–1893) as an Example of the Nature and Function of Absolutes in Religious Symbol System." Ph.D. diss., Boston University, 2001.

Boone, William Cooke. *What We Believe*. Nashville: Sunday School Board of the Southern Baptist Convention, 1936.

Booth, Abraham. *Vindication of the Baptists from the Charge of Bigotry, in Refusing Communion at the Lord's Table to Pedobaptists*. Philadelphia: American Baptist Publication Society, 1778.

Borum, Joseph H. *Biographical Sketches of Tennessee Baptist Ministers*. Memphis: Rogers and Co., 1880.

Brackney, William Henry. *The Baptists*. New York: Greenwood Press, 1988.

Brand, Chad, and R. Stanton Norman eds. *Perspectives on Church Government*. Nashville: Broadman & Holman, 2004.

Breckinridge, Robert. *The Christian Pastor, One of the Ascension Gifts of Christ. To Which Are Added by Way of Appendix, Presbyterian Government Not a Hierarch, but a Commonwealth; and Presbyterian Ordination Not a Charm, but an Act of Government*. Baltimore: by the author, 1845.

—*The Knowledge of God, Objectively Considered*. New York: R. Carter, 1858.

—*The Knowledge of God, Subjectively Considered*. New York: R. Carter, 1859.

Bromiley, G. W. *Zwingli and Bullinger: Library of Christian Classics*, Vol. 14. Philadelphia: Westminster Press, 1953.

Brown, J. Newton. *The Baptist Church Manual: Containing the Declaration of Faith, Covenant, Rules of Order and Brief Forms of Church Letters*. Philadelphia: American Baptist Publication Society, 1853.

—*A New Baptist Church Manual*. Valley Forge: Judson Press, 1895.

Bruce, F. F. *The English Bible: A History of Translations*. New York: Oxford University, 1961.

Brunner, Emil. *The Divine-Human Encounter*. Translated by Amandus W. Loos. Philadelphia: Westminster, 1943.

Bryan, Philip Ray. "An Analysis of the Ecclesiology of Associational Baptists, 1900–1950." Ph.D. diss., Baylor University, 1973.

Buchanan, Colin Ogilvie. *Infant Baptism in Common Worship*. Cambridge: Grove Books, 2001.

Bunyan, John. *The Miscellaneous Works of John Bunyan*. Edited by T. L. Underwood. Clarendon Press: Oxford, 1989.

Burnett, J. J. *Sketches of Tennessee's Pioneer Baptist Preachers*. Vol. 1. Nashville: Marshall and Bruce Co., 1919.

Burrows, J. L. *What Baptists Believe*. Baltimore: H. M. Wharton & Company, 1887.

Bush, L. Russ, and Thomas Nettles. *Baptists and the Bible*. Revised and Expanded. Nashville: Broadman & Holman, 1999.

Calvin, John. *Calvin's Commentaries*. Grand Rapids: Baker Books, 1999.

—*Institutes of the Christian Religion.* in *Library of Christian Classics*, Translated by F.L. Battles, Edited by John T. McNeil. Louisville: Westminster John Knox Press, 1960.

Campbell, Alexander. *Christian Baptism with Its Antecedents and Consequents.* Bethany: Published by the author, 1851. Reprint, Nashville: Gospel Advocate, 1951.

Carroll, J.M. *The Trail of Blood.* Lexington: American Baptist Publishing Company, 1931.

Carson, Alexander. *Baptism in Its Mode and Subjects.* Philadelphia: American Baptist Publication Society, 1848.

Chalmers, Thomas. *Lectures on the Epistles of Paul the Apostle to the Romans.* New York: Carter, 1845.

Chambliss, A. W. *The Catechetical Instructor: A Handbook of Bible Doctrines and Practices for the Use of Families, Sabbath Schools, and Bible Classes.* St. Louis: John T. Smith, 1890.

Chapman, James L. and J. R. Graves. *Defence of the Government of the Methodist Episcopal Church: in His Debate with the Rev. J. R. Graves, at Canton, Miss., May, 1855.* Nashville: Southern Methodist Publishing House, 1860.

Christian, John T. *Close Communion: or Baptism as a Prerequisite to the Lord's Supper.* Louisville: Baptist Book Concern, 1892.

Clark, George W., and J. M. Pendleton. *Brief Notes on the New Testament.* Philadelphia: American Baptist Publication Society, 1884.

Clowney, Edmund. *The Church.* Downers Grove: InterVarsity, 1995.

Cobb, Jesse E. *Baptist Church Manual.* Little Rock: Baptist Publishing House, 1941.

Conant, Thomas Jefferson. *The Meaning and Use of Baptizein, Philologically and Historically Investigated for the American Bible Union.* New York: American Bible Union, 1860.

Conkin, Paul. *Cane Ridge: America's Pentecost.* Madison: University of Wisconsin Press, 1990.

Conner, Walter Thomas. *Christian Doctrine.* Nashville: Broadman, 1937.

Cook, Henry. *What Baptists Stand For.* London: Kingsgate Press, 1947.

Cowen, Gerald. *Who Rules the Church? Examining Congregational Leadership and Church Government.* Nashville: Broadman & Holman, 2003.

Crosby, David Eldon. "Church Government in the Church Growth Movement: Critique from a Historic Baptist Perspective." Ph.D. diss., Baylor University, 1989.

Crowther, Edward. "Southern Protestants, Slavery, and Secession: A Study in Southern Religious Ideology, 1830–1861." Ph.D. diss., Auburn University, 1986.

Curtis, Thomas F. *Communion: The Distinction Between Christian and Church Fellowship and Between Communion and Its Symbols.* Philadelphia: American Baptist Publication Society, 1850.

Dagg, J. L. *Manual of Church Order.* Charleston: Southern Baptist Publication Society, 1858. Reprint, Harrisonburg: Gano Books, 1990.

—*Manual of Theology.* Charleston: Southern Baptist Publication Society, 1857.

Dana, Harvey Eugene and L. M. Sipes. *A Manual of Ecclesiology.* Kansas City: Central Seminary Press, 1944.

Dargan, Edwin C. *Ecclesiology: A Study of the Churches.* Louisville: Chas. T. Dearing, 1897.

Davis, Jonathon. *History of the Welsh Baptists*. Pittsburgh: D. M. Hogan, 1835.

Davison, James E. *Living Water: A Guide to Baptism for Presbyterians*. Louisville: Geneva Press, 2000.

Dayton, A. C. *Pedobaptist and Cambellite Immersions*. Nashville: Graves, & Marks, 1858.

—*Theodosia Earnest, or, The Heroine of Faith*. Chicago: Church and Goodman, 1866.

Dever, Mark. *A Display of God's Glory*. Washington: Center for Church Reform, 2001.

—*Nine Marks of a Healthy Church*. Washington: Center for Church Reform, 2001.

—ed. *Polity: Biblical Arguments on How to Conduct Church Life*. Washington: Center for Church Reform, 2000.

Deweese, Charles W., ed. *Defining Baptist Convictions: Guidelines for the Twenty-First Century*. Franklin: Providence House, 1996.

Dick, John. *Lectures on Theology*. Philadelphia: J. Whetham, 1836.

Doddridge, Philip. *Miscellaneous Works*. London: William Ball, 1839.

Doerries, Hermann. *Constantine and Religious Liberty*. Translated by Roland Bainton. New Haven: Yale University, 1960.

Dulles, Avery. *Models of the Church*. New York: Doubleday, 2002.

Duncan, William Cecil. *A Brief History of the Baptists and Their Distinctive Principles and Practices*. New York: Edward H. Fletcher, 1855.

Durnbaugh, Donald F. *The Believers' Church*. Scottdale: Herald Press, 1968.

Dyer, Larry. *Baptism: The Believer's First Obedience*. Grand Rapids: Kregel, 2000.

Eaton, T. T. *The Faith of Baptists*. Louisville: Baptist Book Concern, 1898.

—"The Life of Rev. James Madison Pendleton." First annual meeting of the *Kentucky Baptist Historical Society* (June 14, 1904). Louisville: Baptist Book Concern, 1904.

Edwards, Peter. *Candid Reasons for Renouncing the Principles of Antipedobaptism*. Aberdeen: George King, 1841.

Engelder, Conrad. "The Churches and Slavery: A Study of the Attitudes Toward Slavery of the Major Protestant Denominations." Ph.D. diss., University of Michigan, 1964.

Engle, Paul, and Steven Cowan, eds. *Who Runs the Church?* Grand Rapids: Zondervan, 2004.

Erickson, Millard. *Christian Theology*. Grand Rapids: Baker, 1998.

Estep, William R. *The Anabaptist Story*. Grand Rapids: Eerdmans, 1996.

Fitzgerald, Allan, ed. *Augustine Through the Ages*. Grand Rapids, Eerdmans, 1999.

Fletcher, Jesse. *The Southern Baptist Convention: A Sesquicentennial History*. Nashville: Broadman & Holman, 1994.

Foot, William. *A Practical Discourse Concerning Baptism*. Warminster: J. L. Vardy, 1820.

Frend, W. H. C. *The Donatist Church*. Oxford: Clarendon Press, 1952.

Frey, Joseph Samuel. *Essays on Christian Baptism*. New York: Printed by the author, 1843.

Frost, J. M. *Baptist Why and Why Not: Twenty-five Papers by Twenty-five Writers, and a Declaration of Faith.* Nashville: Sunday School Board, 1900.

—*The Consistency of Restricted Communion.* Philadelphia: American Baptist Publication Society, 1888.

—*The Memorial Supper of Our Lord.* Nashville: Sunday School Board, 1908.

—*The Moral Dignity of Baptism.* Nashville: Sunday School Board, Southern Baptist Convention, 1905.

Fuller, J. G., ed. *Conversations Between Two Laymen, on Strict and Mixed Communion.* Boston: Lincoln and Edmands, 1832.

Gaines, David P. *Beliefs of Baptists.* New York: Richard R. Smith Publishers, 1952.

Gardner, W. W. *Church Communion, As Practiced by the Baptists, Explained and Defended.* Cincinnati: George E. Stevens, 1873.

Garrett, James Leo, Jr. *Systematic Theology: Biblical, Historical, & Evangelical.* Grand Rapids: Eerdmans, 1990.

Garrison, W. E., and A. T. DeGroot. *The Disciples of Christ.* St. Louis: Christian Board of Publications, 1948.

George, Timothy. *Theology of the Reformers.* Nashville: Broadman & Holman, 1988.

—and David Dockery, eds. *Baptist Theologians.* Nashville: Broadman Press, 1990.

—and David Dockery, eds. *Theologians of the Baptist Tradition.* Nashville: Broadman & Holman, 2001.

—and Denise George, eds., *Baptist Confessions, Covenants, and Catechisms.* Tennessee: Broadman & Holman, 1966.

Gilmore, Alec. *Christian Baptism*. Chicago: Judson Press, 1959.

Graves. James Robinson. *Intercommunion: Inconsistent, Unscriptural, and Productive of Evil*. Memphis: Baptist Book House, 1881.

—*The Lord's Supper: A Church Ordinance, and So Observed by the Apostolic Churches*. Texarkana: Baptist Sunday School Committee, 1881.

—*Old Landmarkism: What Is It?* Texarkana: Bogard press, 1880.

—*What Is It to Eat and Drink Unworthily?* Texarkana: Baptist Sunday School Board, 1881.

Gray, Joan S., and Joyce C. Tucker. *Presbyterian Polity for Church Officers*. Louisville: Geneva, 1999.

Grenz, Stanley. *The Baptist Congregation*. Vancouver: Regent, 1985.

Grudem, Wayne. *Systematic Theology*. Grand Rapids: Zondervan, 1994.

Hailey, O. L. *J. R. Graves: Life, Times and Teachings*. Nashville: O. L. Hailey, 1929.

Hall, Robert. *On Terms of Communion: with a Particular View to the Case of the Baptists and Pedobaptists*. np: G. J. Loomis, 1816.

—*The Works of Robert Hall*. ed. Olinthus Gregory, London: George Routledge and Sons, 1866.

Harvey, Hezekiah. *The Church: Its Polity and Ordinances*. Philadelphia: American Baptist Publication Society, 1879.

Hatch, Nathan. *The Democratization of American Christianity*. New Haven: Yale University, 1989.

Helwys, Thomas. *The Mistery of Iniquity*. London: Kingsgate Press, 1935.

Hibbard, Freeborn G. *Christian Baptism: Mode, Obligation, Import and Relative Order*. New York: Carlton & Lanahan, 1841.

Hill, James Emmett, Jr. "James Madison Pendleton's Theology of Baptism." Th.M. thesis, Southern Baptist Theological Seminary, 1958.

Hilton, James. "Robert Boyte Crawford Howell's Contribution to Baptist Ecclesiology: Nineteenth Century Baptist Ecclesiology in Controversy." PhD diss., Southeastern Baptist Theological Seminary, 2005.

Hiscox, Edward T. *Baptist Church Polity, Doctrines, Confessions of Faith*. Nashville: Historical Commissions, 1856.

—*The Hiscox Standard Baptist Manual*. Valley Forge: Judson Press, 1865.

—*The New Directory for Baptist Churches*. Philadelphia: Judson Press, 1894.

Hodge, Charles. *The Constitutional History of the Presbyterian Church in the United States of America*. Philadelphia: Presbyterian Board of Publication, 1863.

—*Discussions in Church Polity*. New York: Charles Scribner's Sons, 1878.

—*Systematic Theology*. Peabody: Hendrickson, 2001.

Hogue, LeRoy B. "A Study of the Antecedents of Landmarkism." Th.D. diss., Southern Baptist Theological Seminary, 1966.

Holifield, E. Brooks. *The Gentlemen Theologians: American Theology in Southern Culture 1795–1860*. Durham: Duke University Press, 1978.

—*Theology in America.* London: Yale University, 2003.

Hooker, Richard. *Of the Laws of Ecclesiastical Polity.* abridged ed., eds. McGrade Vickers and Brian Vickers. New York: St. Martin's Press, 1975.

Horne, Thomas H. *An Introduction to the Critical Study of Knowledge of the Holy Scriptures.* Philadelphia: E. Littell, 1825.

Houghton, Myron James. "The Place of Baptism in the Theology of James Robinson Graves." Th.D. diss., Dallas Theological Seminary, 1971.

Howell, R. B. C. *The Evils of Infant Baptism.* Charleston: Southern Baptist Publication, 1852.

—*The Terms of Communion at the Lord's Table.* Philadelphia: American Baptist Publication Society, 1846.

Howell, R. B. C., et al. *Both Sides.* Nashville: Southwestern Publishing House, 1859.

Huddleston, William Clyde. "James Madison Pendleton: A Critical Biography." Th.M. thesis, Southern Baptist Theological Seminary, 1962.

Hudson, Winthrop. *Baptist Concepts of the Church.* Chicago: Judson Press, 1959.

Hudson, Winthrop, and John Corrigan. *Religion in America: An Historical Account of the Development of American Religious Life.* New York: MacMillan, 1992.

Jenkens, Charles A. *Baptist Doctrines.* St. Louis: Chancy R. Barns, 1881.

—*What Made Me a Baptist.* Richmond: Virginia Baptist Historical Society, 1901.

Jeter, Jeremiah. *Baptist Principles Reset: Consisting of Articles on Distinctive Baptist Prinicples.* Richmond: Religious Herald, 1902.

—*Campbellism Examined.* New York: Sheldon & Blakeman, 1857.

Jewett, Paul. *Infant Baptism and the Covenant of Grace.* Grand Rapids: Eerdmans, 1978.

Johnson, Lennart. *Baptist Reconsideration of Baptism and Ecclesiology.* New York : P. Lang, 2000.

Johnson, W. B. *The Gospel Developed Through the Government and Order of the Churches of Jesus Christ.* Richmond: H. K. Ellyson, 1846.

Jones, Barry William. "James R. Graves, Baptist Newspaper Editor: Catalyst for Religious Controversy, 1846–1893." Ph.D. diss., Ohio University, 1994.

Jones, Philip. *A Restatement of Baptist Principles.* Philadelphia: Griffith & Rowland, 1909.

Kärkkäinen, Veli-Matti. *An Introduction to Ecclesiology: Ecumenical, Historical & Global Perspectives.* Downers Grove: InterVarsity, 2002.

Kennedy, Crammond. *Close Communion, or Open Communion?* New York: American News Company, 1868.

Kiffin, William. *A Sober Discourse of Right to Church Communion.* London: Geo. Larkin, 1681.

—*Some Serious Reflections on that Part of Mr. Bunyan's Confession of Faith Touching Church Communion with Unbaptized Persons.* London: Printed for Francis Smith, 167.

Klaassen, Walter, ed. *Anabaptism in Outline.* Scottdale: Herald Press, 1981.

Kousser, J. Morgan & James M. McPherson, eds. *Region, Race, and Reconstruction: Essays in Honor of C. Vann Woodward.* New York: Oxford University Press, 1982.

Lane, William Thomas. "Ordination: Its Significance and Meaning for the Southern Baptist Convention Studied in the Context of the Landmark Controversy." Ph.D. diss., Southern Baptist Theological Seminary, 1959.

Leonard, Bill J. *Baptist Ways: A History*. Valley Forge: Judson Press, 2003.

Letham, Robert. *The Lord's Supper: Eternal Word in Broken Bread*. Phillipsburg: P&R Publishing, 2001.

Long, Edward LeRoy, Jr. *Patterns of Polity: Varieties of Church Governance*. Cleveland: Pilgrim Press, 2001.

Love, J. F. *The Baptist Position and the Position for a Baptist*. Nashville: Sunday School Board, 1903.

Lovegrove, Deryck W., ed. *The Rise of the Laity in Evangelical Protestantism*. New York: Routledge, 2002.

Lovett, Michael James. "An Inquiry into the Theological Development of Southern Baptist Communion Thought." Th.M. thesis, Southeastern Baptist Theological Seminary, 1983.

Lull, Timothy. *Martin Luther's Basic Theological Writings*. Minneapolis: Fortress Press, 1989.

Lumpkin, William L. *Baptist Confessions of Faith*. Valley Forge: Judson Press, 1969.

MacArthur, John Jr. *Answering the Key Questions about Elders*. Panorama City: Grace to You, 1984.

Macy, Gary. *The Theologies of the Eucharist in the Early Scholastic Period*. Oxford: Clarendon Press, 1984.

Malone, Fred. *The Baptism of Disciples Alone: A Covenantal Argument for Credobaptism Versus Paedobaptism*. Cape Coral: Founders Press, 2003.

Marcel, Pierre Charles, and Philip Edgcumbe Hughes. *The Biblical Doctrine of Infant Baptism: Sacrament of the Covenant of Grace*. Eugene: Wipf & Stock, 2002.

Maring, Norman H. and Winthrop S. Hudson. *A Baptist Manual of Polity and Practice.* Chicago: Judson Press, 1963.

Matthews, Donald. *Religion in the Old South.* Chicago: University of Chicago, 1977.

Matthews, John F. *Baptism: A Baptist View.* London: Baptist Publications, 1976.

McBeth, Leon. *The Baptist Heritage: Four Centuries of Baptist Witness.* Nashville: Broadman Press, 1987.

McBrien, Richard P. *Catholicism.* San Francisco: Harper Collins, 1989.

McCall, Duke K., ed. *What is the Church?* Nashville: Broadman Press, 1958.

McConnell, F. M. *Pendleton's Church Manual: Designed for the Use of Baptist Churches.* Dallas: B. J. Robert Book Company, 1900.

McDaniel, George W. *The People Called Baptists.* Nashville: Sunday School Board, 1925.

McDermott, John ed. *The Frontier Re-examined.* Urbana: University of Illinois Press, 1967.

Mell, P. H. *Corrective Church Discipline.* Charleston: Southern Baptist Publication Society, 1860.

Moody, Dale. *Baptism: Foundation for Christian Unity.* Philadelphia: Westminster, 1967.

—*The Word of Truth.* Grand Rapids: Eerdmans, 1981.

Moore, David O. "The Landmark Baptists and Their Attack Upon the Southern Baptist Convention Historically Analyzed." Ph.D. diss., Southern Baptist Theological Seminary, 1950.

Moore, Eugene T. "The Background of the Landmark Movement." Th.M. thesis, Southwestern Baptist Theological Seminary, 1947.

Morrison, Barry. "In Spirit and in Truth: The Theology and Spirituality of the Lord's Supper within the Context of Worship in the Baptist Tradition." Th.D. diss., Regis College, 1988.

Moser, N. S. Sr. *Baptist Doctrine in One Year: Based on Pendleton's Church Manual.* Little Rock: Central Baptist Church Publications, 1960.

Moulton, W. Fiddian. *The History of the English Bible.* London: Charles H. Kelly, 1911.

Mullins, Edgar Young. *The Christian Religion in Its Doctrinal Expression.* Nashville: Broadman Press, 1917.

Murray, Iain. *Revival & Revivalism: The Making and Marring of American Evangelicalism 1750–1858.* Bath: Bath Press, 1994.

Nettles, Thomas. *By His Grace and for His Glory.* Grand Rapids: Baker, 1986.

—ed. *Teaching Truth, Training Hearts.* Amityville: Calvary Press, 1998.

Nettles, Thomas, and Russell Moore, eds. *Why I am a Baptist.* Nashville: Broadman & Holman, 2001.

Noel, Wriothesley. *Essay on Christian Baptism.* New York: Harper & Brothers, 1850.

Noll, Mark. *America's God: from Jonathan Edwards to Abraham Lincoln.* New York: Oxford University Press, 2002.

—*The Rise of Evangelicalism*. Downers Grove: InterVarsity, 2003.

Norman, R. Stanton. "A Critical Analysis of the Intentional Efforts of Baptists to Distinguish Themselves Theologically from Other Christian Denominations." Ph.D. diss., Southwestern Baptist Theological Seminary, 1997.

—*More Than Just a Name: Preserving Our Baptist Identity*. Nashville: Broadman & Holman, 2001.

Oden, Thomas. *Life in the Spirit*. Peabody: Prince, 2001.

Odle, Joe T. *Why I am a Baptist*. Nashville: Broadman, 1972.

Orchard, George Herbert. *A Concise History of the Foreign Baptists*. Nashville: Graves & Marks, 1855.

—*Theology and the Kingdom of God*. Philadelphia: Westminster, 1969.

Patterson, T. A. "The Theology of J. R. Graves, and Its Influences on Southern Baptist Life." Th.D. diss., Southwestern Baptist Theological Seminary, 1944.

Pendleton, Garnett. *Semi-Centennial of Upland Baptist Church, 1852–1902, Oct. 8 to 12*. Philadelphia: n.p., 1902.

Piper, John. *Biblical Eldership*, printed material accompanying the tapes. Minneapolis: Desiring God Ministries, 1999.

Porter, Stanley, and Anthony R. Cross. *Dimensions of Baptism*. New York: Sheffield Academic Press, 2000.

Proctor, B. F. *The Life of Rev. James Madison Pendleton*. Louisville: Baptist Book Concern, 1904.

Radbertus, Pascasius. *De Corpore et Sanguine Domini*. Turnholti: Typographi Brepols, 1969.

Ratramnus. *De Corpore et Sanguine Domini*. London: North-Holland, 1974.

Remington, S. *A Defence of Restricted Communion*. Philadelphia: American Baptist Publication Society, 1847.

Renfroe, J. J. D. *Vindication of the Communion of Baptist Churches*. Selma: John West, 1882.

Reynolds, J. L. *Church Polity: or The Kingdom of Christ, in Its Internal and External Development*. Richmond: Harrold & Murray, 1849.

Ripley, Henry J. and Henry Ware. *Sacred Rhetoric; or Composition and Delivery of Sermons*. Boston: Gould and Lincoln, 1849.

Robinson, H. Wheeler. *Baptist Principles*. London: Carey Kingsgate, 1960.

Rodgerson, Phillip Edward. "A Historical Study of Alien Baptism Among Baptists Since 1640." Ph.D. diss., Southern Baptist Theological Seminary, 1952.

Rogers, James. *The Cane Ridge Meeting-house*. Cincinnati: Standard, 1910.

Rosser, Leonidas. *Baptism: Its Nature, Obligation, Mode, Subjects, and Benefits*. Richmond: Published by the author, 1853.

Russell, Brian. *Baptism: Sign and Seal of the Covenant of Grace*. London: Grace Publications, 2001.

Rutherford, Williams. *Church Members' Guide for Baptist Churches*. Atlanta: Jas. P. Harrison & Company, 1885.

Ryland, John. *A Candid Statement of the Reasons which Induce the Baptists to Differ in Opinion and Practice from So Many of Their Christian Brethren*. Philadelphia: Anderson and Meehan, 1820.

Schaff, Philip. *Nicene and Post-Nicene Fathers*, Translated by J. R. King. Peabody: Hendrickson, 1999.

Sheridan, Tom. *The Gift of Baptism: A Handbook for Parents.* Chicago: ACTA Publications, 2003.

Shurden, Walter. *Associationalism Among Baptists in America: 1707–1814.* New York: Arno Press, 1980.

—*The Baptist Identity: Four Fragile Freedoms.* Macon: Smyth & Helwys, 1993.

—*Not A Silent People: Controversies That Have Shaped Southern Baptists.* Nashville: Broadman Press, 1972.

—ed. *Proclaiming the Baptist Vision: Baptism and the Lord's Supper.* Macon: Smyth & Helwys, 1999.

Smith, Harold Stewart. "A Critical Analysis of the Theology of J. R. Graves." Th.D. diss., Southern Baptist Theological Seminary, 1966.

Snay, Mitchell. *Gospel of Disunion: Religion and Separatism in the Antebellum South.* Chapel Hill: University of North Carolina, 1997.

—"Gospel of Disunion: Religion and the Rise of Southern Separatism, 1830–1861." Ph.D. diss., Brandeis University, 1984.Spain, Rufus, and Samuel S. Hill. *At Ease in Zion: Social History of Southern Baptist 1865–1900.* Tuscaloosa: University of Alabama, 2003.

Spencer, J. H. *History of Kentucky Baptists.* Cincinnati: J. R. Baumes, 1885.

Spurgeon, Charles H. *12 Sermons on the Lord's Supper.* Grand Rapids: Baker Book House, 1980.

—*The New Park Street Pulpit.* Pasadena: Pilgrim Publication, 1975.

Srawley, J. H., ed. *St. Ambrose "On the Mysteries" and the Treatise on the Sacraments by an Unknown Author.* Translated by T. Thompson. New York: Macmillan, 1919.

Stacy, R. Wayne., ed. *A Baptist's Theology*. Macon: Smyth & Helwys, 1999.

Staton, Cecil Jr., *Why I Am a Baptist: Reflections on Being Baptist in the 21st Century*. Macon: Smyth and Helwys, 1999.

Strauch, Alexander. *Biblical Eldership*. Littleton: Lewis & Roth, 1988.

Strong, A. H. *Systematic Theology*. Philadelphia: Judson Press, 1909.

Stuart, Moses. *Is the Mode of Christian Baptism Prescribed in the New Testament?* Nashville: Graves, Mark & Rutland, 1856.

Summers, Thomas. *Baptism: A Treatise on the Nature, Perpetuity, Subjects, Administrator, Mode, and Use of the Initiating Ordinance of the Christian Church*. Nashville: E. Stevenson & J. E. Evans, 1856.

Sweet, William Warren. *Religion on the American Frontier*. New York: Cooper Square Publishers, 1964.

Taulman, James E. "Amos Dayton Cooper: A Critical Biography." Th.M. thesis, Southern Baptist Theological Seminary, 1965.

Taylor, James B. *Restricted Communion: or, Baptism an Essential Prerequisite to the Lord's Supper*. Charleston: Southern Baptist Publication Society, 1849.

Taylor, W. C. "James Madison Pendleton: World Landmark of Baptist Devotion to Truth and Loyalty to New Testament Churches." Louisville: The W. C. Taylor Letters, 1990–1991.

Teasdale, Thomas C. *Manual of Baptism and Communion*. Nashville: Baptist Publishing House, 1872.

Tellinghuisen, Rebecca R. "Children and Believer's Baptism: Questions of Proper Age, Readiness and the Role of Faith

Development Theory." M.A. thesis, North American Baptist Seminary, 2000.

Theophilus [pseud.]. *An Appeal to Baptists in Their Necessity and Importance of theMaintenance of Their Denominational Principles as Essential to the Establishment of Their Kingdom of God Upon Earth.* London: G. B. Dyer, 1841.

Thornwell, James Henley. *The Elder Question: Extracted from the Southern PresbyterianReview.* np: privately published, nd.

Torbet, Robert G. *A History of the Baptists.* Valley Forge: Judson, 1950.

Tull, James E. "A Study of Southern Baptist Landmarkism in the Light of Historical Baptist Ecclesiology." Ph.D. diss., Columbia University, 1960.

—*High-Church Baptists in the South.* Macon: Mercer University Press, 2000.

Turner, Paul. *Your Child's Baptism.* Chicago: Liturgy Training Publications, 1999.

Vedder, Henry C. *A Short History of the Baptist.* Philadelphia: American Baptist Publication Society, 1891.

Verduin, Leonard. *The Reformers and Their Stepchildren.* Sarasota: Christian Hymnary, 2000.

Walker, Joseph. *An Essay on the Impropriety of Admitting Persons into Baptist Churches on Paedobaptist Immersions, with a Review of a Letter of Rev. Richard Fuller on the Same Subject.* Macon: Telegraph Steam Press, 1858.

Wall, William. *The History of Infant Baptism.* Oxford: Oxford University Press, 1862.

Wallace, O. C. S. *What Baptists Believe*. Nashville: Sunday School Board of the Southern Baptist Convention, 1913.

Waller, John. *Open Communion Shown to Be Unscriptural and Deleterious*. Louisville: G. W. Robertson, 1859.

Walter, Wangerin, Jr. *Water, Come Down!* Minneapolis: Augsburg Fortress Publisher, 1999.

Wardin, Albert W. *Tennessee Baptists: A Comprehensive History 1779-1999*. Brentwood: Tennessee Baptist Convention, 1999.

Wayland, Francis. *Notes on the Principles and Practices of Baptist Churches*. New York: Sheldon & Co., 1857.

Weatherford, Kenneth Vaughn. "The Graves-Howell Controversy." Ph.D. diss., Baylor University, 1991.

Wells, Tom. *Does Baptism Mean Immersion? A Friendly Inquiry Into the Ongoing Debate*. Laurel: Audubon Press, 2000.

Wesley, John. *The Journal of John Wesley*, ed. Nehemiah Curnock. London: Epworth Press, 1938.

Whitney, S. W. *Open Communion: or, the Principles of Restricted Communion Examined and Proved to be Unscriptural and False*. New York: M. W. Dodd, 1853.

Wile, Mary Lee. *Christ's Own Forever: Episcopal Baptism of Infants and Young Children; Parent/Godparent Journal*. np: Living the Good News, 2003.

Williams, William. *Apostolic Church Polity*. Philadelphia: American Baptist Publication Society, 1874.

Willis, G. G. *Saint Augustine and the Donatist Controversy*. London: S P C K, 1950.

Wilson, Douglas. *To A Thousand Generations: Infant Baptism Covenant Mercy for the People of God*. Moscow: Canon Press, 1996.

Wring, Robert A. "An Examination of the Practice of Elder Rule in Selected Southern Baptist Churches in the Light of New Testament Teaching." Ph.D. diss., Mid-America Baptist Theological Seminary, 2002.

Wuthnow, Robert. *The Restructuring of American Religion: Society and Faith Since World War II*. Princeton: Princeton University, 1988.

Wyatt-Brown, Bertram. *Southern Honor: Ethics and Behavior in the Old South*. New York, Oxford University Press, 1982.

Yarbrough, Slaydon. *Southern Baptists: A Historical, Ecclesiological, and Theological Heritage of a Confessional People*. Nashville: Fields, 2000.

ARTICLES

Briggs, Edward C. "Landmark Views of the Church in the Writings of J. M. Pendleton, A. C. Dayton, and J. R. Graves," *The Quarterly Review* 35 (April 1975): 47–57.

Compton, Bob. "J. M. Pendleton: A Nineteenth-Century Baptist Statesman (1811–1891)," *Baptist History and Heritage* 10 (January 1975): 28–35.

Crowther, Edward R. "Holy Honor: Sacred and Secular in the Old South," *Journal of Southern History* 58 (November 1992): 619–36.

George, Timothy. "Southern Baptist Ghosts," *First Things* 93 (May 1999): 17–24.

Hall, Chad W. "When Orphans Become Heirs: J. R. Graves and the Landmark Baptists," *Baptist History and Heritage* 37 (Winter 2002): 112–27.

Harper, Louis Keith. "Old Landmarkism: A Historical Appraisal," *Baptist History and Heritage* 25 (April 1990): 31–40.

Hudson, Winthrop. "Documents on the Associations of Churches," *Foundations* 4 (1961): 332–9.

Matthews, Donald. "The Second Great Awakening as an Organizing Process, 1780–1830," *American Quarterly* 21 (Spring 1969): 23–43.

Moore, LeRoy. "Crazy Quilt: Southern Baptist Patterns of the Church," *Foundations* 20 (1977): 12–35.

Patterson, W. Morgan. "The Influence of Landmarkism Among Baptists," *Baptist History and Heritage* 10 (January 1975): 44–56.

Smith, Harold S. "The Life and Work of J. R. Graves (1811–1891)," *Baptist History and Heritage* 10 (January 1975): 19–27.

Snay, Mitchell. "American Thought and Southern Distinctiveness: The Southern Clergy and the Sanctification of Slavery," *Civil War History*, 35 (December 1989): 311–28.

Taulman, James E. "Baptism and the Lord's Supper: As Viewed by A. C. Dayton, J. M. Pendleton, and J. R. Graves," *The Quarterly Review* 35 (April 1975): 58–69.

—"The Life and Writings of Amos Cooper Dayton (1813–1865)," *Baptist History and Heritage* 10 (January 1975): 36–43.

Torbet, Robert. "Landmarkism" presented at the Second National Theological Conference in Green Lake, Wisconsin, June 6–11, 1959.

Tull, James E. "The Landmark Movement: An Historical and Theological Appraisal," *Baptist History and Heritage* 10 (January 1975): 3–18.

Wamble, Hugh. "Landmarkism: Doctrinaire Ecclesiology Among Baptists," *Church History* 33 (December 1964): 429–47.

NEWSPAPER ARTICLES

Chapman, James L. "Defense of the Scriptural and Republican Character of the M. Church Government," *Christian Advocate*, May 31, 1855.

—"Defense of the Scriptural and Republican Character of the M. Church Government," *Christian Advocate*, June 7, 1855.

Ford, S. H. "Elder J. M. Pendleton and High Churchism," *Western Recorder*, January 10, 1855.

—"History of the Baptists in the Southern States by B. F. Riley. D. D. —Misstatements—Old Landmarkism—Succession—Irregular Immersions," *Ford's Christian Repository and Home Circle*, July 1899.

Graves, J. R. "Beliefs" *Tennessee Baptist*, February 8, 1867.

—"Letter to Pendleton," *Tennessee Baptist*, April 20, 1861.

—"Reply to S. H. Ford," *Tennessee Baptist*, June 16, 1883.

—"The Goal Won at Last," *Tennessee Baptist*, January 8, 1859.

Manly, Basil Sr. "Immersion administered by Pedobaptist," *South Western Baptist*, May 28, 1857.

McFerrin, John. "Methodist Church Government," *Christian Advocate*, May 31, 1855.

Unsigned announcement. "Theological Chair at Union University," *Tennessee Baptist*, December 6, 1856.

Unsigned article. "Editorial Notes of the Death of J. M. Pendleton," *Western Recorder*, March 12, 1891.

Unsigned article. "Our Associate," *Tennessee Baptist*, July 6, 1861.

Unsigned article. "The Baptist Church in Murfreesboro to the First Baptist Church in Nashville, Tennessee," *Tennessee Baptist*, October 23, 1858.

Unsigned article. "The Baptist Watchman," *Tennessee Baptist*, February 27, 1858.

Unsigned article. "The Tennessee Baptist Irreconcilable," *Western Recorder*, October 31, 1855.

ENCYCLOPEDIAS AND DICTIONARIES

Cathcart, William., ed. *The Baptist Encyclopedia*. Philadelphia: Louis H. Everts, 1881.

Cox, Norman., ed. *Encyclopedia of Southern Baptists*. Nashville: Broadman Press, 1958.

Elwell, Walter., ed. *Evangelical Dictionary of Theology*. 2d ed. Grand Rapids: Baker, 2001.

Kittel, Gerhard. *Theological Dictionary of the New Testament*. Translated and Edited by Geoffrey W. Bromiley, Grand Rapids: Eerdmans, 1965.

CHURCH DOCUMENTS

"Church Minutes." First Baptist Church, Bowling Green, Kentucky.

"Church Minutes." Upland Baptist Church, Upland, Pennsylvania.

Grace Community Church, Sun Valley, CA: "By-laws of Grace Community Church," Sun Valley, CA: Grace Community Church, 1999.

NEWSPAPER ARTICLES RELATED BUT NOT CITED

A Member of the Bible Board. "Dear Bro. Pendleton," *Tennessee Baptist*, January 15, 1859.

Alabama. "Dear Brother Pendleton," *Tennessee Baptist*, July 3, 1858.

Bowling Green Church. "The Junior Editor," *Tennessee Baptist*, April 28, 1860.

Buckner, Daniel. "The 'Old Landmark' Not Removed," *Western Recorder*, July 8, 1857.

Crawford, N. M. "'Doulos' in the New Testament," *Tennessee Baptist*, June 22, 1861.

Creath, J. W. D. "To Elder J. M. Pendleton," *Tennessee Baptist*, April 25, 1857.

Dagg, J. L. "Letter to the Tennessee Baptist," *Tennessee Baptist*, December 25, 1858.

—"Old Landmark Controversy," *Western Recorder*, May 20, 1857.

Dayton, A. C. "New Editorial Arrangement," *Tennessee Baptist*, June 6, 1858.

—"Resignation," *Tennessee Baptist*, May 15, 1858.

Graves, J. R. "Letter from the Senior Editor," *Tennessee Baptist*, June 16, 1860.

—"Our Associate," *Tennessee Baptist*, July 13, 1861.

Gordon, John A. "Eld. J. M. Pendleton," *Tennessee Baptist*, December 8, 1860.

Hawthorne, J. B. "Old Landmark," *Tennessee Baptist*, April 19, 1856.

Howell, R. B. C. "Rev. J. R. Graves—Sin," *Tennessee Baptist*, October 23, 1858.

Jeter, J. B. "Pulpit Communion Again," *Tennessee Baptist*, August 8, 1857.

—"The Policy of the Committee to Nominate New Boards at the Last Meeting of the Southern Baptist Convention," *Tennessee Baptist*, March 2, 1861.

Oliver, John A. "Pendleton on Faith," *Tennessee Baptist*, December 10, 1859.

Lend, S. W. "The Landmark," *Western Recorder*, April 25, 1855.

Mell, P. H. "Corrective Church Discipline," *Tennessee Baptist*, June 16, 1860.

Morehead, R. W. "A Student's Opinion," *Tennessee Baptist*, May 5, 1860.

Morrow, O. H. "Pendleton's Sermons," *Tennessee Baptist*, July 21, 1860.

Pendleton, John. "Self-Defense," *Tennessee Baptist*, April 12, 1860.

Perryman, James. "My Dear Bro. Pendleton," *Tennessee Baptist*, November 20, 1858.

Poindexter, A. M. "Correction," *Tennessee Baptist*, July 16, 1859.

Riley, M. M. "Funeral of Dr. J. M. Pendleton," *The Baptist*, March 12, 1891.

Ross, Z. "The Facts in the Case," *Tennessee Baptist*, June 2, 1860.

Sanders, A. A. "Reply to Elder Sears' Old Landmark not Removed," *Western Recorder*, October 28, 1857.

Unsigned article. "Baptist Church Directory by Hiscox," *Tennessee Baptist*, July 20, 1859.

Unsigned article. "Baptist Highchurchism," *Tennessee Baptist*, September 20, 1854.

Unsigned article. "Baptist Should Circulate Baptist Literature," *Tennessee Baptist*, October 31, 1857.

Unsigned article. "Brother Pendleton Getting Right, But Not Right Yet," *Western Recorder*, November 24, 1855.

Unsigned article. "Death of Rev. J. M. Pendleton, D. D.," *Religious Herald*, March 19, 1891.

Unsigned article. "Death of Prest. Eaton," *Tennessee Baptist*, January 22, 1859.

Unsigned article. "Dr. J. M. Pendleton," *The National Baptist*, March 12, 1891.

Unsigned article. "Editorial Telegrams—on the controversy with Howell," *Tennessee Baptist*, October 9, 1858.

Unsigned article. "Elder H. E. Talliaferro," *Tennessee Baptist*, February 13, 1858.

Unsigned article. "To the Public," *Tennessee Baptist*, May 15, 1852.

Unsigned article. "R. Everts and Rev. J. M. Pendleton," *Tennessee Baptist*, April 21, 1855.

Unsigned article. "Reply to Elder Sears Old Landmark Not Removed," *Western Recorder*, October 28, 1857.

Unsigned article. "Rev. J. M. Pendleton," *Western Recorder*, September 30, 1865.

Unsigned article. "The Convention," *Baptist Standard*, May 21, 1859.

Unsigned article. "The Editors of the Parlor Visitor and Our Correspondent J. M. P.," *Tennessee Baptist*, October 18, 1856.

Unsigned article. "The Landmark Discussion," *Tennessee Baptist*, October 31, 1857.

Unsigned article. "The Old Landmark Controversy," *Western Recorder*, October 28, 1857.

Unsigned article. "The 'Old Landmark' Not Removed," *Western Recorder*, July 8, 1857.

Unsigned article. "The 'Old Landmark' Not Removed," *Western Recorder*, July 15, 1857.

Unsigned article. "The Tennessee Baptist," *Tennessee Baptist,* May 6, 1854.

Unsigned article. "The Tennessee Baptist Reviewed," *Western Recorder*, November 7, 1855.

Unsigned article. "To The Public," *Tennessee Baptist*, May 15, 1882.

Unsigned article. "To the Rev. J. M. Pendleton," *Tennessee Baptist*, June 23, 1855.

Unsigned article. "Union University," *Tennessee Baptist*, February 25, 1860.

Unsigned article. "Union University," *Tennessee Baptist*, June 30, 1860.

Unsigned article. "Union University," *Tennessee Baptist*, July 21, 1860.

Walton, Edward Payson. "Rev. J. M. Pendleton," *Tennessee Baptist*, July 10, 1858.

Reminiscences of a Long Life

By J. M. Pendleton

TABLE OF CONTENTS

Reminiscences of a Long Life

Chapter 1
Ancestry—Charles Thompson—
Henry Pendleton—My Father a Pupil
of Andres Broaddus—Marries
Frances J. Thompson—Removes to
Kentucky—War with England . . .   283

Chapter 2
Childhood and Boyhood—Going to
School—School House—Going to
Mill—Taking Medicine—Fond of
Play—Bashfull—Hunting   291

Chapter 3
Religious Impressions and
Conversion—My Baptism   299

Chapter 4
Licensed to Preach—Taught School
for Some Months   305

Chapter 5
Settlement at Hopkinsville and
Ordination—Sickness—Baptist State
Convention   311

Chapter 6
Removal to Bowling Green,
Kentucky—General Association—
Proposal of Marriage   317

Chapter 7
My Father's Death—My Marriage—
Richard Garnett—Robert Stockton—
Jacob Locke—Birth of a Daughter . .   323

Chapter 8
Death of President Giddings—
Revival—J.L. Burrows—Birth of a
Son—Second Daughter—T.G. Keen
Becomes Pastor at Hopkinsville—
Visit to Philadelphia—Canal
Travel—Triennial Convention   329

Chapter 9
Objects of Interest in Philadelphia—
Independence Hall—Girard
College—Fair Mount—Laurel Hill
Cemetery, Etc.—Mr. Clay Nominated
for the Presidency—Distressing
Stage Ride from Chambersburg to
Pittsburg—Down the Ohio to
Louisville—Thence Home by Steamer
General Warren   341

Chapter 10
Mr. Polk's Election—Texas
Annexed—War with Mexico—Treaty
of Peace—The Question of
emancipation in Kentucky—John L.
Waller—Western Baptist Review . .   349

Chapter 11
Meeting at Green River Church, Ohio
County—Removal to Russellville—
Birth of Our Third Daughter—
Return to Bowling Green—Revival
Under the Preaching of J.R.
Graves—Birth and marriage of Our
Second Son   357

Chapter 12
Removal to Murfreesboro,
Tennessee—Union University—
Theological Department—President
Eaton and Wife—Tennessee Baptist
and Southern Baptist Review—
Charge of Anti-Slavery Sentiments
Brought Against Me—A Little
Discussion with Alexander Campbell.   365

Chapter 13
The Civil War—The States' Rights
Doctrine—The Position of the United
States—The Overthrow of Slavery
God's Work—Slavery in Kentucky
and Tennessee   371

Chapter 14
Leaving Murfreesboro—Exposed to
Danger in Going into Kentucky—
Settlement as Pastor at Hamilton,
Ohio—Death of My Mother—Desire
to Go West—The End of the War—
Mr. Lincoln's Assassination   381

Chapter 15
Removal to Upland, Pennsylvania—
The Crozer Family—The Theological
Seminary—Meeting House
Enlarged—Great Revival   389

Chapter 16
Baptist Publication Society—
Ministers' Conference—Fifty Years
in the Ministry—Authorship—Death
of President Garfield and ex-
President Grant   397

James Madison Pendleton

Chapter 17
Mrs. John P. Crozer's Death—
Resignation of Pastorate—Last
Sermon—Winter of 1883-83 in
Nashville, Tenn.—Wife's Blindness   405

Chapter 18
Austin, Texas—State House—
Monterey—Jubilee of General
Association of Kentucky—Golden
Wedding   411

Chapter 19
Return to Upland—Anniversaries at
Washington—American Baptist
Education Society—Mr. Cleveland's
Reception—Wayland Seminary—
Columbian University—Visit to Dr.
Osgood—Bible Class of My Son—
Death of Mrs. S. A. Crozer—
Conclusion   419

Chapter 20
Last Illness—Death—Funeral and
Memorial Services   427

Reminiscences
CHAPTER 1

ANCESTRY – Charles Thompson, Henry Pendleton – my father a pupil of Andrew Broaddus – marries Frances J. Thompson – removes to Kentucky – war with England.

My information concerning my ancestors goes back no farther than to my grandfathers, who were natives of Virginia and of English descent. They were worthy citizens and honorable men, on whose characters there rests no blemish. My maternal grandfather was Charles Thompson, who had a number of children, the most prominent of whom was William M. Thompson, who, for some years, filled official positions, at Washington, under the Government of the United States. He was the father of Hon. Richard W. Thompson, for many years a member of Congress from Indiana, and Secretary of the Navy under the Presidency of Mr. Hayes. He is now an old man and the most conspicuous member of the Thompson family. In his palmy days he was a captivating orator and a special friend of Hon. Henry Clay.

My paternal grandfather was Henry Pendleton, whose name is mentioned in connection with an important meeting of the freeholders of Culpeper County, Virginia. I quote as follows: "At a meeting of the freeholders and other inhabitants of the County of Culpeper, in Virginia, assembled at the Court House of the said county, on Thursday, the 7th of July, 1774, to consider of the most effective method to preserve the rights and liberties of America." "*Resolved,* That importing slaves and convict servants is injurious to this colony, as it obstructs the population of it with freemen and useful manufacturers; and that we will not buy any such slave or convict servant hereafter to be imported. HENRY PENDLETON, ESQ., Moderator."

I make this extract, second-hand, from "the first volume, 4th Series of American Archives, published by order of Congress." It shows that there was in Virginia, in 1774, a decided anti-slavery feeling and a purpose to oppose the policy of the British Government in the matter referred to. It is to the credit of my grandfather that he presided over the Culpeper meeting and gave his influence in condemnation of the wrong and in approval of the right.

My grandfather afterward became a soldier in the Revolutionary War, and I have before me a letter written by him, dated "Oct. 2, 1780, Guilford, North Carolina." The beginning of the letter is in these words: "My ever Dear and Loving Wife," showing that the spirit of the soldier did not interfere with the affection of the husband. He expresses his gratitude to God that while others had fallen he had been preserved, and he says to his wife, "I hope the Lord has heard your prayers for me." This is a suitable recognition of dependence on God, and there is something beautiful in the thought that while the husband was fighting in the cause of liberty the wife was at home, not only caring for small children, but praying for the success of that cause and the safe return of her husband. Many wives in times of war have done the same thing, and we shall never know our full indebtedness to their prayers. At what time my grandfather returned to his home I am not able to say, but it was an occasion of great joy to him and his family. He then devoted his attention to the pursuits of agriculture during the remainder of his life, and died an honest farmer and a devout Christian. His posterity need not blush in thinking of his name, but should strive to be like him in his patriotism and in his piety. When such men die earth suffers loss, but they are infinitely better off. They are "taken from the evil to come" and enter into the blessedness of "the dead who die in the Lord." (As the letter to which I have referred is signed Henry Pendleton, Jr., and the signature to the Culpeper meeting has not this distinction, it is possible that it was my great grandfather who presided at this meeting. It cannot certainly be known.)

My grandfather had four children, one daughter, Mary, and three sons, Benjamin, Henry, and John, the last of whom was my father. While his brothers devoted themselves to the occupation of farmers, he had literary aspirations and resolved to acquire an education. He became a pupil of the celebrated Andrew Broaddus, of Caroline County, Va. Mr. B. was a popular teacher and the most distinguished pulpit orator of his time. His eloquence was often charming and irresistible. His sermons were long remembered by his hearers and regarded as precious treasures.

My father ever felt his indebtedness to Mr. Broaddus for the assistance he received from him in his educational pursuits. He learned from him to appreciate knowledge more highly than ever before and became a respectable scholar for that day, though education was not then what it is now. His intelligence gained at school and from diligent reading in subsequent years gave him an influence far greater than that of most of his associates. This influence in no doubt felt by his posterity and has had a beneficial effect on their destiny.

After leaving the Academy of Mr. Broaddus my father taught school for some years, and in teaching others added to his stores of knowledge. Tuition fees were then meager, but by rigid economy he saved some money every year, which he invested as judiciously as possible. He looked to that period in the future when his expenses would be necessarily increased; for he had decided that it was not best for "man to be alone."

It was while my father was teaching that he became acquainted with Miss Frances J. Thompson and was enamored of her charms. She was an orphan and was living in the family of relatives. She had a bright, active mind, but her education was imperfect, for she labored under the disadvantages of orphanage. These disadvantages, however, did not eclipse her excellences of character, and her amiable qualities strongly attracted the admiration of her suitor. Admiration ripened into love and proposals of marriage were made. Judging from some things in a diary kept by my father at the time, I may say that he was greatly troubled with doubt and fear as to the acceptance of his offer. The question he had submitted to her was, "Will you marry me?" and when the time for the answer came, he said, "Is your response favorable or not?" She timidly, and with a throbbing heart, replied, "Favorable." He was thrown into such ecstasy that he wrote in his diary the word "FAVORABLE" in glowing capitals. It was, as subsequent years indicated, favorable for him and for her.

In "the course of human events," John Pendleton and Frances J. Thompson were united in marriage in the year 1806. They were very happy in their new relation, and hope painted the future in roseate colors. It is a significant fact that marriage was instituted in Eden before the Fall. It was therefore, in the judgment of God, essential to the perfection of human blessedness ere sin cursed the earth. He said, "It is not good that the man should be alone: I will make a help meet for him." Man was alone among animals of beauteous form and birds of brightest plumage and sweetest voice. Alone amid thornless flowers and richest fruits, shady bowers and limpid waters! Yes, alone, and why? Because woman was not there. There was a vacuum which neither the inanimate nor the animate creation could fill. There was a want to be supplied.

> Still slowly passed the melancholy day,
> And still the stranger wist not where to stray –
> The world was sad! The garden was a wild!
> And man the hermit sighed – till woman smiled.
> —*Campbell.*

Conjugal bliss was no doubt enjoyed in its highest perfection by Adam and Eve in their state of innocence; but their descendants may well rejoice that while it was diminished it was not destroyed by the Fall. There has been much domestic happiness in all the centuries, and still conjugal joy cheers the family circle and brightens the world.

The marriage union between my father and mother was a happy one in its beginning, and so it continued for many years till sundered by the hand of death. Each was especially concerned for the comfort of the other, and this is the best recipe for happiness in married life.

Why my father abandoned teaching after his marriage, I do not know, but he engaged in mercantile pursuits. He rented what was then known, and, I am told, is still known, as "Twyman's Store," in Spottsylvania County, Va. He bought his goods in Baltimore and Philadelphia, and I have the impression that he sometimes rode to those cities on horseback. There were few traveling facilities in those days, and the present generation does not sufficiently appreciate its advantages.

My father's success as a merchant was encouraging, but after a few years he sold his stock of goods, and decided to seek his fortune in what was then the new State of Kentucky. By this time (1812) there were three children around the hearthstone, and their presence no doubt suggested the necessity of providing better for his family than he could do in Virginia. He and my mother consulted on the subject, deliberated long, but finally concluded it was best to seek a new home. They had many sad thoughts about leaving their native State. They loved Virginia, considered the best place to be born, and wished it could be the best place in which to live and die. It was painful to leave their many friends and the graves of their ancestors.

Breathes there a man with soul so dead
That never to himself hath said,
This is my own, my native land?

JAMES MADISON PENDLETON

When I remember that my parents left the land of their birth, encountered the perils of what was then called the "wilderness" on their way to Kentucky, suffered the inconveniences and hardships of a sort of pioneer life—all this that their children might enjoy better advantages than they had enjoyed—no language can express the grateful admiration I feel for them. If it is unmanly for the heart to palpitate with emotion, then I am unmanly, and make no apology for it, but rather glory in it. If I forget those to whom I owe so much, may "my right hand forget her cunning, my tongue cleave to the roof of my mouth," and my name be blotted from the recollections of men.

It was but a short time before my father and mother left Virginia that they made a public profession of their faith in Christ and were baptized by Elder Zachary Billingsley. They had been led to see their lost condition as sinners against God, they repented of their sins, trusted for salvation in the Lord Jesus, and openly espoused his cause.

My father sometimes doubted his acceptance with God, but my mother was not troubled with doubts. She could say, "I know whom I have believed, and am persuaded that He is able to keep that which I have committed to Him against that day." Her Christian confidence and cheerfulness had much to do with her usefulness in the cause of God. She was an unspeakable blessing to her husband and to her children.

As already stated, my parents before their removal from Virginia, had three children, two daughters, Mary and Frances, and one son, and I was the son, born at "Twyman's Store," November 20, 1811. It was during Mr. Madison's Presidency, and as my father greatly admired him as a statesman I was named for him. Whether the name has been of any advantage to me I am not able to say, but probably not, as there is not much in a name. After their removal to Kentucky, there were born to my parents, seven children, namely: John, Caroline, Juliet, William, Waller, Emily, and Cyrus.

It was during Mr. Madison's first term that the encroachments of England on American rights became too flagrant to be born, and Congress, under the leadership of Henry Clay and John C. Calhoun, declared war. The British government claimed what was called "the right of search"— the right to search American vessels on the high seas, to see if British subjects were on board; and, it is said, that American seamen were sometimes "impressed." This was regarded an indignity to which American self-respect and honor could not submit. War was waged for two years, from 1812 to 1814, when, on December 24th, a treaty of peace was concluded at Ghent. There were no telegraphs and steamships then, and it required a long time to receive news from the other side of the Atlantic. It therefore so happened that General Jackson fought his celebrated battle in New Orleans, January 8, 1815, *after* the treaty of peace was made. Men are, in some respects, very much like children. This is seen in connection with the war under consideration. England claimed "the right of search;" we denied it, and the issue was joined. After two year' fighting peace was agreed upon, but the question which brought on the war was ignored in the treaty of peace. England did not relinquish the right she claimed, and the United States did not insist that she should. This was like children's play. "The pen is mightier than the sword." In the correspondence connected with the treaty of Washington, negotiated in 1842 by Lord Ashburton and Daniel Webster, the latter so exposed "the right of search" theory that British statesmen have said that it can be plausibly advocated no longer. The matter stood thus: England claimed the right to exercise jurisdiction over her subjects. The United States acquiesced, but said the jurisdiction could not extend beyond British territory. England, however, insisted that the high seas were embraced in her jurisdiction. Webster said no, but that the high seas are the property of all nations, and "the flag of a vessel is the protection of the crew." England does not, of course, in time of peace, claim the right to invade the territory of the United States in pursuit of her subjects. The existence of an extradition treaty shows this; but every part of the high seas covered by vessels floating the United States' flag is, for the time being, as much the territory of the United States as is the soil of any State in the Union. It follows, therefore, that as England has no right to invade our permanent territory on the land, she has no right to invade our *protempore* territory on the sea. This is the way I argue the case, not pretending to give Mr. Webster's argument, for I have not seen the Ashburton treaty for more than forty years.

England must have modified her views in regard to "the right of search," and hence, in the beginning of the late civil war, when the Captain of a United States' vessel took from a British ship Messrs. Mason and Slidell, agents of the Southern Confederacy, it was regarded by the British government as a flagrant outrage on its dignity. The release of the two captured gentlemen was at once called for, and a suitable apology demanded. That is to say, England wished the United States to apologize for doing what she had often done without making any apology. Secretary Seward, supreme in diplomatic skill, was equal to the occasion. He said, in substance, that in accordance with the English doctrine of "the right of search," Messrs. Mason and Slidell had been taken from a British ship, and in accordance with the American doctrine they would be surrendered.

This may be thought a digression, and so it is, but it has been suggested by my reference to the war with England during Mr. Madison's Presidency. Then, too, as I am writing for my children and grandchildren, I have attempted to place in small compass facts with which they could not become acquainted without examining many pages of history.

CHAPTER 2

CHILDHOOD AND BOYHOOD – GOING TO SCHOOL – SCHOOL HOUSE – GOING TO MILL – TAKING MEDICINE – FOND OF PLAY – BASHFUL – HUNTING.

It was in the Autumn of 1812 that my father and mother left Virginia never to return. With sad hearts they bade adieu to the scenes of their youth, parted with friends, and looked for the last time on the graves of their kindred. Those only who have had an experience of this sort know how painful it is to pronounce the word *farewell*, break up the associations of an old home, and seek a new residence in a distant land. Kentucky was then considered a distant land, for the point of destination was seven hundred miles away. There was an intervening "wilderness," so-called, to be passed through, and it was infested by Indians. The "red men of the forest" were objects of terror even to grown persons, and the most effectual way of quieting the noise made by children was to tell them that the Indians were probably near. Emigrants were often plundered and some were killed. It may well be supposed therefore that passing through the "wilderness" excited gloomy apprehensions.

I do not know how many wagons were provided by my father for the accommodation of his family, but they were under the general superintendence of a cousin of his, Robert T. Pendleton, a young man determined to make Kentucky his home. In after years he often told of the difficulties of the way and of the almost impassable roads. I remember hearing it said that it was sometimes necessary to descend hills so steep that the ordinary locking of wheels was not sufficient, but that branches of trees were fastened to the wagons to make their descent safe. This always impressed me as a strange thing, and it will so impress all who are familiar with good roads.

After a wearisome journey the travelers reached their new home in Christian County, Kentucky. Their number was nine, and among them were three young servants – slaves – for nobody then thought that there was anything wrong in slavery. My father had bought a tract of land, three hundred acres, with an unfinished dwelling house, and his farming operations engaged his attention for some years. I was only a year old at the end of the journey, and the servants gleefully told me afterward that I had been knocked down by the wagging of a dog's tail. They thought it something to laugh at, and I had no recollection of it. My memory goes back no farther than to my sixth year. That date (1817) is indelibly impressed on me by a visit of Rev. Andrew Broaddus (already referred to) to my father. Mr. Broaddus was then considering the question of removal to Kentucky, and was elected Principal of an Academy in Hopkinsville. He, however, decided to remain in Virginia. I remember his walking the floor and calling the attention of my mother to a "shirt" which he said had been "spun and woven and made at home." He referred with evident pride to the fact. While sojourning with my father, Mr. Broaddus preached at the only regular preaching place in the neighborhood. It was then, and I believe is now, called Salubria Spring. I remember nothing of the sermon, but I distinctly remember that at its close was sung the old hymn beginning, "How tedious and tasteless the hours." There was but one line in the hymn that riveted my attention. It was this, "Sweet prospects, sweet birds, and sweet flowers." The "sweet birds" struck my fancy, and if I had known the language of modern childhood I would have thought, if I had not said, "splendid." Mr. Broaddus came out of the pulpit and passed through the congregation "shaking hands" – a thing much more common then, even in the South, than now. He shook hands with my mother, but of course he did not notice so small a child as I. Little did he think that more than seventy years from that time I would be writing about the matter, with tearful eyes, in thinking that of all who composed that congregation only two or three are now living. On all the rest the stroke of mortality has fallen.

After some years my father resumed his former vocation of Teacher. The neighbors built a schoolhouse about a quarter of a mile from his own residence on his own land. It was one of the typical school-houses of that day. It was built of rough logs, the chinks between which were imperfectly filled and daubed with red clay. There were no windows worthy of the name, but parts of logs were cut out to let in the light, and panes of glass were so adjusted as to keep out the cold. The floor was of dirt and the chimney had a fire-place six feet wide and four feet deep. The benches were made of slabs, and these were the outsides of sawed logs. There were no backs to the benches, and everything seemed to be so arranged as to keep the feet of small children from reaching the floor. This, though not so designed, was the refinement of cruelty. Not less than six hours a day were spent in school, and during that time the small children had no support for their backs and feet! I know of no epithet that can describe the injustice of this arrangement, and I say no more about it.

I think I must have been nine or ten years old when I first when to school, though I had learned a little at home. I was required to devote special attention to spelling and reading. Noah Webster's "Spelling Book" was used, and when I got as far as "Baker" I thought my progress considerable, but when at the end of the book I was able to spell and define from memory, "Ail, to be troubled," and "Ale, malt liquor," I supposed myself very near the farthest limit of scholarship. The course of reading embraced Murray's "Introduction to the English Reader," the "Reader" itself, and then the "Sequel" to it. No other book was read in the school. In due time Arithmetic, as far as the "Rule of Three," "Geography and Grammar" were studied, but not thoroughly. My studies were often interrupted, for, when necessity required, I had to work on the farm. I, too, was the "mill boy." I remember well that about three bushels of corn were put into a bag, the bag thrown across the back of a horse, and I lifted on the horse. The "mill" was four miles distant, and I sometimes thought I had a hard time of it. If I had only known that Henry Clay was called the "Mill Boy of the Slashes," it would have seemed quite respectable to go to mill. When the mill stream failed, as it did in the summer, it was necessary to go to more distant mills on larger streams. Then my father would send his wagon, and his servant "Ben" was the driver, while I went along. I remember how Ben cracked his whip, and I thought if I ever became a man, the height of my ambition would be reached if I could drive a wagon and *crack* a whip. I saw nothing beyond this.

I had very few difficulties with my fellow-students, though some of them were irritable, and so was I. My temper was bad in my boyhood, and when mad, the appearance of my face, as I once happened to see it in a glass, was frightful. It was sometimes necessary for my father to whip me, though I believe he never did so in the school. I richly deserved every whipping I ever received. I remember well my last whipping, when I was thirteen years of age. It happened one day that my father wished to avoid the necessity of teaching in the afternoon, and he protracted the forenoon session rather unreasonably, as it seemed to me. When we went home I was mad and hungry, and when my mother asked, "Why are you so late?" I replied, "Because father was so bad." It was an outrageous thing for me to say, and justice human and divine demanded my punishment. I was whipped and for the last time, but it might have been better for me if I had received a few subsequent chastisements.

I was a very bashful boy. In company I was greatly embarrassed and was almost startled at the sound of my own voice. I can remember when I would go out of my way rather than meet a person to whom I would have to speak. No one will ever know how much I suffered from foolish embarrassment, and it was a long time before I recovered from it. When I first gained courage to ask a neighbor about the health of his family I thought the achievement wonderful, and reflected on it with satisfaction for some days.

REMINISCENCES OF A LONG LIFE

I was much afraid of thunder and lightning, so that when there was a storm at night I would get out of my bed and go into the room where my parents were asleep, and there I would remain till the storm was over. Meanwhile I would pray for divine protection, but when the thunder and lightning ceased I thought no longer of my dependence on God. I see now how inconsistent and wicked I was in the days of my boyhood.

My children may feel interested in knowing that there is a section of country about six miles long and three miles wide, embracing parts of Christian and Todd County, in which Jefferson Davis, Roger Q. Mills, J.B. Moody, and myself spent some of our childhood years. How different has been our destiny! All the world knows about Mr. Davis and Mr. Mills has been for years and is now (1890) a member of Congress from the State of Texas. For almost sixty years I have been preaching the gospel of Christ, and I today "thank God who counted me faithful, putting me into the ministry." Mr. Moody is also a preacher.

In looking back to my boyhood, I think of spells of sickness I sometimes had. There was no doctor in less than ten miles, and my mother administered medicine. The two prominent remedies then were "Tartar Emetic" and "Calomel." They were both nauseous, especially the former. It required an effort to swallow it, and I had to take it in several portions, draughts of warm water intervening, and O! How offensive it all was! The object was to produce vomiting, and this followed every portion of the medicine I took. My mother held my head as I threw up the green bile, and when she thought my stomach in a proper condition she gave me a little chicken soup, which was highly exhilarating. Afterward came warm water with toasted bread in it to allay my thirst. However much I suffered from fever, I was lectured as to the danger of taking a swallow of cold water, and was told of a boy who brought on his "death by drinking cold water." No one then thought it possible for cold water to come into beneficial antagonism with the hottest fever, but blood-letting was the resort. I am glad that many changes, in the practice of medicine, have taken place since the days of my boyhood.

My children have sometimes expressed the opinion that I, like Adam, was never a boy. This is a mistake. I was a boy fond of play and fun and frolic, with sufficient perception of the ludicrous to call forth many a laugh. I always appreciated and enjoyed a good joke, even if it was at my own expense. I was usually cheerful, but sometimes had melancholy hours. I thought but little of the future and enjoyed the present. I did not neglect my studies at school, but anticipated with pleasure what was called "playtime." It was delightful to sport and romp with my fellows, and I thought it no little thing that I could outrun most of them, and was quite adroit in avoiding balls that were thrown in some of our plays. But enough: my children will now believe that I was once a boy.

It was in my boyhood that I went with my sisters to a "singing-school." I remember the teacher well. He was a large man and enjoyed in a high degree of feelings and self-satisfaction. His musical abilities were not of the first order, but he thought they were and made his pupils believe it. The different parts of music he called "tenor, treble, and base." To show us what he could do, he sometimes sang what he termed "counter." Seats were so arranged that he could stand and walk between them. I thought it in the wonder of wonders that he could sing any part he pleased. He could help the tenor bench and in a moment go to the failing treble, giving it more life, and pass to the drawling base which badly needed assistance. We had small "singing books," which contained what were called "patent notes," and we sang four tunes, "common, short, and long meter" with "sevens." Sometimes there was discord, and the teacher would stop everything by stomping the floor. Having explained the cause of the discord, he would require us to try again. I do not think we learned much, and to hear such sounds as we made would now excited the risibilities of every musician on either side of the Atlantic. Within the last sixty years there has been, perhaps, as much improvement in music as in anything else. Many changes have taken place in human affairs, but all changes are not improvements.

It may be proper for me to say something of myself as a boy-hunter. My father had a shotgun which I learned to use, which would not be used now, for it had a flint lock and was not attractive in appearance. I often killed squirrels, and this was remarkable, for I could not, in taking sight, shut one eye and open the other, nor can I yet. In a moonlight night I shot an owl that was disturbing the chickens in a tree. On but one occasion did I shoot a wild turkey. There was a better way to capture these turkeys. It was this: A trench about eight feet long was dug, wide enough and deep enough for the turkeys to pass through it. Then a rail pen was made one side of it, crossing the trench midway. The pen was covered and a little brush lay across that part of the trench that was inside. Corn, as bait, was scattered along the trench all the way. The turkeys would pick up the corn outside and then make their way inside, when, coming up, they found themselves in the pen. They looked up, anxious to get out, but could not, for they never looked down into the trench through which they had passed. Poor things, their lives were the forfeit they paid for not looking down. This fact is suggestive.

My way of catching partridges was by means of traps, which I set in suitable places on different parts of the farm. When I went to a trap and saw it down and the birds struggling to get out of it, my boyish heart was filled with joy.

My plan for hunting rabbits was peculiar. On moonlight nights, an hour or two before day, I would go into the woods with dogs, which would very soon find a rabbit and rush in pursuit of it. The rabbit would flee for safety to a hollow tree and go up the hollow. The dogs would stand at the tree and bark. I would go to the tree and run a switch up the hollow to see how far the rabbit was from the ground. Then with my ax I would cut a hole in one side of the tree, pull the rabbit down, and put it alive in a bag. I remember that one morning I caught four rabbits in this way and carried them home alive that they might be more easily skinned as soon as they were killed. Their skins I sold for a trifle.

It was my business as a boy, between thirteen and fifteen years of age, to take care of my father's sheep. One of the ewes died, leaving a lamb which was given to me, and I raised it, feeding it with milk out of a spoon. When it grew up I sold the wool from it, and with the money received, I made my first investment. I bought a Bible, and this was the first thing I ever bought. I prized it highly and found great use for it, as will be inferred from the following chapter.

CHAPTER 3

RELIGIOUS IMPRESSIONS AND CONVERSION – MY BAPTISM.

From my childhood I received as true the fundamental facts of the Bible. I never doubted the existence of God, nor the incarnation, death, and resurrection of Jesus Christ. I believed in an eternal heaven and an eternal hell. It was my purpose from my earliest years to become a Christian at sometime, but I thought length of days was before me and that I had ample time to prepare for eternity. My prominent conception of religion was that it is the means of escaping hell and getting to heaven. Of my obligation to love God and to serve him from the promptings of love, I seldom had a serious thought. My views were very selfish and very mercenary. My first impressions as to the importance of Christianity were made by my mother. She was more accessible than my father, who was somewhat stern and, whether intentionally or not, kept his children at a distance. I could approach my mother, and even when I had a request to make of my father, it was generally done through her. She talked to me about Christ and salvation, and expressed her desire for me to become a Christian. I always listened with respect to what she said, but there was no fixed determination to seek the salvation of my soul. The evil spirit of procrastination had possession of me, but my purpose to be a Christian at sometime in the future was an opiate to my conscience and silenced its clamors.

When fifteen years of age, I decided to give immediate attention to the subject of religion. The decision was brought about in a very strange way; I know of nothing stranger in connection with my life. I visited a boyish companion, older than myself, with whom I had enjoyed the pleasures of sin, expecting a renewal of those pleasures; but, to my astonishment, he told me that he wished to be a Christian. We talked on the subject of religion and as we talked, or rather as he talked to me, I made the decision referred to and adhered to it. Several years, after I met him, told him that I had made a public profession of my faith in Christ, and that my religious impressions had continued from the time or our conversation. He said in reply, "You have been more fortunate than I," and intimated that he was then a careless sinner. I have never heard of his becoming a Christian. How marvelous was all this! The sermons I had heard, the advice of Christian friends, the talks of my mother, and the reading of the Bible had failed to inspire the purpose to turn to God; but the conversation of one whom, so far as I know, lived and died in sin, led me to a decision. I pretend not to explain this farther than to say that God's thoughts are not as our thoughts.

I resolved to read the Bible regularly and to pray every day, and I expected to reach the point of conversion within three weeks. Why I fixed on this time I never knew, but I thought it would be sufficient to enable me to ingratiate myself into the favor of God. Never was there a Pharisee in Jerusalem more self-righteous. At the expiration of the three weeks I saw no improvement in my spiritual condition, and, indeed, I was much discouraged by my inability to control my heart and life as I had determined to do. Still I persevered in seeking salvation, or, I may say, in seeking to save myself; for self-salvation was the idea that occupied my mind. When the thought at times presented itself that I might not be able *fully* to save myself, my plan was for God to do what I could not do. I supposed it would be well for my defects to be divinely supplemented.

As time passed on I saw more and more of the wickedness of my heart. This wickedness showed itself in my rebellious murmurings that I was not saved. I thought God ought to save me, or rather let me save myself. I had been what was called a "moral boy," had never used a profane expression; but now I cursed God in my heart and felt that I would be glad to annihilate Him. I wonder that He did not strike me with some thunderbolt of His wrath. I have that period of my life vividly in my memory and my soul is humbled within me. I was led gradually, month by month, to see myself a great sinner without a shadow of excuse for my sins. My outward sins appeared as nothing compared with the deep depravity of my heart. I saw myself justly condemned by God's holy law and richly deserving His displeasure. I fully justified God in my condemnation and heartily approved the holiness of His law. I loved the righteousness of the divine government and wished to be saved if my salvation could be in accordance with law and justice; but how this could be I had no conception. I thought it impossible and concluded that I must be forever lost. I expected to go to hell and fully determined there to justify God and vindicate His proceedings. I thought I would say to the inhabitants of that lost world, "God is in the right and we are in the wrong, we deserve all that we suffer, we have no reason to complain, and let us think well of God." I was resolved to say this, was never more resolved to do anything. Visionary purpose, it will be said; yes, but the purpose was fully formed. Meanwhile I felt what I may call the calmness of despair and the tranquility of hopelessness, and expected so to feel until I dropped into perdition. Weeks and months passed slowly away and not a ray of light shone on my path. There was no promise in the Bible that I could apply to my case. My prayer was, "God be merciful to me a sinner;" but I did not see how he could have mercy on such a sinner. I have intimated that I did not wish to be saved unless God could save me consistently with His glory and the claims of His righteous law. I thought it would be far better for me to be damned than for God to compromise the honor of His government in saving me. The union of justice and mercy in salvation was what I wished to be possible; but I despairingly said, this cannot be. While in this state of mind I read a sermon by Rev. Samuel Davies from 1 Cor 1: 22-24: "For the Jews require a sign and the Greeks seek after wisdom; But we preach Christ crucified, unto the Jews a stumbling block, and unto the Greeks foolishness," etc. (Davies' Sermons, in three volumes, my father had taken with him from Virginia.) This sermon, delivered in 1759, which I have recently read, is an excellent one, and Mr. Davies was an admirable sermonizer. In the discourse now referred to I was especially impressed with his remarks on the union of mercy and justice in the salvation of sinners through "Christ crucified." This is shown to be happily possible through the atoning death of Jesus, whose obedience and blood "magnified the law and made it honorable." Having read this sermon I went into a forest to pray, and while kneeling by a tree I had new views of the way in which sinners could be saved. I saw that mercy could be exercised consistently with justice through Jesus Christ. I felt a lightness of heart to which I had been a stranger for about two years. Strange to say, the joy I felt was not on my personal account. I was glad that other sinners could be saved, but did not think of myself as a saved sinner. I knew faith in Christ was indispensable to salvation, but I ignorantly thought that to believe in Christ was to believe myself a Christian. The latter thing, with my views, I could not do, and, therefore, for some weeks considered myself out of "the pale of salvation." I was amazed and at times alarmed at my peace of mind. I began to fear that my "conviction" was gone, and that I was worse off than ever. I tried to bring my conviction back. I wished to feel again my sense of guilt and condemnation. I indulged in soliloquy, though I knew not the meaning of the word: "Am I not a sinner? Yes, but Jesus is a Savior. Am I not a great sinner? Yes, but Jesus is a great Savior." Thus there was something in Christ as the Savior which prevented the return of my conviction, kept off my sense of condemnation, and rendered impossible the anguish I had felt and was anxious to feel again.

A few weeks passed away and in the providence of God I had an opportunity of conversing with one of the prominent preachers of that day, Rev. John S. Wilson. He explained the nature of faith in Christ, defining it as a personal and an exclusive reliance on Jesus for salvation. He asked me if my only reliance was on Christ and I was obliged to answer in the affirmative. He told me and convinced me that I was a believer in the Lord Jesus. He also told me that to believe myself a Christian I must examine myself and see if I found a correspondence between my character and the Christian character as delineated in the New Testament.

Thus I saw the difference between believing in Christ and believing one's self to be a Christian, a difference I have never forgotten.

Very soon I was urged to make a public profession of my faith in Christ, and on the second Sunday of April, 1829, I went before the Bethel Church, Christian County, Kentucky, and related my "experience," telling the brethren and sisters how I had been led to the exercise "repentance toward God and faith toward our Lord Jesus Christ." I was received as a candidate for baptism, and as the pastor, Rev. William Tandy, was in feeble health, I was baptized by Rev. John S. Wilson on Tuesday, the 14th day of the month. The ordinance was administered in the creek not far from the meeting house, and the place is sacred to my memory. If my descendants pass that way at any time, I hope they will pause and think of the import of the solemn and beautiful ordinance of baptism, which commemorates the burial and resurrection of Christ, symbolizes the believer's death to sin and his rising to a new life, while it anticipates the resurrection of the Saints on the last day. I of course did not, as a boy, understand the rich significance of Baptism as I do now; but I thought of my baptism as a profession of faith in Christ and a manifestation of my love for Him as shown in obeying one of His commandments. I remained for several years a member of Bethel Church. It no longer meets at the same place, but is now divided into two bands, the one worshipping at Pembroke and the other at Fairview, the latter retaining the name Bethel. The two places are about equidistant from Hopkinsville, the former on the Nashville and the latter on the Russellville road. All the associations of my boyhood, as well as those of subsequent years, cause me to feel a special interest in the two churches.

It is proper to say that in the spring and summer of 1829 the old Bethel Church enjoyed a precious revival, so that the baptismal waters were frequently visited and the church received an addition of about sixty members.

CHAPTER 4

LICENSED TO PREACH –
TAUGHT SCHOOL FOR SOME MONTHS.

As stated in the preceding chapter, a precious revival was enjoyed by the Bethel Church during the spring and summer of 1829. I was numbered among the earliest converts and took a deep interest in those whose conversion followed. It was a source of the sincerest pleasure to me to see my associates convicted of sin, and to hear them inquiring, "What must we do to be saved?" I had never seen a revival before and tried to do something in directing "inquirers" to Christ. The substance of what I said to them was that as Jesus had saved me, he could and would save them. I remember when first called on to pray in public for anxious souls. I was greatly embarrassed, and even alarmed. I trembled at the sound of my voice, and after a few petitions, incoherently expressed, I close my prayer with the words, "O Lord, I am oppressed; undertake for me." Some brother followed me in prayer, and when the meeting was over I was ashamed to look at those who had witnessed my poor attempt to pray.

As my young companions found peace with God by faith in Christ they united with the church and were baptized. Those were precious occasions when converts in the ardor of their earliest love went down into the baptismal waters, professing their death to sin and their resurrection to a new life. The countenances of many of them as they came up out of the water were radiant with smiles, and brethren and sisters, with extended hands, welcomed them to the joys of Christian service. The revival went on till the church received three score members. A feeling of sadness comes over me now when I remember that scarcely any of those sixty converts are in the land of the living. Nearly all of them have "finished their course," and, I trust, their disembodied spirits are in the paradise of God. Why I have been spared till now to refer to them, I know not, but I hold them in loving remembrance.

There were no "protracted meetings" in those days and there was seldom preaching more than two days together, about every two weeks. Still the revival went on and results were certainly as favorable as those connected with "protracted meetings" at the present time.

During the greater part of the years 1829, 1830, and 1831 I was at work on the farm of my father, and manual labor did not interfere with my Christian enjoyment. I call up the fact that one of the happiest days I ever saw was spent in plowing "new ground." The roots and stumps made it very difficult to hold the plow in its proper place, but my soul was full of joy. My thoughts were fixed on that supreme epitome of the gospel contained in John 3:16. "For God so loved the world that He gave His only begotten Son, that whosoever believeth in Him should not perish, but have everlasting life." I wondered that God could love such a world and that the proof of His love was seen in the gift of His Son. I stopped my horse and plow and retired to a secret place that I might pour forth my soul in thanksgiving to God for love so amazing, so infinite. From that day to this I have known that religious joy does not depend on any bodily environment.

I was in the habit of attending prayer meetings, and sometimes led them. Not having much to say, I read largely from the Scriptures, believing that this was the best thing I could do. Some of my friends were kind enough to say that they were interested in my way of conducting meetings.

Time passed on till February, 1830, when, to my astonishment, the church licensed me to preach. I thought it quite uncalled for, and did not believe it possible for me to preach. Sometimes I reluctantly attempted to "exhort" at the close of a sermon, for it was the custom then for an "exhortation" to follow a sermon. Indeed, I often heard two sermons preached without intermission, and then came the exhortation. My exhortations were very short, consisting at times of only a few sentences, but when I had said all I could think of, I sought relief from my embarrassment in prayer. Strange to say, when I had done the best I could I had a tranquil conscience, not because I had done my duty, but because I had *attempted* to do it.

Early in the year 1831 I began to teach a school in the western part of Christian County. It was a small school and I taught only three months. I learned that some of my patrons were dissatisfied because I did not teach longer than six or seven hours in a day, and I gave up the school. When I returned home with three dollars in my pocket, which remained after my board was paid, my sisters were sad, and my father looked as if he thought I had been predestined to fail at everything I undertook. But my mother, with a burdened heart, retired to her place of prayer, and while praying was impressed with the Scripture, "Ye are of more value than many sparrows." Her countenance became cheerful and she afterward said that from that time she did not doubt that the Lord would provide for me. I shall never know how much I owe to the prayers of my mother. O, that I could pray as she did. Her prayers on earth have given place to praises in heaven.

Months passed away, and on the fourth Sunday in September, 1831, I made my first effort at preaching. It was at a church called West Union, about ten miles west of Hopkinsville. The name of the church was afterward changed to Belle View. My text was Acts 17: 30, 31. "And the times of this ignorance God winked at; but now commands all men everywhere to repent; Because he hath appointed a day in which he will judge the world in righteousness by that man whom He hath ordained." I said something in a superficial way about repentance, and urged the people to repent in view of the judgment, that they might be prepared for the solemn day. To call what I said a "sermon" would be flagrant injustice to that term. The next time I attempted to preach the text was Hebrews 2: 3, "How shall we escape if we neglect so great salvation?" I said a few things about the "great salvation" and the danger of neglecting it, but my performance was wretchedly imperfect. Then when I thought of preaching again it seemed clearly impossible; for I had exhausted my scanty store of theology and could think of no other subject on which I could say anything.

After a while, familiar passages of Scripture coming into my mind took some sort of shape, and I attempted to preach on them. But I did not believe I could ever be a preacher. I was sorely troubled. I desired the work of the ministry, but my sense of unfitness was appalling, and at times I dismissed the subject from my mind. I decided positively to give up the idea of preaching, but my decision was soon disturbed. Just as soon as it was made my mind would be shrouded in awful gloom, and I found that in giving up the thought of preaching I had to give up the hope of heaven. My refusal to preach was not compatible with a belief that I was a Christian. That was the predicament in which I was placed – utterly incompetent to preach, and compelled to give up my hope in Christ if I did not. The agony of those days and nights will never be known. "My soul has it in remembrance, and is humbled within me."

After much thought and prayer, I resolved to transfer the responsibility resting on me to the church that had licensed me. I said within myself, I will try to preach, I will do the best I can, and when the brethren see that they have made a mistake, they will candidly tell me so, tell me that while they do not wish to hurt my feelings, they deem it their duty to say to me that I can never make a preacher. I thought if the church so decided I would be relieved of all sense of responsibility, and could with a clear conscience devote myself to agricultural pursuits. The church had monthly meetings for business, and I waited month after month to hear of their decision in my case; but the brethren failed to act. I was painfully tempted to doubt their fidelity because they did not stop my incipient ministerial career. They let me go on, and I have therefore preached for nearly sixty years.

During the years 1831 and 1832 I accompanied different ministers on their preaching excursions. Sometimes they gave me an encouraging word, and at other times what they said was not complimentary. One of them, in referring to my attempts to preach, said, "You certainly could do better if you would try." Another said, "You are scarcely earning your salt." The language of a third brother was, "You say some pretty good things, but your preaching is neither adapted to comfort the saint nor alarm the sinner."

Of course those good men, now in heaven, did not know how depressing the effect of their words was, and how my spirit was crushed. I refer to this matter for the sake of expressing the opinion that old ministers should be careful as to what they say to young preachers.

But the most uncomplimentary and discouraging things were not said about me by ministers. It was a layman, of whom I heard afterward, that said, "As God is omnipotent he of course can make a preacher of that young man." This exhausted the language of depreciation; for it made the possibility of my becoming a preacher entirely contingent on the omnipotence of God.

In October, 1831, I went to Russellville, Ky., and became a pupil of Rev. Robert T. Anderson, who had charge of a school there. I began to study the Latin Grammar, but it was a wilderness to me. I did not understand why nouns had so many cases, why adjectives were declined, and the conjugation of verbs was so complicated. I read a few pages from "Historia Sacra," beginning with extracts from the book of Genesis. It was not long before I was induced to take charge of a little school. I did this that I might make some money to meet necessary expenses. I had taught only a short time when Mr. Peebles, who had charge of a Female Academy, proposed to employ me as an assistant, agreeing to pay me fifteen dollars a month. I taught with him four months, and when in the summer of 1832, at the close of the session, I received sixty dollars I felt quite rich. While I remained in Russellville I was kindly treated and invited to board for a month with each of the following persons: Spencer Curd, George Brown, Thomas Grubbs, Edward Ragan, William Owens, and Hon. E.M. Ewing, whose wife was a Baptist. I have ever felt my obligations to these kind friends.

Having left Russellville in the summer of 1832, I returned to my father's in Christian County, and in October of the same year I went with Rev. John S. Wilson to the Baptist State Convention at New Castle. There I saw Messrs. Silas M. Noel, Ryland T. Dillard, George W. Eaton, U.B. Chambers and other devoted men. Eaton was at that time Professor in Georgetown College, and he impressed me as being a very lovely man. We went from the Convention to Frankfort, where Dr. Noel was pastor. It was arranged of course for Wilson to preach, and strange to say, Dr. Noel had me to preach. He told me, after hearing me, that I "ought to put more life into my sermons." He was no doubt correct in this view. We went to George Waller, who was one of our prominent ministers. While at Lexington we saw Henry Clay, at that time a candidate for the Presidency, and I trembled in approaching him, so deeply was I impressed with his greatness.

At Dr. Dillard's invitation we rode a few miles in a horse-car on the railroad in process of construction from Lexington to Frankfort. This was a new thing, the first road of the kind in Kentucky, looked upon as a wonder marvelous to behold.

We returned, Wilson to his home in Todd County, and I to my father's house, where I remained till the beginning of the next year.

Chapter 5

Settlement at Hopkinsville and Ordination – Sickness – Baptist State Convention.

Elder William Tandy, one of the best of men, had long been pastor of Bethel Church, but for some years his impaired health prevented his preaching with any regularity. To my surprise the church, in the beginning of the year 1833, invited me to preach two Sundays in the month. A similar invitation came from Hopkinsville and I went there, where I remained four years. The arrangement was for me to become a student of the Academy under the charge of Mr. James D. Rumsey, who had a fine reputation as a classical scholar. I was to make a special study of Latin and Greek. The two churches agreed to give me, each a hundred dollars a year, a sum thought sufficient to pay for my board, clothes, books, and tuition. I never knew why it was, but at the end of the first year the Bethel Church added fifty dollars to my salary so that I afterward received two hundred and fifty dollars a year as long as I remained in Hopkinsville. Some may think that this was poor pay; but my deliberate opinion is that the pay was better than the preaching. I knew hardly anything about the construction of sermons. I did not know there was such a word as "Homiletics," and my expositions of Scripture were sadly superficial. I had to preach every Sunday and two Saturdays in each month, for it was the custom then for churches to have a monthly Saturday business meetings preceded by a sermon. The Saturday sermons were addressed specially to church members, while the Sunday discourses were designed for promiscuous assemblies. With all this preaching I had to recite my lessons in the Academy five days in the week. It was more than any mortal man could do as it ought to have been done. All things considered, it is a marvel that the churches endured my preaching; but they were content for "patience to have her perfect work." If the brethren and sisters had been literal descendants of Job they could not have treated me more generously. At this late day I feel and acknowledge my obligations to them. The members of these churches, with very few exceptions, were "sound in faith" and consistent in practice. While they did not claim perfection, they "forgot the things behind, reached to those before, and thus passed toward the mark for the prize of the high calling of God in Christ Jesus." In my long life I have not met with better men and women. I was fortunate in boarding for two years in the family of Dr. Augustine Webber, who had more theological knowledge than any layman I have known, while his general intelligence was quite extensive.

So far as I know there are only two persons now living to whom I preached the four years I resided in Hopkinsville. The rest have passed away and have, I trust, found a home in heaven. "Blessed are the dead who die in the Lord." They are free from all the encumbrances of the flesh and mingle with "the spirits of just men made perfect."

Another surprise was in reserve for me. The church at Hopkinsville, of which I had become a member, called for my ordination. I thought it premature, but with great hesitation gave my consent. The ordaining Council, consisting of Elders Reuben Ross, William Tandy, Robert Rutherford, and William C. Warfield, met November 2, 1833. The examination as to my Christian experience," "call to the ministry," and "views of doctrine" was far from being thorough; but the Council seemed to be satisfied and decided in favor of my ordination. The sermon was preached by Elder Ross from Hebrews 12: 3, "For consider him who endures such contradictions of sinners against himself, lest ye be wearied and faint in your minds." The impression the sermon made on me was, that ministers, to be preserved from discouragement in their work, must consider what Christ endured. How often have I had occasion to think of this in a ministry of almost sixty years! I here record my conviction that the "love of Christ" is the true inspiration to the preaching of the gospel, and that it is the highest wisdom to copy His example.

The men composing the Ordaining Eldership have long since fallen "asleep in Christ." Warfield, though the youngest, was the first to die, then Tandy, next Rutherford, and last Ross. In these men of God were exemplified Christian and ministerial excellencies which commanded the respect and love of all who knew them. I was not present at the funeral of these ministers, but I have been told that Elder Rutherford, who had not been known to weep before in preaching, was so overcome by the death of his "beloved brother Tandy" that he was unable to speak, and left the services with Elder Ross, whose tears rather helped than impeded his speech.

These ministers of God served their generation according to the divine will, but Elder Ross was "easily chief." I have witnessed many impressive sights, but I can call up nothing as impressive as Reuben Ross, in tears, entreating sinners to be reconciled to God. Of commanding person, he exemplified in the pulpit a solemn and majestic dignity that I do not expect to see again. "The fathers, where are they?"

Warfield died in 1835, Ross in 1860 and Tandy and Rutherford in intervening years. It would gratify my curiosity, but it cannot be, to know that the glorified spirits of these men of God, amid the employments of the heavenly world, have taken an interest in my ministerial career. There may be a closer connection between earth and heaven than we suppose; but how many things we do not know!

While living in Hopkinsville, that is to say, in the year 1834, I had the severest spell of sickness I ever experienced. I was taken with bilious fever in August and it was November before I was able to preach again. I was reduced to such a state of emaciation and weakness that I was unable to raise my hands to my head. My friends generally thought I would die; but I did not think my case hopeless, and this may have had something to do with my recovery. Dr. Webber was my physician and did whatever medical skill could do. As August was the month in which my sickness came on me, I have ever dreaded it more than any other month in the year. I have often thought of the man who said that he had always noticed that if he "lived through the month of June he lived all the year." So it has been with me in regard to August.

The year 1835 brought sorrow to my heart; My special friend, Rev. John S. Willson, died in August, and, as already stated, Warfield departed this life. He died in November. Willson was pastor of the First Baptist Church in Louisville, Ky., then worshiping on Fifth and Green Streets. He had been for a short time Agent of the American Bible Society, and while performing his agency became acquainted in Louisville and was called to the pastorate of the church named. This was in 1833, and his labors were crowned with the blessing of God. He was "a burning and shining light," an attractive preacher, full of love and zeal, eloquent and transcendent in exhortation. When he died it was truly said, "A great man has fallen in Israel." The Baptist State Convention met in Louisville in October, 1835, and during its session Dr. Noel preached a sermon commemorative of the "Life and Word" of Willson. It was an appropriate and able discourse, parts of which were very pathetic. Willson died at about forty years of age, and it has always appeared to me that he brought on his death not only by his unwearied labors, but specially by expending unnecessary vocal power in preaching. In the greater part of his ministry he indulged in vociferation, though his loud voice was by no means unpleasant. After his settlement in Louisville he attempted to change his manner of preaching, being convinced that the deepest feeling is not expressed in the loudest tones of voice. It would be well for preachers to remember this fact.

From the Convention in Louisville I went in company with John L. Waller (of whom I shall say more in another place) and others to the Western Baptist Convention in Cincinnati. We went up the beautiful Ohio and it was my first experience in steamboat traveling. I thought for a time of danger, but soon forgot it. The objects of the Convention were the promotion of acquaintance and union among brethren west of the mountains, and the more zealous prosecution of the work of Missions. Here I met for the first time such men as S.W. Lynd, John M. Peck, John Stevens, and many others. I never knew why, but the Organization was not permanent, and I do not think it had meetings except in the years 1834 and 1835. It was a failure rather than a success.

Returning to Louisville I again saw the bereaved family of my friend Willson and I well remember how sad our parting was. Mrs. Willson's face was the picture of sorrow and the children were in tears. Who knows the crushing grief of a widow's heart? Who can adequately sympathize with children bereft of a loving father's care? But our God is the God of the widow and the fatherless ones.

CHAPTER 6

REMOVAL TO BOWLING GREEN, KENTUCKY – GENERAL ASSOCIATION – PROPOSAL OF MARRIAGE.

In the latter part of the year 1836 I was called to the pastorate of the church in Bowling Green, Ky. This call was made in consequence of the lamented death of the former pastor, Rev. William Warder, who died in August, at the age of fifty years. He was an able preacher, happily combining logical strength and hortatory power. He had been pastor of the church from its organization in 1818. He was often the companion of Jeremiah Vardeman and Isaac Hodgen in their tours of preaching; nor has Kentucky ever sent forth an abler triumvirate. Vardeman was eloquent, Hodgen was effective, but in argumentative ability Warder was superior to either of them. It is a pleasure to me to say that Joseph W. Warder, D.D., of Louisville, Ky., and William H. Warder, M.D., of Philadelphia, worthily represent the name of their honored father. They may well feel satisfaction in the reflection that they are the sons of a father whose character was unblemished, and the sun of whose life set in a cloudless sky. May blessings ever rest on his memory! In September, 1836, sermons occasioned by his death were preached, at Russellville, by Rev. Robert T. Anderson and myself. Mine was the first sermon I ever published, and the text was 1 Thess 4: 13, 14: "But I would not have you to be ignorant, brethren, concerning them which are asleep, that ye sorrow not, even as others which have no hope. For if we believe that Jesus died and rose again, even so them also which sleep in Jesus, will God bring with him." I greatly desired to alleviate the sorrows of the bereaved widow by saying something consolatory concerning the pious dead.

I began my ministerial labors in Bowling Green the first day of the year, 1837, and continued them for twenty years, with the exception of a few months. It was considered by many as phenomenon that the church offered me a salary of four hundred dollars a year. No Baptist minister in that part of Kentucky had ever received so large a compensation. It was John Burnam, Esq., who proposed that I should be paid this amount, and all the church thought it impossible to raise it; but when Brother Burnam subscribed one tenth of the sum it was then believed that the thing could be done. "Honor to whom honor is due;" and I record the fact that to John Burnam is due the credit of introducing this new order of things in the compensation of ministers in the Green River portion of Kentucky. He took large views for that day and advocated them with great earnestness. It is to be remembered, however, that I was the first man in Southern Kentucky who abjured all secular avocations, giving myself wholly to the ministry of the word. It was customary for the churches, almost all of them, to have preaching but one Sunday in the month. With this arrangement, a preacher could serve four churches; and he was called, not ironically, but really the pastor of them all. My predecessor had supplied the Bowling Green church with monthly preaching, and his compensation was a hundred dollars a year. If any one should be curious to know how ministers lived in those times, the answer, is, that some of them taught school, while the large majority of them were farmers. Thus five days of the week were devoted to secular affairs, Saturday and Sunday being set apart for preaching. There could of course be no such thing as regular, systematic study; and ministers labored under many disadvantages. Some of them had a great thirst for knowledge, but their books were few. Their reading was confined chiefly to the Bible, and they studied it during the intervals of manual labor. It would fill our eyes with tears if we could go back to those days, and see what was sometimes seen—a man of God, in Winter, having cut down a tree, sitting on its stump to rest, and while resting reading the word of truth with a view to the next Sunday's sermon; and, in Summer, after following the plow until his horse needed rest, stopping to open the blessed book of the Lord. We shall never know how much we are indebted to men of this class for our denominational prominence and prosperity. Their sermons did not illustrate the rules of Homiletics, for the word was not known. They never thought of beauty and elegance of style, but they said wondrous things. They often, without knowing it, broke the rules of grammar, and at the same time they broke the hearts of their hearers. They were sometimes thrillingly eloquent, but their eloquence was not that of the schools. It was born of the inspiration of the Savior's love and melted the hardest hearts. I call to mind one who, attempting to show sinners that they need not perish in their sins, assigned several reasons why they need not, and then with a heavenly countenance and streaming eyes, exclaimed, "CALVARY SAYS NO!" I do not expect to hear anything in the language of mortals more eloquent than that. When I think of the disadvantages under which those good men labored, and that their noble spirits, by an irrepressible elasticity, rose above surrounding circumstances, I feel for them the profoundest veneration. Through my long life I have remembered them, shall remember them till I die, and hope to be with them after I die.

It was not long after I removed to Bowling Green, that is, in the spring of 1837, that there was pecuniary trouble. There were no telegraphs then, and I remember that a post-boy came with all possible haste from Louisville, bringing an order for the suspension of "specie payments" in bank. This was looked on as a calamity of no little magnitude, for it disparaged the paper money in circulation and created a feeling of disquiet everywhere. It was the first year of Mr. Van Buren's Presidency and he was thought responsible for the unsatisfactory state of things. This, however, was not the case. General Jackson had in the preceding year issued what was called the "Specie Circular," requiring the public lands, then selling rapidly, to be paid for in gold and silver. Paper money had been chiefly used in the purchase of these lands and the "Specie Circular" was unexpected and revolutionary. It was seen in a very short time that the demands made on the banks for gold and silver would be so great as to make it necessary to suspend "specie payments." Whether the policy of President Jackson was wise or just it is not for me to say; but it is certain that Mr. Van Buren inherited the unpopularity of the measure, so that in 1840 William Henry Harrison was elected over him by an overwhelming majority. Thus it was that General Jackson, to whom Mr. Van Buren was indebted for his election in 1836, virtually defeated him in his candidacy in 1840. So strange are human affairs.

In August, 1837, my friend, John T. Waller, who was on a visit to Bowling Green, proposed that I should go with him to Russell Creek Association, which was to meet at Columbia, in Adair County. We went and took Glasgow in our way. We spent a night in the family of Richard Garnett, Esq., and here I was introduced to his daughter Catherine S., of whom I shall have much to say in my Reminiscences. I was not very favorably impressed by her at first, but she and her brother Joseph, and another gentleman went with us to the Association. We thought there was no risk in presuming on Kentucky hospitality and unannounced we, five of us on horseback, stopped with a friend to spend a night. It made no difference and everything in the family circle went on without a ripple. At Columbia my home was with William Caldwell, Esq., with whose family from then till now I have had a pleasant acquaintance. When the Association was over I parted with my friend Waller and returned with Miss Garnett and her brother to Glasgow. The ride of more than thirty miles gave me a fine opportunity of conversation with her and I was impressed with the excellences of her character and her general intelligence. When I left Glasgow I thought it probable that my admiration for her would result in feelings of a different kind; but more of this hereafter.

In October, 1837, I went to Louisville, where the General Association of Kentucky Baptists was formed. The Baptist

State Convention had not been a success, and it was thought better to have a new organization. As introductory to the business of the meeting, a sermon was preached by that prince of preachers, Rev. William Vaughan, from Acts 20: 24: "To testify the gospel of the grace of God." It was the first time I saw and heard Mr. Vaughan, and my many years of acquaintance with him greatly endeared him to me and convinced me that there was no minister in Kentucky superior to him.

Spencer, in his History of Kentucky Baptists, says, "The meeting was called to order by Elder W.C. Buck, when, on motion, Elder George Waller was appointed Chairman, and brethren John L. Waller and J. M. Pendleton, Secretaries, *pro tempore*." It was a day of small things, for only fifty-seven messengers were present. A Constitution was adopted which has remained substantially the same for more than fifty years.

Having performed my little part in forming the *General* Association I returned home by way of Glasgow, where I was especially interested in forming a *particular* association. My feelings of admiration for Miss Garnett had ripened into feelings of love, and I so informed her. I rather think my proposal of marriage took her by surprise, for she said nothing. I tried of course to construe her silence into a favorable omen, and insisted that she should not give an immediate answer, but take ample time for consideration. A suitor generally gains an important point when he can so present his case as to induce consideration. It was so with me as will be seen in the next chapter.

CHAPTER 7

My Father's Death and My Marriage – Richard Garnett – Robert Stockton – Jacob Locke – Birth of a Daughter.

My father died in January, 1838. He had suffered for weary months with inflammatory rheumatism. I had seen him several times during his illness, and on one occasion had a special conversation with him. I asked him what were his feelings in prospect of death. I well remember his answer: He said, "I am like Abraham, going into a country I know not, but willing to trust my Leader." He spoke of the plan of salvation through Christ as the only conceivable plan suited to the necessities of lost sinners. Referring to the Cross as his refuge, he repeated, amid tears and in broken accents, the stanza of Dr. Watts:

> Should worlds conspire to drive me thence,
> Moveless and firm this heart should lie;
> Resolved, for that's my last defense,
> If I must perish, there to die.

He died trusting in Christ, and the family withdrew, leaving kind friends to prepare the body for burial. I remember the countenance of my mother. Oh, what sadness! What bitter tears were hers! I made a great effort to suppress my feelings that I might comfort her, and when duty required me to return to my field of labor, then sixty miles distant, no language can describe my grief in leaving my mother in the desolateness of widowhood. I rode alone, leaving my horse oftentimes to proceed in a way perfectly familiar to me, which tears did not then permit me distinctly to see. Years have fled since then, the duties of a life not inactive have engrossed my thoughts, and yet the feelings of that sad morning return in measure today, and my eyes not much accustomed to tears, will weep again. I stood by the grace of my father and prayed that I might follow him as he followed Christ, and hear at last those words of commendation, "Well done, good and faithful servant." Years after, I saw by my father's resting place the grace of my eldest sister, in whose piety I had the fullest confidence. With more than telegraphic rapidity my thought ran back to the days of our childhood and youth, the time of our union with the church, the period of her last affliction, etc., etc. In looking at the grace of my father and that of my sister, one thing deeply touched my heart. I saw between the two a space reserved for another grace. How suggestive! It was not necessary to inquire why that space was left. I knew my mother wished it so; and after thirty-five years of widowhood she was laid to rest between the husband of her love and her first-born.

My father was a man of vigorous intellect, the distinctive peculiarity of which was its logical strength. He had read much and possessed large information. He was distinguished for an ample share of common sense, a very sound judgment, and often expressed himself in sentences so remarkable for their wisdom as to remind me of the Proverbs of Solomon. I give but one of his utterances: "If a man has done you an injury he will be your enemy." In pondering these words I think I have seen the philosophy of the matter. He who has done you an injury will ordinarily have feelings of shame and mortification, and it is some relief to him for these feelings to be supplanted by those of positive hostility.

Miss Garnett, having considered my proposal of marriage, was kind enough by the end of the year to give me a favorable answer, and it was arranged that we should be married during the month of March. It is proper for me to say something of her parents. Her father was one of the most respected citizens of Glasgow, and for many years filled the office of Clerk of the Barren County Circuit Court. When he became a Christian his predilections were in favor of the

Presbyterian Church. His mind, however, was not settled on the subject of baptism, and it was arranged for Dr. Lapsley, of Bowling Green, to visit Glasgow and preach a sermon on Baptism. The effect of the sermon was not according to expectation. Dr. Lapsley was a learned man and the ablest Presbyterian preacher in the Green River country. He was unfortunate, or rather fortunate, in saying in the early part of his sermon that he believed Jesus was immersed in the Jordan; but he went on to say that sprinkling would do as well, that it was more convenient, etc. Mr. Garnett took hold of the fact that Christ was immersed and said to himself, "I ought to copy His example. Why should I do what he did not do?" The question was settled at once and forever. He joined the Baptist Church in Glasgow, of which he remained a member till his death, which occurred when he was ninety-seven years of age. He was baptized by Rev. William Warder, and was the most influential member of the church as long as he lived. Dr. Lapsley, in conceding that Jesus was immersed, laid the Baptists under many obligations.

Mr. Garnett some year before had married Miss Theodosia Stockton, daughter of Elder Robert Stockton, a Baptist minister, who had been imprisoned in Virginia for preaching the gospel without "Episcopal orders." His imprisonment for such a reason was a greater honor than to wear a monarch's crown and sway a monarch's scepter. Peace to the memory of Robert Stockton. His daughter was a lovely woman with a heart full of unselfish love. She died at sixty years of age and was the mother of twelve children, only two of whom are now living. William Garnett, Esq., deacon of the First Baptist Church, Chicago, is one of the two, and she whom I proudly call my wife is the other. The ten children, whose names were John, Robert, Reuben, Joseph, Benjamin, James, Richard, Fanny, Elizabeth, and Maria, have all passed away. Children as well as parents must die.

It was on the 13th of March, 1838, that Miss Catherine S. Garnett and I were united in marriage. The ceremony was performed by Elder Jacob Locke, who was a kind patriarch among the Baptists in his wide sphere of labor. I was very slightly acquainted with him, but he must have been a remarkable man. It is said that his wife taught him to read, but he rose to eminence in the ministry. In proof of this I need only say that Judge Christopher Tompkins and Joseph R. Underwood, after being in Congress for years, in its palmy days, said that Jacob Locke was the most eloquent man they ever heard. It was untutored eloquence, the outburst of love to God and to the souls of men. "The fathers, where are they?"

The married pair, after a day or two, left Glasgow for their home in Bowling Green and spent a night on the way with special friends, Edmund Hall and family, whose cordial hospitality was all it could be. We often shared their kindness in after years. When we reached Bowling Green we were heartily welcomed by Mr. and Mrs. Richard Curd, who had prepared for us an elegant dinner. We never had better friends than they, and we boarded with them for more than two years, until we were ready to go to "housekeeping." We have never forgotten their many acts of kindness to us.

We of course visited my mother in Christian County, who received her daughter-in-law with much affection and continued to love her as long as she lived. My brothers and sisters were much pleased with the addition I had made to the family, and they thought me very fortunate in my choice.

We visited Hopkinsville and I was delighted to see my friends there so favorably impressed with my bride. They thought I had reason to be a happy man.

We returned to Glasgow and then took our principal "bridal tour," on horseback, to Louisville. This was our only way of traveling, till in a short time I bought a buggy. It will amuse young people now to hear that a bridal trip of several hundred miles was taken on horseback; but we were very happy and had much pleasant conversation. At Louisville we stopped with our friends, the Wilson family, and were made to feel perfectly at home. We spent an evening with the Rev. W. C. Buck, then pastor of the First Church, and heard him preach an evangelical sermon. He was a strong man in the pulpit, and some thought stronger on the platform. It was very inspiring to hear him in debate with "a foeman worthy of his steel." His sermons were generally able presentation of divine truth, but at times his ideas were rather nebulous, and on one occasion they suffered so total an eclipse that he could say nothing, and he sat down. This I learned from Dr. Vaughan, who was present. The Baptists of Kentucky are greatly indebted to Mr. Buck for his arduous labors. He was for several years Editor of the *Baptist Banner*. He improved as a writer, though there was in some of his editorials a tendency to prolixity. When he left Kentucky he became Secretary, at Nashville, of the Bible Board of the Southern Baptist Convention. After two or three years he sojourned for a time in Alabama, editing a small paper which he called *The Baptist Correspondent*. He went from Alabama to Texas, where, after reaching his four-score years, he died of cancer and found a grave, where he had found a home, at Waco.

During the visit to Louisville, just referred to, I was invited to preach. My text was 2 Cor 6: 2: "Behold, now is the accepted time; behold, now is the day of salvation." I thought it a poor, inanimate sermon, but learned, years afterward, that a man in the congregation was convicted under it, who subsequently became a church member and a deacon. I mention this to emphasize the fact that we sometimes do good when we are not aware of it. Probably the revelations of eternity will develop many instances of this kind.

Returning to Bowling Green I gave myself to my work as pastor, preaching twice on Sunday and attending prayer-meeting during the week, visiting the people and especially the sick. My wife aided me in every suitable way and became a favorite with those who made her acquaintance. Nothing remarkable occurred during the year 1838, though the General Association met with us in October. It was not very well attended.

January 8th is celebrated in commemoration of the battle of New Orleans in 1815. The victory achieved there was decisive of General Jackson's destiny. It made him President and was far-reaching in its influence. On this date in 1839 an event occurred which makes it impossible for us to forget the 8th of January. Our first child was born. We named her Letitia after a dear friend. She was a weakly child and we feared that she would not live. The Lord preserved her life and in the days of her youth she became a Christian and received baptism at my hands. She did not go to school till she was fifteen years of age, but was taught by her father and mother at home. Here I may say, parenthetically, that her mother was very competent to teach, for she had been educated by Elder P.S. Fall at his "Female Eclectic Institute," near Frankfort, Ky., and graduated with the highest honor. When Letitia was fifteen years old she entered the Mary Sharp College, at Winchester, Tenn., under the Presidency of Z.C. Graves, LL.D., and graduated at the expiration of four years. There was at that time, if there is now, no Woman's College with a curriculum so extensive and so thorough.

Letitia returned to our home, which was then in Murfreesboro, Tenn., and remained with us till February, 1860, when she was married to Rev. James Waters. Their married life now embraces a period of more than thirty years and they have lived in Tennessee, Pennsylvania, New Jersey, New York, and Delaware. They are now (1891) in Denver, Colorado. Mr. Waters is an able, impressive preacher of the word, and I hope he will accomplish much good in his present field of labor.

CHAPTER 8

DEATH OF PRESIDENT GIDDINGS – REVIVAL – J.L. BURROWS – BIRTH OF A SON – SECOND DAUGHTER – T.G. KEEN BECOMES PASTOR AT HOPKINSVILLE – VISIT TO PHILADELPHIA – CANAL TRAVEL – TRIENNIAL CONVENTION.

The General Association met in Shelbyville in October, 1839. There was a feeling of sadness in the hearts of the brethren, for Rev. Rockwood Giddings was on his dying bed. He was a short distance from the town at the home of his father-in-law, Mr. Hansborough. I visited him and saw him for the last time, and saw the power of Christianity in supporting while "flesh and heart failed." Mr. Giddings was a young man full of promise. He was for a short time President of Georgetown College and infused new life and hope into the Institution. The friends of the College looked for a long and prosperous administration of its affairs. But he died October 29, 1839. From then till now his death has been to me one of the unsolved mysteries of Providence. A thousand times I have wondered why I was not taken and he left to fulfill what seemed so bright a destiny. But God is often pleased to remind us of what he said by His prophet long ago: "For My thoughts are not your thoughts, neither are your ways My ways, says the Lord." (Isa 40: 8.) We must adjourn dark problems to the last day, and then they will receive a solution so bright as to call forth rapturous hallelujahs in heaven.

About the first of March, 1840, we began a protracted meeting in our church at Bowling Green, which continued for a month. Rev. J.L. Burrows was the preacher. He was at that time pastor in Owensboro, and was in the full enjoyment of his young manhood. He exhibited pulpit talents of the first order, as he has continued to do. His sermons were profound in argument and persuasive in exhortation. He showed his sanctified common sense in preaching first to the church and to reclaim it from its backslidden state and to inspire it with zeal for the glory of God in the salvation of sinners. Not till the church was revived did he preach to the impenitent. Then he earnestly urged on them the claims of the gospel, and the Holy Spirit made his sermons effective. Sinners were convicted and began to ask, "What must we do to be saved?" Conviction was followed by conversion, and the songs of rejoicing converts were heard. The meeting went on day and night until the church had sixty members added to its number. We had no "baptistery" then and the ordinance of baptism was administered in Big Barren River not very far above where the Louisville and Nashville Railroad now crosses the river. I remember one Sunday morning that Bro. Burrows and I were in the water together, alternately baptizing, as the candidates were presented. As we "went down into the water" and "came up out of the water" it seemed to me then, and it seems to me yet, that we did just what Philip and the eunuch did. (See Acts 8: 38, 39.) There was a large crowd to witness the administration of baptism, and there was suitable solemnity, as there should be on such occasions. Bro. Burrows, I think, baptized more gracefully than I, for I have never had the talent to do things gracefully.

There were more than twenty sermons preached during the meeting, and not one of them was mediocre. Bro. B. was a fine specimen of a gospel preacher, and when the time of his departure came it was with sad hearts that brethren and sisters bade him adieu. It was not long after that he visited his friends in the East, and while there was called to the pastorate of the old Sansom Street Church, Philadelphia. After some years of ministerial labor in the city of "Brotherly Love" he was called to Richmond, Va., where he served the First Church for twenty years. After this he became pastor of Broadway Baptist Church, Louisville, Ky. He is now pastor in Norfolk, Va. (He has resigned since this was written.) He is feeling the infirmities of age and the First Church, Richmond, has most gracefully offered him a home, promising him care for the rest of his days. God bless him as the beneficiary of such a church!

In the early part of the year 1840 my wife and I went to Glasgow to be present at the marriage of her brother William to Miss Eugenia Tompkins, daughter of Judge Tompkins. The occasion was a pleasant one, and the two who became husband and wife were congenial spirits, and have enjoyed a happy life. Chicago has been their home for many years. I retuned home soon after the wedding, but my wife, on account of her mother's feeble health, and for other reasons, remained. Her mother had been the marked victim of consumption for some years, but the disease had not been rapid in its progress; but now it became evident that death was not far distant. Mrs. Garnett died in the month of April and found her final resting-place in the family "burying-ground." Her memory is most fondly cherished by those who knew her best.

My wife being with her sick mother, was not in the revival at Bowling Green, and before her return, that is, on the 5th of May, 1840, our second child was born. We named him John Malcom, after my father and our friend Rev. Howard Malcom. He was a bright, promising boy and, at a suitable age, became a student of Bethel College, Russellville, Ky. There he remained till my removal to Murfreesboro Tenn., in 1857. He entered Union University at that place and graduated in 1860. It was in the latter part of the year 1859 that he gave satisfactory evidence of conversion, and was baptized in what has since become the historic "Stone's River." I had baptized him before, when he was very young, but he and I were soon convinced that he labored under a mistake in supposing himself a Christian. I therefore did not hesitate to baptize him a second time, considering his first baptism, so-called, a nullity.

In the fall of the year 1860, my son went to West Tennessee and opened a school at or near Brownsville, employing the intervals between school hours in studying Law. He was thus engaged till rumors of war in 1861 unsettled every thing. Young men were urged to enlist as soldiers in the Confederate cause, and my son yielded to the advice of his legal preceptor and exchanged civil for military life. He became a Confederate soldier. We were on opposite sides of the question that convulsed the nation. Why I was on the side of the United States will be shown in another chapter. The different views held by my son and me made no difference in our relations of love. We kept up a correspondence as long as we could, and there was not an unkind word in any of our letters. I refer to this because the supreme slander perpetrated against me in my long life had connection with my son. It was even published in a newspaper that I had pronounced a curse on him, expressing the hope that he might be killed in the first battle. Satan himself never instigated a more flagrant falsehood, though in so doing he availed himself of a professed Christian and a preacher, whose name I in mercy withhold.

My son acted as commissary for some time and was never engaged in a battle, though he was a private in the ranks when General Bragg made his expedition into Kentucky in 1862. While Bragg was at Glasgow my son obtained leave to visit his mother, who was with her sister a few miles in the country. He spent a night with her and with two of his sisters and his younger brother. Nearly the whole night was spent in conversation, and when in the early morning he had to return to his regiment there was a very sad, but a most affectionate farewell. It was the last time his mother saw him and I had not seen him since he left Murfreesboro in 1860. The two armies (Bragg's and Buell's) made their way to Perryville, Ky., and while they were seeking favorable positions and my son was reclining on the grass, the fragment of a shell struck his classic forehead, and in a moment the bright hopes of his parents were extinguished forever. Language has no epithets to describe the calamitous event. It is a mournful satisfaction, however, that my son the day he was killed sent a message to his mother by one of his comrades. The message was this: "Tell my mother, if I die, that I have died trusting the same Savior in whom I have trusted." We therefore believe that his active spirit, escaping from the mutilated tabernacle of the body, ascended to the heavenly mansions where all is peace. This blessed assurance has been a balm to wounded hearts till now, and will be till these hearts cease to throb with the pulsations of life. My son died October 8, 1862.

It was in 1842 that I did what has always afforded me great satisfaction. My special friend, Rev. T.G. Keen was teaching a Female School in Russellville, and while so engaged was called to the pastoral charge of the Baptist church in Hopkinsville. He wrote to me informing me of the fact and adding: "I leave the matter entirely in your hands. You know the church and you know me. I shall be guided by your decision." I wrote by return mail, "Accept the call by all means," and thus I brought into active ministerial work one of the best sermonizers that has ever filled a Kentucky pulpit. After a comparatively long life of usefulness, Mr. Keen died at Evansville, Indiana, in the home of one of his daughters in September, 1857. He was buried in Hopkinsville by the side of the wife of his love. I with many others was at his funeral and thousands remember him with fond affection.

On the 11th of March, 1844, our daughter Fannie was born. She was about perfect in bodily form and brought sunshine into the family circle. She grew up and was greatly beloved by her parents and sister and brother. Her education began at home, and she did not go to school till we removed to Tennessee in 1857. She was for a time in Murfreesboro schools and was then sent to the Mary Sharp College, at Winchester, where she remained till the war disturbed everything in 1862. A diploma was subsequently given her. When we went to Ohio (an account of which will be given in another place) she went with us, but afterward returned to Kentucky and was employed by Mr. Charles Barker to teach his children. When through with her engagement, she rejoined the family then at Upland, Va. June 27, 1867, she was married to Prof. Leslie Waggener, then connected with Bethel College, Russellville, Ky. She found in him a congenial spirit and theirs has been a happy married life. They have seven children, as bright as any that could be found in a long summer day.

After a number of years devoted to the interests of Bethel College, of which Mr. Waggener was President, he was called to a professorship in the University of Texas, at Austin. He was recommended as suited to the position by scholars of distinction, one of whom was Dr. John A. Broadus. He has been for several years Chairman of the Faculty, and is recognized as having a special talent for the management of students. The University is prosperous and will, no doubt, be well endowed, as it owns two million acres of Texas lands. Mr. and Mrs. Waggener and their three eldest children are members of the Baptist church in Austin.

On April 11, 1844, I started to Philadelphia to attend the old Triennial Convention for Foreign Missions. It was the last meeting of the body, as it was afterward superseded by the Baptist Missionary Union. This was my first visit to the east, and my leaving home to go such a distance was thought to be an important event. My wife therefore suggested, and she has made many good suggestions, that the deacons of the church be invited to our house (for we had been housekeeping since the summer of 1840) to hold a little prayer-meeting. They accepted the invitation and were present, six in number, John Maxey, John Burnam, J.C. Wilkins, F. Vaughn, W.D. Helm and John L. Shower. They all prayed. So fraternal were their allusions to me, so eloquently did their voices falter when they mentioned my departure, so earnestly did they ask God that I might return in safety, the whole scene made an indelible impression on my mind. This was the night before I left, and the afternoon of the next day I called my family together, read the forty-sixth Psalm, called on God in prayer, commending us to His care during our contemplated separation. Then taking leave of my wife, kissing our sweet children, and giving a word of religious advice to the servants, I took passage in the stage for

Louisville and reached there in *twenty-eight* hours. The next day, which was Saturday, after calling on some friends, I took passage at 11 o'clock A.M. on the steamer "Pike" for Warsaw, where I was to preach on the morrow. I was met at the wharf at 8 P.M.. by Mr. Hawkins and his sister Mildred, who conducted me to their mother's residence to enjoy her hospitalities. She was the mother of Col. P.B. Hawkins, then and now of Bowling Green. I preached at 11 o'clock and at 4, then at 8 stepped on the steamer "Ben Franklin," went to my state-room, committed myself, my family and friends to God in prayer, and slept sweetly till morning. When I awoke I found myself in Cincinnati and took passage on the boat "Clipper" for Pittsburg. I had as companions in travel Drs. Sherwood, Lynd, Cressy, Brisbane, and Robert. We of course talked and read on our way, but nothing impressed me so deeply as the fact that our steamer, instead of doing justice to its name, ran aground and remained stationary for some hours. We had need of patience, but bore the disappointment as well as we could.

When we reached Pittsburg we found that Dr. Lynd's brother, living there, had secured seats in the stage for the Dr. and two others, but Dr. Sherwood, Robert, and myself were left to go by a canal boat. We had to stay in what was then the "smoky city" from 9 o'clock A.M. to 9 P.M. before the boat would start. Determined to utilize the day, we visited "glass works," "coal mines," and "iron works." It is wonderful into what forms liquid gas can be blown. Bowls, tumblers, and bottles are made sooner than some persons get money out of their pockets to throw into a contribution box. We went into a coal mine five hundred yards, stooping all the way. There is a railroad on a small scale, and the coal is hauled out in little cars drawn by mules. Dr. Sherwood gave the miners some good advice and expressed the hope that we all might meet above where there is no darkness, but unclouded light.

But to our boat. It was drawn by three horses and we went four miles an hour. It required some philosophy to bear this cheerfully. We went, I think, through thirty locks and one tunnel before we reached the foot of the Alleghany Mountains. The railroad car was in readiness, we took our seats, and up and up we went. By means of five inclined planes we ascended to the summit, and the same number of planes took us down to the level again. The scenery on the mountain, some of it at least, is majestic. Tall cliffs raise their heads magnificently and straight pines point to the heavens. I enjoyed the descent from the mountain exceedingly. A strange exhilaration of spirit seized me and I thought of Longinus' definition of the sublime.

Descending from the mountain, at Hollidaysburg we took the canal again and we were well prepared to draw a contrast between its slow progress and the rapid descent of a car on an inclined plane. Sunday came and brethren Sherwood and Robert stopped on the way, but advised me to remain on the boat and preach. I did so and was heard with respect by most of the passengers, though some read papers. Monday morning I awoke at Harrisburg, the capital of Pennsylvania, and had a welcome view of the railroad to Philadelphia. It was an exquisite pleasure to turn away from the canal with the firm belief that I would never travel on it again. Still canal traveling furnishes some good opportunities of learning something about human nature. It is soon seen that there are among men, and especially among women, different dispositions and different wishes. It is next to impossible to please all passengers. Elder Alfred Bennett told me this anecdote: There were two women on a boat, one of whom wished fresh air and the other did not. The name of the chambermaid was Tabitha. In the night the cry was heard, "Tabitha, raise the window; I shall be suffocated." Tabitha obeyed, but in a little while the other woman cried, "Tabitha, let down that window or the fresh air will kill me." Thus the thing went on with alternate demands that the window be opened and shut, till an ungallant man, not willing longer to have his sleep disturbed, cried out, "Tabitha, close that window till one of these women dies, and then open it till the other dies, and let us have some peace."

We passed through so many locks between Pittsburg and Harrisburg that I will not mention the number, lest somebody may doubt my veracity.

Leaving Harrisburg on the railroad it was not many hours before we reached Philadelphia. The city was beautiful to behold, but it is much more beautiful now and very much larger.

I met my friend Burrows at the Publication Rooms, 530 Arch Street, and he took me to his home to share his hospitalizes. His other guests were men of mark, J.B. Jeter, Daniel Witt, and Cumberland George, all from Virginia. The anniversaries were held in Dr. Ide's church, then, I think, about two squares from the Delaware River. The American and Foreign Bible Society held its meeting first, and Dr. Spencer H. Cone presided. He was a very competent presiding officer, familiar with parliamentary rules. I have seen no man in the North his superior in this respect, but do not think he was equal to Dr. Boyce or Dr. Mell. Dr. B.T. Welch, of Albany, New York, preached the Annual Sermon before the Bible Society. I was especially impressed with one thing in his sermon, namely, that his illustrations were drawn from the Bible. I wish some other preachers were like him.

The Triennial Convention for Foreign Missions met April 24. Dr. W.B. Johnson, of South Carolina, was in the chair. He called the meeting to order and it was found that four hundred and fifty messengers were present — more than ever before. Nothing of special importance was done after the organization. The next day Dr. Francis Wayland was chosen President, and Dr. J.B. Taylor, of Virginia, and R.H. Neale, of Massachusetts, Secretaries.

Rev. Eugenio Kincaid, returned Missionary from Burma, and Dr. Richard Fuller, of South Carolina, made interesting addresses. Kincaid made no effort to be eloquent, but gave a simple account of what he had seen in his missionary life. A plain statement of facts, as he gave them, brought tears to many eyes.

Dr. Fuller was one of the best looking men in the Convention and made a capital speech. He was tall and commanding in his person, graceful in his manner, and impressive in his elocution. Nature did much for him and education supplemented the work of nature, while piety placed its sanctifying impress on both.

The Home Mission Society met on the 26th, and it was the occasion of great excitement. Hon. Herman Lincoln, of Boston, was President, and he found much difficulty in maintaining order. The question of slavery was introduced and the Abolitionists urged that the Society should not appoint any slaveholder as a missionary. Dr. Colver was the leading speaker on this side of the question. He was a man of talent, but exceedingly discourteous and rough in his remarks. He utterly failed to exemplify the amenities of Christian debate. He used a number of *ad captandum* arguments, but did not meet the question with fairness and magnanimity. Dr. Welch said that he considered it inexpedient for slaveholders to be employed as missionaries. Dr. Jeter and Dr. Fuller were the principal speakers on the opposite side. Dr. Jeter stood up straight as an arrow and said, "Mr. President." Attempts were made to interrupt him, but he stood immovable. Mr. Lincoln, interposed, crying with his peculiar voice, "Order, brethren, Dr. Jeter, of Virginia, has the floor." Some one replied, "He always has it." He made an able speech. Dr. Fuller spoke with great power and his gentlemanly bearing made its impression on every body. He was logical and eloquent.

The slavery discussion continued at times till the 29th. On this day the excitement and interest were so great that there was no adjournment at noon and Deacon Wattson had a barrel of "crackers" rolled in, that brethren might partially satisfy their appetites. The aisles of the church were pretty well filled by Friends (Quakers), who, being anti-slavery, were much interested in the discussion. I well remember the expression of their countenances. When the final decision came it was resolved that ministers in slave-holding States were eligible to appointment as missionaries. The vote stood *a hundred and thirty-one to sixty-two*. Thus was the matter disposed of for the time.

On Sunday most of the Protestant pulpits of the city were filled by Baptist ministers in attendance on the Anniversaries. To my surprise I was appointed to preach, at night, at the North Baptist Church. Dr. J.B. Taylor, of Virginia, having his lodgings near this church, and having been appointed to preach in the Presbyterian Church on Tenth Street, kindly proposed an exchange with me. I therefore preached to a Presbyterian congregation, not a person in which did I know. I gave them sound doctrine, for I preached on the value of Christ's sacrifice. The Elders were pleased to express their approval, and their courtesy led them to express a desire to hear me again. There was in the congregation a remarkable man, whose face was expressive of intelligence and studious habits. He was a voluminous writer, and some of his views in his "Notes on Romans" were not satisfactory to many of his brethren, and he was charged with heresy, but the Philadelphia Synod acquitted him. That man was Rev. Albert Barnes, who died suddenly more than twenty years afterward. Calling to see a family, he was invited to take a seat, and as he sat down his spirit left the pale clay and soared upward to its God.

CHAPTER 9

OBJECTS OF INTEREST IN PHILADELPHIA – INDEPENDENCE HALL, GIRARD COLLEGE, FAIR MOUNT, LAUREL HILL CEMETERY, ETC. – MR. CLAY NOMINATED FOR THE PRESIDENCY – DISTRESSING STAGE RIDE FROM CHAMBERSBURG TO PITTSBURG – DOWN THE OHIO TO LOUISVILLE AND THENCE HOME BY STEAMER GEN. WARREN.

Every one who visits Philadelphia must of course see Independence Hall, so called because there the Declaration of Independence was adopted in 1776. This is thought by many to be the grandest uninspired document ever published. It required Mr. Jefferson's best ability to write it, and it required the sublime moral courage to adopt it. The men who voted for it placed themselves in advance of the civilized world and showed their superior knowledge of the philosophy of liberty. They levied a large contribution on the gratitude and admiration of succeeding generations. The building in which they deliberated and acted has in itself no special attractions. What was done in it gives the structure a sort of earthly immortality.

The Anniversaries being over, my friend Burrows kindly procured a horse and buggy and we rode to Girard College. This was at the time said to be the finest building in the United States. It is of marble, four stories high. The roof projects several feet and rests on magnificent columns, which cost $14,000 a piece, and there are thirty-four of these columns. The roof is covered with marble slabs four feet wide. The distance from the eaves to the comb of the roof is fifty-six feet. It is said that Girard in his will expressed a desire to have a plain and substantial building erected, gave a plan, and added, "let it be according to this plan or any other that good taste may suggest." The Philadelphians have availed themselves of the latitude given in the phrase "good taste," and have already expended one million eight hundred thousand dollars, and the building is not yet completed. They, however, justify themselves in this extravagant outlay in the following manner: They say that Girard knew that he would soon be forgotten unless he did something extraordinary, and that he wished a splendid edifice reared out of the most durable material, that his name might be handed down to posterity.

Fair Mount, with its large reservoir, was well worth seeing. The water is thrown up from the Schuylkill and thus the city is supplied with an indispensable article. Some other cities, no doubt, now have more attractive "water works" than Philadelphia, but at the time to which I refer Fair Mount reservoir was considered a great affair. It may perhaps admit of debate whether the Schuylkill in supplying the city with water is not of greater utility than the Delaware on which the shipping rides so majestically. I do not enter into the discussion, but simply express the opinion that the Delaware might furnish better water, as it now does to Chester.

Laurel Hill Cemetery was the most beautiful repository of the dead I had then seen. It was a most enchanting place. The trees waved their branches, the grass carpeted the ground, the shrubbery was tastefully arranged, and everything was in perfect order. Along how many gravel walks we made our way I know not, for who in admiring the monuments could think of numbers? The specimens of sculpture are very fine, some of one form and some of another, exhibiting beautiful diversity. One monument I noticed with much interest. A fond husband and father had it erected in memory of his wife and seven children. There was on it a very impressive representation of an open rose and seven buds. Ah, how does that bereaved man feel when thinking of the rose and the buds!

I saw a column most elegantly finished and most naturally broken about six feet from the ground—an affecting symbol of the broken hopes of the parents who had there deposited the remains of a dear child. One tomb I saw and long did I gaze on it. The marble out of which it was constructed was beautiful, and on the slab was the exact image of a little boy—pale, emaciated, his eyes closed in death, his hair lying in graceful ringlets on his neck, and his head resting on a pillow. Nothing in the cemetery affected me so much as this. I began to think how I should feel on seeing my own dear boy motionless in death. There is an inexpressible tenderness in a father's feelings when a thousand miles from his children.

I visited the monument erected to the memory of Charles Thompson, a prominent man in our Revolutionary struggle, Secretary to Congress, and Translator of the Old Testament from the Greek Septuagint into English. He was a native of Ireland. After his arrival in America he received many marks of kindness from Dr. Franklin.

But I must not enlarge on these objects of interest farther than to say that we visited the House of Refuge, and the Philadelphia Library, which contained a hundred and forty thousand volumes. Doubtless it has been greatly enlarged since then, for "of making many books there is no end."

It was my full purpose to go to Washington that I might for the first time see the capital city of the nation; but I was told that there would be great difficulty in getting a seat in the stage from there to Wheeling in less than two weeks. This was owing to the large number who, it was supposed, would be returning from the great Whig Convention in Baltimore. So I abandoned my purpose to visit Washington.

By the way, that Convention met May 1, 1844, and it was well known beforehand that Henry Clay, of Kentucky, would be nominated for the Presidency. No other man was thought of. The nomination was unanimous and enthusiastic. I found that Mr. Clay was almost idolized in Philadelphia. His praises were heard in all parts of the city. I remember that in going into a bank to cash a check, the teller, learning that I was from Kentucky, said, "You are from his own State." He seemed to think that everybody would know who was meant. Orators declaimed on Mr. Clay's greatness and his transcendent fitness for the Presidency and poets made songs. All of these songs were not perfect in poetic merit and some of them were not much above doggerel. This made no difference. They were sung with the greatest zest and with enthusiastic vociferation. I cannot now call up a single one of those songs, but I well remember the refrain of one. It was this:

> Get out of the way – you are all unlucky;
> Clear the track for old Kentucky.

These lines, in ordinary times, would hardly create even moderate excitement, but in 1844 they stirred the staid city of Philadelphia. Circumstances are often material things.

Having decided to return home without visiting Washington, I took leave of Bro. Burrows and his family. There was a railroad as far as Chambersburg, but from there the public way of travel was by stage and I had the most distressing ride of my life. There were nine inside passengers who had an accidental advantage over me; that is, their names were first on the list. I had of course to ride on the outside. Some of the inside passengers, four of whom were preachers who had attended the Anniversaries, told me that they would exchange places with me from time to time, and that everything would be pleasant. One of them took my place soon after we left Chambersburg late in the afternoon, for he said he would like to have a good view of the scenery. The sun was shining then and everything looked beautiful; but soon it began to rain and my friend called for his inside seat. I surrendered it and taking my seat by the driver, and owing, no doubt, to the almost continuous rain, I heard no more about an exchange of seats. We were forty-eight hours from Chambersburg to Pittsburg, and for a considerable part of the way I was wet to the skin. I became so tired and weary and sleepy that I was obliged to nod, and in the nodding process my hat fell off, but the driver was kind enough to stop and let me pick it up. I was roused up and kept my eyes open for a time, and I cannot forget in the midst of a heavy rain, the stage broke down. The driver said he would have to go a short distance to get the damage repaired, and asked if some passenger would stand before the horses till he returned. There was a man from Boston on the top of the stage who was protecting himself as well as he could. He generously offered his services on condition that some one would lend him an umbrella. There was only one umbrella not in use and that belonged to one of the preachers. I suppose he had bought it in Philadelphia; but however that was; he refused to lend it, and gave as his reason that "it had never been wet." This made the Boston passenger indignant and he said that the horses might do what they pleased. I do not remember all his words, but some of them probably were not strictly evangelical. From that day to this I regarded the refusal to lend the umbrella as the most striking proof of selfishness I ever saw. During our delay I went to some iron works not far away and tried to dry my wet clothes by a glowing fire. The damage being repaired we proceeded on our way, and after a little more than forty-eight hours, two days and two nights, we reached Pittsburg at 9 o'clock P.M. Friday, having left Chambersburg a little before sundown on Wednesday. I have no pleasant memories of that ride, and hope that no one, saint or sinner, will ever be subjected to the calamity of suffering as I suffered.

From Pittsburg I descended the Ohio on the steamer "Majestic" and at Wheeling many who had been to the Baltimore Convention came on board, full of patriotic zeal, and perfectly assured of Mr. Clay's election. Some talked eloquently of what his administration would be, and some sang Whig songs, not forgetting the lines quoted:

>Get our of the way – you are all unlucky;
>Clear the track for old Kentucky.

I reached Louisville May 7th and visited the families of my friends, Halbert and Heth, who had married into the Wilson family. On the 8th, in the afternoon, I left Louisville for Bowling Green on the steamer General Warren and met several acquaintances on board, among them Judge E.M. Ewing. The boat reached the mouth of Green River early on the 9th and passed through two locks during the day. These locks are incomparably better than any on the Pennsylvania Canal. Green River is a very fine stream, though not very straight. The distance from where Big Barren River empties into Green River to Bowling Green is not great. I therefore arrived at home on the 10th, after an absence of twenty-nine days. My family had just returned from Glasgow. There was no concert between us, for there was no certainty then as to the time of a boat's arrival, but we all reached home about the same hour – a very agreeable coincidence. We devoutly thanked God for his preserving goodness during our separation, and for our re-union amid favorable circumstances.

On a review of my journey I feel glad that I attended the Triennial Convention. It gave me an opportunity of seeing many men of whom I had often heard, but whom I had not seen. Among these were Spencer H. Cone, Francis Wayland, Daniel Sharp, William R. Williams, Bartholomew T. Welch, Richard Fuller, George B. Ide, Jeremiah B. Jeter, J.B Taylor, William Hague, Rufus Babcock, William W. Everts, Adiel Sherwood, Daniel Dodge, Nathaniel Colver, and many others. Concerning a few only of these I record my opinion: I think Dr. Wayland was the most profound man among them. I had studied his "Moral Science" with no little interest and felt a great veneration for him. He had a wonderful power of analysis, and could easily show the component parts of a subject. When introduced to him I inquired concerning his health: He replied, "I am as stiff as a cow," and I thought if the President of Brown University knows about cows I need not be afraid of him.

Dr. Williams was no doubt the most learned man I saw. He was a student from his boyhood, and being lame he could not play at school and spent "playtime" in reading. This may have had something to do with his life-long love of books. He was the most diffident man I have ever seen. I heard him make a speech and it was some minutes before he could raise his eyes and look at his hearers, who were eager to catch every word that fell from his lips. His sentences were beautiful rhetoric, but at times somewhat artificial. I think this may be seen, too, in his books. His style is by no means so clear and forcible as Dr. Wayland's. Other persons may not think so.

I have already referred to Dr. Fuller as eloquent. He easily broke away the palm of pulpit oratory in his best days. He was well versed in logic and at home in rhetoric, apt in illustration and pathetic in appeal. His person was commanding, his voice charming, his elocution impressive, his gesticulation natural. It was in the year 1845 that he and Dr. Wayland had their written discussion on slavery. Published at first in the *Reflector* of Boston, it was afterward published in book form, and everybody ought to read it to see with what dignity a discussion can be conducted, and how men can differ and still respect each other.

Alas, of the brethren I have named not one of them is now in the land of the living. They have all fallen under the stroke of death. They had their trials and sorrows while here, but they are free from them now. They had their struggles with temptation and sin, but they have gone where temptation does not assail, and where there is no sin.

> Part of the host have crossed the flood,
> And part are crossing now.

Of all the distinguished brethren I met in 1844, I know of no one now alive except Dr. Robert Ryland of Lexington, Kentucky – venerated and beloved by all who enjoy his acquaintance. His hoary head is a crown of glory.

CHAPTER 10

MR. POLK'S ELECTION – TEXAS ANNEXED – WAR WITH
MEXICO – TREATY OF PEACE – THE QUESTION OF
EMANCIPATION IN KENTUCKY – JOHN L. WALLER –
WESTERN BAPTIST REVIEW.

The general impression had been that Mr. Clay would be elected President. So confident was Judge Ewing that he thought it doubtful whether Mr. Polk would receive the electoral vote of a single State in the Union. He did not carry his own State of Tennessee, but he was elected, to the astonishment of the nation and of the civilized world. Mr. Clay had had Presidential aspirations from 1824, when he, John Quincy Adams, Andrew Jackson, and William H. Crawford were candidates. There never was a time when he could have been elected except in 1840, when William Henry Harrison was the successful Whig candidate. Mr. Polk was a man of respectable talents, had been a member of Congress for some years, was Speaker of the House of Representatives, but was not to be compared, in ability, with Mr. Clay. He, however, received a majority of the electoral, and also of the popular vote.

It is the impression of many, even to this day, that as the result of Mr. Polk's election, Texas was annexed to the United States. This is a mistake, for the annexation took place just before the expiration of Mr. Tyler's term of office. Mr. Tyler became President on the death of General Harrison. In the latter part of his administration he made Mr. Calhoun Secretary of State, and thus he had a very able man to engineer the annexation of Texas. This was done not by treaty, but by a joint resolution of both Houses of

Congress. It could not be expected that Mexico would quietly submit to this, and soon were heard rumors of war. Whigs and Democrats differed very widely as to the origin and even the righteousness of the war. Whigs considered the river Nueces the boundary between the United States and Mexico, while Democrats made the Rio Grande the dividing line. Mr. Polk ordered General Taylor, with the army under his command, to the Rio Grande, and there was not found a Texas family between the river and the Nueces. This fact is stated by General Grant in his "Personal Memoirs," and he was with General Taylor. The Whigs therefore believed that Mr. Polk was quite unreasonable in assuming that the territory of the United States extended to the Rio Grande. While General Taylor's troops were opposite Matamoras a few Mexicans crossed the river and in a little skirmish a little blood was shed. This was enough for Mr. Polk and he issued a proclamation in which he declared, "American blood has been shed on American soil." This statement was believed by Democrats and earnestly denied by Whigs. Hon. J.J. Crittenden applied to it the plain Anglo-Saxon term "lie," for he did not believe that there was any "American soil" between the Nueces and the Rio Grande. War with its attendant horrors came, and I think now, as I thought then, that the two political parties exemplified the two kinds of insanity, mental and moral. That is to say, Democrats were *mentally* insane in believing that the territory between the two rivers belonged to the United States, and Whigs were *morally* insane in voting for and urging the prosecution of a war which they pronounced unjust. While Whig members of Congress, with Democrats, voted supplies for carrying on the war, such men as Cassius M. Clay, Thomas F. Marshall, Henry Clay, Jr. and many others, belonging to the Whig party, volunteered their services and made their way to Mexico. General Taylor was of course ordered to cross the Rio Grande and to engage the Mexican forces. He was very successful in his battles, became the idol of the army and very popular in the United States, so that he was in a short time heir *apparent*, and afterward *real* heir to the Presidency. Mr. Polk was annoyed for fear the glory of the war would not inure to the Democratic party, and for a time he was anxious to put Col. Thomas H. Benton in command of the army; but this could not well be done. General Scott was first in military authority and was ordered to Mexico. He sailed for Vera Cruz, bombarded and captured the place, and then proceeded without very much fighting to the city of Mexico. By this time it was known that the army of the United States was victorious and Gen. Scott rode on a high horse into the capital city of the enemy with all the pomp and display of which he was childishly found.

In due time a treaty was made in which the Rio Grande was named as the boundary line (although Democrats said it was the line before) and New Mexico and California were ceded to the United States.

The consequences resulting from the treaty were unexpected and far-reaching. The purpose of Mr. Polk and his party was that the territory ceded should enlarge the area of slavery; but in this they were disappointed. When the matter came before Congress for discussion and decision, California was admitted into the Union as a *free* State, and there was a failure to establish *slavery* in New Mexico. The discussion was earnest and even vehement. Mr. Jefferson Davis in the Senate insisted that there should be recognition of slavery in New Mexico; but Mr. Clay said that no earthly power could make him vote to send slavery where it was not. Mr. Webster argued in his celebrated speech of March 7, 1850, that it would be needlessly offensive to the South to declare New Mexico free, because God in the physical conformation of the territory had virtually made slavery impossible, and that no action of Congress was called for. For this speech Mr. Webster was denounced by many of his former friends, but at this day we can see he was patriotic and wise. The oil of vitriol so copiously poured on his head was out of place and posterity will do him justice.

General Taylor was at this time President, having been elected in 1848, but he died July 9, 1850, leaving Mr. Fillmore to take his place.

JAMES MADISON PENDLETON

One of the results of the treaty with Mexico was the discovery of gold in California, and this affected the condition of things not only in the United States but throughout the world. Many persons went in hot haste to California in pursuit of gold, the city of San Francisco was built up, and railroads reaching the shores of the Pacific have been constructed. There has been a Divine providence in all this which reminds us that God can bring good out of evil. A war, unjustifiable on the part of the United States, has resulted in many beneficial consequences. We need not now speculate as to what the state of things would have been if California had not been admitted into the Union.

The year 1849 was an important year in Kentucky. A new Constitution was to be formed, and the friends of Emancipation hoped that some provision might be inserted in it for the gradual abolition of slavery in the State. Mr. Clay wrote an able letter on the subject which was extensively circulated. The plan he advocated was that all slaves born in the State after a certain time should be free at certain ages – males at twenty-eight years and females at twenty-one. I was not satisfied with these numbers, for, in my judgment, they deferred the period of freedom for too long. Having business in upper Kentucky in the summer of 1848, I visited Mr. Clay and conversed with him on the subject. He insisted that without a large concession to the pro-slavery feeling of the state nothing could be done, and he was right in this view. Indeed, it was afterward seen that no concession would have been satisfactory to the advocates of slavery. During the canvass for Delegates to the Constitutional Convention in 1849, the Emancipation party thought it wise to vote for men in favor of what was significantly called the "open clause." By this it was meant that if the Convention failed to adopt any measure of Emancipation, the adoption of the "open clause" would enable the Legislature at any time to submit the question to the people, untrammeled by any other question.

I was deeply interested in the subject of Emancipation, for all the pulsations of my heart beat in favor of civil liberty. There was an Emancipation paper, called *The Examiner*, published in Louisville, and I wrote for it more than twenty articles signed "A Southern Emancipationist." I incurred the ill will of many, and an old friend said to me, "I do not see how an honest man can be in favor of Emancipation." I bore it quietly. It may surely be said that some of the ablest men in the State were on the side of Emancipation, such men as Henry Clay, President Young of Center College, Dr. Malcom of Georgetown College, Drs. R.J. and W.L. Breckinridge, Dr. E.P. Humphrey, Dr. Stuart Robinson, Judges Nicholas, Tompkins, Underwood, Graham, and many others. But the influence of these strong men was unavailing. The pro-slavery party was triumphant at the election of delegates by a very large majority. My spirit sank within me and I saw no hope for the African race in Kentucky, or anywhere else without the interposition of some Providential judgment. The thought did not enter into my mind that a terrible civil war would secure liberty to every slave in the United States. That God brought slavery to an end I shall attempt to show in another place.

It was in the summer of 1849 that I resigned the care of the church in Bowling Green. I thought it best to do, as I supposed that my views of Emancipation were not acceptable to some of the members. The church, however, was unwilling to receive the resignation, requested me to remain pastor, and I did so remain till the end of the year. Persons at this day cannot easily imagine how strong the pro-slavery feeling was in Kentucky before and at the election of Delegates to the Constitutional Convention. When it was known that Dr. Malcom had voted the Emancipation ticket, some of the Trustees of the College gave him to understand that his resignation of the Presidency would be acceptable. He did resign and went East. There was some discussion in the papers concerning the resignation and I think the Trustees regretted the treatment Dr. Malcom received. I defended him in some newspaper articles, and it is a satisfaction to me that years after he said to me, "You are the man who defended me in Kentucky." I think I may say that I have always had a propensity to defend my friends when unjustly assailed.

After the result of the election was known those opposed to Emancipation, being in an overwhelming majority, felt that they could afford to be courteous and magnanimous toward their opponents. I attended the General Association in October of that year, at Lexington, and was treated with great kindness. It was arranged, too, for me to attend the ordination of Rev. J.W. Warder at Frankfort in November, and preach the sermon. I saw clearly that there was no intention to ostracize me. Most of the men of that time have passed away. I am left to pen these lines.

I have failed to say, in the proper place, that in the year 1845, Re. John L. Waller, editor of *The Baptist Banner*, began the publication of the *Western Baptist Review*, a monthly magazine. It was published at Frankfort, Ky. I had written occasional articles for the *Banner* for some years, and Mr. Waller was pleased to ask me to become a contributor to his *Review*. I did so, and find from an examination of the four volumes before me that if I did not have the pen of a ready writer, I had a pen that was often in use. My articles are rather numerous, and I may say that in writing for the *Review* I learned to write with greater care than I had exercised in writing transient pieces for newspapers. I found this an advantage, by way of concentrating my attention on a subject, and I have tried to write carefully ever since. I may have carried this thing to a greater length than most writers for I have written nothing a second time. All my books have been written *once* and then printed. It is impossible to write with requisite care if a writer knows that he is going to re-write his manuscript, or make any important interlineations in it. Some of my descendants may profit by these views after I am gone.

Mr. Waller was probably the ablest writer among the Baptists of Kentucky. He wielded a vigorous pen, and on the chain of his logic he often hung festoons of beautiful rhetoric. Many of his productions in this *Review* exhibit transcendent power and, though written more than forty years ago, may be read with profit now. There are, however, but few copies of the *Review* in existence. Mr. Waller did not preach very much, but his sermons were very instructive. There was one, easily first of all his discourses. Its title it, "The Bible Adapted to the Spiritual Wants of the World," and it was preached before the Kentucky and Foreign Bible Society, Danville, October 16, 1846. It is published in the second volume of the *Review*, and is Mr. Waller's masterpiece as a sermon.

As a debater Mr. Waller was quite celebrated. He had a discussion, afterward published, with Mr. Pingree on Universalism, and with several Pedobaptists on Baptism. Among these were Rev. N.L. Rice, and when these two champions came together they were foemen worthy of each other's steel. I have heard that Dr. Rice pronounced Waller abler than Alexander Campbell on the baptismal question.

Mr. Waller did in 1849 what I and many of his friends regretted. He became a candidate, in Woodford County, for a seat in the Constitutional Convention and he was elected over the brilliant Thomas F. Marshall. I am sorry to say that the pro-slavery element decided the election. Mr. Waller made a pro-slavery speech in the Convention which I reviewed, anonymously, in the *Louisville Courier*. Our friendly relations were not disturbed.

Mr. Waller was a strong advocate of the revision of the Bible, and it was through his influence that I was appointed to deliver an address before the American Bible Union, in New York, in October, 1854. Having performed the duty, I returned by way of Niagara, and on reaching Louisville I learned that Mr. Waller was dead. He died October 10, 1854, and the funeral sermon was preached by Dr. W.W. Everts. There is no protection from the grave.

CHAPTER 11

MEETING AT GREEN RIVER CHURCH, OHIO COUNTY –
REMOVAL TO RUSSELLVILLE – BIRTH OF OUR THIRD
DAUGHTER – RETURN TO BOWLING GREEN – REVIVAL
UNDER THE PREACHING OF J.R. GRAVES – BIRTH AND
MARRIAGE OF OUR SECOND SON.

My pastorate at Bowling Green ended for a time with the end of the year 1849. I had promised my friend Rev. Alfred Taylor to aid him, as soon as I could, in a meeting with his church at Green River, Ohio County. I therefore complied with my promise early in January, 1850. Brother Taylor and I had been for many years on terms of intimate friendship. I regarded him one of the best men I ever knew. He was a sound evangelical preacher and great success attended his ministry. It is said that he baptized more young men who became preachers than any other minister in Kentucky.

In the meeting referred to I was required to do the preaching, and in three weeks I preached twenty-one sermons. The Lord was pleased to grant His blessing. The church was revived and sinners were converted. I do not remember how many were baptized, but the number was considerable.

After the meeting was over Brother Taylor told me of a compliment paid me by a plain farmer, which I have prized more than anything of the kind ever said about me. Men of learning and distinction have sometimes said favorable things concerning my preaching; but I have appreciated nothing so much as the remark of the farmer. He said, "Any one who cannot understand that preaching will not be held accountable at the judgment." However this may be, every preacher should make it a point to preach plainly as well as earnestly, faithfully, and lovingly.

I cannot say certainly whether I ever saw Brother Taylor after this meeting. He died October 9, 1855, leaving three sons in the ministry. Happy man, to go up to heaven with three lineal and spiritual representatives to plead the cause of Christ on earth!

After the meeting at Green River Church I visited different parts of the State, but was thinking all the while about removing north of the Ohio River. Having this matter under consideration, friends at Russellville requested me to make no engagement, and in due time I was called to the pastorate there. I accepted the call and was settled the latter part of July. While at Russellville, that is to say, on the 25th of August, our third daughter, whose name is Lila, was born. She was a delicate child from her birth and for some years was a great sufferer, so that she could not enjoy the pleasures of other children. In consequence of the calamities of the war we could not send her to college as we had done with our other daughters. She was therefore taught at home. She made very respectable proficiency in English under the instruction of her mother, while an older sister gave her lessons in French, and I took her through the Latin course.

In the year 1868 she professed conversion and was baptized at Upland, Pennsylvania. By mingling in the best society she has overcome the disadvantages of her childhood and youth, and acts well her part in any circle in which she is called to move. On the 9th of November, 1876, she was united in marriage with Mr. Benjamin F. Procter, of Bowling Green, a prominent lawyer, who has been very successful in his profession. They are congenial spirits and enjoy as much domestic happiness as falls to the lot of mortals. Mr. Procter has served for several years as Superintendent of the Sunday-school of the First Baptist Church in Bowling Green, and Lila has been a zealous teacher. A Presbyterian preacher has pronounced her the best teacher he ever saw.

Reminiscences of a Long Life

My sojourn at Russellville was pleasant, so far as the church and congregation were concerned, but the "parsonage" was not at all comfortable, and we were anxious to get some other house, but could not. It was while I was at Russellville that the Bethel Association decided on the establishment of a High School, which some years after became Bethel College. No one at the time thought of a college, and there are many now who think Georgetown the only Collegiate Institution needed by the Baptists of Kentucky. But Bethel has done, and is still doing a good work, and it is useless to talk, as some do, about transferring its endowment to Georgetown. This will not be done.

All the time I was in Russellville the Church of Bowling Green was without a pastor, and my house there was not rented. In thinking of the discomforts of the "parsonage" we naturally thought of the comforts of our home and wished to be in it again. While occupied with these thoughts, I was invited to resume my former place in Bowling Green, and accepted the invitation.

Everything went on in the ordinary style till February, 1852, when Rev. J.R. Graves, of Nashville, held a meeting with us. The prospect was, at first, by no means bright. The truth is, the church was not far from a state of Laodicean lukewarmness. Brother Graves at once saw this, and this sermons for the first week of the meeting, were addressed exclusively to the church. He said he "could not preach to impenitent sinners over a dead church." Brethren and sisters were awakened from their spiritual apathy, and the spirit of prayer took possession of them. They called mightily on God, confessed their backslidings, and sought a restoration of the joy of Salvation. When this joy was restored, and not till then, they were prepared to labor for the salvation of sinners. This is in perfect accordance with the language of David: "Restore unto me the joy of Thy salvation; and uphold me with Thy free Spirit. Then will I teach transgressors Thy ways and sinners shall be converted unto Thee." (Psalm 51: 12, 13.) Brother Graves well understood the true philosophy of a revival or religion. By the time saints were revived, sinners were awakened and began to inquire, "What must we do to be saved?" There was a sense of guilt and danger. Inquirers felt that sin had proved their ruin, that they were justly condemned, that they could not save themselves, and that, if saved, it must be by the grace of God. The way of salvation through Christ was presented and one anxious soul after another saw it and rejoiced in it. The seats of inquirers, vacated by happy converts, were filled again and again by anxious souls. Thus the meeting went on from day to day and from week to week until about seventy-five persons, young and old, were baptized and added to the church. Truly it was a time of refreshing from the presence of the Lord. Our old meeting-house was not large, but the members of the church now filled all the seats at the Lord's Supper, and we began to plan for a new house of worship. It was not long before a lot was bought on Main Street at what now appears a marvelously cheap price (seven dollars a foot) and a building was erected, into which we entered in 1854. This house is still occupied.

I may say of Brother Graves that no man ever conducted a meeting more judiciously. His sermons were able and instructive, his exhortations were powerful, and his advice to inquirers and young converts just what it should be. There was considerable excitement among Pedobaptists on the subject of Baptism and several sermons were afterward preached by Methodist and Presbyterian ministers. Before the excitement subsided I was called on to preach a dedication sermon at Liberty Church, Logan County, and I gave my reasons for being a Baptist. These were afterward expanded into a little book styled "Three Reasons Why I Am a Baptist." This book was published in 1853 and was my first attempt at authorship. It had a good circulation, and I subsequently sold the copyright and stereotype plates to Graves, Marks & Co., of Nashville. After twenty-eight years, when the copyright had fully expired, I revised and enlarged the book, and it was published in the year 1882 by the American Baptist Publication Society, with the title, "Distinctive Principles of Baptists." I wish my descendants and others to consider this volume as my testimony in favor of Baptist Principles.

From the time of the meeting above referred to, I became a regular contributor to the *Tennessee Baptist*, a weekly sheet published in Nashville, J.R. Graves, editor. I wrote on various subjects and was requested to write several articles on this question: "Ought Baptists to Recognize Pedobaptist Preachers as Gospel Ministers?" I answered in the negative, and wrote four articles which were afterward published in pamphlet form under the title, "An Old Landmark Re-set." Bro. Graves furnished the title, for he said the "Old Landmark" once stood, but had fallen, and needed to be "re-set." So much for the name. This tract had a wide circulation, for the copy now before me has on the title page the words, "Fortieth Thousand." The position I had taken was most earnestly controverted by a large number of brethren. Drs. Waller, Burrows, Lynd, Everts, and Prof. Farnam, among Baptists, took part in the discussion, and Drs. Cossitt and Hill, who were Presbyterians. I replied to them all in an Appendix to the "Landmark," and after more than thirty years have passed away, I still think that I refuted their arguments. I do not wonder therefore, that Dr. N.M. Crawford, of Georgia, said that I had never been answered. The "Old Landmark" has been out of print for many years and it would be very difficult to obtain a copy, but the discussions connected with it have modified the views of many Baptists in the South, and of some in the North.

The controversy was and is a strange one: in one sense, all Roman Catholics and all Protestant Pedobaptists are on the side of the "Landmark." That is to say, they believe, and their practice of infant baptism compels the belief, that baptism must precede the regular preaching of the gospel. This is just what Landmark Baptists say, and they say, in addition, that immersion alone is baptism, indispensable to entrance into a gospel church, and that from such a church must emanate authority, under God, to preach the gospel. All this is implied in the immemorial custom, among Baptist churches, of licensing and ordaining men to preach. But I will not enlarge: I have said this that my children and grandchildren may know what the "Old Landmark" was, and why I wrote it. Baptists can never protest effectually against the errors of Pedobaptists while the preachers of the latter are recognized as gospel ministers. This to me is very plain.

The birth of our second son, the last birth in our family, occurred on the 24th of May, 1855. We called him Garnett that he might preserve the maiden name of his mother. He was a healthy, good child and soon became a favorite in the family. We of course took him with us when we removed to Tennessee in 1857, and to Ohio in 1862, and to Pennsylvania in 1865. An account of these removals will be given in future chapters. Garnett, like our other children, was taught by his mother for several years, and then went for a time to the academy of Mr. Aaron, at Mt. Holly, New Jersey. This was with a view to his preparation for college, but he was very imperfectly prepared. Before he left home, at a time of some religious interest, he made profession of his faith in Christ and was baptized with his sister Lila the 12th of January, 1868. They both went down into the water together and it was a happy time for their father. It has so happened that I have baptized all my children and married them all, except the one who died unmarried.

My exalted opinion of President M.B. Anderson decided me to send my son to the University of Rochester, New York. He was there four years, and though he did not take the "first honor," so-called, he had a respectable standing in the graduating class of 1875. On his return home, he became a student of law in the office of E. Coppee Mitchell, of Philadelphia. Here he remained three years, attending, in the meantime, the Lectures in the Law School of Pennsylvania University and graduating at the expiration of that period. His purpose, at first, was to open an office in Philadelphia; but on due reflection he decided to settle in Chester, Pennsylvania, where he now lives (1891) and has a respectable practice. There is no lawyer of his age who prepares his cases more laboriously and exhaustively, and there is no one who has a better faculty of analysis, or can make a stronger logical argument.

Garnett was married in the First Baptist Church, Philadelphia, December 30, 1879, to Miss Helena Ward, daughter of Rev. William Ward, D.D., missionary to Assam. She was born on the Island of St. Helena, and hence her name. One bright child, Emma, now six years old, whom her blind grandmother taught to read, is the fruit of this marriage. Where the great Napoleon found a prison, and Mrs. Sarah B. Judson a grave, Helena first saw the light. Years afterward she saw in Philadelphia the light of salvation and was baptized by Rev. Mr. Rees, pastor of the Tabernacle Baptist Church.

There is nothing pertaining to Garnett that gratifies his parents more than the fact that he is a useful member of the Upland Baptist Church and the teacher of a Bible class of about seventy grown persons. He is highly appreciated as an expositor of the Sunday-school lessons. May there be long years of Christian usefulness before him! It will probably devolve on him to write at the end of these Reminiscences the date of the death of their author.

CHAPTER 12

REMOVED TO MURFREESBORO, TENNESSEE – UNION UNIVERSITY – THEOLOGICAL DEPARTMENT – PRESIDENT EATON AND WIFE – TENNESSEE BAPTIST AND SOUTHERN BAPTIST REVIEW – CHARGE OF ANTI-SLAVERY SENTIMENTS BROUGHT AGAINST ME – A LITTLE DISCUSSION WITH ALEXANDER CAMPBELL.

On the first day of January, 1857, I left Bowling Green and removed to Murfreesboro, Tennessee. Nothing had been more unexpected by me. The explanation of the matter is this: The Trustees of Union University decided to establish a Theological Department in the Institution, and, to my amazement, they appointed me professor. When informed of the fact I promptly declined the appointment and told the Trustees that I was utterly incompetent, having never been to a theological school, and knowing nothing of theology except what I had learned from the Bible. I thought this would end the negotiation, but the Trustees said they wanted a man who had learned his theology from the Bible. I then replied that preaching the gospel was my business and that I could not give it up for any thing in the world. I supposed that this would settle the matter, but the Trustees were ready to meet this state of the case. They said that the Baptist church in Murfreesboro was without a pastor, and that I would be chosen to the pastorate, so that I could preach every Sunday and teach theology during the week. They argued that in this way my usefulness would be increased, and this consideration alone induced the acceptance of the professorship offered me. I thought it my duty to God to place myself in a position promising greater usefulness. I therefore, with a sad heart, resigned my pastorate at Bowling Green, and, in broken accents, preached my last sermon, which was heard by many whose eyes were filled with tears. It was a day of sorrow.

It is proper to say that, at the time, the Southern Baptist Theological Seminary had not been established, and it was thought wise to have theological instruction in colleges. Thorough teaching was, of course, out of the question, and the plan was for instruction in theology to be interspersed with literary pursuits through the collegiate course. This was the best that could then be done, but the work of the Seminary now supersedes this arrangement.

While connected with Union University I had, first and last, between forty and fifty ministerial students under my instruction. The different classes could not be so arranged as to give me more than an hour a day for my class in theology; and it was not long before other classes were given me, so that I had to teach five hours a day. Marvelous to say, I had to teach many things of which I knew absolutely nothing, except what I had learned myself without the aid of any one. I had therefore to go ahead of the classes, and it is a wonder to me to this day how I was able to conceal my ignorance so as to avoid the ignominy of its exposure. In the Theological Department, the text-books I used were Horne's Introduction, Ripley's Sacred Rhetoric, Dagg's and Dick's Theology. One brother, rather more candidly than encouragingly said that the department was a "one-horse concern." Even so; but the reason students had to learn what they could from one teacher was they could not go to a regular theological seminary. The greatest improvement I saw in the young preachers was in the art of sermonizing. They studied Ripley to great advantage, and listened attentively to my extemporaneous explanations. I trust they received some benefit, and some of them became useful.

Dr. Joseph H. Eaton was President of the University. He was a man of intellectual power and broad scholarship, not inferior, as I think, to his brother George W., who died

President of Madison, now Colgate University. Dr. Joseph H. was a very laborious teacher, enthusiastic in his work, and almost compelled by the cares of the Presidency to do overwork. When I first knew him he was a fine specimen of manly beauty, and his sermons and addresses were replete with vigor and eloquence. But his noble physical frame succumbed to disease and he died in the prime of his life, January 1859, leaving a bereaved University, a bereaved church, and a more bereaved family. It devolved on me to preach the funeral sermon and the text was, "Lord Jesus, receive my Spirit." (Acts 7:59) The general feeling was, "A great man has fallen in Israel." Mrs. Eaton, left to feel the desolateness of widowhood, was a remarkable woman, equal in intellectual and spiritual qualities to her husband. She spent many years of her life in teaching, and left her impress on the minds of many young ladies. She lived a widow more than twenty-five years and died in Louisville in 1886. I preached her funeral sermon also, from Rev. 14:13: "Blessed are the dead who die in the Lord," etc. Two children survive, Rev. T.T. Eaton, D.D., and Mrs. J.E. Peck, who are worthy representatives of their parents, and who are occupying positions of usefulness.

After President Eaton's death the faculty consisted of Professors George W. Jarman, Paul W. Dodson, and A.S. Worrell, with all of whom my relations were especially pleasant. For two years I acted as Chairman of the faculty and therefore presided on commencement occasions, and handed to the graduates their diplomas in testimony of their scholarship.

Rev. J.R. Graves had long been editor of the *Tennessee Baptist*, published at Nashville, and in 1858, Rev. A.C. Dayton and I became joint editors with him. Dr. Dayton (not a D.D. but an M.D.) is best known as the author of "Theodosia Ernest," a book of great celebrity, having had a wide circulation, and which was written, as I know, to show that there is, in the republic of letters, a realm which sanctified fiction should claim as its own.

JAMES MADISON PENDLETON

My becoming editor did not impress on me the necessity of writing more than I had done; for I had been for several years engaged to supply two columns a week for the paper, and was one of the editors of the *Southern Baptist Review* for the six years of its existence, immediately preceding the war. It may be inferred that mine was not an idle life in Tennessee. My body would probably have sunk under the mental strain if I had not taken active exercise on my little farm. I often plowed by way of recreation in the afternoon, and did other work which needed to be done. Usually I finished my editorials by nine o'clock Saturday night. I did too much for any mortal man to do. I advise no one to copy my example except in part.

While engaged in performing these onerous duties, I was charged with being an "Abolitionist." The charge, so far as I know, was first made by Dr. Dawson, then editor of the Alabama Baptist paper. In justice to him it is proper to say that he had, as he stated it, no feeling against me "*personally*;" but he declared boldly that no man of my anti-slavery views ought to belong to the faculty of any Southern college. I suppose he made no distinction between an "Abolitionist" and an "Emancipationist." The latter was in favor of doing away with slavery *gradually*, according to State Constitution and law; the former believed slavery to be a sin *in itself*, calling for immediate abolition without regard to consequences. I was an Emancipationist, as I have said, in Kentucky in 1849; but I was never for a moment an Abolitionist. The application of this term to a man was, at the time referred to, the most effectual way of creating hostility to him. I suppose one fact intensified the hostility in my case. In 1859 John Brown made his raid into Virginia, and as Greeley says in his "American Conflict," "The fifteen slave States were convulsed with fear, rage, and hate." The excitement in Tennessee was great and, father South, still greater. Then it was that articles which I had published in Kentucky in 1849, in connection with the Emancipation movement there, were republished in a Nashville paper to excited prejudice against me, with a view to my dismissal from the faculty of the University. The thing was as cruel as the grace, and I did not know till the war was over who furnished the articles for publication. Then I learned that they were furnished by a brother who had delivered a course of lectures to our theological students, and whose traveling expenses had been paid in part by me. This was the poetry of the case. He was, in spite of his strong pro-slavery feeling, a good man, a just man, his recent death has no doubt released him from all earthly imperfections and introduced him into the blest region where "the spirits of just men are made perfect."

The Trustees did not dismiss me. As an honorable man I told them that if my views of slavery were unsatisfactory to them, and they thought my influence was injuring the University, they could have my resignation at any time, and that there was no earthly power that could compel me to remain in my position. The Trustees did not wish me to offer my resignation, and I did not. I therefore continued in my place till the Institution suspended in April, 1861.

It was while I was in Murfreesboro, that is, in my forty-ninth year, that I began to feel the need of spectacles. I first detected my failure of sight by my inability to see the figures opposite to the first lines of hymns in the Psalmist, which book we then used. I wondered why figures could not be as plain as letters, not thinking that there was anything the matter with my eyes. From my forty-ninth year till now (1891) it has not been necessary to change my eye-glasses. This, I suppose, is something unusual, and my children may be interested in knowing it. They need not be told that I have used my eyes by day and by night.

It was during my residence in Tennessee that I had a little discussion with Alexander Campbell. He was a celebrated man and quite adroit in controversy. I wrote an article for the *Tennessee Baptist*, in which I argued the priority of repentance to faith. Mr. Campbell published a long reply in his *Millennial Harbinger*. To my astonishment, he treated me with marked respect, a thing he did not always do with

JAMES MADISON PENDLETON

his opponents. He insisted that faith must precede repentance. In proof of my position I quoted such Scriptures as these: "Repent and believe the gospel," "Testifying repentance toward God, and faith toward our Lord Jesus Christ." (Mark 1: 15; Acts 20: 22.) Mr. Campbell said that the mention of repentance *first* was a matter of no significance. I insisted that in explaining Scripture it is often indispensable to take things first that come first. In proof of this I quoted 1 Timothy 5: 14, "I will therefore that the younger widows marry, bear children," etc. The point I made was of course that younger widows should marry before bearing children. There was, there could be no reply to this.

Mr. Campbell was a great man, had a high reputation for scholarship, but this reputation was somewhat impaired by his Revision of Acts of the Apostles for the American Bible Union.

Having referred to Mr. Campbell, I will now quote a long sentence from him in his written controversy with a "Clergyman," as published in the *Harbinger*. Bishop Smith, of Kentucky, was no doubt the "Clergyman." The Bishop contended that the validity of gospel ordinances depends on their administration by men Episcopally ordained. Mr. Campbell in reply used these words, which made such an impression on my memory that I have not forgotten them in thirty years. I quote them that my children may have an unsophisticated laugh. The long sentence is as follows:

"If my salvation depended on a pure administration of baptism, I would rather have a pure, godly man to immerse me, on whose head the hands of Romish or British prelate were never laid, than to be baptized by any Bishop under these heavens, whose sacerdotal blood has run through ecclesiastic scoundrels ever since the flood which the fiery dragon issued out of his unsanctified mouth to drown the apostolic church in its early youth."

A premium may well be offered for any sentence equal in all respects to this.

CHAPTER 13

THE CIVIL WAR – THE STATES' RIGHTS DOCTRINE – THE POSITION OF THE UNITED STATES – THE OVERTHROW OF SLAVERY GOD'S WORK – SLAVERY IN KENTUCKY AND TENNESSEE.

The election of Mr. Lincoln to the Presidency in 1860 was the occasion of the secession of most of the Southern States from the Union. They did not wait to see how he would fill his high office, but with impatient haste decided that he should not preside over them. The Southern Confederacy was organized at Montgomery, Alabama, in February, 1861, and adopted measures to maintain its separate existence. The Confederacy wished to do this without war and asked to "be let alone;" but this was impossible, especially after Fort Sumter was fired on. The sound of the first gun was heard in every part of the nation, for it reached every nook and corner of the land. The people were roused as never before since the Revolutionary uprising. Some, even in the North, were willing for the "wayward sisters," as they were called, to "go in peace;" but the great majority of the nation was zealous for the integrity of the Union. It is proper to refer to the differences of opinion which were antagonistic, hostile, and implacable. In the South the doctrine of "States' Rights" was espoused and earnestly advocated. All that vigorous logic and fiery rhetoric could do was done. It was urged, in accordance with the "States' Rights" view that a State could, at its option, withdraw from the Union. The celebrated Resolutions of 1798-99, adopted by Virginia and Kentucky, were appealed to in support of this view. It is the part of candor to admit that these Resolutions embody a theoretical justification of secession, though in the history of the Government they had received no practical endorsement. Many Southern Democrats had been for years in favor of them, but no National Convention of the party declared its adherence to them till 1856, when Mr. Buchanan was nominated for the Presidency. After that it was natural for Democrats of the South to believe that, in case of their secession from the Union, they would be justified by the entire party. Had this turned out to be so, the result of the secession movement would probably have been very different; but Northern Democrats failed to act in convert with their brethren of the South. Indeed, many of them were not only on the side of the Union, but fought under the "star-spangled banner."

The Resolutions referred to declare that when there is a difference of judgment between a State and the United States the State may decide for itself as to its course of action. On this point my friends Dayton and Graves differed from me most materially. They believed the Government of the United States was oppressive and tyrannical, and their conclusion was that the Southern States should secede from it. The argument of Dr. Dayton amazed, and would have amused me, if the times had not been too serious for amusement. He insisted that as the "people" made the Constitution of the United States, they could alter or abolish it. This is doubtless true of the whole people: but Dr. Dayton said, *therefore* the people of Tennessee have the right to revoke their allegiance to the Government of the United States. I need not say that neither logic nor common sense authorizes the use of the particle *therefore* in such a connection.

My friend Graves visited me and spent hours in trying to persuade me to declare myself in favor of the Confederacy. He thought my influence and usefulness would be greatly increased if I would do so, and would be ruined if I did not. I told him that if the Confederacy established itself I would either obey its laws or remove from its jurisdiction. This was not satisfactory, and after saying many things he asked me if

I could not say that I preferred the Confederate Government to that of the United States? My answer was, "I can't lie." This closed our interview.

I make all allowances for the anxiety of Graves, Dayton, and others on my account; for they honestly believed that the Confederacy would be a success, and that I would occupy the place of a "Tory" of the Revolution. The only question with me was, "What is right?" Having settled this question in favor of the United States, I took my stand, and there were very few who stood with me. Those were dark days. Tennessee, in the year 1860, was largely on the side of the Union, but the next year espoused the Confederacy.

I had no difficulty in deciding my allegiance to the United States superior to any allegiance that could be due to a State. It was only necessary for me to read in the Constitution of the United States the second section of Article VI: "This Constitution, and the laws of the United States which shall be made in pursuance thereof, and all treaties made, or which shall be made, under the authority of the United States, shall be the supreme law of the land; and the Judges in every State shall be bound thereby, anything in the Constitution or laws of any State to the contrary notwithstanding."

This is what the Constitution says of itself, and it is absurd for any State government to assume an attitude hostile to "the supreme law of the land." This, the Confederate States did and vainly attempted to justify themselves. There were individuals in the South who, denying the right of secession, claimed what they called "the right of Revolution." I think Hon. John Bell belonged to this class. That he was wrong I have no doubt.

Against the right of Revolution, when the masses of the people are oppressed under monarchial and aristocratic forms of government, I have nothing to say. I recognize sovereignty as inherent in the people and revolution is sometimes the only way in which down-trodden humanity can throw off its burdens. But I deny that the right of revolution can exist under a Republican form of government. This view, so far as I know, is original with me. In a Republican government the majority must rule. This is its foundation principle. Very well. Then if the majority wishes to make any change in the method of government, they can do so peaceably, and without the violence which the term revolution implies. The right of revolution, then, does not belong to the majority, and if it did it would be superfluous, for the reason indicated, to exercise it. But can the right belong to the minority? Not unless the minority has the right to govern, which is absurd. Contemplate, then, the right of revolution in connection with either a majority or a minority in a Republican government, and it has no existence; for the people have adopted their form of government and can change it, if they please, without any revolutionary violence. The matter seems too plain to need elaboration.

Believing the Confederacy, whether regarded as secession or revolution, had no right to exist, I had no sympathy with it, and heartily wished its overthrow by the Army and Navy of the United States. I am no advocate of war, but I say this, that with the exception of wars waged by command of God, of which we are told in the Old Testament, history contains no account of any war more justifiable than that waged by the United States against the Confederacy. The South had as much to do as the North in making the National Constitution, but refused to abide by the provisions of that Constitution when a President, whom the South disliked, was elected under it. For no one denied that Mr. Lincoln was constitutionally elected, and his oath of office certainly required him to put forth the power of the government to maintain the Union in its integrity, and this was done. So much concerning the position of the United States.

It was about midsummer in 1861, when the Confederate flag was hoisted on the Court House in Murfreesboro, and there it waved for nine months, but I seldom saw it. I was unwilling to look at it, because it was usurping the place of the flag of the United States—the flag of my heart's love. The "stars and bars" were utterly distasteful to me. I was known to be a Union man, and it was no advantage to me that nearly all my family connections, my blood and marriage, were on the other side. I suppose I was in greater danger of personal violence than I thought at the time. It is said that a citizen offered to head any company that would undertake to hang me, and that my name, accompanied by no complimentary remarks, was sent to the daring John Morgan. I knew not what might happen to me. I supposed that if measures of personal violence were resorted to, it would be done in the night; and how often, before going to bed, did I arrange a back window and shutter, so that I could escape in a noiseless way! My wife would put up a parcel of something for me to eat; and I remember well how sad her tones were when she said, "You may need this."

I do not know how long I suffered from fear, but I know how well I was relieved. Everything being disorganized by the war, my means of support were cut off, and I went to work on my farm. I knew of nothing else I could do; so I worked during the week and preached on Sunday to the very few that were willing to hear me. One day, while at work, there occurred something of which I have not often spoken. I do not claim that it was a vision; I do not believe it was, but my imagination was deeply impressed. I thought I was standing in the midst of a circle of demons incarnate and that they were rushing toward me to tear me in pieces; but they seemed to stop, and with gnashing teeth stretched forth their murderous hands to seize me, and could not. Amid the exciting scene, I thought that God was sitting in serene majesty above, and that He spoke to the demons saying, "You can't touch him unless I permit." When I returned from the field members of my family said that my face, though covered with sweat, was *shining*. I know not as to that, but I know that I was relieved from fear, and could afterward sleep as sweetly as a child. I was fully satisfied that God would suffer no one to injure me unless it would be for the glory of His name, and then I was ready to endure anything, even death itself.

JAMES MADISON PENDLETON

After the Confederate flag had floated over the Court House in Murfreesboro for nine months, General Mitchell, with his magnificent division of the Army of the Cumberland, entered the town. Very soon was the flag of the Union unfurled, displaying its starry glory. When I first saw it, my eyes filled with tears of love and joy. I do not expect ever again in this world to see anything so beautiful as that flag appeared to be. How I admired its "red, white, and blue!" From that day, it has been no wonder to me that patriotic soldiers are willing to follow that flag into any danger and to die for it; for it is the symbol of greater glory than Greece or Rome ever saw.

I now anticipate one of the results of the war to emphasize the fact that the overthrow of slavery was God's work. I mean by this that in the early part of the war there was no reference to the extermination of slavery. The South of course had no such object in view, nor had the North. Mr. Lincoln's supreme purpose was to preserve the Union without interfering with slavery. When he issued his Proclamation, September 22, 1862, he offered the seceded States the opportunity of coming back into the Union. In proof of their coming back they were to send members to Congress. Had they done this there would have been an end of the conflict. The opportunity was not accepted and the war went on. The Emancipation Proclamation of January, 1863, was made because the Proclamation of September, 1862, was disregarded. That is to say, it was seen that the preservation of the Union required the abolition of slavery by a successful prosecution of the war. It was an overruling Providence that permitted things to reach this point. It was reached in opposition to Mr. Lincoln's wishes and purposes in the first years of the war, and it disappointed the expectations entertained in all parts of the country. This being the case, it is evident that the overthrow of slavery was not man's work. There was a God in heaven, presiding over all, and causing, "the wrath of man to praise Him," accomplishing His purpose by thwarting the designs of men, and even using them as instruments in His hands. The overthrow of American slavery was an epoch in the world's history, and it is the providence of God that creates epochs. Now, that slavery is abolished, there are no regrets, but rejoicings rather, both in the North and in the South. The North is glad that an institution in conflict with the Declaration of Independence no longer exists, and the South concedes that hired labor is better than slave servitude. Being pretty well acquainted in the South, I may be permitted to say that I know no man who would have slavery re-established. It is true that some of the emancipated slaves, perhaps many, have had a worse time in the early years of their freedom than when in slavery, but brighter days are before them. Then, too, they have the proud satisfaction of knowing that liberty, with its priceless blessings, will be transmitted as a rich legacy to their posterity. For all this God deserves the glory and it should be given to Him.

It is appropriate for me in closing this chapter to say something of slavery as I saw it in Kentucky and Tennessee before the war. No doubt it existed in these States, particularly in Kentucky, in its mildest form. I knew slaveholders who sustained this relation for the good of their slaves rather than for any personal profit. They were willing to set their slaves free if it would improve their condition, but on this point they doubted. They did not see that the free colored people were any better off than the slaves. In addition to this, there was, as the result of the Abolition excitement, a law passed in Kentucky forbidding emancipation. This was, I think, between 1850 and 1860.

As to the sinfulness of slavery in itself, Southern slaveholders did not believe the doctrine. They generally held the view expressed by Dr. Richard Fuller in his discussion with Dr. Francis Wayland, though some thought that view too moderate. Dr. Fuller shows very clearly that a distinction was to be made between slavery and the abuses of slavery. This distinction was certainly recognized in Kentucky. The law gave the master the right to separate husband and wife, but no master did this without injury to his reputation; for it was considered an abuse of slavery. There was a class of men called by the odious designation, "negro traders," but they were not received in the best circle of society. They bought slaves, conveyed them farther South, and sold them to cotton and sugar planters. They were an odious class.

The opinion of slaveholders generally was that they were not responsible for the existence of slavery, because it was introduced into the country before they were born. For its introduction the North was as accountable as the South, and the South felt that it must adjust itself to the circumstances of the case. There was always an Emancipation party in Kentucky, and if in making the second Constitution in 1799, the sagacious policy of Henry Clay had been carried out, the State would have been free before the war.

As to the Negroes, I saw among them in the days of slavery as pious Christians as I ever saw anywhere. They attended church, occupied the place assigned them in the meeting-house, and partook of the Lord's Supper with their white brethren.

I take pleasure in testifying that slavery in Kentucky and Tennessee, and I was not acquainted with it elsewhere, was of the mild type. When I went north nothing surprised me more than to see laborers at work in the rain and snow. In such weather, slaves in Kentucky and Tennessee would have been under shelter. It will astonish some of my friends to learn that at the death of my mother in 1863, I by the will of my father became a slaveholder. In the distribution of the estate a young girl was assigned to me. The law did not permit me to emancipate her, and the best I could was to hire her out. I paid her the amount for which she was hired and added to it ten per cent. When slavery was abolished I rejoiced in the severance of the relation I had sustained to her. I was not a slave-holder *morally* but *legally*. My children may be interested in knowing these facts, and the additional fact that my conscience is clear.

There is hope for the African race in this country. Its improvement, since the abolition of slavery, has been, all things considered, wonderful. The improvement has not of course been universal, but history records no such progress as has been made by the race since the war. In proof of this I may refer to a volume before me, styled, "The Negro Baptist Pulpit," containing sermons of which no white preacher need be ashamed. These preachers were slaves till the Emancipation Proclamation gave them liberty. The elevation to which they have risen is "the Lord's doing and it is marvelous in our eyes."

CHAPTER 14

LEAVING MURFREESBORO – EXPOSED TO DANGER IN GOING INTO KENTUCKY – SETTLEMENT AS PASTOR AT HAMILTON, OHIO – DEATH OF MY MOTHER – DESIRE TO GO WEST – THE END OF THE WAR – MR. LINCOLN'S ASSASSINATION.

I remained in Murfreesboro till General Bragg left Chattanooga on his Kentucky expedition, and General Buell moved his forces from near Huntsville, Alabama, to thwart General Bragg's plans. I concluded that by the time two such armies passed though Middle Tennessee it would be a desolation, and rapid preparation was made for our departure.

Strange to say, United States' soldiers had something to do in making our departure a necessity. They began to appropriate the little crop that I had raised, and they did this, I have no doubt, without official authority; but, in one sense, it was the same to me. But there was official authority at a later day. After the battle of Stone River General Rosecrans' army occupied Murfreesboro and must have fuel. My farm was fenced with valuable cedar rails and the soldiers were ordered to take only the *top* rail. They obeyed and took the top rail till there was not a rail left. The United States Government in compensating me put the rails in the category of green cord wood. This was a little business for a great nation. How I was to support my family became a serious question.

Here I may record some things, a few of which, so far as I know, have not been published in any "History of the War," and probably will not be published, as they are not very creditable to two United States' Colonels.

During the summer of 1862, two regiments, 9th Michigan (Colonel Parkhurst) and 3d Minnesota (Colonel Lester), were stationed at Murfreesboro. The two regiments were encamped for a time near my house; but it was said the Colonels disagreed about something, and one of them removed his regiment more than a mile from the other. This fact was naturally communicated to the Confederate General Forrest, who was not far away. He took advantage of the circumstances, and, with his "Texas Rangers" and others, dashed into Murfreesboro at day break Sunday morning (the second Sunday in July) and captured the regiment near my house. There was some fighting, not a great deal, and a few balls struck the house. General Forrest, having captured this regiment, moved on the other, which surrendered. Now, the fact not creditable to the Colonels is this: If their regiments had been together, General Forrest could have done nothing, for his success grew out of the disagreement of the Colonels. Who can tell how many of the disasters of the war may be traced back to quarrels among officers? This may be considered an episode in my narrative.

The last day of August, 1862, we left our home in Murfreesboro to occupy it no more. As the Federal forces had possession of the railroad to Nashville, it was deemed safer for me to go on the train. My family went in a barouche in charge of Rev. G.W. Welch, a theological student. The horse was well-known in and around Murfreesboro and not much progress was made on the way before a "halt" was called by one of a guerrilla band. He made inquiries of Mr. Welch and finally said, "You are not the man I thought you were," and permitted him to proceed. My wife heard all that passed, and has never had a doubt that the man supposed that I, as usual, was driving my horse, and intended to capture me. Providence ordered that I should be elsewhere. We reached Nashville in safety and there Mr. Welch took the stage and I took his place in the barouche. I could go by the railroad no farther, for Gen. John Morgan had destroyed the tunnel near

Gallatin. In going by private conveyance to Bowling Green I was exposed to the danger of which I learned more afterward. I was entrusted at Nashville with more than thirty letters from officers and soldiers, to be mailed at Bowling Green for the North. As we passed along we sometimes had a view of men whom we took to be guerrillas, and if they had obtained possession of the letters, I know not what would have been the consequence; but we were not molested. In passing through Franklin, Simpson County, we met our friend Judge Ritter of Glasgow, who was holding Court. We had a short conversation, and to our consternation we learned afterward that guerrillas dashed into Franklin the next morning, captured the Judge, and conveyed him to some unknown place. Surely I was mercifully preserved.

At Bowling Green we met old friends, but none of us could feel as in other years, for a pall of gloom rested on the country. We tarried a day or two and then my wife, under the protection of Mr. Welch, proceeded to Barren County to sojourn for a time with her only sister, Mrs. Eubank, near Glasgow. My friends said it would not be safe for me to go, for General Bragg's army was about passing through that county, and it was thought important for me to get north of the Ohio River as soon as possible. Fortunately for me the railroad to Louisville was in possession of the United States' forces, and I found no difficulty in reaching the city. National flags were flying, which cheered a heart considerably depressed, for the parting with my wife was very sad, and she, to this day, refers to it as one of the saddest partings of her life. I saw a few friends in Louisville, among whom was Hon. J.J. Crittenden, who inquired if I knew anything about his son, the Federal General.

From Louisville I went to Indianapolis and called on my friend, Rev. Henry Day, formerly professor in Georgetown College, Kentucky. It was arranged for me to preach on Sunday, and I did so. During the week I visited my cousin, Hon. R.W. Thompson, of Terre Haute, whom I had not seen from my boyhood. He is a man of extensive information and fascinating in conversation. He told me a great many things about Mr. Clay and others, which occurred when he was in Congress. He was very fluent and words came out of his mouth with such graceful volubility that I was tempted to ask him if he ever lacked a word? His wife said, "I can answer, *never.*" I have not met with a man of more fluent speech, and when years afterward, while Secretary of the Navy, he lectured at Chester, Pennsylvania, on "Adams, Jackson, and Clay," I was confirmed in my impression that no man had command of language more forcible, more elegant, more beautiful. He yet lives, several years older than I. His accomplished wife is dead.

From Terre Haute I returned to Indianapolis, preached the next Sunday, then made my way to Cincinnati, where I first saw Mr. Lincoln's preliminary Proclamation. From Cincinnati I went to Lebanon, a place I had visited years before, and where something had been said to me about the pastorate of the Baptist church. I then discouraged a call, but now I was willing to be called, for above all things I wished a quiet place in which to labor, and I knew no place quieter than Lebanon. The church was without a pastor, but I was not called, because there was some suspicion on the part of one or more of the influential members as to my views of slavery. From Lebanon I went to Hamilton, the county-seat of Butler County, to attend the meeting of the Little Miami Association. The brother appointed to preach the introductory sermon did not make his appearance, and I was requested to take his place. This church, too, was without a pastor, but I did not suppose that a call would be given me. I remember waking the next morning before day and bursting into tears, under the impression that the Lord had nothing more for me to do, and that there was no place for me in his vineyard.

I remained in Hamilton a few days and preached several times. It pleased the church to call me to the pastorate, and I accepted the call. I have never regarded this pastorate as a success. It seems more like a parenthesis in my ministry. My predecessor left me a legacy of trouble. There were two parties in the church, almost equally divided. The difference between them involved considerations of great delicacy, and it was not advisable for matters to be talked about. Many imprudent things had no doubt been said privately on both sides, which had given mutual offense. The question arose: How can the breach be healed if it will not do to talk about what caused it? The general opinion was that nothing could be done. I suggested a plan of settlement, and one brother thought that God must have put it into my heart, for nothing like it had ever been heard of before in the adjustment of church troubles. The plan was this: For the church to meet at a certain time and for the members to take certain designated seats, in doing which it was to be understood that they retracted everything they had said offensive to any brother or sister and asked forgiveness, pledging themselves to hold their peace in future as to the matters about which they had differed. The plan was a success and I refer to it because I had never known anything like it before.

It was while in Hamilton, that is, on the 2d of November, 1863, that I received from my youngest brother a startling dispatch, which read, "Mother is dangerously ill – come by first train." The message reached me on the morning of the 3d, and in less than one hour I started for the home of my childhood. What a time for reflection! The place of my destination was three hundred miles distant. There was a crowd of passengers most of the way, strangers, to whom I could not tell my tale of grief. Thought I, how little they know of the sadness of my heart, and how little would they care, if they did know! The hours passed slowly away, and the revolutions of the rattling wheels were too tardy for me. Alas! What mode of travel is fast enough to satisfy the desires of one who wishes to reach a dying bed? At length I had gone as far as I could by railroad, and still I was fifteen miles distant from the place then of all places most replete with solemn interest to me. Night was coming on and I could get no traveling conveyance till morning. There was not a moment's hesitation. Thankful to God for strength to walk, I went on foot, hoping to be in time to hear that voice which had so often sounded as music in my ears. For a time hope predominated, and then fear, and between the two there was a short, but a sharp conflict. The conflict was soon ended, and *such an end!* "She died yesterday," were the first words that terminated my painful suspense. I sat by the motionless form of my mother, and looked and looked at her pale face. It seemed as if the death-sealed lips would open and speak to me as in other days. They did not open, and spoke not a word. I never saw my mother's countenance more pleasant than it was in death. The spirit appeared to have been so joyous in making its exit from the body as to leave a placid smile on the pale clay. The body lay in serene dignity, as if it could well afford to yield to the temporary dominion of death and the grave, in prospect of a triumphant resurrection.

I wish I could do justice to the character of my mother. She was distinguished for common sense, sound judgment, and earnest piety. She was not an educated woman in the present acceptation of the words, for thorough female education was unknown in the days of her youth. But when I remember how she, amid the disadvantages incident to a newly settled country, exerted herself that her children might enjoy privileges which she never enjoyed, no language can express my admiration and love for her, and my deep sense of obligation to her.

My mother was a praying woman and enjoyed nearness of access to the throne of grace. She prayed much and had power with God. I doubt not I am receiving blessings to this day in answer to her prayers. Truly I can say, in the language of Cowper:

> My heart boast is not that I deduce my birth
> From loins enthroned and rulers of the heart;
> But higher far my proud pretensions rise,
> The son of parents passed into the skies.

Becoming convinced that Hamilton ought not to be my permanent residence, I was anxious to go West, and hoped to be called to the pastorate of a church in a flourishing town in Illinois. But I was disappointed and the disappointment was clearly providential. I therefore remained at Hamilton till the latter part of the year 1865. It was in April of this year that the war ended in the surrender of General Lee at Appomattox. It was arranged for the surrender to be celebrated at Hamilton, and I will be excused for saying that this was the only time in my life when I gave a dollar to be used in buying powder to be used in firing cannon. I was jubilant in view of the fact that the "old flag" was to wave in triumph over an undivided people.

I sympathized with General Lee in the humiliation of his surrender, but my joy very nearly extinguished my sympathy. In the beginning of the civil conflict General Lee had written to his sister, "I recognize no necessity for this state of things;" yet his views of the pernicious doctrine of "States' Rights" led him to renounce his allegiance to the United States and identify himself with the Confederacy. If he had accepted the supreme command of the Army of the United States, offered him by Mr. Lincoln, in how different a light would his name appear on the page of history! In that case, General Grant would scarcely have been heard of, and General Lee would have been the favorite and the President of the nation. His name would have gone down to posterity in honorable conjunction with that of Washington. But he made a fatal mistake and General Grant reaped the honors of the war. What strange things affect the destinies of men! General Grant, in his tour round the world, received from more nations greater honors than were ever conferred on any other man from Adam to this day.

Not long after General Lee's surrender, an event occurred which threw the nation, and indeed the civilized world, into consternation. Mr. Lincoln was assassinated at Washington on the 14th of April. The fatal shot was fire by J. Wilkes Booth, of whom it is best to say nothing more.

During his Presidency a thousand things were said by his enemies in disparagement, and even in ridicule, of Mr. Lincoln, but he was a great man with a heart full of kindness. No one could more truly than he use the words which have become immortal: "WITH MALICE TOWARD NONE, WITH CHARITY FOR ALL." His name will go down to posterity clothed with glory, historians will record what he did, and the millions of the African race in the United States will thank God that he lived.

CHAPTER 15

REMOVAL TO UPLAND, PENNSYLVANIA – THE CROZER
FAMILY – THE THEOLOGICAL SEMINARY – MEETING HOUSE
ENLARGED – GREAT REVIVAL.

As intimated in the preceding chapter, my desire and purpose to go west were not carried into effect. I therefore directed my attention to the East, hoping there to find a suitable field of labor. This led me to attend the Philadelphia Association, which met October, 1865, with the Fifth Church on Eighteenth and Spring Garden Streets.

At that time Rev. William Wilder had resigned the pastorate of the Upland Baptist Church, which he had filled for eleven years, and Dr. Griffith arranged for pulpit supplies. He invited me to preach and I did so on the first Sunday in October, attending the Association during the week. On the second Sunday I preached in Camden, New Jersey, and on the third, at Upland again. The church, at the evening service, was requested to remain after the congregation was dismissed. I of course did not remain, though I did not know what business would come before the church. That night, as I retired, the venerable John P. Crozer put a letter in my hands informing me that I had been called to the pastorate. I remember well kneeling down and thanking God that in His gracious providence He had indicated that there was still work for me to do. As there was something peculiar about this call, I may explain. Mr. Crozer was not in favor of electing a pastor at that time, but wished to wait till his eldest son, Samuel A., reached home from Europe; for he, next to his father, was the most influential member of the church. Mrs. Crozer said to her husband (this she told me years after) that it would be necessary to act at once if my services were secured. Her favorable opinion of my preaching led her to believe that some other church would give me a call, and that with the Upland Church it was *now* or *never*. She carried her point with her husband, and thus I was indirectly indebted to her for the eighteen happy years of my pastorate at Upland. My opinion of Mrs. Sallie L. Crozer I need not here express; for in the dedication of my "Christian Doctrines" to her, I have told the public the estimation in which she was held by me. Her husband, John P. Crozer, was a remarkable man. He had risen from comparative obscurity and poverty to prominence and wealth. He had great energy and was the architect of his own fortune. His life, as written by J. Wheaton Smith, D.D., shows what he was from his boyhood till his death. At fourteen years of age he heard of a funeral sermon, preached by the celebrated Dr. William Staughton, and was led to see himself a sinner in need of salvation. After his conversion he united with the Marcus Hook Baptist Church, of which he remained a member till the Upland Church was constituted in 1852. A house of worship was indispensable and one was built at his expense and afterward enlarged. He was very successful in his business, which was the manufacture of "cotton goods," and he early learned to give as the Lord prospered him. His contributions for Missions, Education, the American Baptist Publication Society and kindred benevolent objects were large, and his hospitality knew no limit. He was Superintendent of the Sunday-school, filled his place in the prayer-meeting, and was in the sanctuary on the Lord's day. It is a fact worthy of notice that he and his gardener, Mr. John Pretty, were for years the only deacons of the church. They acted in harmony, and their last interview, when Mr. Crozer was on his dying bed, was very affecting. Mr. Pretty often spoke of it with deep feeling.

Mr. Crozer lived but a few months after I first knew him in 1865, for he died in March, 1866. His death created a deep sensation, but not only in Upland, but in Philadelphia and the surrounding country. The general feeling was that a benefactor of his race had been taken away. His funeral was largely attended and was very solemn and impressive. It devolved on me to preach the sermon, and the text was 2 Tim 4: 7, 8: "I have fought a good fight, I have finished my course; I have kept the faith: Henceforth there is laid up for me a crown of righteousness, which the Lord, the righteous Judge, shall give me at that day: and not to me only, but unto all them also that love His appearing." Appropriate remarks were made by Bishop Lee, of Delaware, and Dr. J. Wheaton Smith, of Philadelphia. The body was buried in the Upland Cemetery to await the resurrection of the last day.

Mr. Crozer, at his death, left seven children, four sons and three daughters. The names of the sons who still live (1891) are Samuel A.J. Lewis, George K. and Robert H. His daughters were Margaret (Mrs. Bucknell), Elizabeth (Mrs. Griffith) and Emma, who afterward became Mrs. Gustavus W. Knowles. Mrs. Bucknell died a few years after her father and was buried near him. The children now living are worthy representatives of their father and mother, and though the inheritors of wealth, it is to be said to their credit that they never assume airs which some rich people take on themselves. They do not boast of their wealth, but they use it to promote benevolent objects. This reminds me that after Mr. Crozer's death, his family, by a donation of fifty thousand dollars to the American Baptist Publication Society, established what is called "The Crozer Memorial Fund," in honor of the husband and father. The interest on this fund is used year by year to promote the religious welfare of the colored people of the South, and the good it is doing will not be fully known till it is disclosed by the revelations of eternity.

In the year 1868 "Crozer Theological Seminary" was established. The large building which it occupies had been put up by Mr. Crozer for school purposes, but for some reason those purposes had not been satisfactorily carried out. The best thing to do with the structure was not determined on till there was a family consultation. Then it was decided to make the building the seat of a theological school. To endow it Mrs.

Crozer and her seven children gave twenty-five thousand dollars each, and Mr. Bucknell added twenty-five thousand dollars. This endowment was ample at the beginning, for the faculty consisted of only three instructors, Henry G. Weston, D.D., President, and Drs. Howard Osgood and G.D.B. Pepper, Professors. In the course of human events changes have taken place, and Dr. Weston is the only man who has been identified continuously with the institution till now (1891). The faculty has been enlarged, so that it now consists of the President, George R. Bliss, J.C. Long, E.H. Johnson, J.M. Stifler, B.C. Taylor and M.G. Evans. Something has been added to the original endowment, but it needs to be augmented, and I have reason to know that this will be done while some of its founders live, or when their wills are executed.

As I have been for a number of years one of the Trustees of the Seminary, it would not be in good taste for me to profuse in its praise. I may say, however, that it has done, and is still doing a good work. The members of the faculty are men of God, sound in faith, and apt to teach. The number of students is increasing year by year, and many of its graduates are filling important places in this country and some are Missionaries in Foreign lands. The Crozer Seminary is in friendly relations with other Seminaries, and while it does not ask to be compared with them, it does not recoil from a comparison. Its motto is ONWARD, UPWARD; onward to larger attainments in the knowledge of the Bible; upward to brighter heights in spirituality.

The location of the Seminary is all that can be desired, fourteen miles from Philadelphia, one mile from Chester, on the Baltimore & Ohio Railroad. Thus it escapes the severity of Northern winters and the enervating effects of Southern climates.

In the year 1873 it became necessary to enlarge the meetinghouse in Upland, and an addition of thirty feet was made to it at an expense of fourteen thousand dollars. A new baptistery was constructed and everything was made attractive. It was gratifying to see that the house, though enlarged, was not too large for the congregation. By the end of the year there was an increase of interest in the services of the sanctuary, and early in the year 1874, there were promising indications of a revival. These indications were first seen in cottage prayer-meetings held in different parts of the village. The spirit of prayer came upon the church, parents became interested for the conversion of their children, and meetings were commenced in the Sunday-school chapel. These meetings were held every night of the week except Saturday night and continued about two months. They were chiefly devoted to prayer and exhortation, and a few sermons only were preached, though there was a regular preaching on the Lord's day. Soon many were inquiring, "What must we do to be saved?" They were the old, the middle-aged, and the young. They were convicted of sin, they felt their lost condition, and earnestly cried to God for mercy. It was not long before anxious inquirers became rejoicing converts, telling what the Lord had done for their souls. Thus the meeting went on for weeks, and wintry weather, at times severe, did not keep the people away. An opportunity was given each week for persons who had found peace with God to unite with the church. Old-fashioned "experiences" of the grace of God were related, and some of them were very affecting. The ordinance of baptism was administered nine consecutive Sunday nights, and the additions to the church were about two hundred. In my long life I have never seen a revival equal to this. I do not claim that I had any special agency in it. My preaching was as it had been for years, though more earnest. The same gospel was preached. The revival was God's work, in answer to the prayers of brethren and sisters. It is prayer that brings down the blessing of heaven. The keynote of the meeting was, perhaps, struck in the beginning by the pastor's remarks on the words of Jesus, "Father, glorify Thy name." The glory of God was referred to as the supremely important thing to be aimed at during the meeting, and the salvation of souls was to be sought as promotive of that glory. I never saw church members more forgetful of everything not immediately connected with the glory of God. Of the number baptized a hundred and twenty were over twenty years old, eighty were thirty years of age, twenty-five over forty, twelve over fifty, nine above sixty, and two above seventy. The remainder was between ten and twenty years old with the exception of one who was nine. Twenty-five husbands and wives were baptized, twelve husbands whose wives were members before, and six wives whose husbands were members before. I have never heard of a revival in which so large a proportion of the converts were over twenty years of age.

This meeting modified my views as to what are called "Protracted Meetings" and "Evangelists." I think there should never be a "protracted meeting" until there is a spiritual interest in a church and congregation that calls for it. To appoint such a meeting "in cold blood," as the saying is, cannot be justified. I may say also, that where a church has regular preaching every Sunday and prayer-meeting during the week, a protracted meeting is unnecessary. Nor has such a church need of the labors of an "evangelist." It is better to look for the blessing of God on the ordinary means of grace. As to "evangelists," it is their special business to labor where there are no churches with a view to build up churches. This seems to be forgotten by most of them.

Though I shall refer to Upland church again, I may take occasion here to say that it has an honorable history. During my connection with it there went forth two colonies which became churches, namely, South Chester and Village Green. At an earlier date it furnished constituent members for the First Church, Chester, which sent out as her daughter, North Chester Church, so that the latter is the grand-daughter of Upland. All this is an honor not to be despised.

Upland's liberality is known far and near. It is impossible to ascertain certainly what sums of money the Crozers give away, for they do not tell. For the first ten years of my pastorate I tried to find out the amount of their pecuniary gifts, but I made only an approximate estimate. I decided that they gave a hundred thousand dollars a year, making a million for the ten years. It is a great thing to have money to give, but as I once heard Mr. Samuel Crozer say, "It is a greater thing to have the disposition to give it."

CHAPTER 16

BAPTIST PUBLICATION SOCIETY – MINISTERS' CONFERENCE – FIFTY YEARS IN THE MINISTRY – AUTHORSHIP – DEATH OF PRESIDENT GARFIELD AND EX-PRESIDENT GRANT.

When I went to Upland in 1865 the American Baptist Publication Society was not what it is now. Its headquarters were at 530 Arch Street Philadelphia, and it was plain enough that there was not sufficient room for the convenient transaction of the business of the Society. No one was more fully convinced of this than Dr. Griffith, the Secretary of the Society. He therefore began to agitate the question of a new building. He was the man who engineered the whole matter, and in doing so was fortunate in availing himself of the pecuniary liberality of the Crozers and of Mr. William Bucknell. Without their aid it is evident that there would have been no new building. Dr. Griffith's connection by marriage with the Crozer family has been an inestimable blessing to the Publication Society. The site selected for the new edifice is 1420 Chestnut Street, and the structure extends from Chestnut to Sansom Street. It is worthy of the important objects of the Society. I was placed on the Board of Managers, and for about eighteen years rendered some service, chiefly on the Committee of Publication. This Committee had a laborious work to perform in the examination and recommendation of manuscripts. The plan was for a manuscript to be referred to two members of the Committee, and if reported on favorably it was ordered to be published; if not, it was declined. If the two members differed in opinion the manuscript was given to a third brother, whose opinion decided the matter.

I think I can safely say that I read ten thousand pages of manuscript, and I often wished that some persons could write more legibly. The Publication Society has done, and is doing a great work in the publication of books and Sunday-school literature. Its issues embrace a Commentary on the whole New Testament and the tiny leaflet, with all intermediate publications. Baptists may well thank God for the operations of the Society. Their principles are ably discussed and advocated.

"The Baptist Ministers' Conference," of Philadelphia and vicinity is an important and interesting organization. It meets every Monday, and ministers fatigued by the labors of Sunday enjoy rest and recreation. Some brother is appointed beforehand to prepare and read an essay, which becomes the subject of discussion and criticism. The essays are generally good and the discussions edifying. Sometimes the themes written on are not very suitable and excite but little interest. Still the Conference is the means of doing much good in bringing to light views which are discussed in a fraternal spirit. Dr. Wayland, the editor of the *National Baptist*, is generally present and gives in his paper a synopsis of what is said, though he does not report the wit with which he often enlivens discussions.

At the expiration of my "Fifty Years in the Ministry," the conference was pleased to request me to prepare an essay on the subject. This I did, and read it November 21, 1881. It was a day of solemn interest to me, and the brethren said some very kind things. I copy, for the satisfaction of my children, the following:

"P.S. Henson, D.D., said, I have witnessed many scenes of interest in this room, but none so august as that we have just witnessed. I have felt as though we were looking on the face of Moses as he came down from the mount."

"I have heard it said that reverence for age and wisdom is decaying among us. I am glad that the spectacle of to-day puts the brand of falsehood on that libel. When I see the tribute paid to our brother, I say, 'There is hope for us, if we keep our hearts young, as he has done.' For myself, while I touch my hat to the young lieutenant in the ministry I take off my hat and bow in reverence to the Captain of the Lord's host, who has served for three score years and ten. I offer the following:

"*Resolved*, That the Conference has listened with the deepest interest and pleasure to the review of 'Fifty Years in the Gospel Ministry,' which our honored brother and father, J.M. Pendleton, D.D., has read at the invitation of the Conference, a paper marked alike by wisdom, ripened experience, and good taste: we thank God who has granted to our brother the distinguishing privilege of preaching Christ for half a century, and who has crowned his labors with a rich blessing to the Church of Christ; it is our earnest prayer that the Lord will be pleased long to spare to us his counsels, his prayers, and his example of matured piety and unswerving patriotism, and that the evening of a day so full of beneficent labor may be made bright and glorious by the softened effulgence of the Sun of Righteousness."

The Minutes state that "The resolution was adopted by a unanimous rising vote."

I may add that I would be much less than a Christian man and minister not to appreciate these kind sentiments of brethren with whom I had met for many years. May the blessings they invoked on me fall richly on their own souls.

My children and grand-children will also read with interest the following letter from President Anderson:

"ROCHESTER, December 1, 1881.

"MY DEAR BROTHER: -- I have just read with the greatest interest your paper reviewing your life as a pastor and teacher. I beg leave to congratulate you on this protracted and efficient service rendered to Christ and His people. The difficulties which you have overcome in your long career have given you a vigor of mind and character, which has made you respected by the entire Baptist denomination in the United States. Your fidelity to our Union in the time which so tried the souls of loyal men in the South, is worthy of remembrance for all time. Your fidelity to your convictions, whether moral, religious, or political, has won for you the profoundest respect wherever you are known. It matters little what I think of your honorable career; but I have felt an impulse which I could not restrain to write as I have; and I pray God to give you still many years of life to defend Christian truth by your voice and pen, and to illustrate it by your example.

Very truly yours,

"M.B. ANDERSON."

What I read in my "Fifty Years in the Ministry" was copied by several papers, and I have made extracts from it in other portions of these Reminiscences.

It was while I lived at Upland that I became more of an author than I ever expected to be. My first book, as I have said elsewhere, was written at Bowling Green, Ky., and bore the title, "Three Reasons Why I Am a Baptist." In 1868 I wrote my "Church Manual" which bears the imprint of the Publication Society. It is of course gratifying to me that it has attained a circulation of more than thirty thousand copies, and that it has been translated into the German language. My best and most important book, as I think, was published in 1878. Its title is, "Christian Doctrines," containing a "Compendium of Theology." There is something singular as to the origin of this book. I was urged by Dr. Howard Osgood to write it, and he was almost the only person who encouraged me to undertake it. He was pleased to say that I had command of a clear, simple style, easily understood, and that I could make many Bible truths plainer than they are sometimes made by theological writers. I wished to write a book suitable to the comprehension of colored ministers in the South, and at the same time acceptable to other classes of readers. I knew that simplicity of style, while important for colored ministers, would be no objection with white ministers.

I supplied myself with materials for my task and attempted to arrange chapters and a table of contents. I was utterly unable to do this and gave up the matter for a whole year. Then I undertook it again, and the result is before the public. When the book made its appearance I asked Dr. Griffith what he would consider "a success." He said, "If there are a thousand copies sold within a year that will be a success; and if two thousand are sold in all time that will be a success." Not a year ago he told me that he would have discouraged the publication if I had not been his pastor. In view of all this I need not say that it is especially gratifying to me that the circulation of the volume has reached about eleven thousand copies, and that it is used as a text-book in most of the colored Theological Institutes of the South. Nor is this all; for I have reason to know that Doctors of Divinity, when they wish to refresh their memories on theological topics, and have not time to examine larger works, are accustomed to refer to "Christian Doctrines." The smallness of the volume, in connection, I trust, with its merits, has had something to do in making it acceptable.

In the year 1881 Dr. John W. Ross, of the United States Navy, informed me that his father, James Ross, recently dead, had left a manuscript styled, "Life and Times of Elder Reuben Ross." His descendants were anxious for its publication, and the Doctor said it would never be done unless I would consent to edit it and see it through the press. I hesitated to assume the task, for I knew something of the labor it would impose on me, but at last I consented. The book was published in 1882, fifteen hundred copies, but the sales were slow. It was expected that it would be in great demand in certain parts of Tennessee and Kentucky, where Elder Ross had been well known. This expectation was not met. He had been dead more than twenty years, and a generation had risen up that "knew not Joseph." When the book had about ceased to sell, Dr. Ross authorized me to dispose of the copies remaining (about one-half) as I thought best. I gave them away to institutions and to individuals. I sent quite a number of copies by mail to Maine and Oregon and intervening States. Though my labor was all gratuitous, I am gratified to know that I have had something to do in sending the name of a good and great man down to posterity. The memory of Elder Reuben Ross is blessed.

Another book which I published is styled "Distinctive Principles of Baptists," which is, as I have said, an enlargement of my first book, "Three Reasons Why I Am a Baptist." The object of this work is to show wherein Baptists differ from other religious denominations and to demonstrate that their principles are identical with those of the New Testament. This book has not had so large a circulation as I expected, but I have the satisfaction of knowing that it has been translated into the Swedish language and is useful in the propagation of Baptist principles among the Swedes. No one can tell how much good may result from the circulation of one book.

In the year 1883 George W. Clark, D.D., of New Jersey, and I were appointed to write "Brief Notes on the New Testament." The arrangement was for Dr. Clark to furnish Notes on the Gospels, and for me to write on the remaining portion of the New Testament. We did our work, and the volume published, the cheapest of the Society, has had a satisfactory circulation. The object of Dr. Clark and me has been to furnish, in small compass, the results of our studies on the New Testament, and we hope our labors will do good while we live and after we are dead.

In the winter of 1884-85 I wrote a book on "The Atonement of Christ," which I of course think presents that subject in its proper light. It treats of the "Nature," "Necessity," "Value," "Extent," and "Results" of the Atonement, with "Concluding Addresses to Ministers of the Gospel, to Christians, to Awakened Sinners, and to Impenitent Sinners." The New

York *Examiner*, in noticing this volume, has been pleased to say that there is no better book of its size on this great subject. Its circulation is not what it should be.

In 1886 the Publication Society issued my last book, entitled, "Notes of Sermons," which I wrote with a view chiefly to aid young preachers in the construction and arrangement of their discourses. Kind friends are of opinion that the themes discussed are naturally deduced from the texts, and that the language used is full of simplicity, so that everybody can understand it.

I have now referred to all that I have done in the line of authorship. In my early life nothing was farther from my thoughts than that I should ever write a book. I do not now see how I could ever have attempted it but for my large experience in writing for newspapers. I trust it is not vanity that makes me hope that some persons, while I live, and others, after I die, will thank God that I employed my pen.

During the period reviewed in this chapter two important and solemn events occurred, namely, the death of President Garfield and that of Ex-President Grant. The former was shot in July, 1881, by a disappointed office-seeker, who had a badly balanced mind, and who said that his name would go "thundering down to posterity." I choose not to mention his name.

President Garfield was an able statesman, and began his Presidency under favorable auspices. What would have been the results of his administration, had he lived, it is impossible to say. His death shrouded the nation in gloom and called forth many expressions of sorrow.

In August, 1885, General Grant died, beloved by his friends and admired by his political enemies. His name and deeds will fill a large space on the pages of history. I have referred to him in another place.

The names, Lincoln, Garfield, and Grant, remind us that in the United States of America, citizens may rise from obscurity and poverty to the most exalted station. This fact exhausts encomium on our Republican form of government, showing that there is no barrier in the way of eligibility to the highest office.

CHAPTER 17

MRS. JOHN P. CROZER'S DEATH – RESIGNATION OF
PASTORATE – LAST SERMON – WINTER OF 1883 AND 1884 IN
NASHVILLE, TENNESSEE – WIFE'S BLINDNESS.

In August, 1882, Upland was made sad by the death of Mrs. John P. Crozer, who, as she was born in the year 1800, had reached her four score years. She was a remarkable woman, with sound judgment and a large measure of good sense. In all the relations of life she acted well her part. As a wife, her devotion to her husband was beautiful, and he felt her influence in amassing his fortune. He ever consulted her as his safest counselor. As a mother she was loving and judicious in training her children, and they thought no other mother equal to her. They were devoted to her while she lived, and her death intensified their reverence for her character. Their memories have a fond place for her. As a neighbor she was kind, and gave many proofs of her thoughtful consideration. She was dignified and ladylike in her manners, commanding the respect of all who knew her. Her Christian character was lovely in youth, in middle age, and supremely lovely in her old age. For many years she taught the large infant class in the Upland Sunday-school, and "even down to old age" she was present at the prayer-meetings and at the public services on the Lord's day. During the years of her widowhood she gave thousands and tens of thousands of dollars to benevolent objects. I have known no woman her equal in pecuniary liberality.

Mrs. Crozer's death was preceded by protracted and painful disease, but her mind was clear and peaceful. I saw her not long before her death; it was Sunday morning, and I repeated the text I was going to preach from, "These things I have spoken unto you, that in Me ye might have peace." (John 16: 33.) She added, "I have that peace," and these words are on her tombstone. Her funeral was largely attended on a beautiful Saturday afternoon; remarks were made by Dr. Bliss and others, and the sermon by the pastor the next day was commemorative of her life and character. It was from Rev 14: 13; "Blessed are the dead who die in the Lord," etc.

I gratefully recognize my obligations to Mrs. Crozer, for she had much to do in making my Upland pastorate of eighteen years a pleasure and a joy. Her long life, full of good deeds, is ended, and she rests by her loved one. Being for many years united in the busy activities of life, they now have the silent companionship of the grace. This concerns their bodies only, and we think of their spirits as among "the spirits of just men made perfect."

In the month of June, 1883, I resigned my pastorate. I knew that judicious ministers had expressed the opinion that a man should not be pastor after reaching seventy years of age. I had transcended the limit by nearly two years, but I feel no special regret that my resignation did not bear an earlier date, in view of the fact that, after I had reached my "three score years and ten," there was a quiet revival, in which I baptized more than forty persons.

The following is my letter of resignation:

TO THE UPLAND BAPTIST CHURCH:

Dear Brethren and Sisters – I now have to perform one of the most painful duties of my life. I have more than reached my "three score years and ten," and the weakness of old age is coming on me. You need as a pastor a man of greater physical, mental, and spiritual vigor, and I therefore resign my pastorate, the resignation to take effect the last of October. I fix on this rather remote date that you may have ample time to select my successor, and that I may complete eighteen years of service among you. I ask that my resignation be quietly accepted, and that no "resolutions" be passed. I know that your kind feelings for me will not permit you to vote resolutions of censure, and I have done nothing which calls for resolutions of commendation. I leave you as I came among you, nothing but a poor sinner, "saved by grace." I trust you will cast the mantle of your charity over the many imperfections you have seen in me, and if my ministry has been a blessing to any of you, to God belongs the glory.

I have received uniform kindness at your hands, and if any one of you has done or said anything with a view to hurt my feelings, I have never known it.

Whatever becomes of me in the short space of life that remains to me, I shall ever rejoice in your prosperity, and my prayer is that God will give you in my successor a better man, a better Christian, a better minister. My dear brethren and sisters, the Lord abundantly bless you, and grant you the consolations of that gospel which, for nearly a score of years, I have preached to you. As your names come into mind tears come into my eyes, and you will please think of these tears as proofs of a love which words cannot express.

Most affectionately yours in the Lord,

J.M. PENDLETON.

The resignation was accepted, and in spite of my request that it should not be so, commendatory resolutions were adopted.

The months passed away, and the fourth Sunday in October came. What a day was that! – a day of sadness and sorrow to my heart. I number it with the days when I saw my father and my mother buried, and heard of the death of my first-born son. Ties were to be broken that touched the nerve of the heart. It was painful to leave the friends of my love, but I say without hesitation that the supreme sorrow of that day grew out of the fact that I was closing my work in the ministry of the gospel. I knew that in future I could only expect to preach occasionally; for not many congregations are willing to hear an old man. I was therefore obliged to consider my work of preaching *virtually* done. This thought with its excruciating power agitated my soul. Language was not invented to express the feelings of my heart on that day of sorrow. No miser ever loved his gold more than I have loved my work of preaching. This love has not wavered for more than half a century. I have not seen the day during that time when, if the option had been given me to go over life again, I would have chosen any other calling but that of a minister of God. I think I have proved my love for my work. For the first twenty-five years of my ministry my salary ranged from two hundred to six hundred and fifty dollars, and often I had to study, as hard as I studied theology, how to meet my pecuniary obligations, knowing that nothing but positive immorality more cripples a minister's usefulness than debt. I preached regularly during those twenty-five years when my support was a scanty one; I have preached since when my support has been ample; and I preached during the war with no prospect of support. The greater part of my ministerial life, my salary did not enable me to educate a child or to bury a child, though I did both in another way. I mention these things to emphasize my love of the work of preaching the gospel of the grace of God.

In view of all this, it is not strange that my heart was crushed with sorrow when I preached for the last time as pastor at Upland. It seemed that the burden resting on me would sink me into the earth. But I remembered the words, "Cast thy burden on the Lord, and He shall sustain thee." (Psalm 40: 22.) I think I have often proved the truth of the declaration, "He shall sustain thee." It is not said what will become of the burden, and this is a matter of little consequence, while it is said, "He shall sustain THEE."

I survived the day of sorrow and the next day departed, bearing with me the generous gifts of the Crozer family, to whom I shall ever feel my indebtedness. My wife and I, with sad hearts, left dear Upland for Nashville, Tennessee, to spend the approaching winter with our son-in-law, Rev. James Waters. After reaching there, one of the first things I did was to baptize three of my grand-daughters into the fellowship of the Edgefield Baptist Church, of which Rev. Wm. Henry Strickland was then pastor. The ordinance was administered in the presence of a large and deeply interested congregation. I remember well my feelings in saying to the eldest of the three, "My grand-daughter in the flesh, but my sister in the Lord, I baptize thee," etc. Not often does a grandfather enjoy such a privilege as this. I spent the winter chiefly in writing my "Brief Notes on the New Testament," and finished them March 4, 1884. As I began the work on the patriotic 4th of July, I completed it in precisely eight months. As my health was feeble, and as I had heard of the death of several brethren in Philadelphia, I began to fear that I might die leaving my task unfinished. I therefore wrote with great industry and energy, even to the disadvantage of my health.

There was another sorrow before me. My wife's eyes were failing, and it was necessary to see an optician who, we had no doubt, could furnish suitable glasses. The optician advised that an oculist be consulted, and to our dismay he, on examination, said that there was a cataract on each eye. The information penetrated the depths of our hearts and excited the deepest grief. My wife soon became tranquil and expressed her gratitude to God that the affliction had not come on her during my pastorate. Having been a Sunday-school teacher for more than fifty years, she took a class in the Edgefield School and taught for some weeks before the class knew she was blind. Her way of preparation was to have one of her grand-daughters, Lila Belle, read over the lessons to her, and then she was competent to teach. What woman of a thousand would, in these circumstances, have preserved in attending a Sunday-school? I record this fact to her credit and for the gratification of her children and grand-children.

In 1885 we made a visit to Professor Irby and family in Jackson, Tennessee. Dr. Savage, now of Vanderbilt University, was recommended to us as an accomplished oculist. He removed the cataract from the left eye, thinking that the more hopeful of the two. He was very skillful, and everything seemed to be going on well, but inflammation set in and the eye was lost. We have never attached the least blame to Dr. Savage. In 1888 we were advised to engage Dr. Risley, of the Pennsylvania University, to remove the cataract from the other eye. He did so and pronounced the healing process "perfect." The eye appeared as natural as ever, but the sight did not return. There is only a glimmer of light which makes a little difference between day and night, but does not avail to the recognition of the face of the dearest friend. The Doctor thinks there is some weakness in the eye, the cause of which cannot be found out. Thus hope is gone, and she who once gazed with delight on the works of nature and of art will never see them again. In this dark providence we find the only recipe for comfort in the words of Jesus: "Even so, Father; for so it seemed good in thy sight."

The wise man said, and the foolish man knows it, "Truly light is sweet, and it is a pleasant thing for the eyes to behold the sun." No one enjoys the pleasures of vision more than would my wife, if it were the Lord's will, but I have heard from her no murmuring word on account of the deprivation she suffers. Her spiritual vision seems more distinct and clear, and I trust that "beholding as in a mirror the glory of the Lord, she will be changed into the same image from glory to glory, even as by the Spirit of the Lord."

It would be an unpardonable omission in these Reminiscences if I did not record my high appreciation of my wife. She has been more than all the world to me. In times of prosperity and times of adversity, in days of joy and days of sorrow, I have ever heard her voice encouraging and blessing me. We have trodden together the path of life for more than half a century, and I trust that we shall walk the streets of the New Jerusalem together.

I shall have more to say of her when I refer to our "Golden Wedding."

CHAPTER 18

AUSTIN, TEXAS – STATE HOUSE – MONTEREY – JUBILEE OF THE GENERAL ASSOCIATION OF KENTUCKY – GOLDEN WEDDING.

The Winter of 1884-85 I spent in Austin, Texas, and while there wrote my book on "The Atonement of Christ." The time passed pleasantly, for I was in the family of my son-in-law, Prof. Leslie Waggener. He and his wife did everything necessary to the comfort of my wife and myself; and their seven children contributed not a little to our pleasure.

Austin, the capital of the State, is a beautiful place of fifteen thousand inhabitants, on the Colorado River. It does not appear to advantage from every point; but when I went into the University building and, from the third story, took in all the surroundings, I pronounced it the most beautiful city I ever saw, nor have I changed my opinion. It will be gratifying to some for me to say that Bowling Green, Kentucky, as it appears, with its environment, from its reservoir is, in my judgment, next to Austin in beauty. What I think of the two places is, however, a matter of little importance.

While I was in Austin, that is in the spring of 1885, I witnessed the laying of the corner-stone of the State House. The ceremony attracted a large crowd. The building is now complete, and is thought superior to any State Capitol in the Union. Texas may well be proud of it.

In April, 1885, the energetic Dr. O.C. Pope arranged and superintended an excursion to Monterey, to attend the dedication of the Baptist meeting-house in that city. This was the first house of worship erected by Baptists in the Republic of Mexico. I was in the excursion, and Dr. Pope generously met all the expense incident to my going, and I also went by request of Dr. H.L. Morehouse, Corresponding Secretary of the American Baptist Home Mission Society.

I was greatly disappointed on the trip when I reached Laredo and saw the historic river Rio Grande. I was looking for a large stream, not as wide as the Mississippi, but comparable to the Ohio or the Cumberland. It is much smaller than the Cumberland at Nashville. Soon after leaving the Rio Grande I thought we would encounter terrific storms, for very dark clouds seemed to be rising in different directions. I learned that what I thought clouds were dark mountains, and I saw neither storm nor rain in Mexico.

Rev. Thomas M. Westrup, pastor of the church in Monterey, arranged for the dedication services, which were full of interest. Dr. Powell preached the sermon in Spanish, not ten words of which did I understand. Several of the visiting brethren made addresses in English, which were translated by Mr. Westrup into Spanish. My topic was, "Through Christ to the Church," and when I spoke a sentence I paused, and M.W. translated it. I was told afterward that a Presbyterian Missionary criticized what I said; but I still think that Baptists alone can truly say, "Through Christ to the Church." Pedobaptist denominations must say, "Through the Church to Christ."

Dr. W.C. Wilkinson, of Tarrytown, New York, was present at the dedication, and we, having been sent to the same hotel, occupied the same room. I have ever since regarded this as a very fortunate thing for me. I thus became acquainted with a very intelligent Christian gentleman, from whom, if I did not learn many things, it was my fault. Dr. Wilkinson has acted a prominent part in the preparation of a number of volumes for the Chautauqua course of reading, and he has an enviable place in the republic of letters.

We of course heard a good deal about the capture of Monterey by General Taylor's forces in the Mexican War, and some memorable places were pointed out. The excursion made a visit of a few hours to Saltillo, the headquarters of Dr. Powell's missionary operations. Everything seemed hopeful and prophetic of success.

The civilization of Mexico is strikingly different from that of the United States. The houses are different, and their flat roofs give them an Oriental appearance. In leaving Monterey I felt almost as if I were leaving some city in Syria. My imagination was at work, as I never saw Syria.

Returning from Mexico to Austin, I enjoyed for a few days the company of kindred and friends, among whom were Dr. William Howard, pastor of the church, and Drs. J.B. Link and O.C. Pope, editors of *"The Texas Baptist Herald."*

Early in May I left Austin with my wife for Murfreesboro, Tennessee, where we spent the Summer with Mr. and Mrs. Waters, and the next Winter with Mr. and Mrs. Proctor, Bowling Green, Ky. Here I wrote my last book, "Notes of Sermons," which was published during the year 1886. It has had a respectable circulation. In January of the year there was at Bowling Green the coldest weather I ever felt. That is to say, the thermometer was twenty degrees below zero, and the snow was *twenty-seven* inches deep. I had never seen the thermometer so low, by a number of degrees, nor the snow so deep.

In May of this year we returned to Pennsylvania, spent the summer with our son and family, and saw many old friends. In the absence of the pastor, Rev. Willard H. Robinson, I preached for the First Baptist Church, West Philadelphia, five Sundays, and was frequently at the Minister's Conference.

In November, 1886, we returned to Austin and passed the winter very pleasantly.

The summer of 1887 found us again at Murfreesboro, where we remained till we went to the Jubilee meeting at Louisville, Kentucky in October. Here an explanation is necessary. The General Association of Baptists was formed at Louisville, October 20, 1837, and at the approach of its fiftieth year, it was decided to hold a Jubilee October 20, 1887. The arrangement was for all who were Messengers in 1837, to be guests of the Association at the Jubilee. The number of survivors was small, namely, J.L. Burrows, E.G. Berry, George Robertson, M.W. Sherrill, John Handsborough, and myself. We only had lived through the fifty years that had just expired.

The meeting was held in the Walnut-street Church, and Rev. Green Clay Smith presided. Dr. John A. Broadus made an address of welcome, to which it was expected that Dr. T.G. Keen would respond, but he had died the month before. The response was therefore made by Dr. Henry McDonald, of Atlanta, Georgia, formerly a resident of Kentucky.

Instructive papers were read by Drs. J.H. Spencer, William M. Pratt, D. Dowden, J.L. Burrows, and W.H. Felix; and interesting addresses were made by Drs. A.D. Sears, R.M. Dudley, George C. Lorimer, and Brother Thomas C. Bell.

I had been appointed to prepare and read a paper on "The Condition of the Baptist Cause in Kentucky in 1837." It was rather adventurous in me at the close of my paper to refer, as I did, to my wife, and I felt some anxiety about the matter. When, however, the Moderator and Dr. Broadus told me I was justifiable, I was relieved. Another brother said that it would not do for every preacher thus to refer to his wife, but that in this case "there was a WOMAN behind what was said." I regarded this as a high compliment. I quote in part what I read, as follows:

"She, the wife of my young manhood, of my middle age, and of my old age, is here to-day to enjoy these exercises. Deprived of sight, she can only hear your voices. How glad she would be to see your faces, and specially the face of the Walnut-street pastor, whose father and mother she so much admired and loved thirty years ago. But it cannot be. Still, there is comfort unspeakable in the thought that there is in reserve what the 'old theologians' called the 'beatific vision.' The Saints are to 'see God;' they are to serve Him and 'see His face.' They are to behold the Lamb in the midst of the throne, His head once crowned with thorns, now wearing a crown of glory brighter than the sun; His hands, once stretched forth in quivering agony on the Cross, now swaying the scepter of universal empire, while all the hosts of heaven shout His praise. To see Him of Calvary enthroned in majesty, what a vision will that be! How will it compensate for all the disabilities and privations of physical blindness!"

When I read this, it was grateful to my feelings to witness the sympathetic emotion excited in the audience.

After the Jubilee was over we went to Bowling Green, where we staid till the 13th of March, 1888, the time of our "Golden Wedding." This day would probably have passed unnoticed if the editor of the *Western Recorder*, Dr. T.T. Eaton, had not suggested the propriety of celebrating it. Arrangements were made for its celebration. Cards of invitation were sent to many friends, and more than a hundred responsive letters were received. The celebration occurred in the Baptist church in Bowling Green. Prayer was offered by the pastor, Rev. M.M. Riley, and the opening address was made by Dr. Eaton. In referring to other days at Murfreesboro, when his parents were there, his feelings became so much excited as to impede his utterance and to make it evident to all that he could not say what he intended to say. His broken accents and his silence were eloquent. Inability to speak is sometimes more effective than speech.

I had to respond, and the following is the substance of what I said:

I am embarrassed, and yet much obliged by the kind things Dr. Eaton has said. It is appropriate that the son of Joseph H. and E.M. Eaton should speak on this occasion. They were our friends of other years, and we cannot better express our estimate of them than by saying that when they died earth was impoverished and heaven enriched. We are gratified that their son is here to contribute so much to the interest and pleasure of this fiftieth anniversary of our married life.

Fifty years ago the two persons most deeply interested in this occasion had no expectation of living to see this hour. We did not enjoy vigorous health and did not anticipate long life. God has been pleased to disappoint us, and we can look back to twenty years spent here, five in Tennessee, three in Ohio, and eighteen in Pennsylvania. The last four years have been spent in four States in which our four children live.

In looking back for half a century we see a thousand things to be thankful for. We have found comparatively few thorns in our pathway and many beautiful flowers. Over our heads birds of bright plumage have sung their sweet songs. With delight we have heard these songs, though one of us in recent years has not been able to see the lovely flowers. But there is no murmuring on this account. We prefer to think of our mercies rather than of our blessing, not a curse; a joy, not a sorrow; a privilege, not a misfortune; a benediction, not a calamity. For all this, we give devout thanks to God; nor are we less thankful that we have been permitted to tread together the path of life for fifty happy years. We know that only a short space of time is before us, but from this fact we extract the precious consolation that when one of us is called away, the survivor will have to weep only a little while, a very little while, at the grave of the dead. Yes, we must both die, but we do not wish our children, grand-children, and friends to think of us as dead, but rather as having gone from the land of the living. Through riches of grace in Christ Jesus the Lord we expect a home in the bright realms of immortal glory.

Now, dearest one, it is fitting that I speak a word to you. There is no earthly object so dear to my heart. You are not as you were fifty years ago to-night. Then with elastic step you walked with me to the marriage altar, and we pledged to each other our vows of loyalty and love. I do not recognize that elastic step now. Then your face was fresh and blooming; now the freshness and bloom are gone, and wrinkles have taken their place, while gray hairs adorn your head. Then, and forty-six years afterward, the expression of your mild blue eyes was always a benediction; now that expression is no longer seen, for blindness has taken the place of sight.

But, with these changes in you, my love has not changed. Bodily affliction has not eclipsed the intellectual and spiritual excellences of your character. You are the same to me, and no kiss during half a century has been more deeply expressive of my love than the one I now give you.

At the close of my remarks, the program required a song from the choir; but deep feeling made music impossible, and not a note was heard. I do not know how it was, but it was stated in a paper the next day, that when I kissed my wife, the audience was dissolved in tears.

CHAPTER 19

RETURN TO UPLAND – ANNIVERSARIES AT WASHINGTON – AMERICAN BAPTIST EDUCATION SOCIETY – MR. CLEVELAND'S RECEPTION – WAYLAND SEMINARY – COLUMBIAN UNIVERSITY – VISIT TO DR. OSGOOD – BIBLE CLASS OF MY SON – DEATH OF MRS. S.A. CROZER – CONCLUSION.

In May, 1888, I returned to Upland, but remained only a short time before going to the Anniversaries at Washington held the latter part of the month. They were numerously attended and were full of interest. Many persons will go to the capital city when they would go nowhere else. This is not strange, for everybody wishes to see the headquarters of the nation. Congress was in session at this time, and it was a matter of interest to look at the lawgivers of the people. They deserve respect, and always have it, when they act worthily of their station. I saw and heard some of the leading men of both political parties. Among Democrats were such men as Samuel J. Randall, W.C.P. Breckinridge, R.Q. Mills and others, while T.B. Reed and W. McKinley were prominent among Republicans. All these were in the House of Representatives, and Edmunds, Sherman, Ingalls, Hoar, Hampton, Vance, Harris, and Cole figured in the Senate. But the Senate is not what it was in the days of its glory, when the eloquence of Clay, Webster, and Calhoun not only electrified its Chamber, but was felt in the remotest parts of the nation. Who can tell the influence of great statesmen?

I must not forget the Anniversaries: The Missionary Union, the Home Mission Society, and the Publication Society, all held their sessions, made their annual reports, and transacted important business. In addition to all this, "The American Baptist Education Society" was formed. There was a difference of opinion as to the necessity of this Society. The majority of the brethren thought it necessary, and it was organized. A minority was of opinion that we already had societies enough. I was in the minority and voted accordingly, but the success of the Society has convinced me that I was wrong, and now I am its friend. It has accomplished great good, and the prospect of much greater good is bright and cheering.

During the meetings President Cleveland was pleased to tender a reception to the many Baptists who were in attendance. They went in large numbers, and the handshaking must have been a burden to the President. After getting through with my part of it I found myself in front of the White House, and the crowds were still coming. I saw so many personal friends to whom I spoke, that I facetiously told them I was holding an opposition reception.

Mr. Cleveland's face did not strike me as being intellectual, but this shows that we ought not to judge according to appearance. Mr. Cleveland is a man of ability and honesty. He acts from principle, and certainly did so in assuming his position on the tariff question, with the majority of his party, at that time, against him. He deserves credit for his patient investigation of "pension cases," and his vetoes of unjust "pension bills." In short, his administration has promoted the interests of the country.

While at Washington I visited Wayland Seminary and was pleased to see its prosperity under the wise management of President King. He has done a great work in the education of colored ministers, and has much cause for satisfaction with the results of his patient labors. It is no longer a question whether the negro intellect can be improved. The fact has been demonstrated.

Washington is now a beautiful place, and it is thought by many, that when all the plans for its improvement are carried into effect, it will be the most beautiful capital city of the world. It is becoming more and more attractive. Columbian University is a very important institution, and if it could receive an addition of two million to its endowment it would then be able to avail itself of Government facilities worth fifteen millions of dollars. It is to be hoped that this object of earnest solicitude will be realized in the near future.

Returning from Washington, I spent the Summer with old friends at Upland, with the exception of the time occupied in a visit to Dr. Osgood's, at Rochester, New York. My wife and I have ever found it delightful to be in the family of Dr. Osgood. Our frequent visits have been *oases* in the desert of life. Dr. Osgood, though a close student and a learned man, is versed in all the proprieties and amenities of the first circle of society; and Mrs. Osgood is our ideal of an accomplished and lovely woman, while their children have had a training nearer perfection than we have seen in any other family. The Lord bless the attractive household.

In November, 1888, we went again to Austin, Texas, to spend the winter, and to be present at the marriage of our eldest grand-daughter. She was married to Mr. Alexander S. Walker, son of Judge Walker, a prominent man in Texas. The marriage took place November 27, in the First Baptist Church, and was witnessed by a crowded audience. Everything passed off with the utmost propriety and dignity. It is not often that a man marries his grand-daughter, but I officiated at her request. May heaven's select blessings rest on the happy pair while they tread the pathway of life.

Remaining in Austin till the middle of January, 1889, and not finding the weather sufficiently wintry, we made our way to Bowling Green, Kentucky, in pursuit of winter, but we did not find it and have not yet found it; for to this day (January 19, 1891) we have had no really cold weather.

We enjoyed the affectionate hospitalities of Mr. and Mrs. Procter till May and during our sojourn with them saw a few of our old friends, and the children of those we knew forty years ago. This has been the case whenever we have been here, within the last few years. The friendships of fathers and mothers have been inherited by their descendants, and we are treated with considerate kindness. My feelings prompt me to say that I have had pleasant ministerial intercourse with brethren M.M. Riley, M.F. Ham, J.G. Durham, and R. Jenkins. They are men of God and are useful in his cause. The church and congregation here have greatly increased during the pastorate of Brother Riley, the house of worship has been made very attractive and a beautiful parsonage has been built.

Elders Ham and Durham are advanced in life, and their work will soon be done; brethren Riley and Jenkins are in the vigor of manhood, and there are probably many years before them.

From Bowling Green we went early in May to Murfreesboro, Tennessee, and enjoyed the kind attentions of Mr. and Mrs. Waters till October. I went to the Southern Baptist Convention at Memphis and saw many of the brethren whom I had known in other years, and some whom I had never seen before.

We returned to Bowling Green in October and remained till April, 1890, when we went to Upland for the fourth time since the resignation of my pastorate. Our son and his wife made us more than welcome, friends called to see us, and we were glad to worship where we had so often worshipped in years past. We were pleased to hear persons of all classes speak in terms of commendation of the pastor, Rev. C.L. Williams. He evidently holds a high place in the esteem and love for the people.

The Twenty-first Anniversary of Crozer Seminary took place in June. Dr. E.G. Robinson preached the Baccalaureate Sermon, so called, and it was an able discourse. Dr. Robinson, though considerably over "three score years and ten," shows no sign of intellectual decadence. His mind is bright as ever and he expresses his thoughts in vigorous language. Nothing of very special importance came before the Board of Trustees except the election of Mr. Evans to a place in the faculty. His professorship has to do with the study of the Bible in English. There were fifteen graduates nearly all of whom made speeches that did them credit and reflected honor on their teachers. Dr. Weston, with his usual dignity on such occasions, presented their certificates of theological scholarship to the graduates, and Dr. Long made a parting address rich in thought and full of sound advice.

Dr. Weston is to be congratulated on having presided, without interruption, at the Crozer Anniversaries for twenty-two years, even from the establishment of the Seminary. He has much to be thankful for when he considers what has been done under his administration.

During this sojourn at Upland I was honored, as I had been twice before, by the Bible class taught by my son. The class numbers about seventy, all adults, and meets in the Sunday-school chapel in the afternoon of Sunday. The honor referred to was a call by the class to see me, and it was arranged that I should be taken by surprise. This had been done before, but I did not believe it could be done again, nor did I think that it would be attempted. But the thing was done, and the surprise was complete. I suppose nearly every member of the class was present and I was found in my slippers with an old coat on. By the way, I would like to know what element in human nature it is that makes one person enjoy the surprise of another. I do not understand the matter. My wife knew the purpose of the class, as did my son and his family, but all were charged to keep it a profound secret from me, and they really seemed to enjoy my embarrassment and confusion. There was an abundance of ice cream, and cakes of various kinds and sizes. There was a short speech made to me by the pastor, Rev. C.L. Williams, who was invited to be present. He spoke very appropriately, but my response was a poor thing. Much of the time was spent in conversation and singing, and the occasion was a happy one. I have a suitable appreciation of the honor conferred on me, and may those who bestowed it be blessed for time and eternity.

It is a great gratification to me that my son has charge of this Bible class. It furnishes him an opportunity of doing good, and I may say, great good. It will never be fully known in this world what beneficent results follow a judicious exposition of Scripture. The effect of the exposition is not only felt by those who hear it, but it may be transmitted through them to coming generations. This suggests the idea of solemn, yet delightful responsibility on the part of Bible class teachers.

While in Upland this summer, that is, on the 13th of July, an event occurred which created a deep sensation and spread a pall of gloom over the community. Mrs. Samuel A. Crozer died on that day. It was a day of sorrow and mourning. Sad faces, symbolic of sad hearts, were seen everywhere. On the day of the funeral appropriate remarks were made by the pastor, and Dr. Weston and Dr. Wayland. The pastor suggested that I say something, but I preferred reading the Scripture, and pouring forth my heart in prayer for the bereaved husband, the motherless children, and a large circle of relatives and friends. The time of sorrow is emphatically the time for prayer. God says, "Call on me in the day of trouble."

Mrs. Crozer was a remarkable woman, with bright intellect, of find conversational powers, literary taste, and a capacity to entertain both old and young in the social circle. But it is the sphere of her Christian activities to which I wish to make special reference. She had charge of the church music and performed on the organ for more than thirty years. She taught a large class to sing by note and made them accomplished singers, so that they lead the congregation in the music of the sanctuary. I may say, too, that in all my travels from Pennsylvania to Texas, I have heard no congregational singing equal to that of Upland. There is a spiritual heartiness in it that I have not witnessed elsewhere.

Mrs. Crozer also, for several years, taught the infant class in Sunday-school. She loved children and was at home in her class of between one and two hundred. She required each child to give a penny every Sunday, and thus she directed attention to the great cause of Foreign Missions.

Mrs. Crozer had pecuniary means at her command, and used them for the benefit of the needy. Many shared in her benefactions, and in her the poor found a friend. Even since her death some of her deeds of kindness, of which she said nothing, have come to light.

Mrs. Crozer was in feeble health for months before her death, but she was bright and cheerful, and filled her places of usefulness as long as she was able. Indeed, her energetic spirit seemed at times to compel her body to do what it had not strength to perform. When the last hour drew near and she knew she must die, her mind was calm, and among her last words were these, "Jesus is my Savior." What a blessed thing it is to have such an assurance in the dying hour! It is worth much more than all the honors and riches of the world.

In August, 1890, my wife and I went on the broad Delaware to Cape May Point to spend a week. We found "old ocean" as grand as ever, rolling its majestic waves to the shore as in all past years. This is a sight of which one never tires. The Christian hears the voice of God in the waters of the mighty deep and thinks of the day when the "sea will give up its dead."

While at the Cape, we were near President Harrison's Cottage and I saw him several times. He went in bathing, and attended church, as every man should do. The President is a man of very respectable talents, though he is not entitled to a place among the first of statesmen. He is honest and is striving to use his great office for the benefit of the people. I could but be struck with the fact that he is not magnetic as Henry Clay was, and as James G. Blaine is; but magnetism is a rare quality.

Returning from the Cape, we remained at Upland till November, when we came to dear old Bowling Green, where we now are (January, 1891) and where we find our friends as kind as in other days.

JAMES MADISON PENDLETON

Conclusion

In closing these Reminiscences, written at the special request of my son, I wish to say that the affectionate kindness of our children renders the old age of my wife and me bright and cheerful. We divide our time among them and are obliged; from the treatment we receive, to believe that each one of them would like to have us all the time. We have everything to be thankful for and nothing to complain of.

It may be a satisfaction to the children to know that I began to write these Reminiscences on my seventy-ninth birthday, November 20, 1890, and that I finish them in two months.

Bowling Green, Ky., January 20, 1891.

CHAPTER 20

LAST ILLNESS – DEATH – FUNERAL AND MEMORIAL SERVICES.

The pen has fallen from the hand of him who wrote the preceding pages, and it now devolves upon me to chronicle the fact and the date of his departure. This is done at his request; but filial devotion will not suffer the simple mention of an event that forms an epoch in so many lives.

It will prove of interest to his absent children and his friends to know something of the last months and the last days of his earthly existence.

Upon his arrival at Upland, in the spring of 1890, his appearance was such as to awaken in the hearts of friendly observers a fear that his days on earth were numbered. He was evidently failing in health. As the summer advanced he seemed to grow weaker. At times, his sufferings were acute and intense. He bore them, however, with an almost sublime patience. While the ills of the flesh weighted heavily upon him, his spirit showed a peacefulness and serenity that indicated a ripening for heaven.

In view of the manifest approach to the closing of this eventful life, his friend, Dr. John C. Long, who had previously more than once made the suggestion, now again urged that Father should reduce to some permanent form the scenes and incidents of other days, many of which he had witnessed, and in many of which he had participated. Because of his habit of close observation and of his remarkably retentive memory, it was felt that he must possess a fund of information, which, unless thus imparted by him, would be lost to history. Absorbed as he was in his duties as a student and a teacher of Divine truth, he yet found time to feel and to express, throughout all the years of his active life, an eager interest in current politics. By profession a theologian, he yet possessed knowledge and a grasp of public affairs that would have secured for him no mean rank as a statesman or constitutional lawyer.

It has been remarked by some of his friends that he knew nothing but theology, but knew that, well. It is true that he ever declined to lay claim to scholarship or breadth of culture; but, whenever induced to enter upon the discussion of a given question, whether political, social, moral, metaphysical, or linguistic, it was generally discovered that his ignorance, if such it may be termed, was more blissful to himself than to his opponent. The secret of his success as a debater was the perfect accuracy of his information and his absolute mastery of the subject in hand.

Possessing such qualities of mind, he could not fail to throw valuable light upon the burning questions, the momentous issues, and the wondrous achievements of the era in which he lived. Such was the opinion of those who desired him to add his contribution to the history of his times.

But, urgent as was the request, so great was his fear of incurring the charge of egotism that he repeatedly refused to undertake the work.

It was my good fortune to strike a responsive chord in his affectionate heart; and this was by the suggestion that such a sketch of his life of observation and experience would be a source of interest and profit to his children.

It was then a labor of love on which he entered, when, on the 20th day of November, 1890, when just seventy-nine years of age, he set himself to the formidable task of recounting, unaided by memoranda, the ample outlines of a not inactive career of four score years.

Having decided to write his Reminiscences, he applied himself to the work with characteristic energy – with a system and regularity equally characteristic, devoting two hours a day to this particular subject. The last line was written on the 20th day of January, 1891.

This he called his winter's recreation. It did not interfere with his literary activity in other lines, as the columns of the denominational press for the period will testify. His pen was in constant use, until the day when attacked by his fatal illness. After his death I found among his papers on unpublished article on "The Woman of Canaan."

While he felt that the Reminiscences would prove the last of his extended literary efforts, he did not at first believe that his illness, contracted on the 10th day of February, would terminate fatally. It was pronounced by his physicians to be capillary bronchitis, and from the first, they offered no hope of recovery. When informed of his condition, he remarked, "Well, gentlemen, you may be right; but I do not feel like a dying man."

The progress of the disease was rapid, and he soon passed into a state semi-conscious and, at times, delirious. For the greater part of his illness he was mercifully spared acute suffering. Now and again, full consciousness would return. Then he recognized the different members of his family and exhibited perfect clearness and strength of intellect. It was upon two of these occasions, so precious to those hovering about him that he gave his parting messages to family and friends, and, with all the solemnity surrounding the dying bed of a Christian, testified to the strength of his faith and hope and to the gospel's efficacy to support, when flesh and heart fail.

It is fitting that his words, uttered in this impressive manner, and taken down as they fell from his lips, should be recorded for the comfort of that devoted inner circle, now broken, and of that larger circle that loved him living, and now venerate him departed. (It is thought best to omit special messages to the children and grand children, these having been preserved in another form.)

"I have very little to say of myself. My letter of resignation expresses it. A poor sinner saved by grace. I have performed some labor in my day, but everything has been tinctured with imperfection and impurity. If God should speak to me and tell me that if I could find one sermon that I had preached in all these sixty years that was free from imperfection, I might depend on that, I would not listen to it for a moment. It is grace, grace, from first to last. I just expect to go into eternity, saying: Lord, here I am, a poor, weak, sinful creature, having no claim, and the only hope of being saved is that Jesus Christ died in the place of sinners. I know no other hope. I believe what I did sixty years ago, just exactly. Yes, it is the same old story, not one particle of change in my views. In March, 1865, when I thought I was going to die, I felt this way, and that is my feeling yet. Tell the other children the same. They may know that I think about them every day; pray for them every day; for years and years have done that. My prayers have been that my descendants to the remotest generations may be found among the servants of God.

"I have published a great many things in my day. You may say that I have never had the first regret that I devoted myself to the ministry. I have had a good many trials, in one way and another, in connection with it."

Speaking to his daughter, Mrs. Procter, who had nursed him so faithfully, day and night, throughout his illness, he said: "You could not have done more than you have done. If my death should occur here, it seems fitting that I should end my career where I began it pretty much – where I brought my bride, once so cheerful and happy, now so sad. She cannot see those she loves most. If I should die I would wish her to remain in this family. It will be but a little while. It is not worth while for me to say to any of you, be kind to your mother. I know you will be. Be kind, be kind, be kind."

"My object has been to be an accomplished debater; claiming nothing unjust, yielding to nothing unjust. My grand supreme purpose has been the establishment of truth. I have never attempted to disparage any other brother. My hope is as strong as it ever was. I do not know that my hope is as bright as, when a boy, I hitched my horse and went into the woods to thank God that He sent His Son into the world to die; but it is as strong as ever. You young people may lay too much stress upon the joy of religion. I do not suppose it is necessary for me to say more. I have written so much. Give my love to Dr. Robinson, Dr. Weston, and the members of the faculty of the Seminary. Give my love to the pastor and church, and Sunday-school and Bible class at Upland."

As the days passed away, he seemed more fully to realize his condition. After attending to some little matters of business, and having expressed his desire as to mother's earthly future, his spirit was calm and peaceful. He seemed to have done with the things of earth, save the evident enjoyment of listening to the conversation of the members of his family present, and the solicitous messages of the absent ones. It was a source of grief to his eldest daughters that they were unable, because of distance and ill health, to be with him. Yet it will comfort them to be assured that he fully appreciated the cause of their absence, and felt that they acted wisely.

He was greatly surprised and pleased by the visit of his brother-in-law and friend of more than half a century, Uncle William Garnett, of Chicago. He and mother are the survivors of a family of twelve. How deep and tender the solicitude of the brother as he ministered words of comfort to the sister entering the shadows of widowhood.

Father greatly enjoyed the seasons of prayer, and was interested in the Scripture selections. He asked upon one occasion, for the one hundred and sixteenth Psalm, remaking: "They generally read the one hundred and fifteenth at such times, but I prefer this." He was the only one unmoved at the reading of the verse: "Precious in the sight of the Lord is the death of His saints."

At another time he suggested the reading of the seventh chapter of Revelation. His soul was then yearning for the land of the redeemed. He longed for a sight of that multitude come out of great tribulation. He wished to be with them. "For the Lamb which is in the midst of the throne shall feed them and shall lead them unto living fountains of waters, and God shall wipe away all tears from their eyes." This was a favorite passage with him, and more than once have I heard him say that Robert Burns, wicked man that he was, could not read the verse with tearless eyes.

Two hours before his death, he sent a message to his second daughter: "Tell Fannie, 'Call upon Me in the day of trouble and I will deliver thee.' That is indefinite. It does not say what *kind* of trouble, nor *when* He will deliver." Highly favored one, to receive the last words of such a Father! With a heart ever throbbing with love and sympathy for his children, his ruling passion was strong in death.

He spoke not again, but from his eyes there shone a depth of affection more eloquent than words. The inevitable end was approaching. It was fitting that the faithful servant of the Prince of Peace should sink to rest in the presence of his loved ones. The family sat by the bedside and watched the ebbing away of that life so full of precious significance to them and to the world. There, in the background, in tearful silence, stood representatives of that race for whom he had done and suffered not a little. Close at hand were the friend and brother of his youth, and he whose devotion, as that of a son in the flesh, had brightened the sunset of life. Still nearer was a scene that must have moved the least impressible. Son and daughter supported the mother as her sightless eyes seemed to strain after even a passing glimpse of her loved one. The hand of the blind was clasped in the hand of the dying – the eloquence of a voiceless, sightless grief.

Thus came the hour of departure. So gently did he pass away that mother knew not when his spirit fled. At high noon, on the 4th day of March, he closed his eyes, and peacefully and painlessly entered that land that is fairer than day.

REMINISCENCES OF A LONG LIFE

To his two children who were present, it was a new and strange experience. Death is pictured as the King of Terrors. It is often attended by the most excruciating physical suffering, which, in the case of the godless man is aggravated by the most fearful spiritual convulsions. Death is to such the King of Terrors, but not so to him who serves the King of kings. So tranquil, so easy the exit of the soul from the body, we could but exclaim: Can this be death! Well might we inquire, "Where, O death, is thy sting; where, O grace, thy victory!"

The sun shone in noontide splendor. Nature gave glad response to its genial warmth. Stern winter had melted into smiling spring. Winter, emblematic of trials and bereavements, forever past; Spring, the foregleam of that restful vision on which his eyes had opened. Blessed closing! Blissful opening! To the cares of the earth, forever closed; to the joys of heaven, forever open.

Whatever the bereavement of those left behind, they possess this priceless consolation, that he has achieved the two-fold object of his sanctified ambition: He is like Jesus, for he has seen Him as He is. Blessed the pure in heart, for they shall see God. He saw Him, on earth, even in the midst of dark providences. Now, in unbeclouded light, and with the problems of life made plan, he sees Him face to face.

When father crossed the Ohio River, in the fall of 1862, he had little idea of ever returning to the South. He had then reached middle age. The land was convulsed by a fratricidal war that bade fair to rend the nation into irreclaimably hostile sections. He feared that his usefulness was ended. Borne down by the grief of a patriot over the distracted condition of his beloved country, and overwhelmed by the sore bereavement in the loss of his son, he probably did not look for length of days.

Brighter days, however, came. The war closed. His usefulness had been re-established; but in a different climate and among new surroundings. As the years glided away and old age came on apace, it was his desire, when death should come, to find a resting place in the little cemetery at Upland, among those to whom he had devoted the latter years of his ministry.

But it was decreed otherwise. He resigned his charge in Pennsylvania, and he and mother found it congenial to their feelings to divide their time among their children. Upon her marriage in 1876, his daughter, Mrs. Procter, became a resident of Bowling Green, Kentucky, and still resides there.

Thus, by a succession of events, unforeseen and altogether improbably, at the date of his leaving Bowling Green, in 1857, he returned to his former home, after thirty-three years of life in Tennessee, Ohio, and Pennsylvania. There is a poetic fitness in the providence that turned the heart of the old man toward scenes of his youth; that brought him back to the State of his first love, there to rest in the bosom of the land sacred with the precious dust of his kindred.

It was in January of 1837 that he began his ministry at Bowling Green. It was at Bowling Green, on the 25th day of January, 1891, that he preached his last sermon. His text was taken from the fourth verse of the fifty-first Psalm. His topic was "Sinning Against God." God was the center of his preaching. His first sermon treated of repentance; his last, of sin. Sin is sin against God. Repentance is repentance toward God.

The funeral services were held at two o'clock, March 6th, in the Baptist church at Bowling Green. It was appropriate that in this building, the scene of his faithful and efficient labors, should be gathered a multitude to do honor to his memory: fellow ministers of the Word; descendants of the friends of other days; his children in the faith; with here and there the whitened locks and streaming eyes of those who with him had borne the burden and heat of the day, and will soon again meet him in the Celestial City.

It was his expressed desire that Dr. T.T. Eaton, of Louisville, should conduct the services. For the parents of Dr. Eaton he had performed the like mournful duty.

The services were opened with the singing of the hymn, "Servant of God, well done." A Scripture selection was read by Rev. A.M. Boone. Rev. M.M. Riley, the pastor, offered a fervent and touching prayer in behalf of the widow and children. Mrs. Lucien D. Potter most effectively rendered the beautiful solo, "This Place is Holy Ground," being No. 1099 of the Psalmist. How appropriate the close of the second stanza:

Life so sweetly ceased to be,
It lapsed in immortality.

Dr. Eaton delivered an address drawn from the words of 2 Tim. 4: 7: "I have fought a good fight, I have finished my course, I have kept the faith." He dwelt with special emphasis upon the last clause of the verse, and, defining "faith" in this connection, as the body of doctrine, illustrated the truth of the assertion as applied to Father, in that he had ever felt himself to be set for the defense of the Gospel; had ever proved himself the champion of orthodoxy; had ever contended for the faith once delivered to the saints, and had thus accompanied that "grand, supreme purpose" of his life, "the establishment of truth." It is impossible to furnish an adequate outline of the discourse. It can only be said that it was chaste in diction; vigorous in thought; eloquent in delivery; full of tender feeling and appropriate in eulogy; worthy of him who uttered it; just to its subject and grateful to the family and friends.

Then was sung that hymn, the comfort of the living and the dying saint:

"How firm a foundation."

It was a source of regret that because of the distance, no representative of Crozer Theological Seminary could be present to participate in the services.

JAMES MADISON PENDLETON

Father had been a Trustee of that institution since its foundation, and had ever felt and shown a more than official interest in its welfare; ever rejoiced in its prosperity, and thanked God for the work accomplished by its faculty and graduates.

It had been the habit of Dr. Weston to ask him, when present, to offer special prayer for the graduating class at Commencement; and there are many who will remember how earnest were his petitions, and how more than once he expressed the regret that he was not again young, to join with them in the well-loved work of preaching the Gospel. How he loved that work, and how righteously envious of those who were going forth with physical and mental vigor, to toil in the fields white to the harvest!

It was, however, doubly gratifying that Dr. William H. Whittsitt could be present, and on behalf of the Southern Baptist Theological Seminary as well as of Father's former students, offer his tribute of respect and veneration to his departed friend and instructor. Few, but touching and appropriate were his words. As to courage of conviction and stern fidelity to duty, the eulogist drew a parallel between his subject and the prophet Elijah; and gazing into heaven, whither the spirit of God's servant had fled, could well exclaim with Elisha: "My Father, my Father, the chariot of Israel and the horsemen thereof."

A memorial service was held in the Baptist church at Upland, on Sunday, the 22nd day of March. Dr. Bliss and Dr. Weston offered special and earnest prayer for the widow and family. The choir sang the appropriate anthem, "Blessed Are the Dead Who Die in the Lord;" also the beautiful hymn, "It Is Well With My Soul." Rev. C.L. Williams, the pastor, delivered a memorial address, wherein he spoke of transparency of character, fidelity of friendship, tenderness of his wife and unflinching devotion to the Gospel of Christ as among the striking traits of his predecessor in the Upland pulpit.

The discourse was eloquent, able, polished, and was couched in language tender, beautiful, and fully appreciative of the life and character of its subject. It was a just tribute to him who was devoted in his love to that church, and was a fitting chaplet to lie upon his grave.

In view of Father's long and intimate connection with that body, it will not be considered out of place to insert in this sketch the following minute, which was adopted by the Philadelphia Conference of Baptist Ministers, on the 9th day of March, 1891:

The Conference places on record the deep feeling with which it has learned of the death of James Madison Pendleton, D.D.

We recall with profound gratitude the high privilege of intimate intercourse with him during a quarter of a century, since he joined the Conference November 6, 1865.

We have loved and honored him as a man of exalted piety, of large scriptural knowledge, of undeviating fidelity to conviction, of tender and loving spirit.

He has been a pillar in the Temple of our God, in the Conference and in the Denomination, a pillar of strength, a column of beauty.

As we bid farewell to this good and great man, we look forward with hope and cheer to the renewed and endless union amid the Church of the First-born in the world that lies

> Beyond the smiling and the weeping,
> Beyond the sowing and the reaping.

At the annual meeting of the Board of Trustees of The Crozer Theological Seminary, held on the 10th day of June, 1891, the following action was taken on the recommendation of Rev. George Dana Boardman, D.D., Chairman of the Committee on Resolutions:

JAMES MADISON PENDLETON

"In making a minute of the death of our late colleague, James Madison Pendleton, Doctor of Divinity, we hereby place on record our deep appreciation of his eminent worth as a Christian, his reverent conscientiousness as a Bible student, his signal fidelity as a preacher and a pastor, his conspicuous loyalty as a Baptist, and especially his indefatigable devotion as a Trustee of the Crozer Theological Seminary."

In the midst of the family bereavement, our love and sympathy cluster about her who is the central figure in the scene of mourning. God gave her as a helpmate to her husband. Her unceasing devotion to him and to his work; her unflagging interest and zealous efforts in the cause nearest his heart; her sympathy and her prayers, proclaim her the ideal wife. Nothing in their later years has been more touching or beautiful than the lover-like devotion of the old man to the one who, though stricken with blindness and the infirmities of age, ever remained to him the bride and the love of his youth.

To her has come the saddest day of earth. To him, the lifetime-keeper of her heart's profoundest love, she must say farewell. She sorrows, but in the sweetness and the assurance of her faith, sorrows not as they that have no hope. She must say "Farewell," but it is "Farewell, till we meet again." She misses the strong arm and the loving voice, but can say and feel, "The Lord is my refuge and strength; a very present help in trouble." He is the comforter of the widow. He is eyes to the blind. And so, she calmly waits by the riverside. It is the late afternoon of life. The sun is approaching its setting. She waits for the coming of the hour when the darkness of earth shall be exchanged for the clear light of heaven; when her heart and its great treasure shall again be united, and so shall husband and wife be ever with the Lord.

To our mother and her children very grateful have been the many kind and sympathetic words that have been spoken and written by those whom Father loved and honored. We rejoice to believe that his work has not been in vain; that the Lord has prospered his preaching of the Word; that in the crown which the Righteous Judge shall give him, will appear many stars as seals to his ministry.

The body of our Father sleeps in the beautiful cemetery, well called Fairview, a mile outside Bowling Green. There the birds sing, the branches wave, the flowers bloom, and the summer breezes chant a requiem. But *he* is not there. He is absent from the body. He is present with the Lord.

To the heavenly visitants that stand guard over his consecrated dust, he speaks forth the language of that hymn, the comfort of his last hours, the consolation of his bereaved ones, and the prophecy of his resurrection:

> Ye angels that watch round the tomb,
> Where low the Redeemer was laid,
> While deep in mortality's gloom
> He hid for a season his head.
>
> Ye saints who once languished below,
> But long since have entered your rest,
> I pant to be glorified too,
> To lean on Immanuel's breast.
>
> O, sweet is the season of rest,
> When life's weary journey is done;
> When the blush spreads over its West,
> And the last lingering rays of the sun.
>
> Though dreary the empire of the night,
> I soon shall immerge from its gloom,
> And see immortality's light
> Arise on the shades of the tomb.
>
> Then welcome the last rending sighs
> When these aching heart strings shall break,
> When death shall extinguish these eyes
> And moisten with dew the pale cheek.
>
> No terror the prospect begets,

James Madison Pendleton

I am not mortality's slave,
The sunbeam of life as it sets
Paints a rainbow of peace on the grave.

The Funeral of Dr. J. M. Pendleton

M. M. Riley

THE FUNERAL OF DR. J. M. PENDLETON[1]
March 12, 1891

Rev. James M. Pendleton, D.D., so widely known as a great and good man died of capillary bronchitis, at noon on March 4th, at the home of his son-in-law, Mr. B.F. Proctor in Bowling Green, Ky.

He was born in Spottsylvania County, Va., November 20, 1811, and removed when quite young with his parents to Christian county, KY.

When seventeen years of age he professed faith in Christ and joined the Bethel church, near Pembroke, Ky., and was baptized April 11th, 1829, by Rev. J. S. Wilson.

He preached his first sermon in September, 1831. He served the Bethel and Hopkinsville churches jointly as pastor for some time, having been ordained November 2, 1833 and was called to Bowling Green in 1837, where he was pastor for twenty years.

He was married march 13th, 1838, to Miss Catherine Garnett, of Glasgow, KY. Only nine days more would have given them fifty three years of life together. He removed to Murfreesboro, TN., in 1837, where he was theological professor in Union University and pastor of the Baptist church for five years. From Murfreesboro he removed to Dayton, Ohio, and subsequently to Upland, PA., where he

---

[1] M. M. Riley, "Funeral of Dr. J. M. Pendleton," *The Baptist*, March 12, 1891.

was pastor for eighteen years. Owing to advancing years he resigned the pastorate a few years ago and has since spent his time with his children, writing, and occasionally preaching. He is the author of several very valuable books. "Three Reasons Why I Am a Baptist," "Christian Doctrines," "Distinctive Principles of Baptist," "Brief Notes on New Testament," "Church Manual." "Pendleton's Sermons," and others. He had only six weeks completed his "Reminiscences," which will doubtless be published soon.

He spent last summer in Upland, and returned to Bowling Green in October, quite feeble and greatly reduced in flesh. He had, however, become more vigorous, and preached for us twice, the last time being on Sunday morning, Jan. 25, his text being Ps. 51:4, subject, "Sinning against God." It was an excellent sermon, delivered with great earnestness and tenderness. We shall never forget his closing appeal while enforcing the "awfulness of sinning against God." It was a fitting close of a life-work preaching the "gospel of grace."

He was announced to preach for us on Sunday morning, Feb. 15, but was taken ill on the night of the 10th, and gradually grew weaker until death. He was conscious and calm, with momentary exceptions, up to within an hour of death, and passed away as a child falling asleep.

The funeral services were held in the Baptist church at 2 p.m. on the 6th. The church and Dr. Pendleton's chair in the audience were draped in mourning. The large room was filled with admiring friends of Dr. Pendleton from this and other communities, representing not only Baptists but other denominations and non-professors. His son, from Pennsylvania, had been with him for several days, but his daughters in Colorado and Texas were not able to be here.

The services were begun by an instrumental voluntary, as the procession entered the church preceded by the ministers who took part in the services.

Dr. W. H. Whitsitt announced the first hymn, "Servant of God, well done," (648 Hymnal), Rev. A. M. Boone read 2 Cor.

4:6 to 5:10. Rev. M. M. Riley, the pastor, offered prayer. A beautiful and appropriate solo was sung by Mrs. L. D. Potter, at the conclusion of which Rev. Dr. T. T. Eaton, a life long intimate friend of Dr. Pendleton, announced his text, 2 Tim. 4:7 from which he delivered a forcible sermon and an appropriate eulogy of the deceased. He said no one could take Dr. Pendleton's place, he had filled his place here and had gone to take his place on high. At the conclusion of his remarks, the choir and congregation sang, "How firm a foundation," after which Dr. Whitsitt, who also had been a pupil and friend of Dr. Pendleton, spoke feelingly on behalf of the Seminary and of the pupils in former years. His remarks were brief, appropriate, tender, and true. The remains were then taken to our beautiful Fairview Cemetery, followed by a very long procession, where they were interred in a lot previously procured by Dr. Pendleton and his son-in-law.

Our sympathy and admiration for dear Sister Pendleton we cannot express. Such calm resignation we have never seen. She held his hand till life had fled; and, owing to her blindness, knew not the end had come till a child removed his hand from hers. She and her children have the sympathy of many thousands. Truly had he fought the good fight, finished the course, and kept the faith. May God give us more such men as was J. M. Pendleton.

M. M. Riley

THE BAPTIST STANDARD BEARER, INC.
A non-profit, tax-exempt corporation
committed to the Publication & Preservation
of The Baptist Heritage.

SAMPLE TITLES FOR PUBLICATIONS AVAILABLE IN OUR VARIOUS SERIES:

THE BAPTIST *COMMENTARY* SERIES
Sample of authors/works in stock or in production:
John Gill - *Exposition of the Old & New Testaments (9 Vol. Set)*
John Gill - *Exposition of Solomon's Song*

THE BAPTIST *FAITH* SERIES:
Sample of authors/works in stock or in production:
Abraham Booth - *The Reign of Grace*
John Fawcett - *Christ Precious to Those That Believe*
John Gill - *A Complete Body of Doctrinal & Practical Divinity (2 Vols.)*

THE BAPTIST *HISTORY* SERIES:
Sample of authors/works in stock or in production:
Thomas Armitage - *A History of the Baptists (2 Vols.)*
Isaac Backus - *History of the New England Baptists (2 Vols.)*
William Cathcart - *The Baptist Encyclopaedia (3 Vols.)*
J. M. Cramp - *Baptist History*

THE BAPTIST *DISTINCTIVES* SERIES:
Sample of authors/works in stock or in production:
Abraham Booth - *Paedobaptism Examined (3 Vols.)*
Alexander Carson - *Ecclesiastical Polity of the New Testament Churches*
E. C. Dargan - *Ecclesiology: A Study of the Churches*
J. M. Frost - *Pedobaptism: Is It From Heaven?*
R. B. C. Howell - *The Evils of Infant Baptism*

THE *DISSENT & NONCONFORMITY* SERIES:
Sample of authors/works in stock or in production:
Champlin Burrage - *The Early English Dissenters (2 Vols.)*
Albert H. Newman - *History of Anti-Pedobaptism*
Walter Wilson - *The History & Antiquities of the Dissenting Churches (4 Vols.)*

For a complete list of current authors/titles, visit our internet site at
www.standardbearer.org or write us at:

The Baptist Standard Bearer, Inc.
No. 1 Iron Oaks Drive • Paris, Arkansas 72855

Telephone: (479) 963-3831   Fax: (479) 963-8083
E-mail: baptist@arkansas.net
Internet: http://www.standardbearer.org

www.ingramcontent.com/pod-product-compliance
Lightning Source LLC
Chambersburg PA
CBHW021813300426
44114CB00009BA/159